VIZ GRAPHIC NOVEL

...ndants of Darkness™

Yami no Matsuei

Time for a break.

Haste makes waste.

Story & Art by **Yoko Matsushita**

4

Descendants of Darkness
Yami no Matsuei

Vol. 4
Shôjo Edition

Story & Art by
Yoko Matsushita

English Adaptation/Lance Caselman
Translation/David Ury
Touch-Up & Lettering/Gia Cam Luc
Graphics & Cover Design/Hidemi Sahara
Editor/Pancha Diaz

Managing Editor/Annette Roman
Production Manager/Noboru Watanabe
Editorial Director/Alvin Lu
Sr. Director of Acquisitions/Rika Inouye
Vice President of Sales & Marketing/Liza Coppola
Executive Vice President/Hyoe Narita
Publisher/Seiji Horibuchi

Printed in the U.S.A.

Published by VIZ, LLC
P.O. Box 77064
San Francisco, CA 94107

Shôjo Edition
10 9 8 7 6 5 4 3 2 1
First printing, February 2005

For advertising rates or media kit, e-mail advertising@viz.com

store.viz.com

www.viz.com

Table of Contents

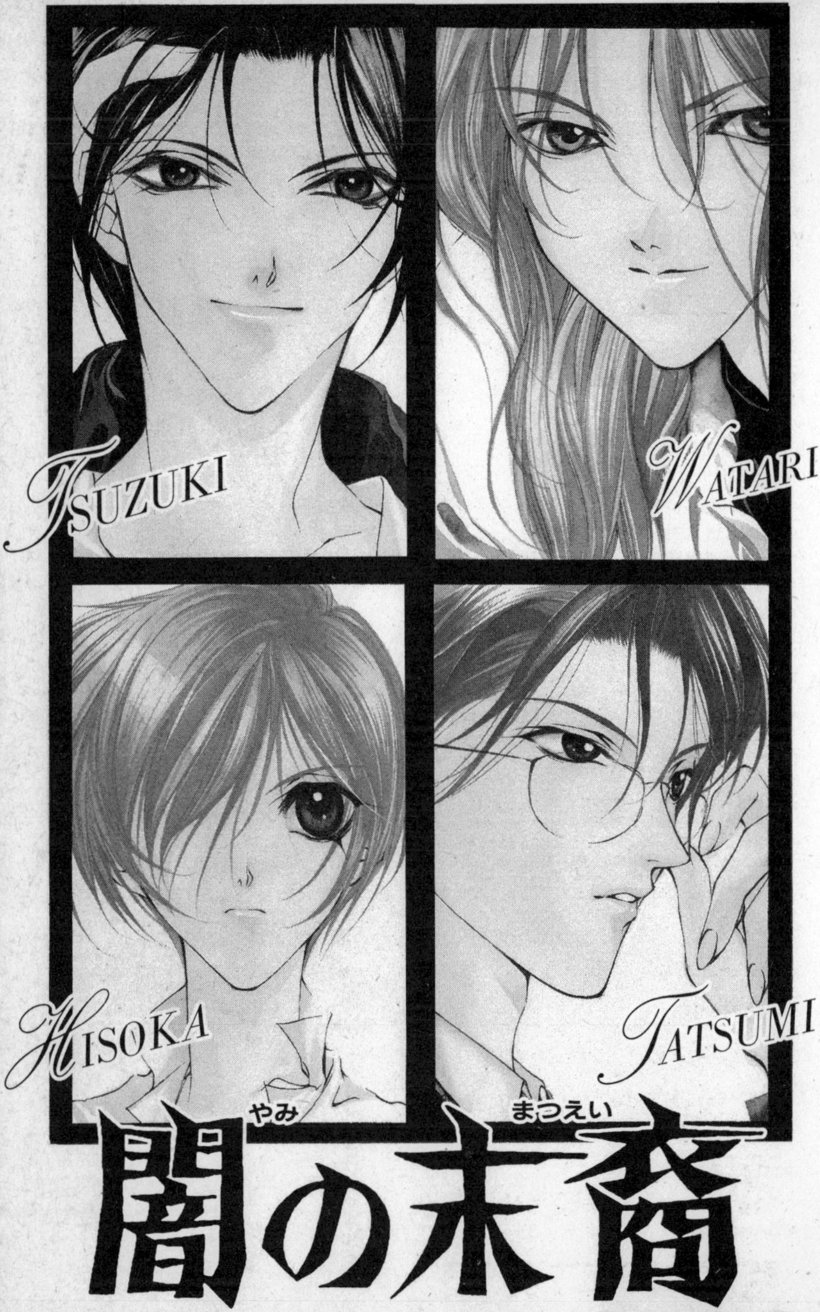
WATARI
TSUZUKI
TATSUMI
HISOKA

闇の末裔

やみ まつえい

DESCENDANTS OF DARKNESS
YAMI NO MATSUEI

CHAPTER 1

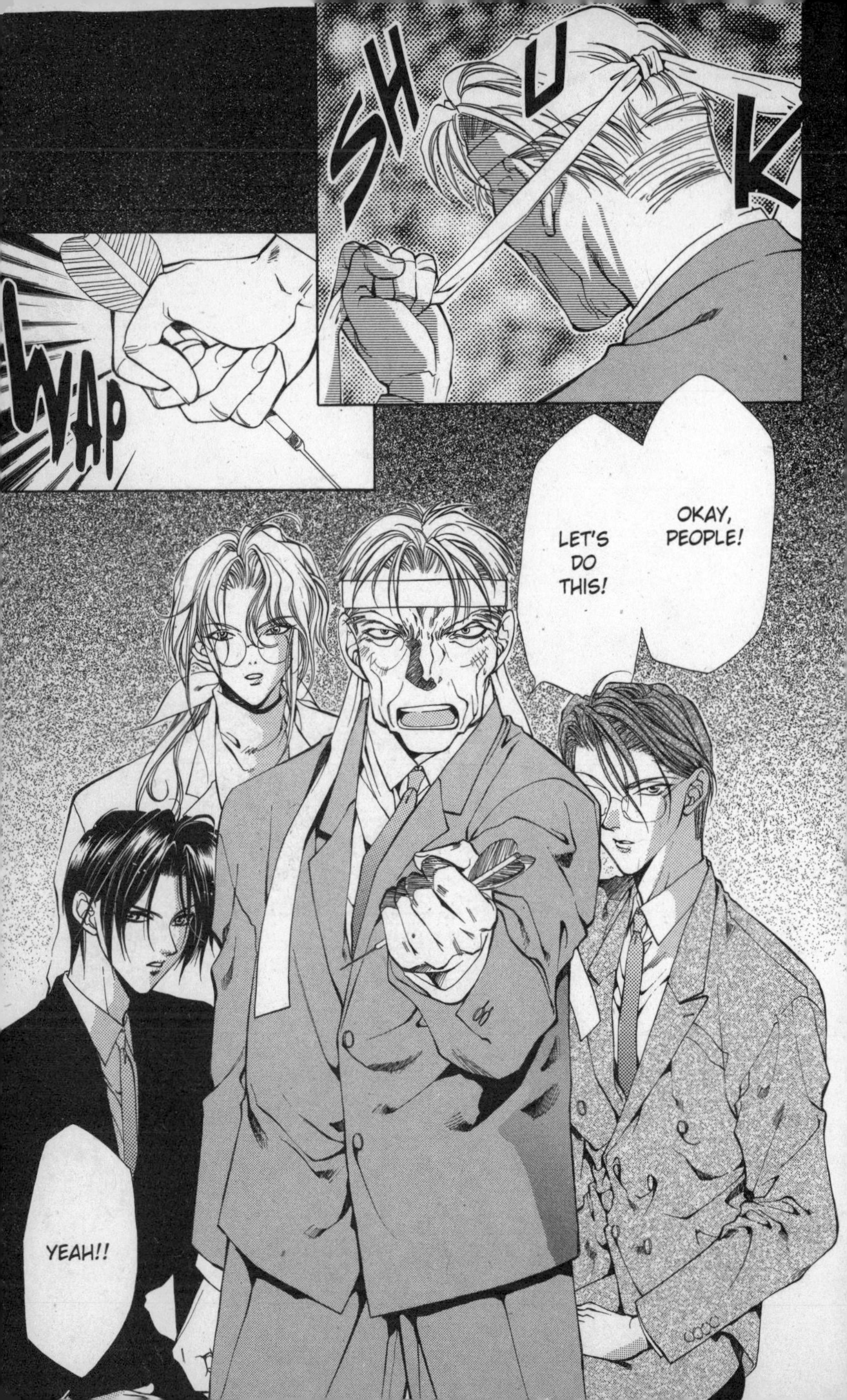
SHUK
WAP
OKAY, PEOPLE!
LET'S DO THIS!
YEAH!!

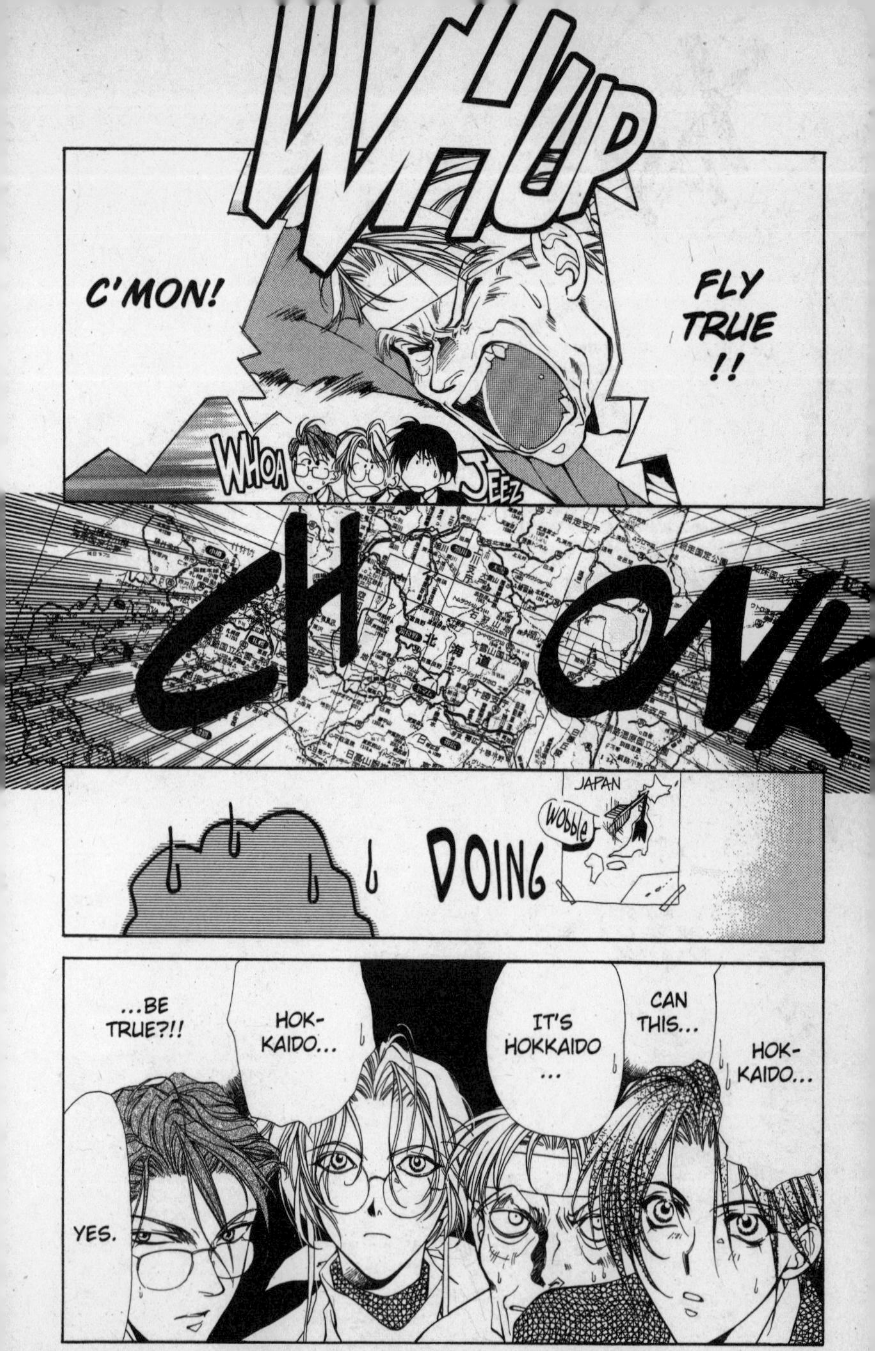
WHUP
FLY TRUE !!
C'MON!
JEEZ
WHOA
CHONK
JAPAN
WOBBLE
DOING
HOK-KAIDO...
CAN THIS...
IT'S HOKKAIDO ...
HOK-KAIDO...
...BE TRUE?!!
YES.

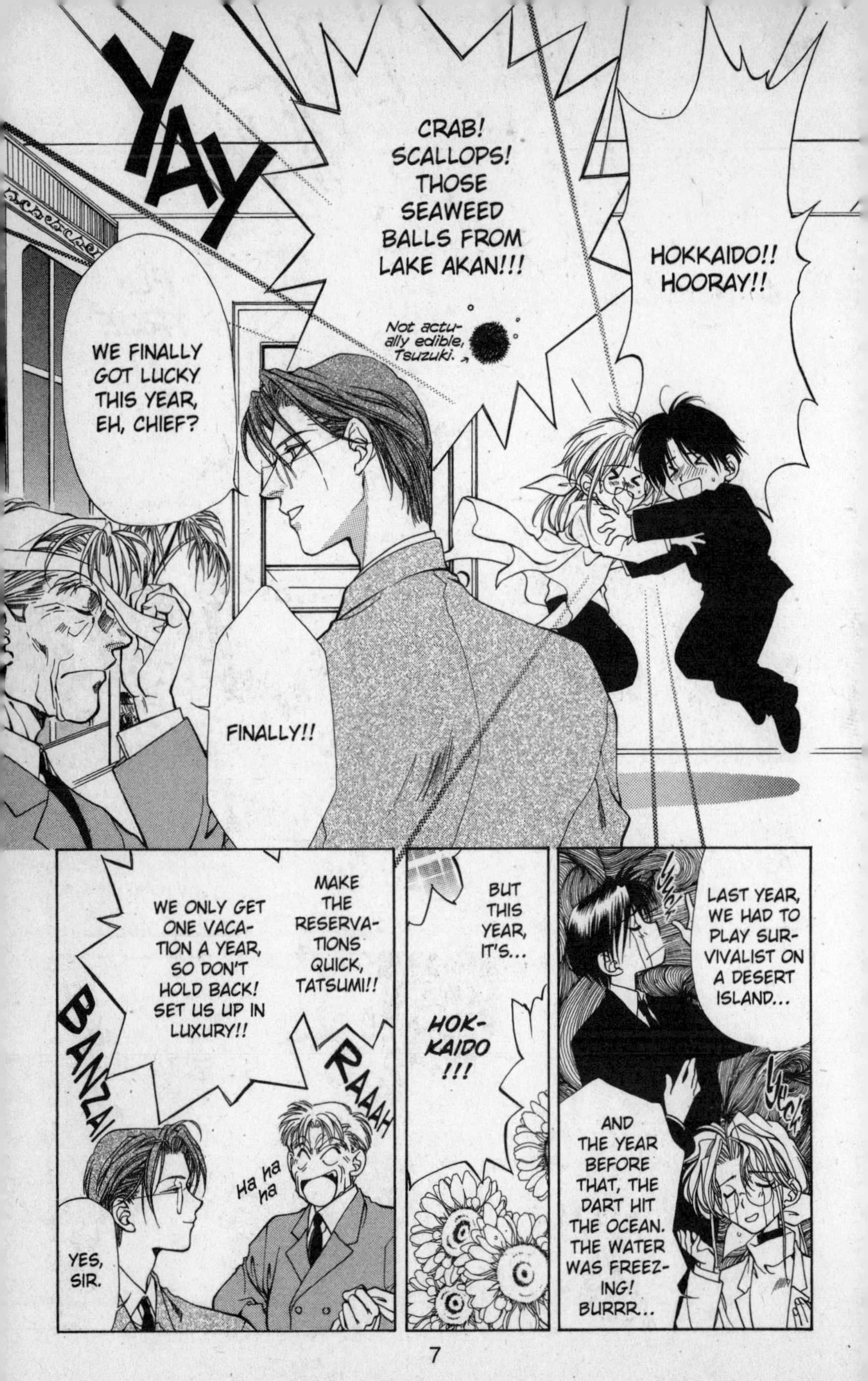
HOKKAIDO!! HOORAY!!
CRAB! SCALLOPS! THOSE SEAWEED BALLS FROM LAKE AKAN!!!
Not actually edible, Tsuzuki.
YAY
WE FINALLY GOT LUCKY THIS YEAR, EH, CHIEF?
FINALLY!!
LAST YEAR, WE HAD TO PLAY SURVIVALIST ON A DESERT ISLAND...
AND THE YEAR BEFORE THAT, THE DART HIT THE OCEAN. THE WATER WAS FREEZING! BURRR..
BUT THIS YEAR, IT'S...
HOKKAIDO!!!
MAKE THE RESERVATIONS QUICK, TATSUMI!!
RAAAH
WE ONLY GET ONE VACATION A YEAR, SO DON'T HOLD BACK! SET US UP IN LUXURY!!
BANZAI
Ha ha ha
YES, SIR.

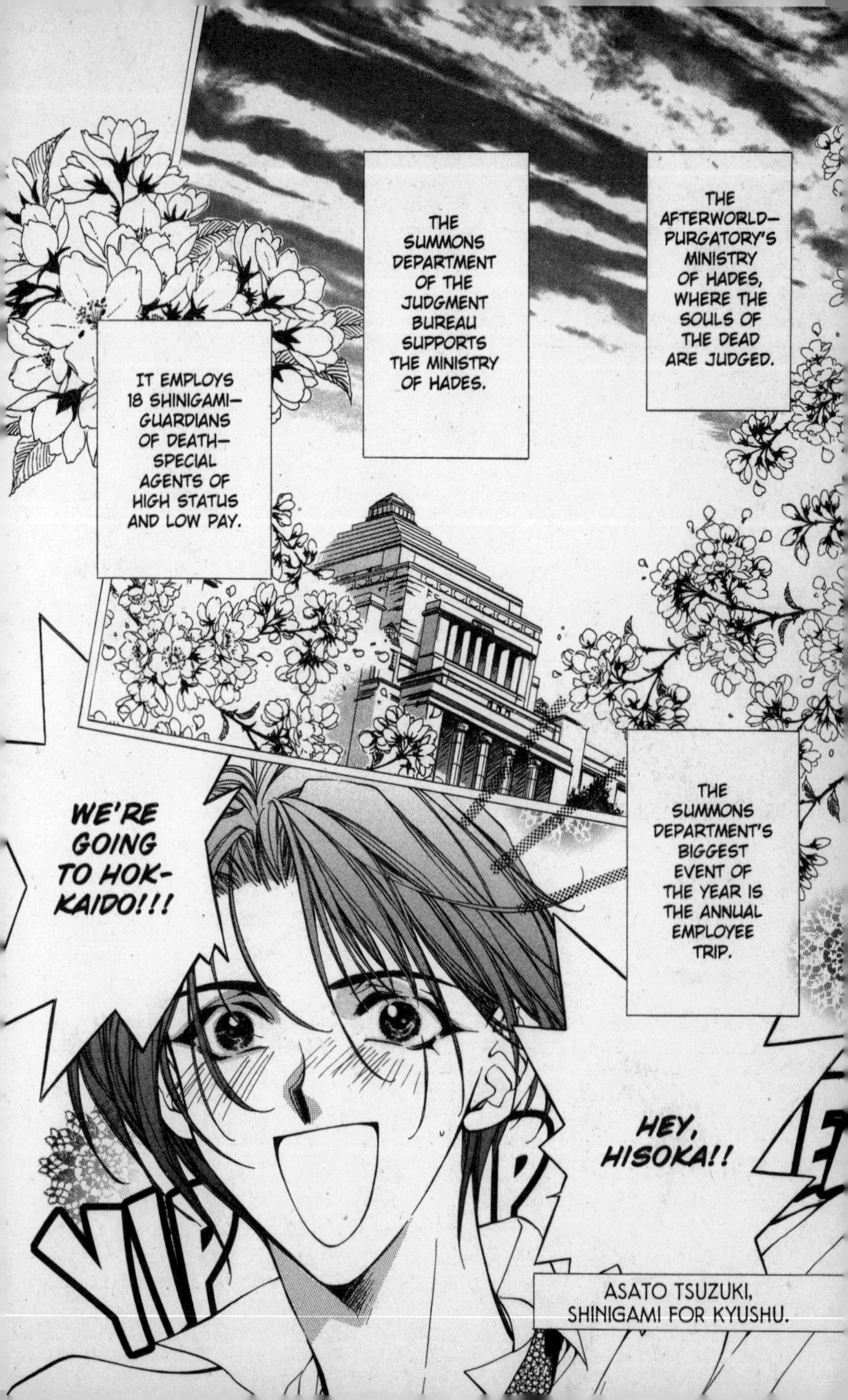
THE AFTERWORLD—PURGATORY'S MINISTRY OF HADES, WHERE THE SOULS OF THE DEAD ARE JUDGED.
THE SUMMONS DEPARTMENT OF THE JUDGMENT BUREAU SUPPORTS THE MINISTRY OF HADES.
IT EMPLOYS 18 SHINIGAMI—GUARDIANS OF DEATH—SPECIAL AGENTS OF HIGH STATUS AND LOW PAY.
THE SUMMONS DEPARTMENT'S BIGGEST EVENT OF THE YEAR IS THE ANNUAL EMPLOYEE TRIP.
HEY, HISOKA!!
WE'RE GOING TO HOK-KAIDO!!!
ASATO TSUZUKI, SHINIGAMI FOR KYUSHU.

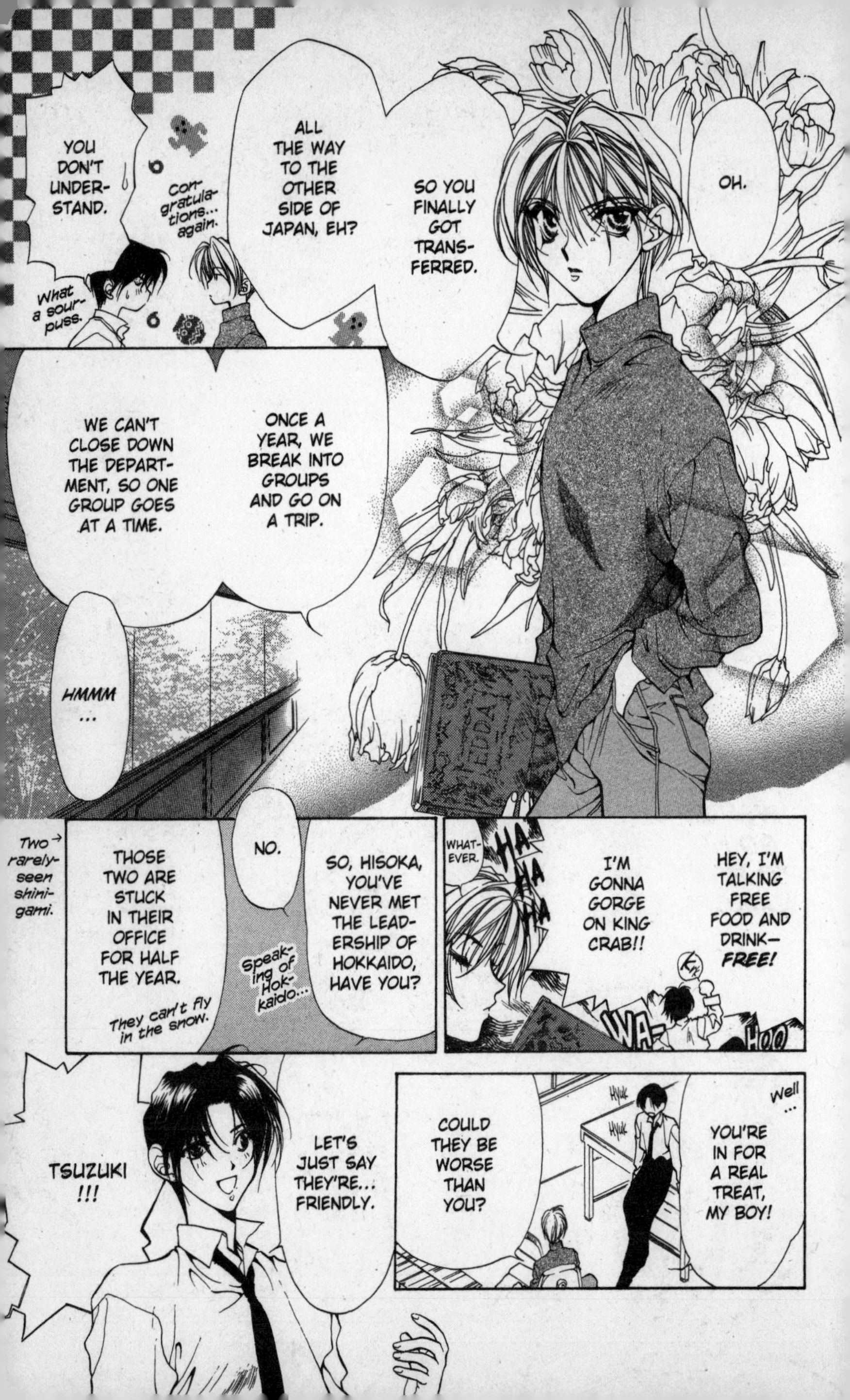

OH.
SO YOU FINALLY GOT TRANS-FERRED.
ALL THE WAY TO THE OTHER SIDE OF JAPAN, EH?
con-gratula-tions... again.
YOU DON'T UNDER-STAND.
What a sour-puss.
ONCE A YEAR, WE BREAK INTO GROUPS AND GO ON A TRIP.
WE CAN'T CLOSE DOWN THE DEPART-MENT, SO ONE GROUP GOES AT A TIME.
HMMM ...
HEY, I'M TALKING FREE FOOD AND DRINK—FREE!
I'M GONNA GORGE ON KING CRAB!!
HA HA HA HA
WHAT-EVER.
WA-HOO
SO, HISOKA, YOU'VE NEVER MET THE LEAD-ERSHIP OF HOKKAIDO, HAVE YOU?
Speak-ing of Hok-kaido...
NO.
THOSE TWO ARE STUCK IN THEIR OFFICE FOR HALF THE YEAR.
They can't fly in the snow.
Two rarely-seen shini-gami.
Well ...
YOU'RE IN FOR A REAL TREAT, MY BOY!
HYUK HYUK
COULD THEY BE WORSE THAN YOU?
LET'S JUST SAY THEY'RE... FRIENDLY.
TSUZUKI !!!

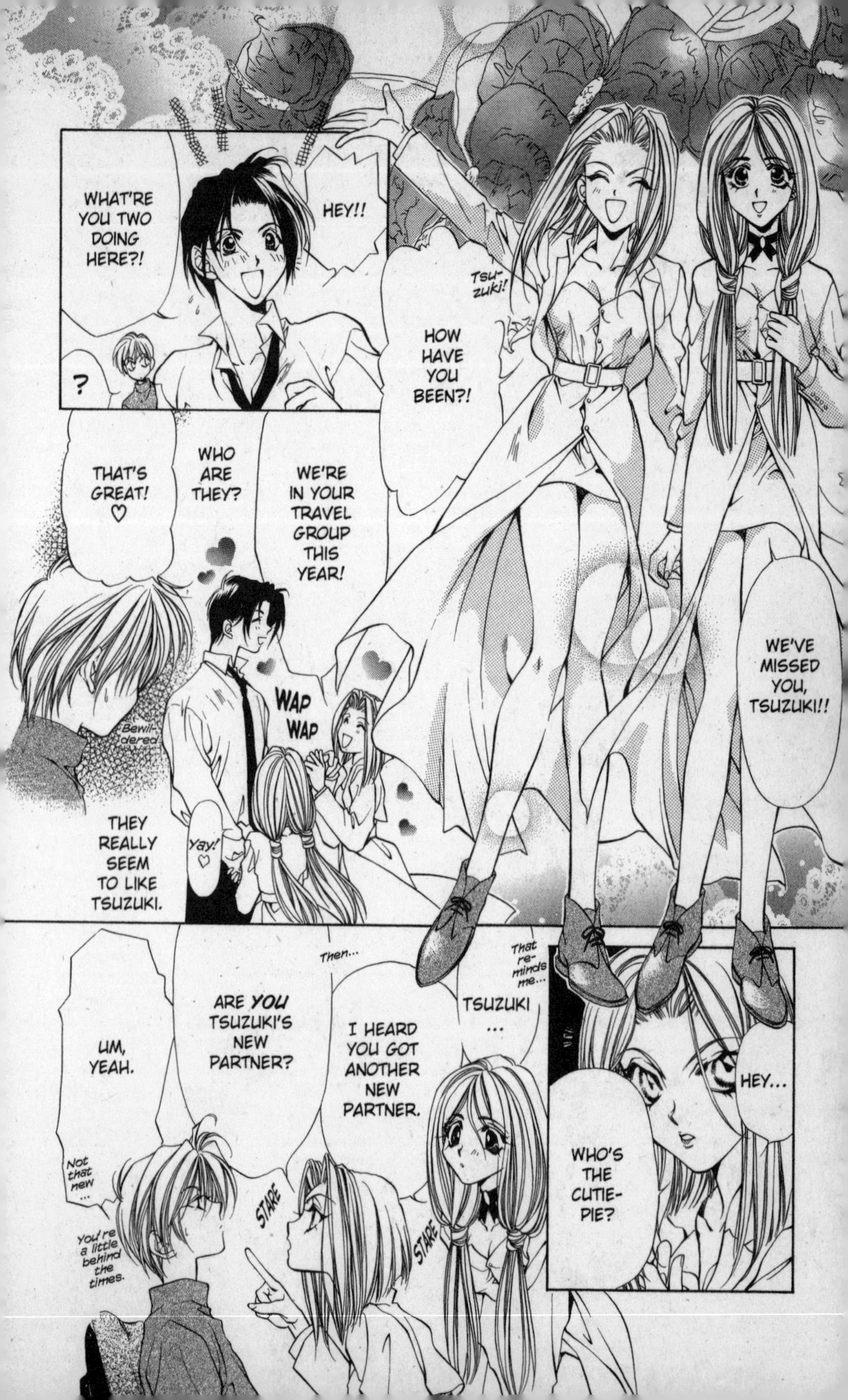
Tsu-zuki!
HOW HAVE YOU BEEN?!
WE'VE MISSED YOU, TSUZUKI!!
HEY!!
WHAT'RE YOU TWO DOING HERE?!
?
WE'RE IN YOUR TRAVEL GROUP THIS YEAR!
WHO ARE THEY?
THAT'S GREAT! ♡
WAP WAP
Bewildered
Yay! ♡
THEY REALLY SEEM TO LIKE TSUZUKI.
HEY...
WHO'S THE CUTIE-PIE?
That re-minds me...
TSUZUKI ...
I HEARD YOU GOT ANOTHER NEW PARTNER.
Then...
ARE *YOU* TSUZUKI'S NEW PARTNER?
STARE
STARE
UM, YEAH.
Not that new ...
You're a little behind the times.

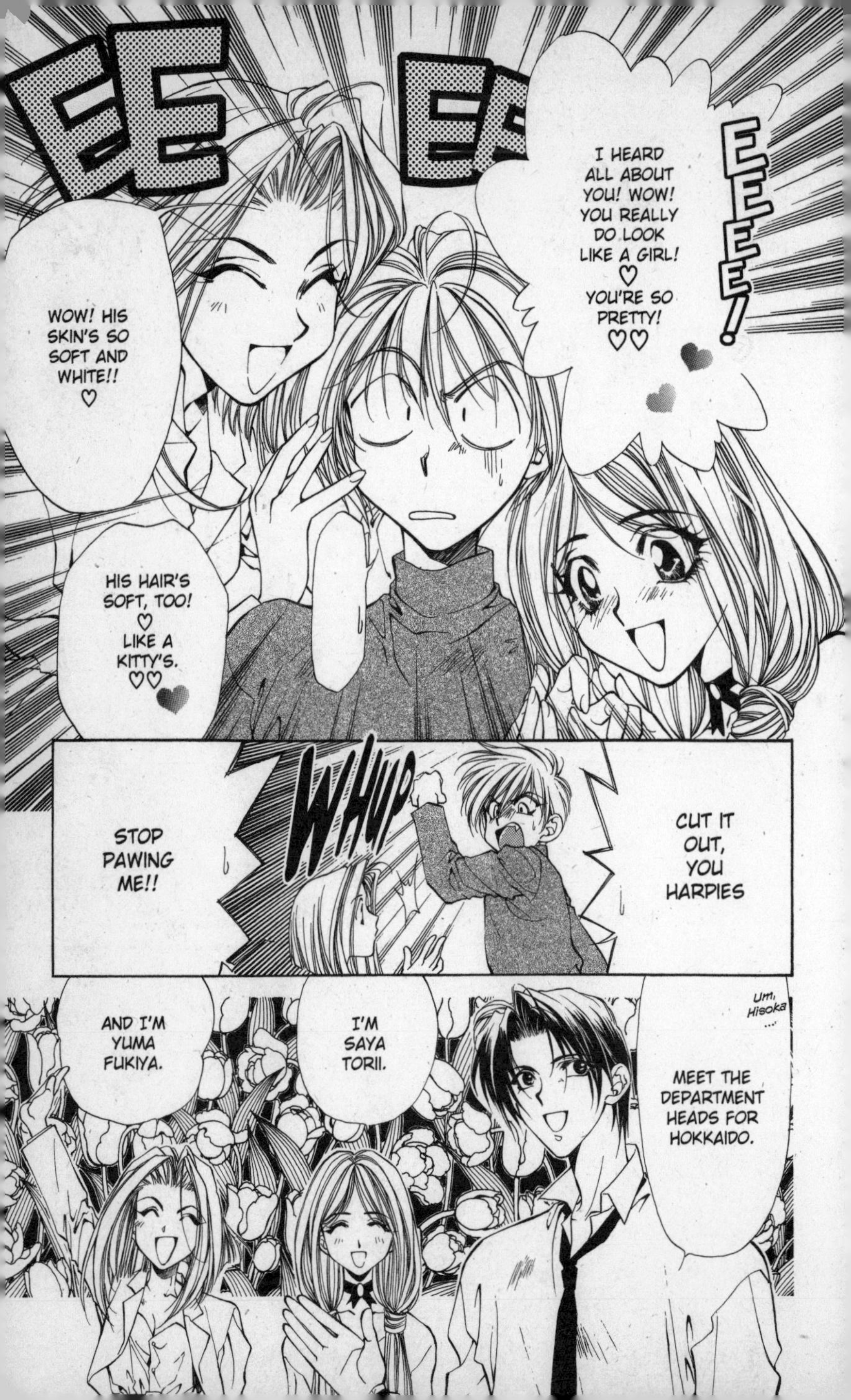
EEEEE!
I HEARD ALL ABOUT YOU! WOW! YOU REALLY DO LOOK LIKE A GIRL! ♡ YOU'RE SO PRETTY! ♡♡
WOW! HIS SKIN'S SO SOFT AND WHITE!! ♡
HIS HAIR'S SOFT, TOO! ♡ LIKE A KITTY'S. ♡♡
CUT IT OUT, YOU HARPIES
WHUP
STOP PAWING ME!!
Um, Hisoka...
MEET THE DEPARTMENT HEADS FOR HOKKAIDO.
I'M SAYA TORII.
AND I'M YUMA FUKIYA.

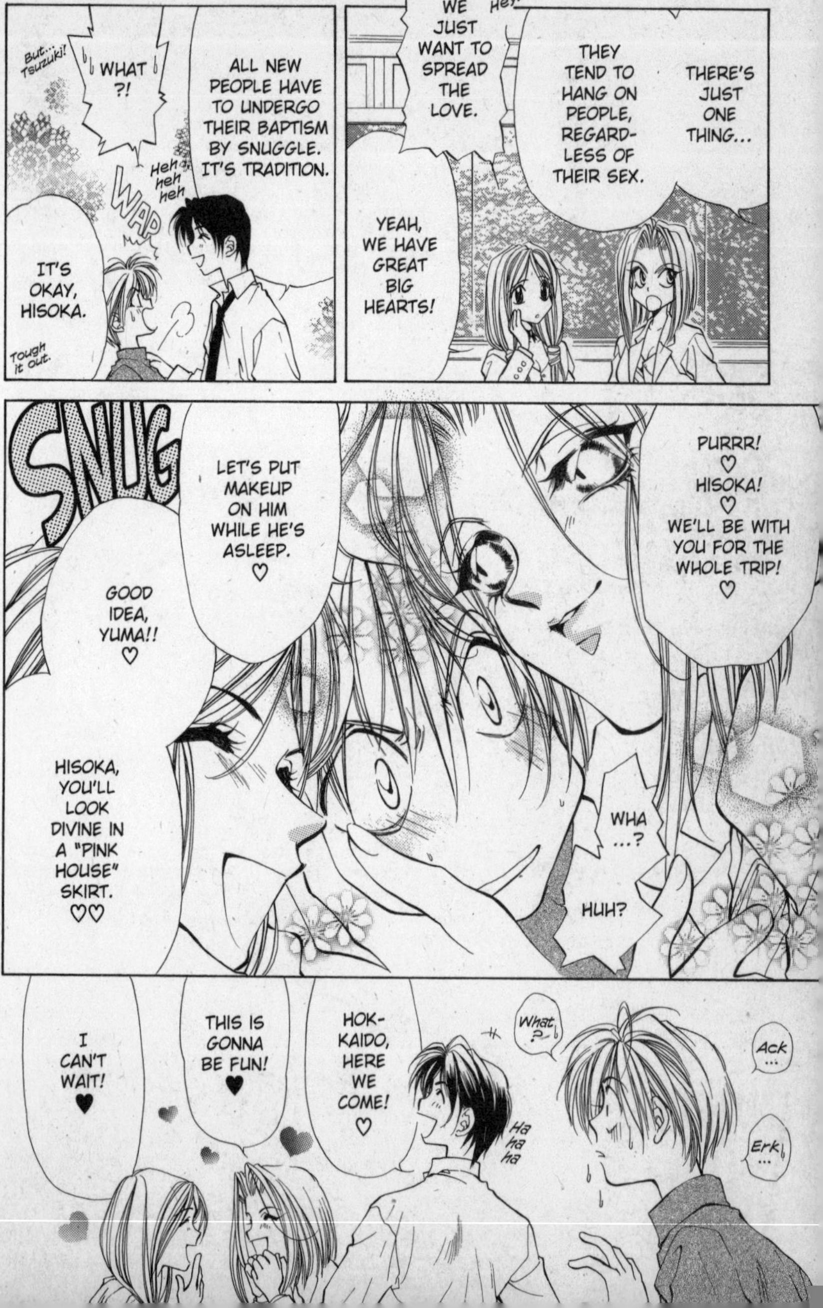
THERE'S JUST ONE THING...
THEY TEND TO HANG ON PEOPLE, REGARDLESS OF THEIR SEX.
Hey!
WE JUST WANT TO SPREAD THE LOVE.
YEAH, WE HAVE GREAT BIG HEARTS!
ALL NEW PEOPLE HAVE TO UNDERGO THEIR BAPTISM BY SNUGGLE. IT'S TRADITION.
WHAT ?!
But... Tsuzuki!
Heh heh heh
WAP
IT'S OKAY, HISOKA.
Tough it out.
PURRR! ♡ HISOKA! ♡ WE'LL BE WITH YOU FOR THE WHOLE TRIP! ♡
WHA ...?
HUH?
LET'S PUT MAKEUP ON HIM WHILE HE'S ASLEEP. ♡
SNUG
GOOD IDEA, YUMA!! ♡
HISOKA, YOU'LL LOOK DIVINE IN A "PINK HOUSE" SKIRT. ♡♡
Ack ...
Erk ...
What ?
Ha ha ha
HOK-KAIDO, HERE WE COME! ♡
THIS IS GONNA BE FUN! ♥
I CAN'T WAIT! ♥

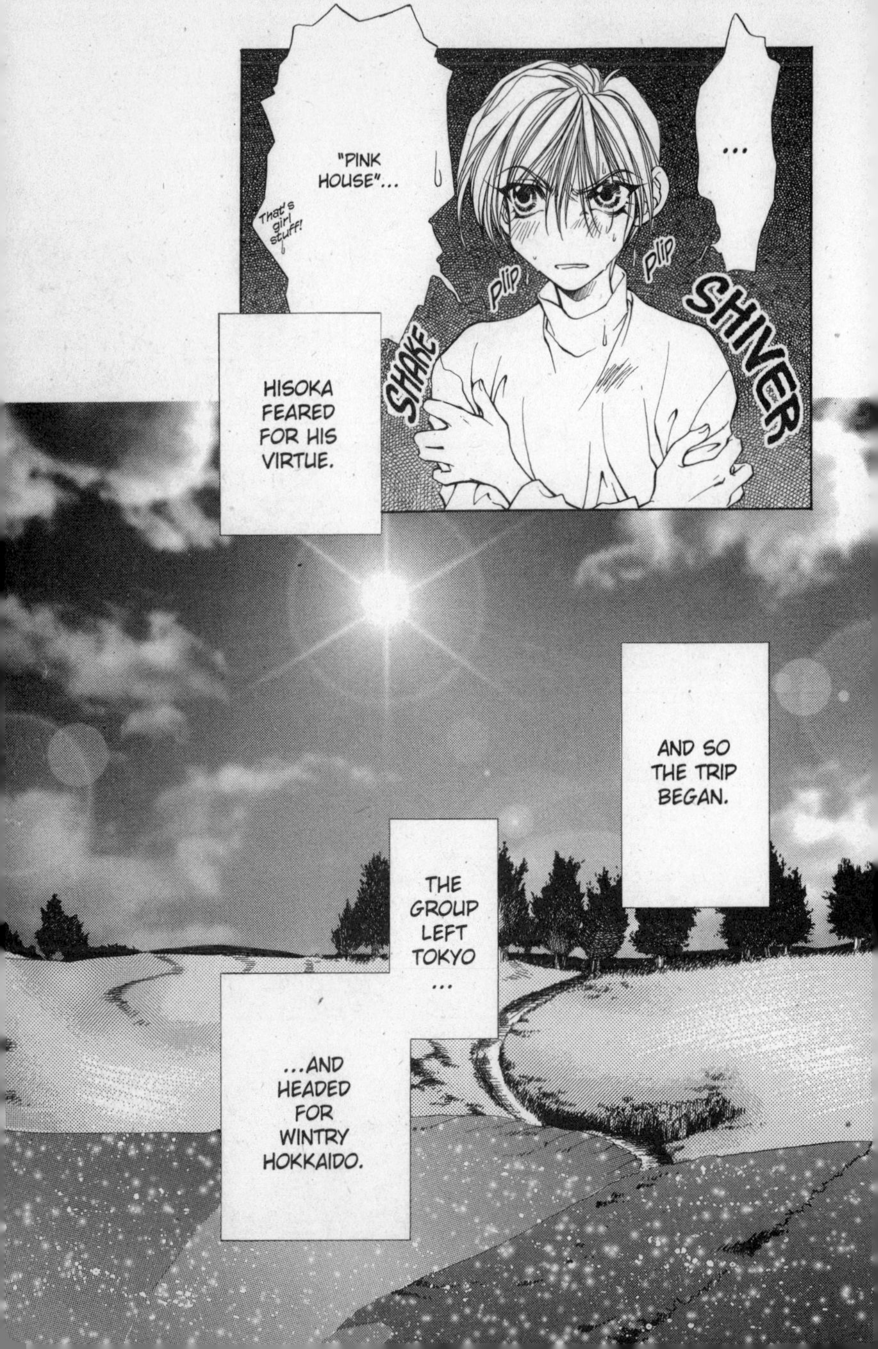
...
"PINK HOUSE"...
That's girl stuff!
plip plip
SHIVER
SHAKE
HISOKA FEARED FOR HIS VIRTUE.
AND SO THE TRIP BEGAN.
THE GROUP LEFT TOKYO ...
...AND HEADED FOR WINTRY HOKKAIDO.

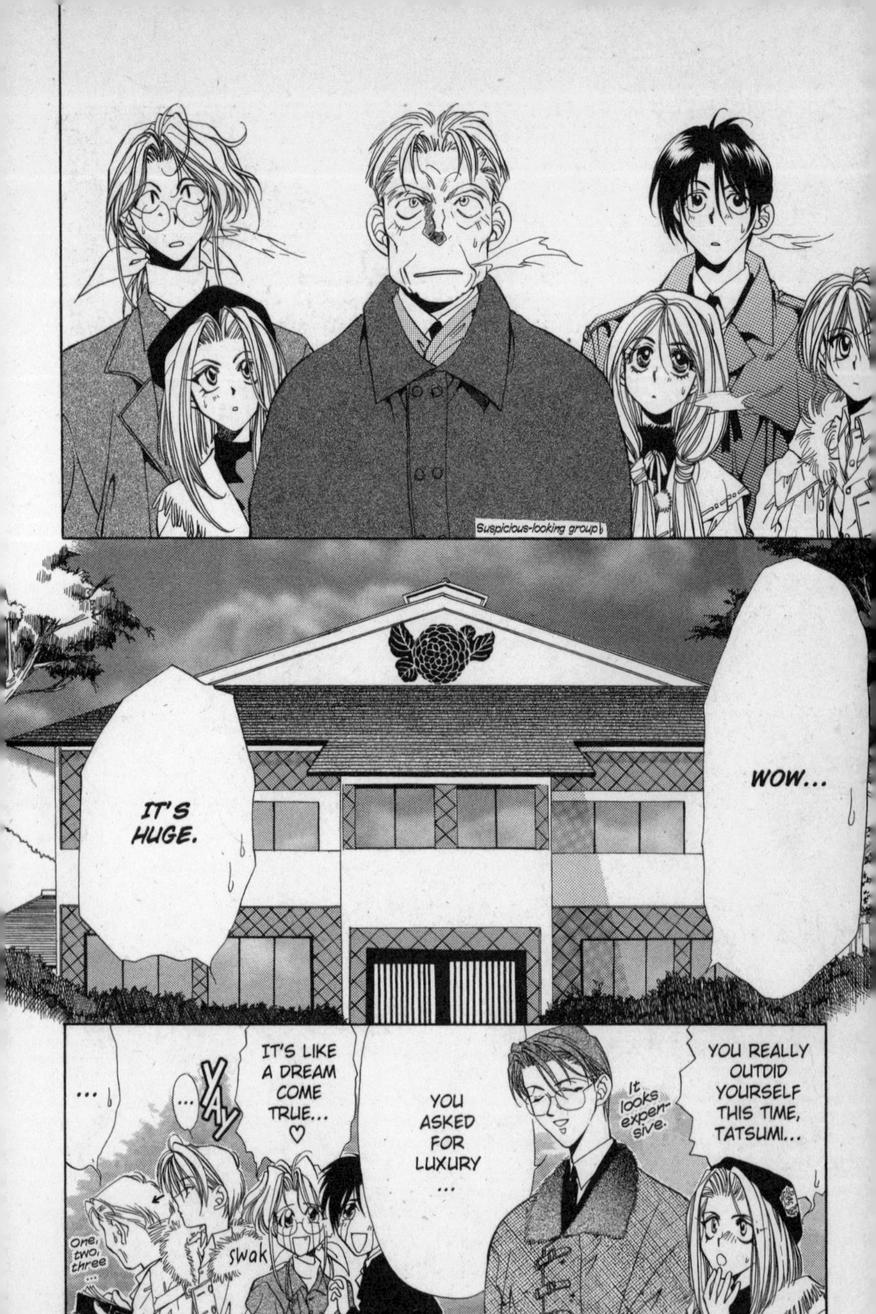
Suspicious-looking group
WOW...
IT'S HUGE.
YOU REALLY OUTDID YOURSELF THIS TIME, TATSUMI...
It looks expen-sive.
YOU ASKED FOR LUXURY...
IT'S LIKE A DREAM COME TRUE... ♡
YAY
...
...
swak
One, two, three...

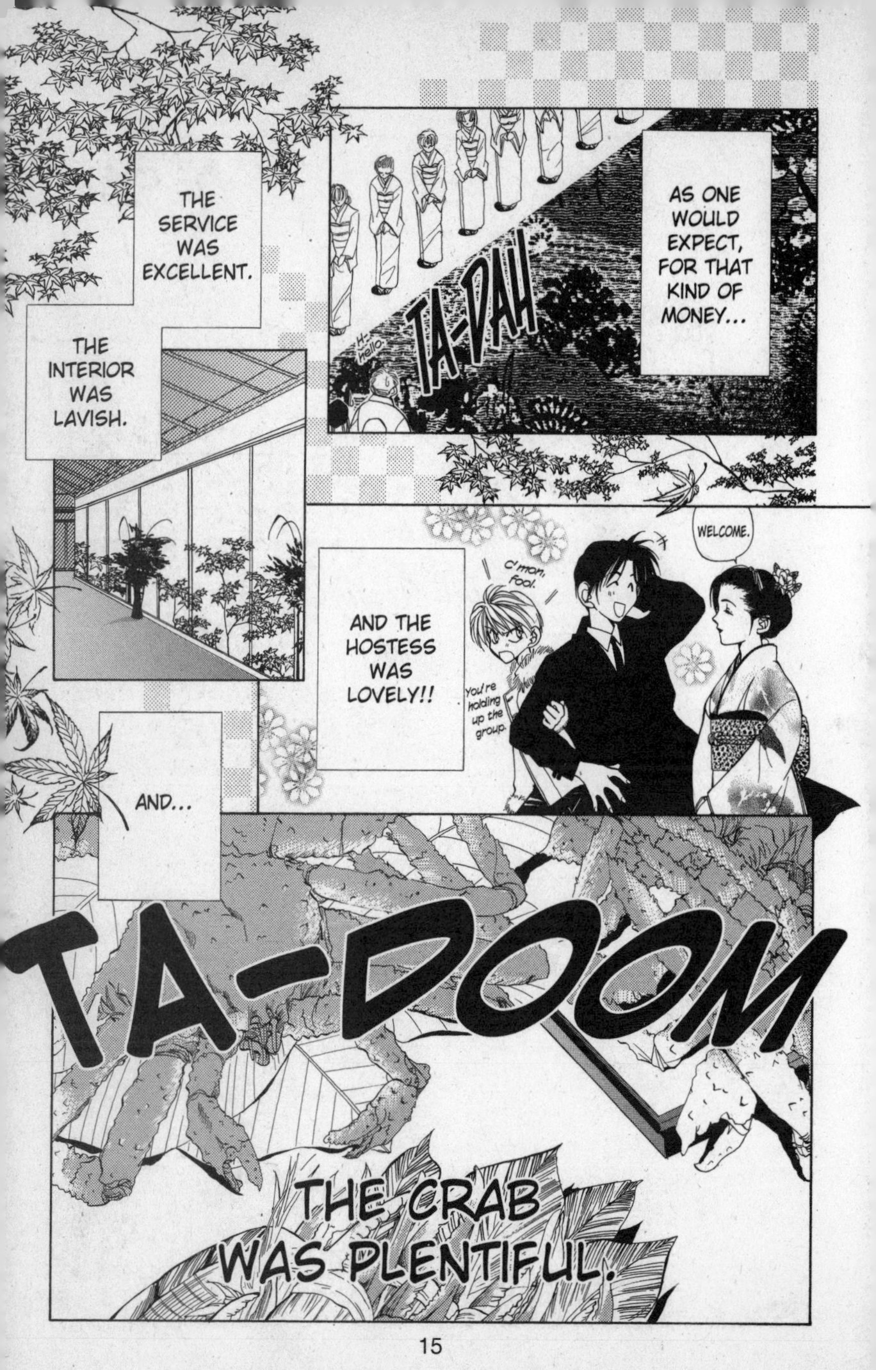
AS ONE WOULD EXPECT, FOR THAT KIND OF MONEY...
TA-DAH
H-hello.
THE SERVICE WAS EXCELLENT.
THE INTERIOR WAS LAVISH.
WELCOME.
C'mon, fool.
You're holding up the group.
AND THE HOSTESS WAS LOVELY!!
AND...
TA-DOOM
THE CRAB WAS PLENTIFUL.

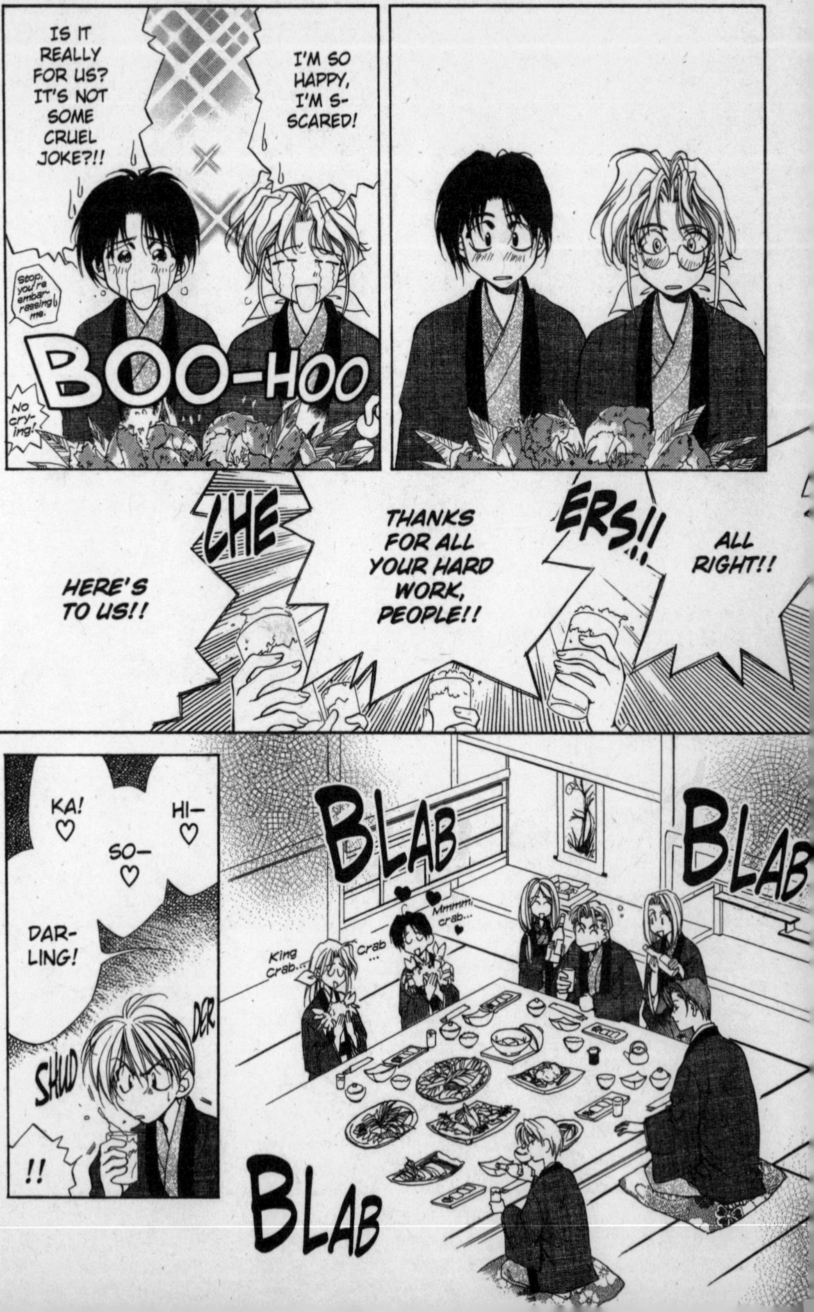
I'M SO HAPPY, I'M S-SCARED!
IS IT REALLY FOR US? IT'S NOT SOME CRUEL JOKE?!!
Stop, you're embarrassing me.
BOO-HOO
No crying!
ALL RIGHT!!
CHE ERS!!
THANKS FOR ALL YOUR HARD WORK, PEOPLE!!
HERE'S TO US!!
BLAB
BLAB
Mmmm, crab...
Crab ...
King Crab...
BLAB
KA! ♡
HI– ♡
SO– ♡
DAR-LING!
SHUD DER
!!

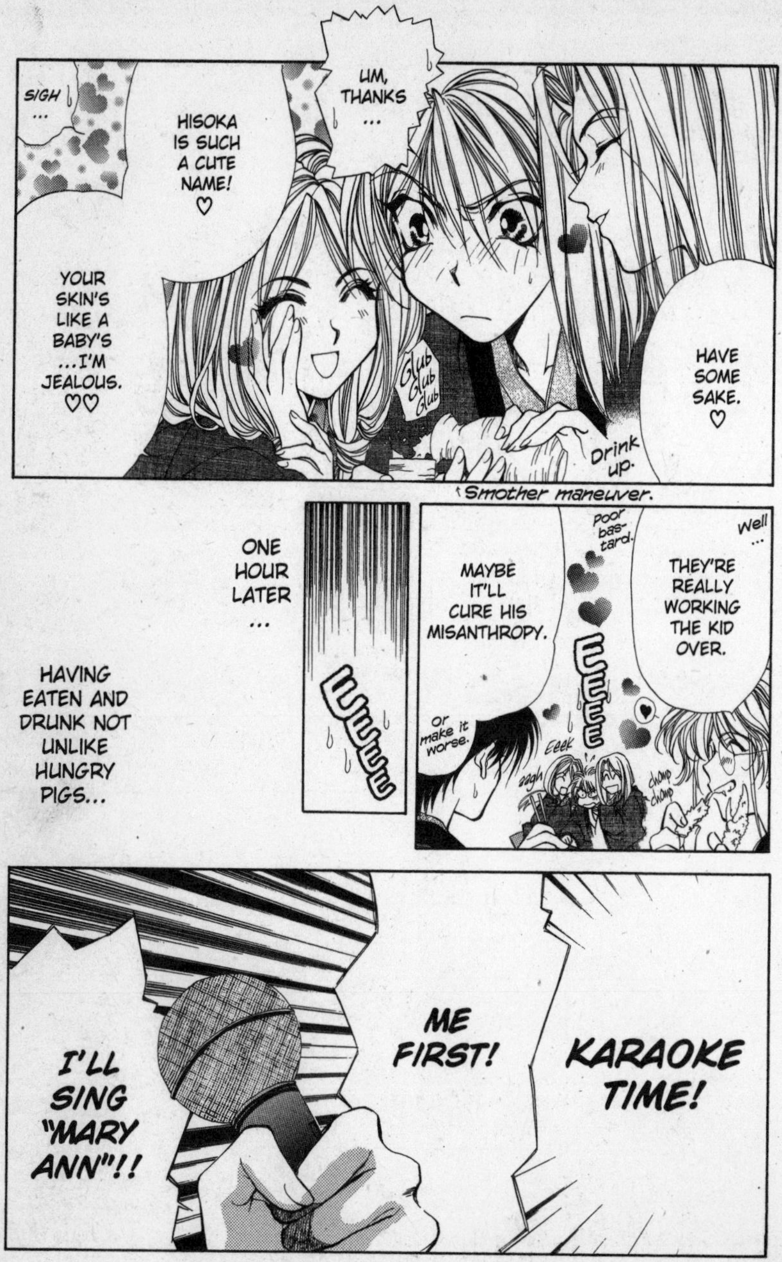
UM, THANKS ...
HAVE SOME SAKE. ♡
Drink up.
HISOKA IS SUCH A CUTE NAME! ♡
SIGH ...
Glub Glub Glub
YOUR SKIN'S LIKE A BABY'S ...I'M JEALOUS. ♡♡
Smother maneuver.
Well ...
THEY'RE REALLY WORKING THE KID OVER.
Poor bastard.
MAYBE IT'LL CURE HIS MISANTHROPY.
EEEE
Or make it worse.
Eeek
aagh
chomp chomp
ONE HOUR LATER ...
HAVING EATEN AND DRUNK NOT UNLIKE HUNGRY PIGS...
KARAOKE TIME!
ME FIRST!
I'LL SING "MARY ANN"!!

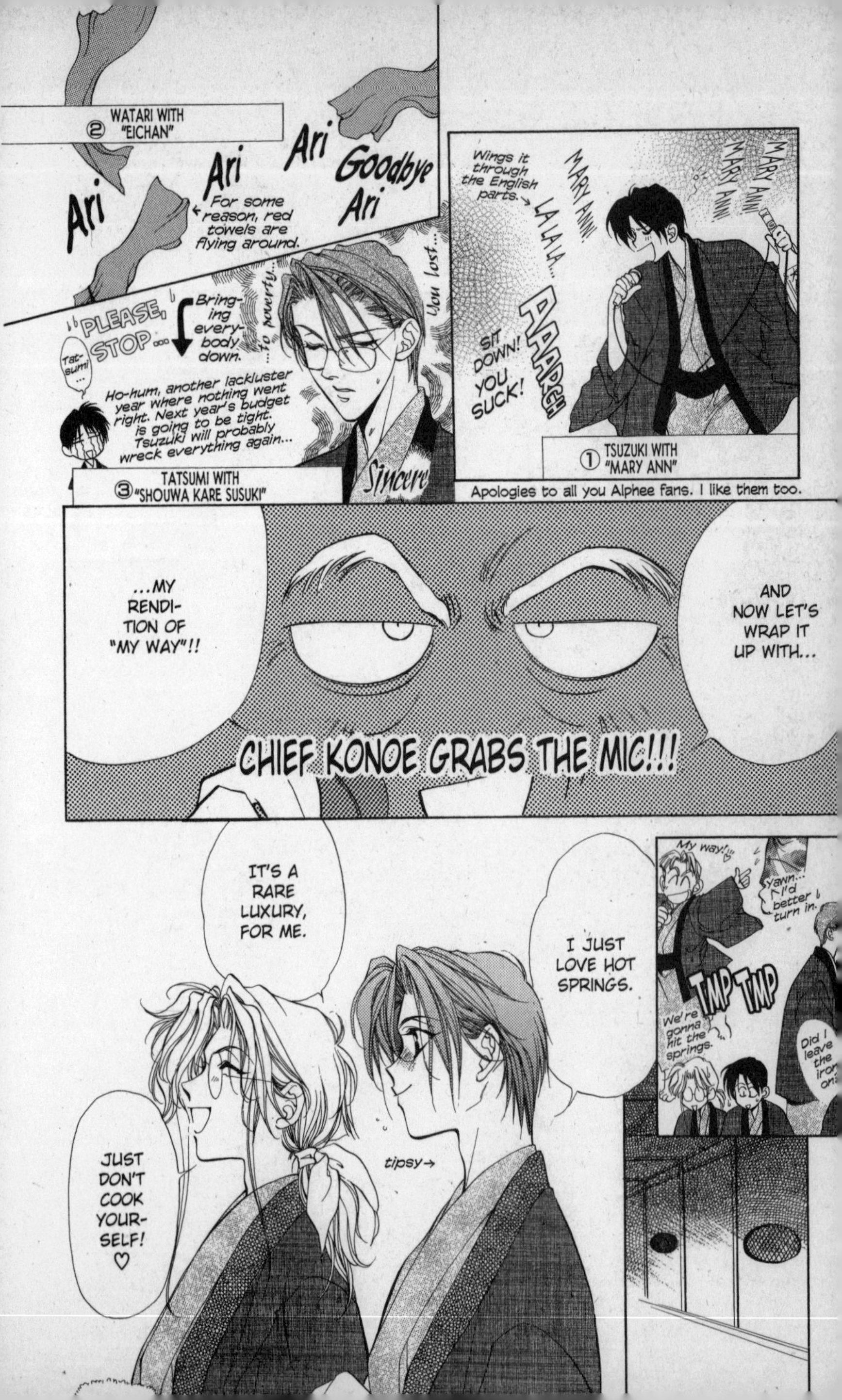

MARY ANN MARY ANN
Wings it through the English parts.→
MARY ANN!
LA LA LA...
AAARGH
SIT DOWN! YOU SUCK!
① TSUZUKI WITH "MARY ANN"
Apologies to all you Alphee fans. I like them too.
② WATARI WITH "EICHAN"
Goodbye Ari
Ari
Ari
Ari
For some reason, red towels are flying around.
You lost...
...to poverty...
Bringing everybody down.
PLEASE, STOP...
Tatsumi...
Ho-hum, another lackluster year where nothing went right. Next year's budget is going to be tight. Tsuzuki will probably wreck everything again...
Sincere
③ TATSUMI WITH "SHOUWA KARE SUSUKI"
AND NOW LET'S WRAP IT UP WITH...
...MY RENDITION OF "MY WAY"!!
CHIEF KONOE GRABS THE MIC!!!
My way!
Yawn... I'd better turn in.
TMP TMP
We're gonna hit the springs.
Did I leave the iron on?
I JUST LOVE HOT SPRINGS.
tipsy→
IT'S A RARE LUXURY, FOR ME.
JUST DON'T COOK YOURSELF! ♡

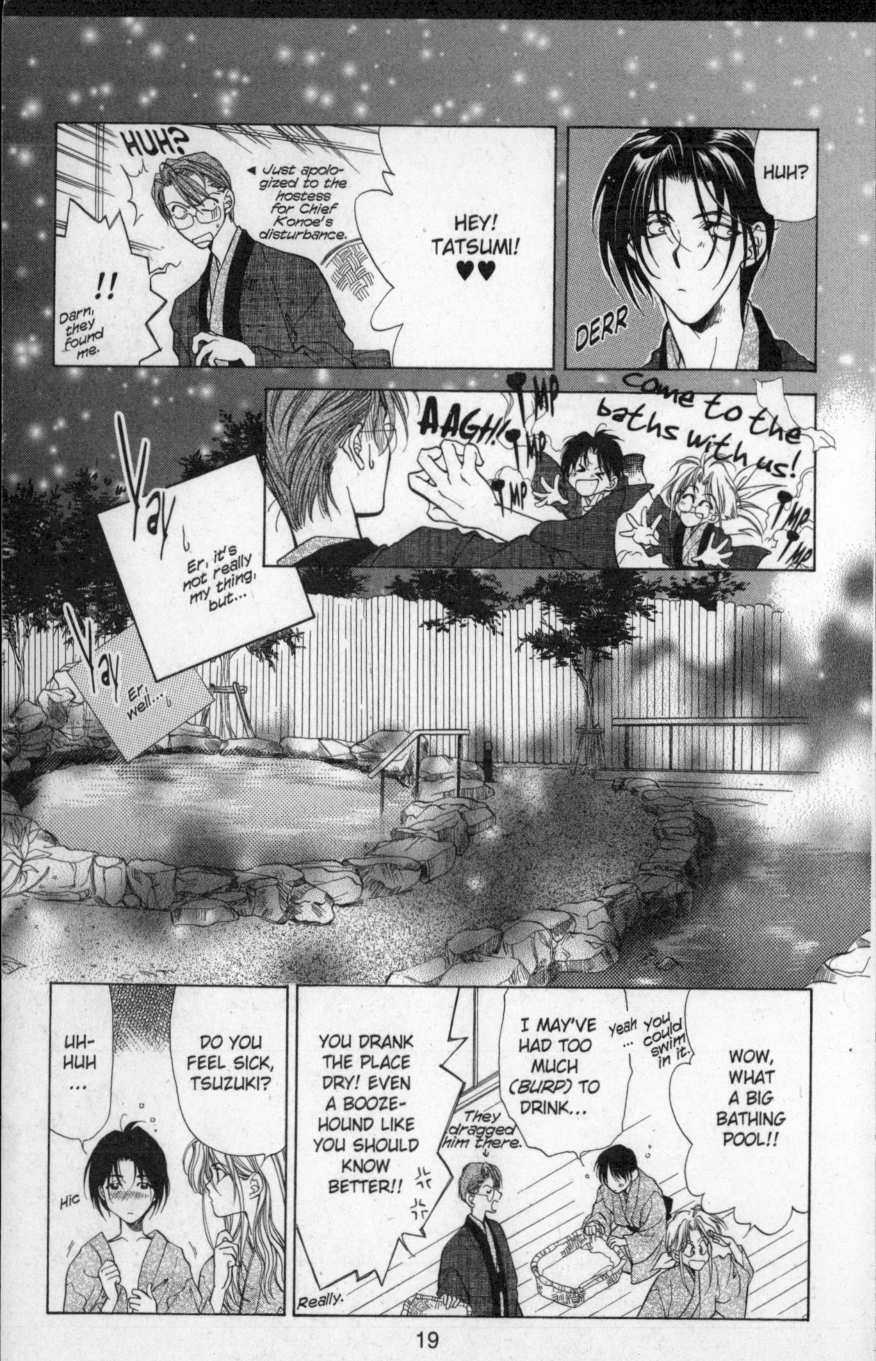
HUH?
DERR
HEY! TATSUMI! ♥♥
◀ Just apologized to the hostess for Chief Konoe's disturbance.
HUH?
!!
Darn, they found me.
Come to the baths with us!
TMP TMP
AAGH!
TMP TMP
Yay
Er, it's not really my thing, but...
Yay
Er, well...
WOW, WHAT A BIG BATHING POOL!!
Yeah ... you could swim in it.
I MAY'VE HAD TOO MUCH (BURP) TO DRINK...
They dragged him there.
YOU DRANK THE PLACE DRY! EVEN A BOOZE-HOUND LIKE YOU SHOULD KNOW BETTER!!
Really.
DO YOU FEEL SICK, TSUZUKI?
UH-HUH ...
Hic

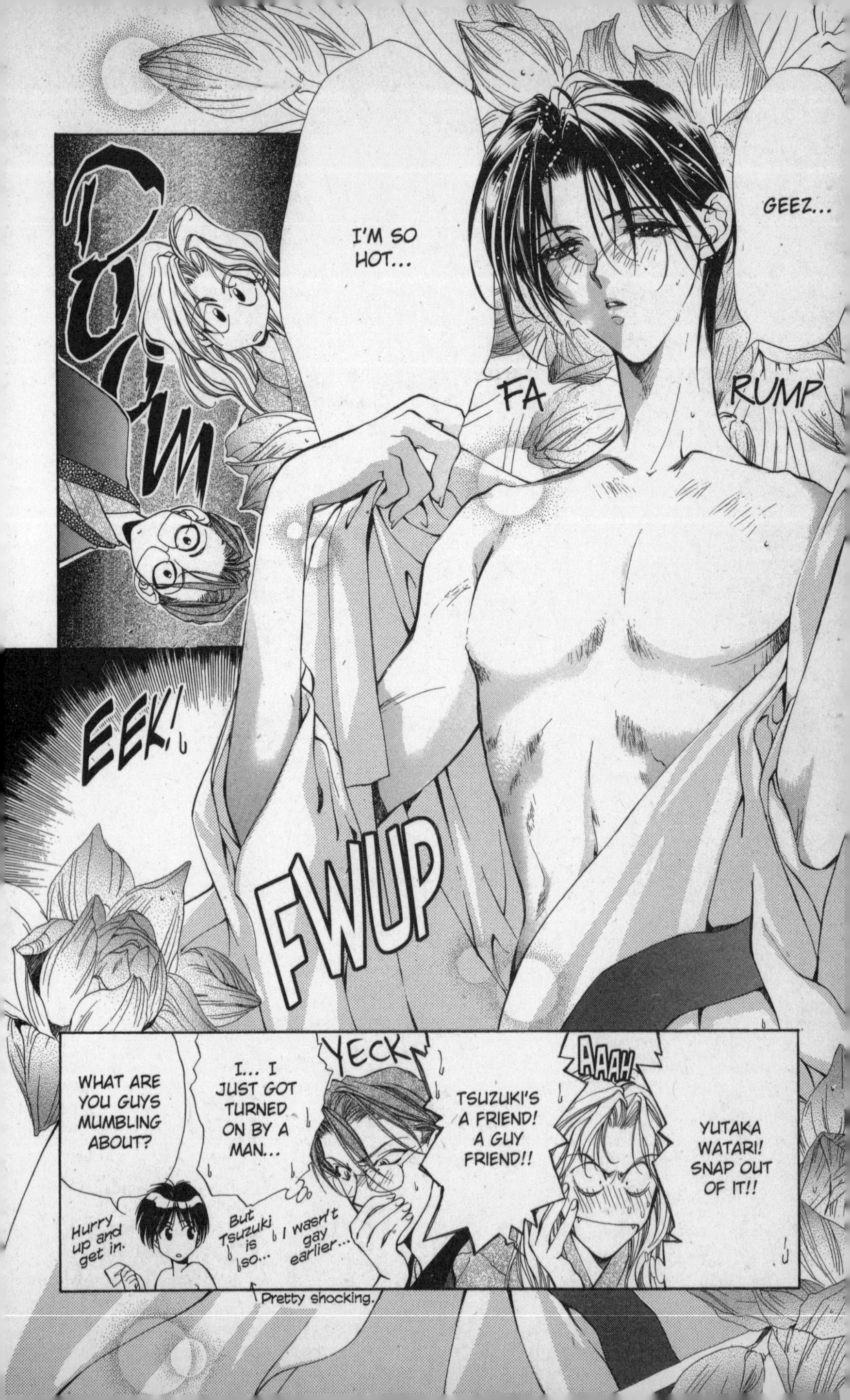
GEEZ...
I'M SO HOT...
FA
RUMP
EEK!
FWUP
YUTAKA WATARI! SNAP OUT OF IT!!
AAAH
TSUZUKI'S A FRIEND! A GUY FRIEND!!
YECK
I... I JUST GOT TURNED ON BY A MAN...
I wasn't gay earlier...
But Tsuzuki is so...
WHAT ARE YOU GUYS MUMBLING ABOUT?
Hurry up and get in.
Pretty shocking.

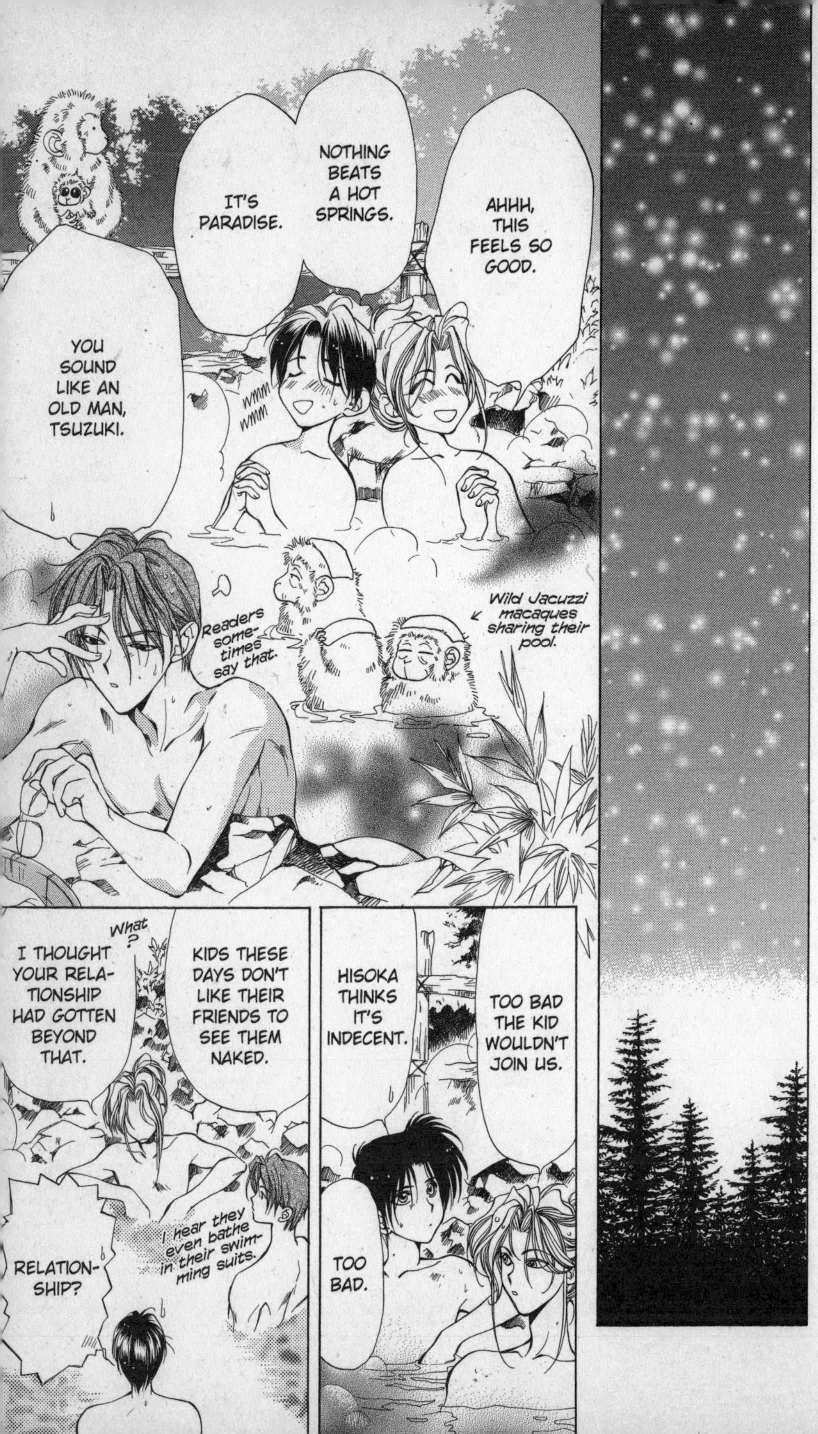
AHHH, THIS FEELS SO GOOD.
NOTHING BEATS A HOT SPRINGS.
IT'S PARADISE.
YOU SOUND LIKE AN OLD MAN, TSUZUKI.
WMM WMM
Wild Jacuzzi macaques sharing their pool.
Readers sometimes say that.
TOO BAD THE KID WOULDN'T JOIN US.
HISOKA THINKS IT'S INDECENT.
TOO BAD.
KIDS THESE DAYS DON'T LIKE THEIR FRIENDS TO SEE THEM NAKED.
What?
I THOUGHT YOUR RELATIONSHIP HAD GOTTEN BEYOND THAT.
I hear they even bathe in their swimming suits.
RELATIONSHIP?

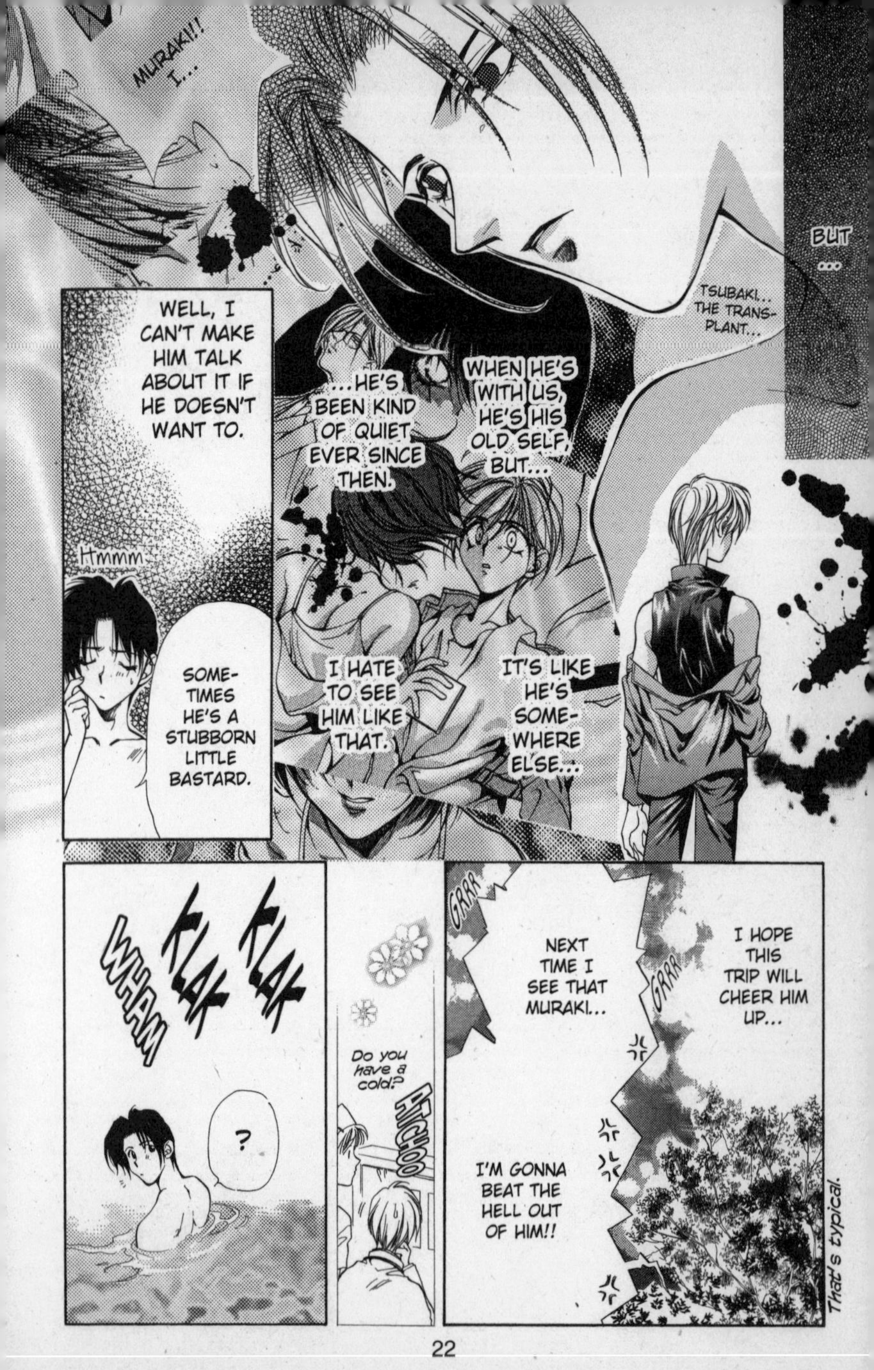
BUT...
TSUBAKI... THE TRANSPLANT...
MURAKI!! I...
WHEN HE'S WITH US, HE'S HIS OLD SELF, BUT...
...HE'S BEEN KIND OF QUIET EVER SINCE THEN.
IT'S LIKE HE'S SOMEWHERE ELSE...
I HATE TO SEE HIM LIKE THAT.
WELL, I CAN'T MAKE HIM TALK ABOUT IT IF HE DOESN'T WANT TO.
Hmmm
SOMETIMES HE'S A STUBBORN LITTLE BASTARD.
That's typical.
I HOPE THIS TRIP WILL CHEER HIM UP...
GRRR
NEXT TIME I SEE THAT MURAKI...
GRRR
I'M GONNA BEAT THE HELL OUT OF HIM!!
ATCHOO
Do you have a cold?
KLAK
KLAK
WHAM
?

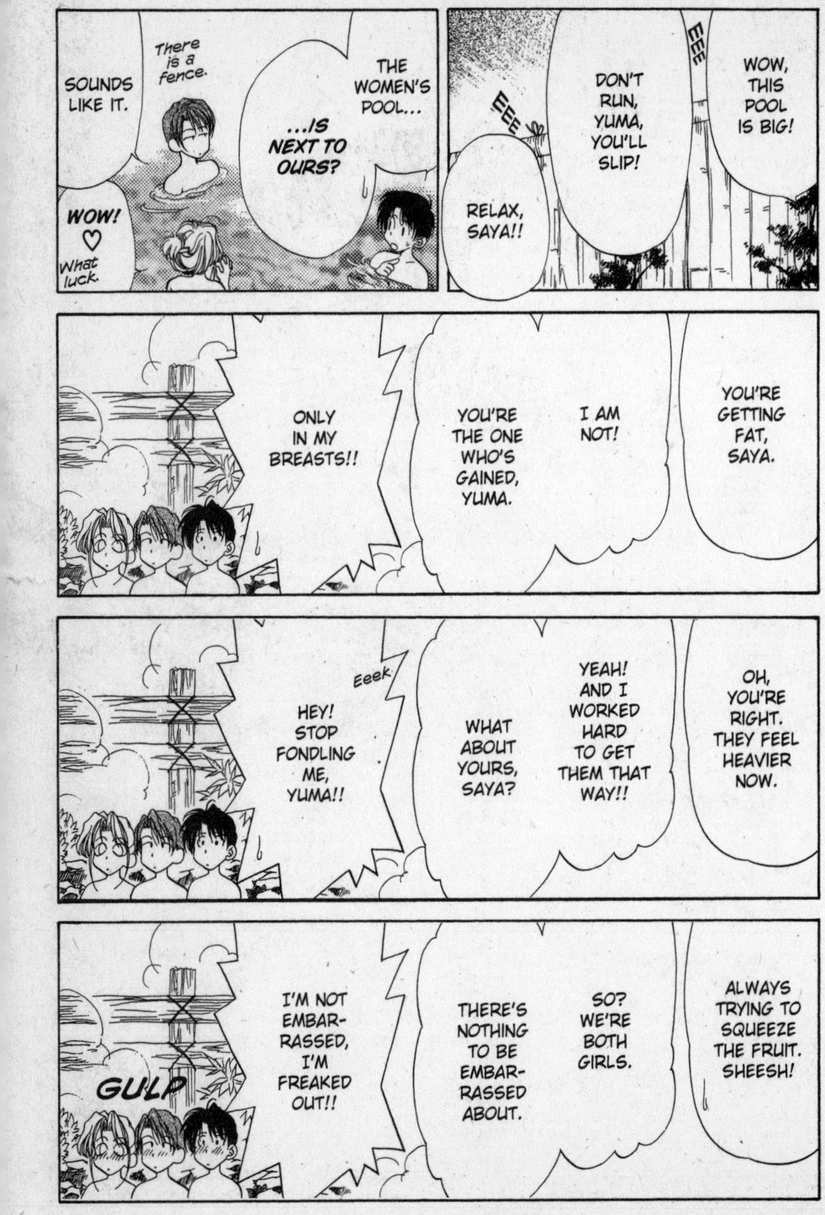
WOW, THIS POOL IS BIG!
EEE
DON'T RUN, YUMA, YOU'LL SLIP!
EEE
RELAX, SAYA!!
THE WOMEN'S POOL...
...IS NEXT TO OURS?
There is a fence.
SOUNDS LIKE IT.
WOW! ♡ What luck.
YOU'RE GETTING FAT, SAYA.
I AM NOT!
YOU'RE THE ONE WHO'S GAINED, YUMA.
ONLY IN MY BREASTS!!
OH, YOU'RE RIGHT. THEY FEEL HEAVIER NOW.
YEAH! AND I WORKED HARD TO GET THEM THAT WAY!!
WHAT ABOUT YOURS, SAYA?
Eeek
HEY! STOP FONDLING ME, YUMA!!
ALWAYS TRYING TO SQUEEZE THE FRUIT. SHEESH!
SO? WE'RE BOTH GIRLS.
THERE'S NOTHING TO BE EMBARRASSED ABOUT.
I'M NOT EMBARRASSED, I'M FREAKED OUT!!
GULP

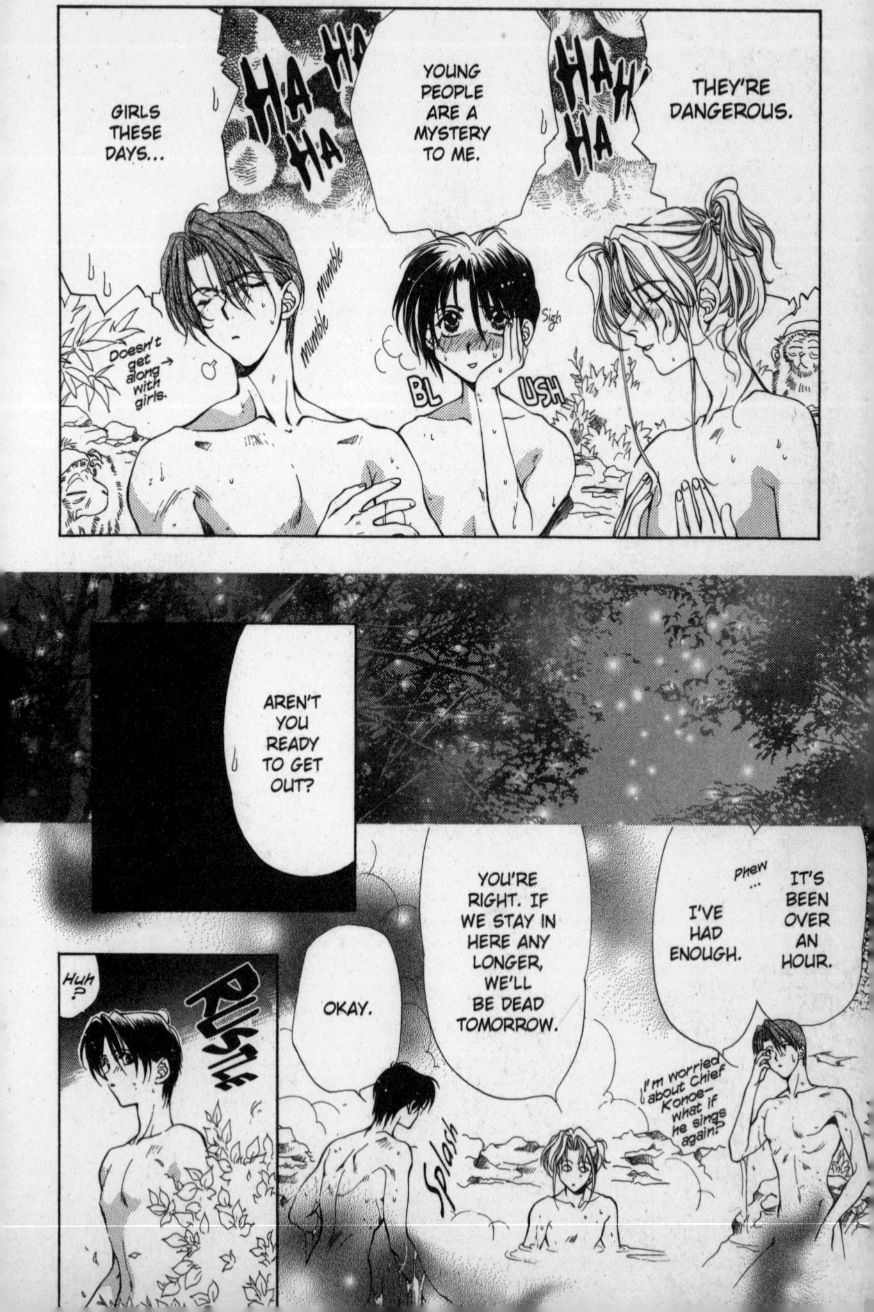
THEY'RE DANGEROUS.
HA HA
YOUNG PEOPLE ARE A MYSTERY TO ME.
HA HA HA
GIRLS THESE DAYS...
Sigh
BLUSH
mumble mumble
Doesn't get along with girls.
AREN'T YOU READY TO GET OUT?
IT'S BEEN OVER AN HOUR.
Phew...
I'VE HAD ENOUGH.
YOU'RE RIGHT. IF WE STAY IN HERE ANY LONGER, WE'LL BE DEAD TOMORROW.
I'm worried about Chief Konoe—what if he sings again?
OKAY.
Splash
RUSTLE
Huh?

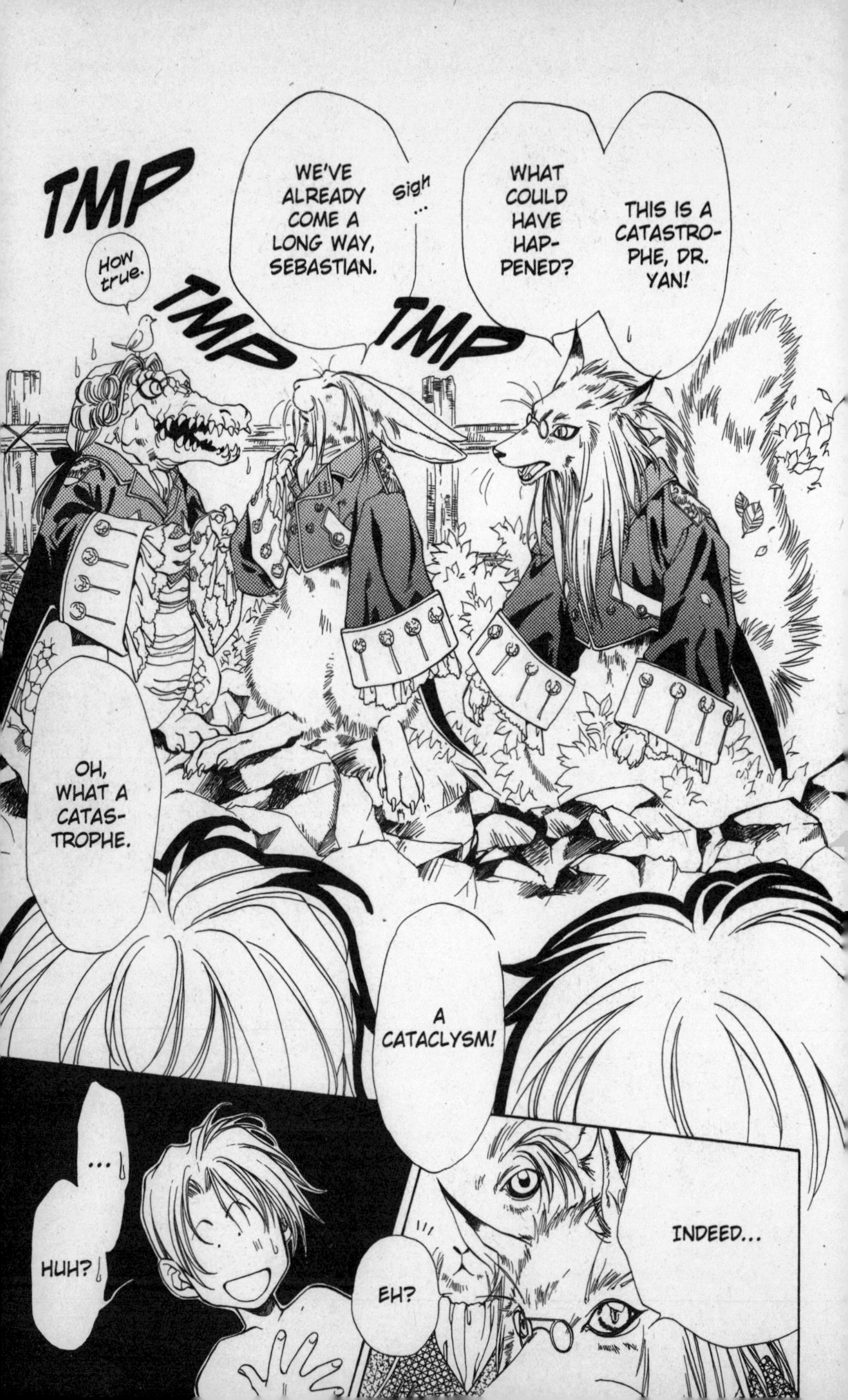
THIS IS A CATASTROPHE, DR. YAN!
WHAT COULD HAVE HAPPENED?
Sigh ...
WE'VE ALREADY COME A LONG WAY, SEBASTIAN.
TMP
TMP
TMP
How true.
OH, WHAT A CATASTROPHE.
A CATACLYSM!
INDEED...
EH?
...
HUH?

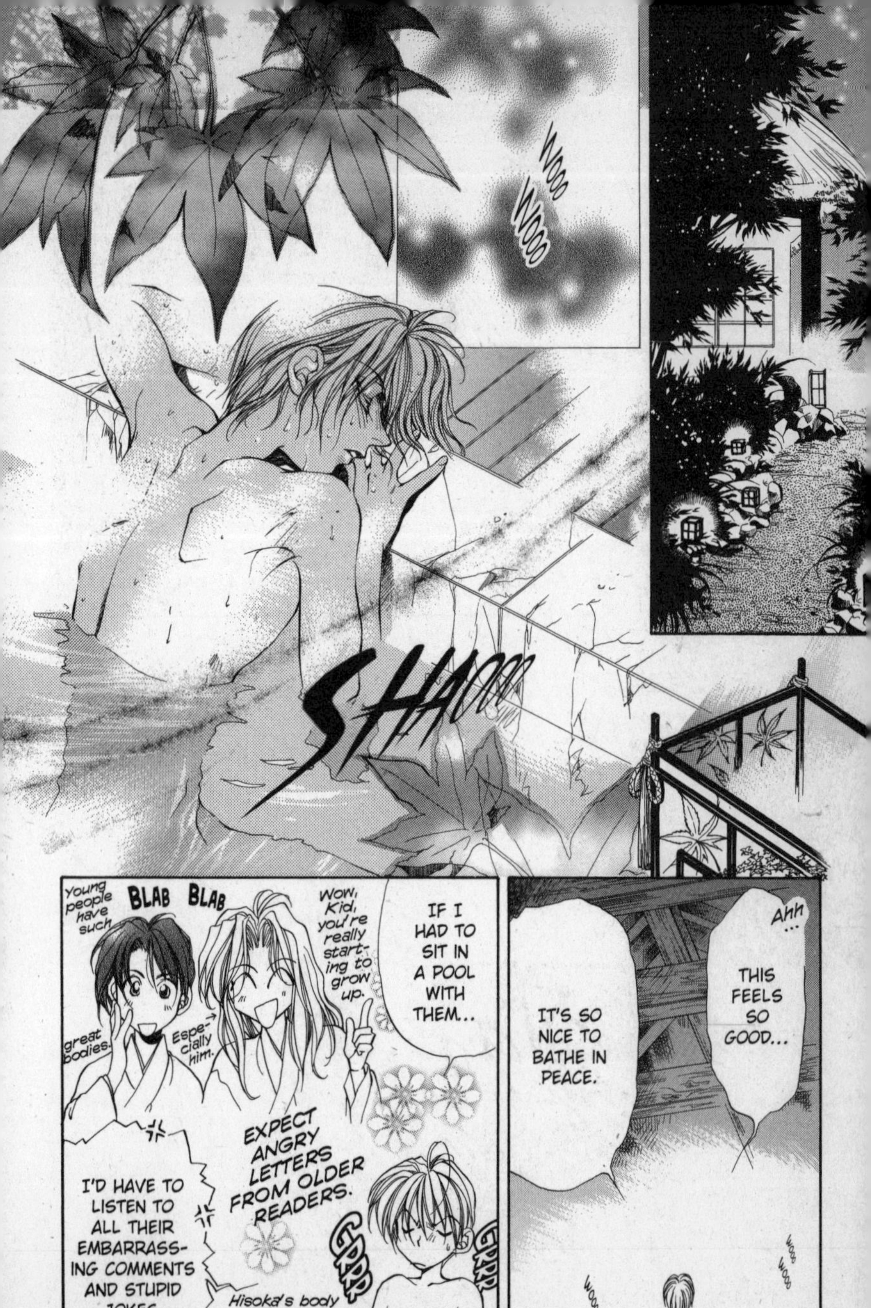
WOOO
WOOO
SHAOO
Ahh...
THIS FEELS SO GOOD...
IT'S SO NICE TO BATHE IN PEACE.
WOO WOO
WOO
IF I HAD TO SIT IN A POOL WITH THEM...
Wow, Kid, you're really start-ing to grow up.
BLAB BLAB
Young people have such great bodies.
Espe-cially him.
I'D HAVE TO LISTEN TO ALL THEIR EMBARRASS-ING COMMENTS AND STUPID JOKES.
EXPECT ANGRY LETTERS FROM OLDER READERS.
GRRR GRRR
Hisoka's body isn't very developed.

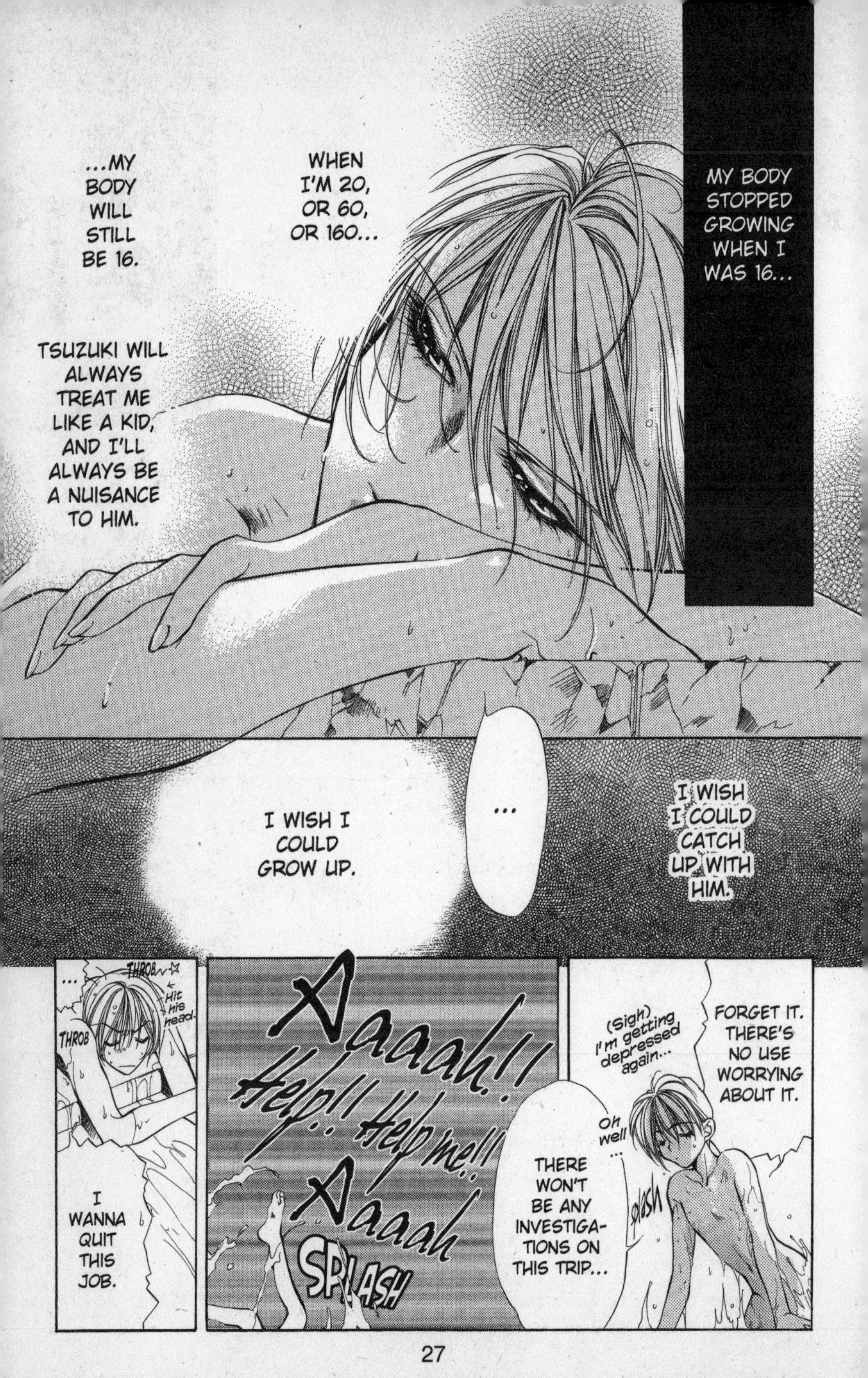
MY BODY STOPPED GROWING WHEN I WAS 16...
WHEN I'M 20, OR 60, OR 160...
...MY BODY WILL STILL BE 16.
TSUZUKI WILL ALWAYS TREAT ME LIKE A KID, AND I'LL ALWAYS BE A NUISANCE TO HIM.
I WISH I COULD CATCH UP WITH HIM.
...
I WISH I COULD GROW UP.
FORGET IT. THERE'S NO USE WORRYING ABOUT IT.
(Sigh) I'm getting depressed again...
Oh well...
THERE WON'T BE ANY INVESTIGA-TIONS ON THIS TRIP...
splash
Aaaah!! Help!! Help me!! Aaaah
SPLASH
THROB
← Hit his head.
...
THROB
I WANNA QUIT THIS JOB.

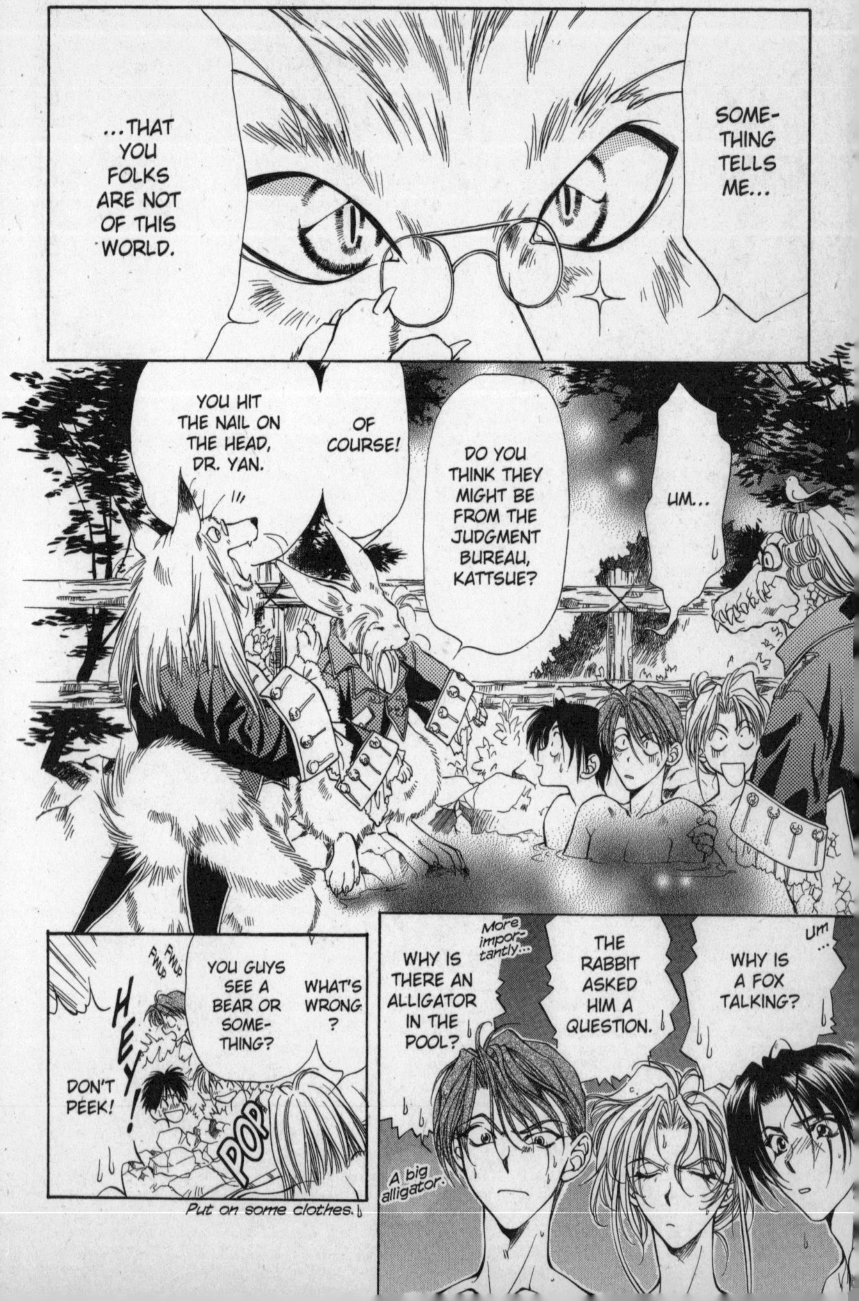
SOME-THING TELLS ME...
...THAT YOU FOLKS ARE NOT OF THIS WORLD.
UM...
DO YOU THINK THEY MIGHT BE FROM THE JUDGMENT BUREAU, KATTSUE?
OF COURSE!
YOU HIT THE NAIL ON THE HEAD, DR. YAN.
Um...
WHY IS A FOX TALKING?
THE RABBIT ASKED HIM A QUESTION.
More importantly...
WHY IS THERE AN ALLIGATOR IN THE POOL?
A big alligator.
WHAT'S WRONG?
YOU GUYS SEE A BEAR OR SOMETHING?
FWUP FWUP
HEY!
DON'T PEEK!
POP
Put on some clothes.

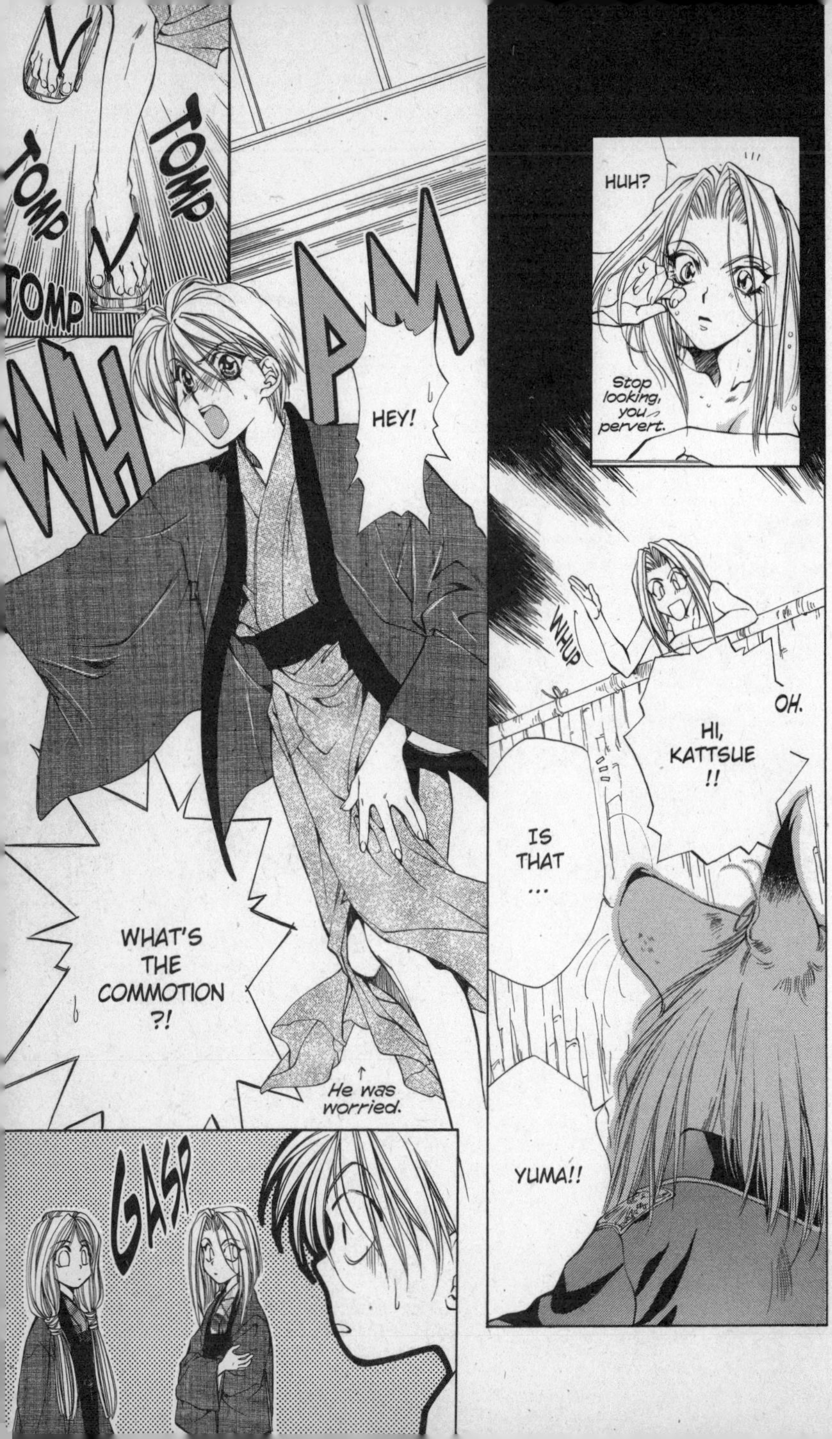
HUH?
Stop looking, you pervert.
WHUP
OH.
HI, KATTSUE !!
IS THAT ...
YUMA!!
TOMP
TOMP
TOMP
TOMP
WHAM
HEY!
WHAT'S THE COMMOTION ?!
↑ He was worried.
GASP

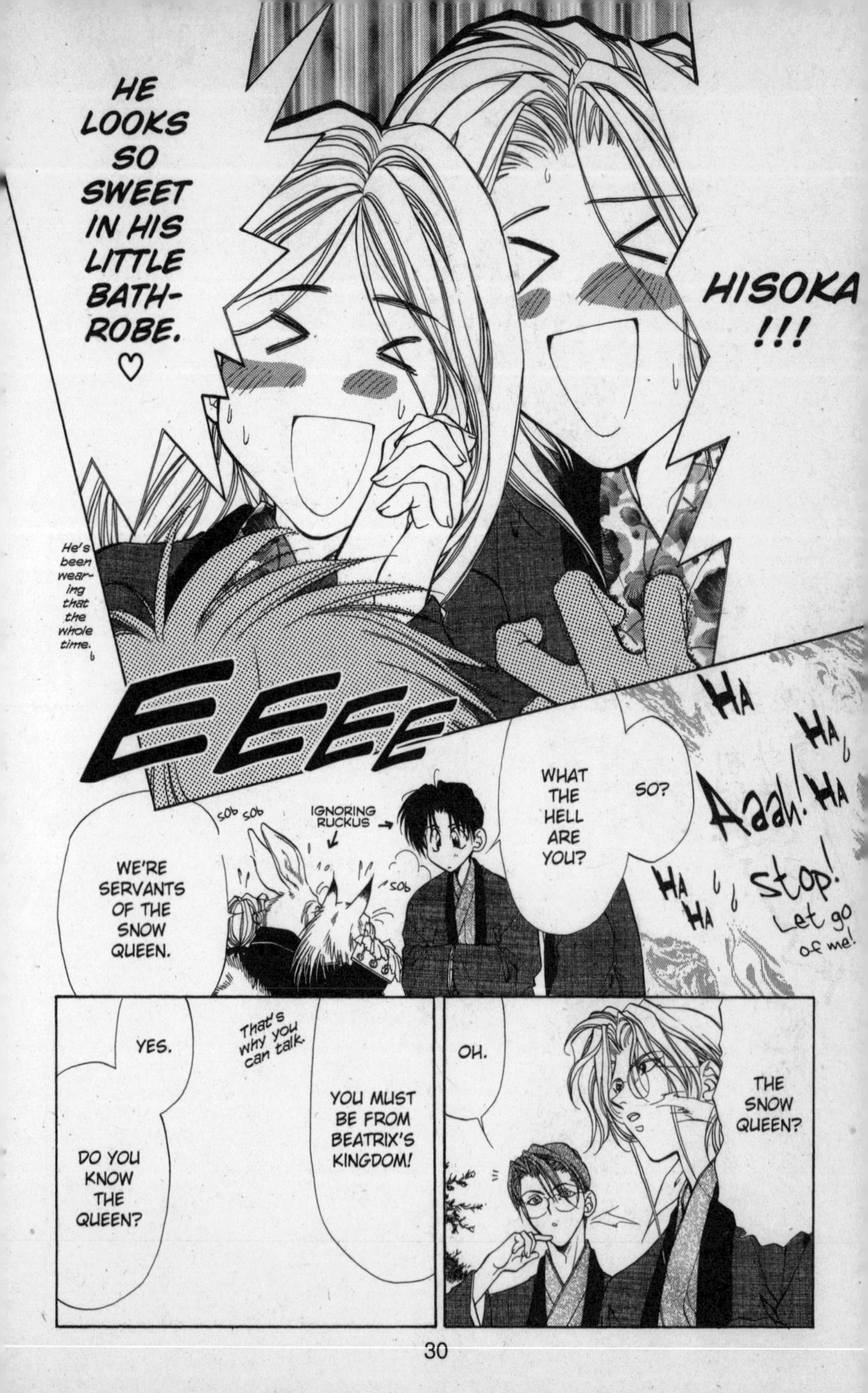
HISOKA!!!
HE LOOKS SO SWEET IN HIS LITTLE BATH-ROBE. ♡
He's been wear-ing that the whole time.
EEEE
HA HA HA HA HA
Aaah! Stop! Let go of me!
SO?
WHAT THE HELL ARE YOU?
IGNORING RUCKUS
sob sob sob
WE'RE SERVANTS OF THE SNOW QUEEN.
THE SNOW QUEEN?
OH.
YOU MUST BE FROM BEATRIX'S KINGDOM!
That's why you can talk.
YES.
DO YOU KNOW THE QUEEN?

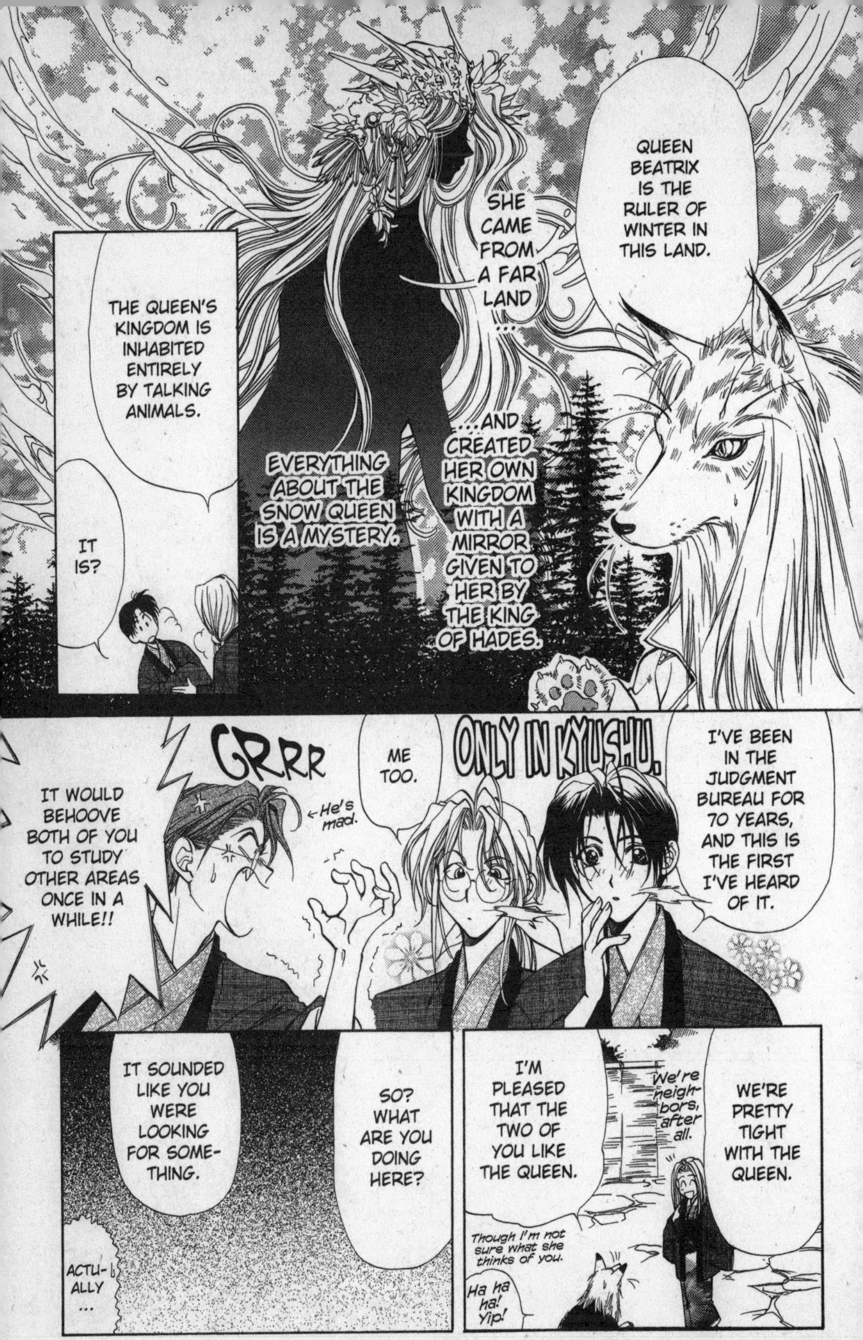
QUEEN BEATRIX IS THE RULER OF WINTER IN THIS LAND.
SHE CAME FROM A FAR LAND...
...AND CREATED HER OWN KINGDOM WITH A MIRROR GIVEN TO HER BY THE KING OF HADES.
EVERYTHING ABOUT THE SNOW QUEEN IS A MYSTERY.
THE QUEEN'S KINGDOM IS INHABITED ENTIRELY BY TALKING ANIMALS.
IT IS?
I'VE BEEN IN THE JUDGMENT BUREAU FOR 70 YEARS, AND THIS IS THE FIRST I'VE HEARD OF IT.
ONLY IN KYUSHU.
ME TOO.
GRRR
←He's mad.
IT WOULD BEHOOVE BOTH OF YOU TO STUDY OTHER AREAS ONCE IN A WHILE!!
WE'RE PRETTY TIGHT WITH THE QUEEN.
We're neighbors, after all.
I'M PLEASED THAT THE TWO OF YOU LIKE THE QUEEN.
Though I'm not sure what she thinks of you.
Ha ha ha! Yip!
SO? WHAT ARE YOU DOING HERE?
IT SOUNDED LIKE YOU WERE LOOKING FOR SOME-THING.
ACTUALLY...

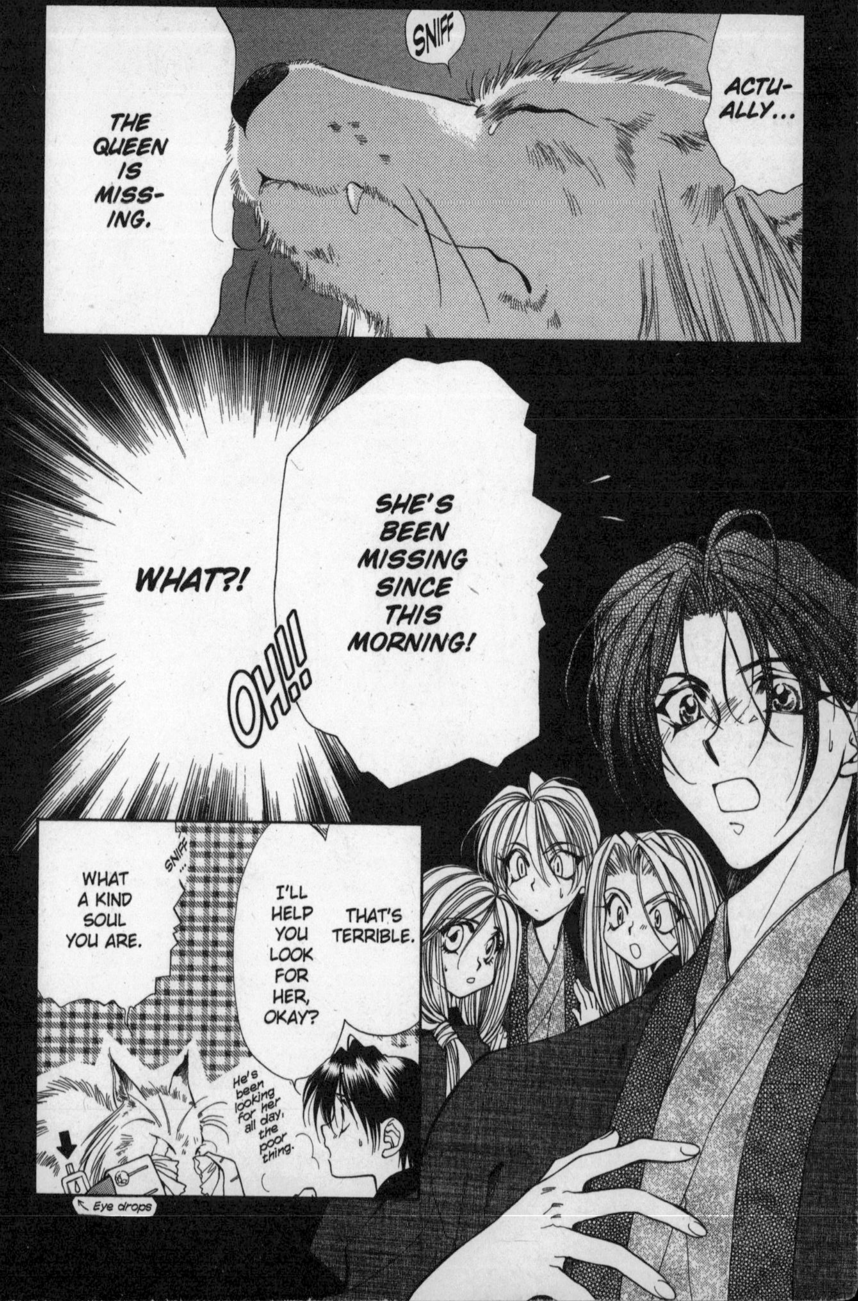

ACTU-ALLY...
SNIFF
THE QUEEN IS MISSING.
SHE'S BEEN MISSING SINCE THIS MORNING!
OH!!
WHAT?!
THAT'S TERRIBLE.
I'LL HELP YOU LOOK FOR HER, OKAY?
SNIFF...
WHAT A KIND SOUL YOU ARE.
He's been looking for her all day, the poor thing.
Eye drops

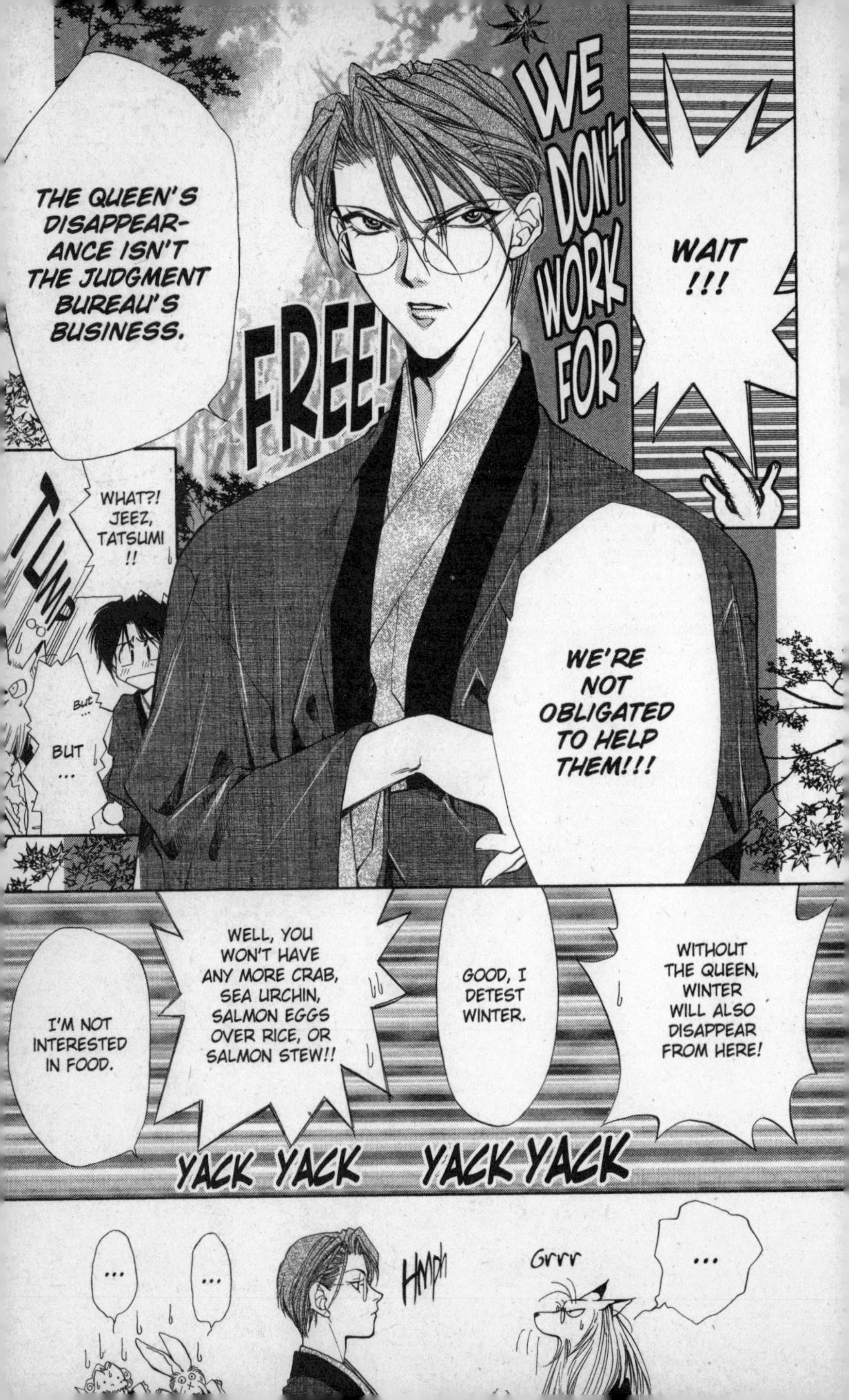
WAIT !!!
WE DON'T WORK FOR FREE!
THE QUEEN'S DISAPPEARANCE ISN'T THE JUDGMENT BUREAU'S BUSINESS.
WE'RE NOT OBLIGATED TO HELP THEM!!!
WHAT?! JEEZ, TATSUMI !!
TUMP
But ...
BUT ...
WITHOUT THE QUEEN, WINTER WILL ALSO DISAPPEAR FROM HERE!
GOOD, I DETEST WINTER.
WELL, YOU WON'T HAVE ANY MORE CRAB, SEA URCHIN, SALMON EGGS OVER RICE, OR SALMON STEW!!
I'M NOT INTERESTED IN FOOD.
YACK YACK YACK YACK
...
Grrr
Hmph
...
...

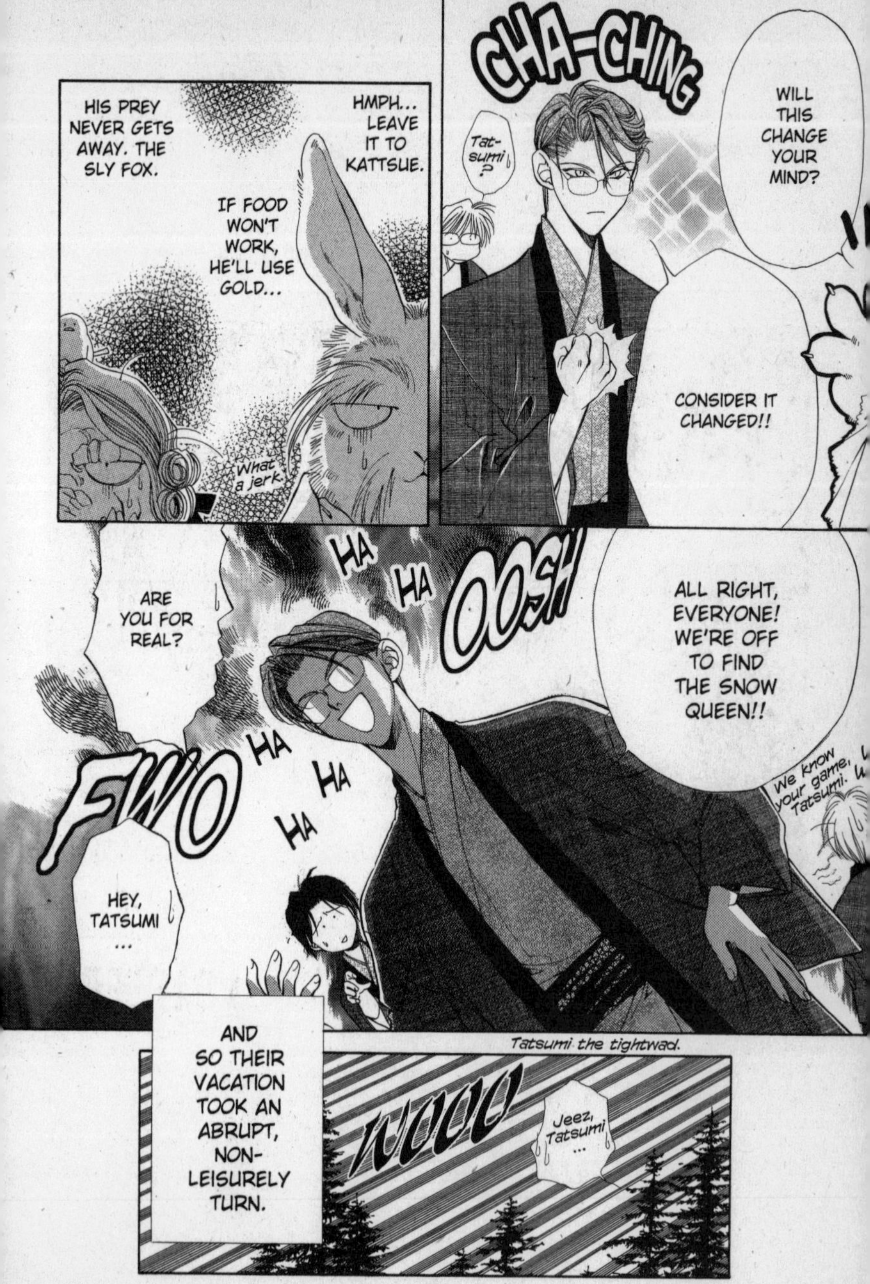
CHA-CHING
Tat-sumi?
WILL THIS CHANGE YOUR MIND?
CONSIDER IT CHANGED!!
HMPH... LEAVE IT TO KATTSUE.
HIS PREY NEVER GETS AWAY. THE SLY FOX.
IF FOOD WON'T WORK, HE'LL USE GOLD...
What a jerk.
ALL RIGHT, EVERYONE! WE'RE OFF TO FIND THE SNOW QUEEN!!
OOSH
HA HA
We know your game, Tatsumi.
ARE YOU FOR REAL?
FWO
HA HA HA
HEY, TATSUMI...
Tatsumi the tightwad.
AND SO THEIR VACATION TOOK AN ABRUPT, NON-LEISURELY TURN.
WOOO
Jeez, Tatsumi...

CHAPTER 2

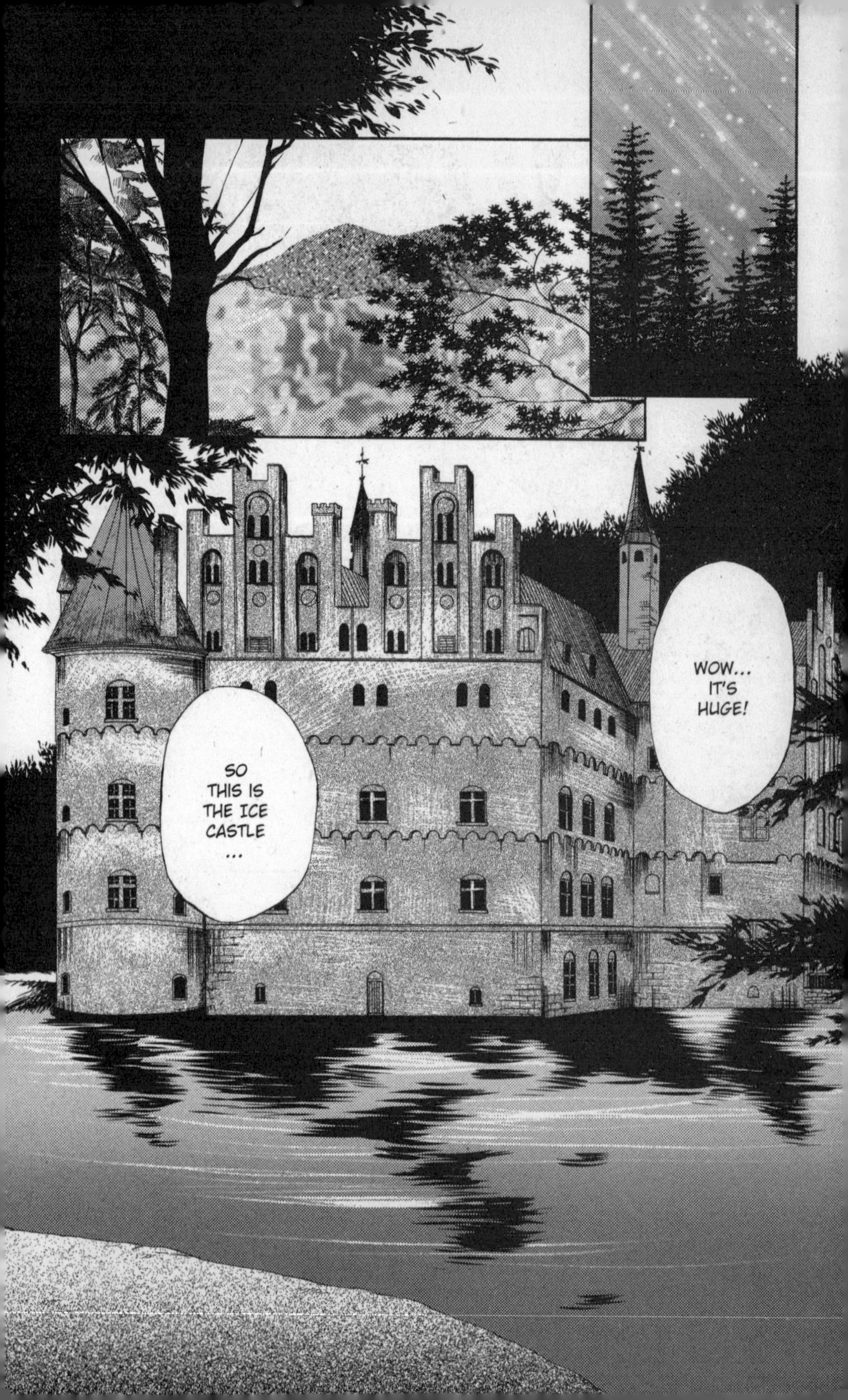
WOW... IT'S HUGE!
SO THIS IS THE ICE CASTLE ...

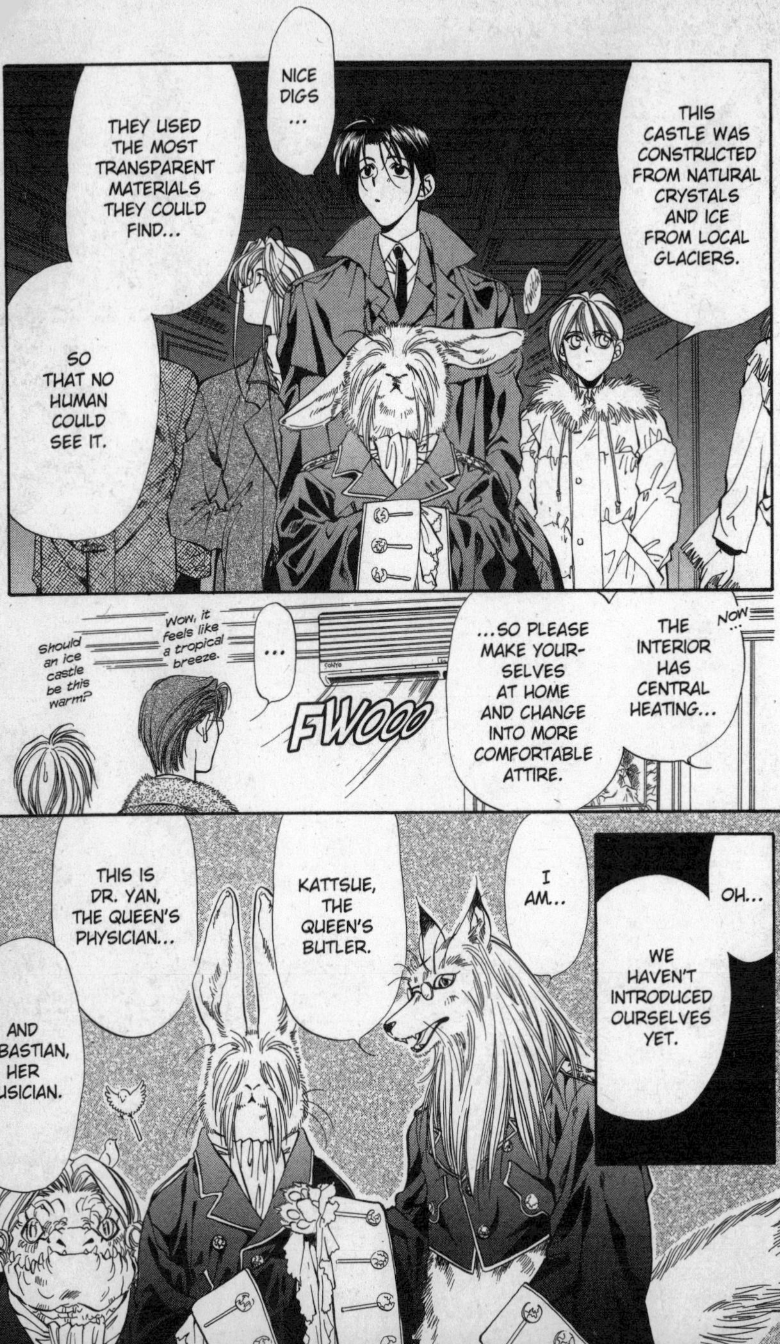

THIS CASTLE WAS CONSTRUCTED FROM NATURAL CRYSTALS AND ICE FROM LOCAL GLACIERS.
NICE DIGS ...
THEY USED THE MOST TRANSPARENT MATERIALS THEY COULD FIND...
SO THAT NO HUMAN COULD SEE IT.
NOW...
THE INTERIOR HAS CENTRAL HEATING...
...SO PLEASE MAKE YOUR-SELVES AT HOME AND CHANGE INTO MORE COMFORTABLE ATTIRE.
FWOOO
...
Wow, it feels like a tropical breeze.
Should an ice castle be this warm?
OH...
WE HAVEN'T INTRODUCED OURSELVES YET.
I AM...
KATTSUE, THE QUEEN'S BUTLER.
THIS IS DR. YAN, THE QUEEN'S PHYSICIAN...
AND SEBASTIAN, HER MUSICIAN.

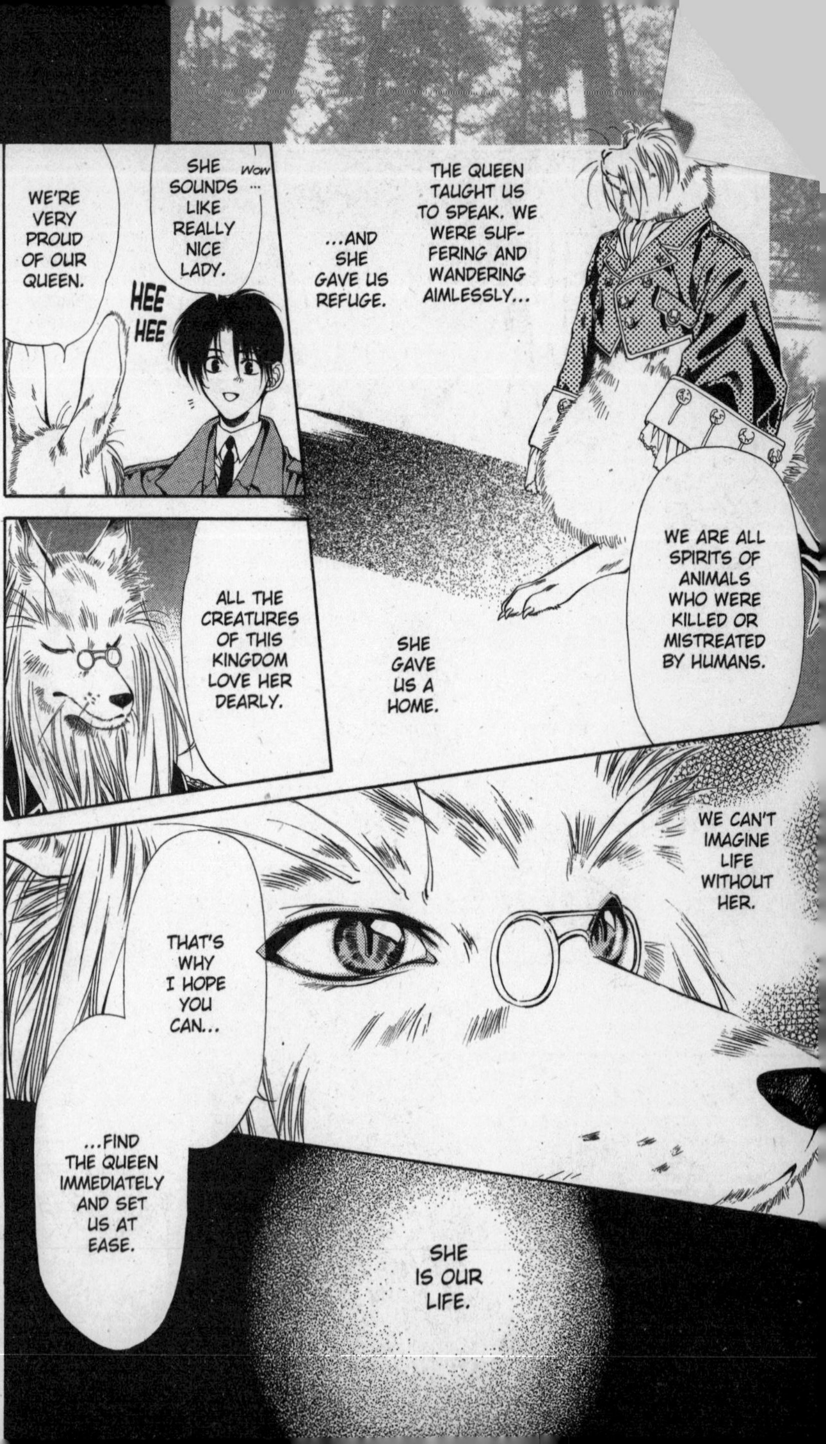
THE QUEEN TAUGHT US TO SPEAK. WE WERE SUFFERING AND WANDERING AIMLESSLY...
...AND SHE GAVE US REFUGE.
WE ARE ALL SPIRITS OF ANIMALS WHO WERE KILLED OR MISTREATED BY HUMANS.
SHE GAVE US A HOME.
WOW...
SHE SOUNDS LIKE REALLY NICE LADY.
WE'RE VERY PROUD OF OUR QUEEN.
HEE HEE
ALL THE CREATURES OF THIS KINGDOM LOVE HER DEARLY.
WE CAN'T IMAGINE LIFE WITHOUT HER.
SHE IS OUR LIFE.
THAT'S WHY I HOPE YOU CAN...
...FIND THE QUEEN IMMEDIATELY AND SET US AT EASE.

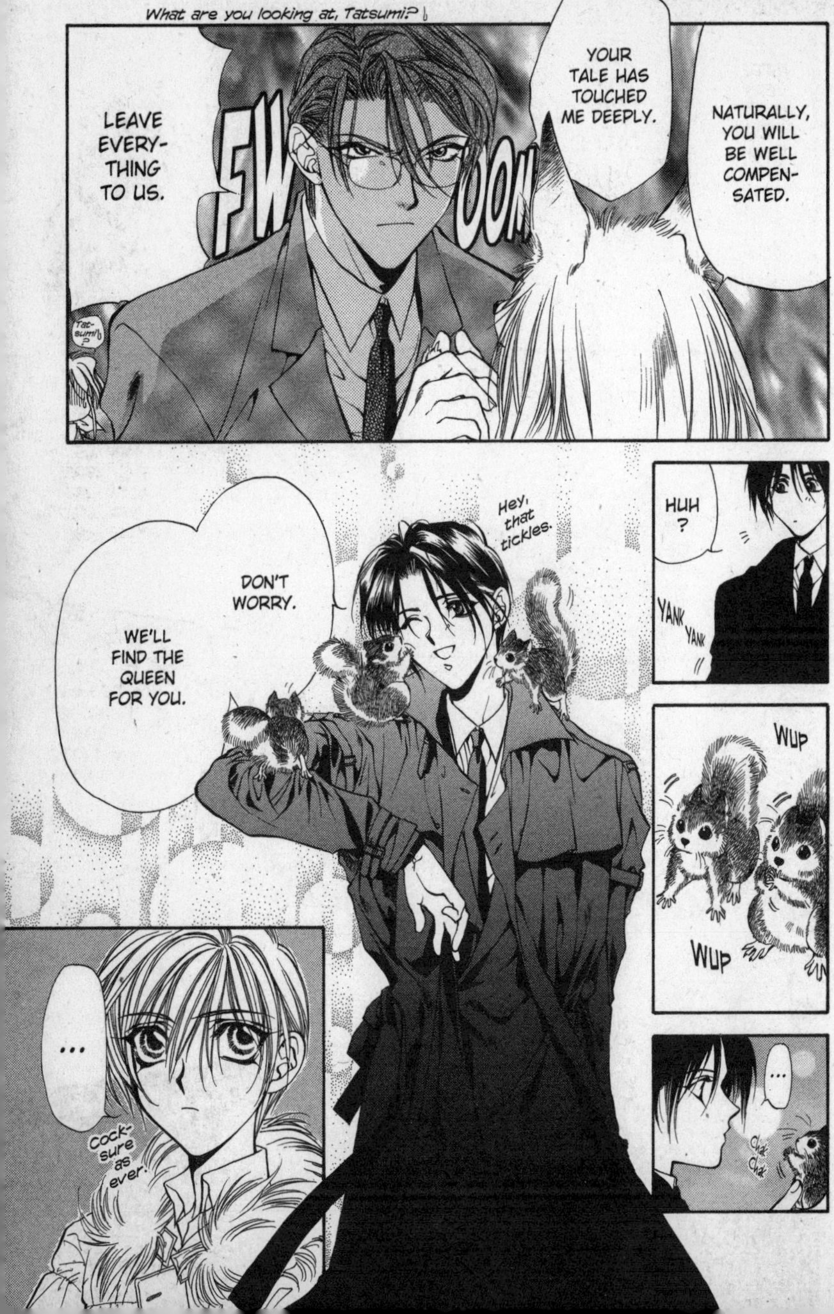
What are you looking at, Tatsumi?
NATURALLY, YOU WILL BE WELL COMPEN-SATED.
YOUR TALE HAS TOUCHED ME DEEPLY.
FWOOOM
LEAVE EVERY-THING TO US.
Tat-sumi?
HUH?
YANK YANK
WUP
WUP
...
Hey, that tickles.
DON'T WORRY.
WE'LL FIND THE QUEEN FOR YOU.
...
Cock-sure as ever.

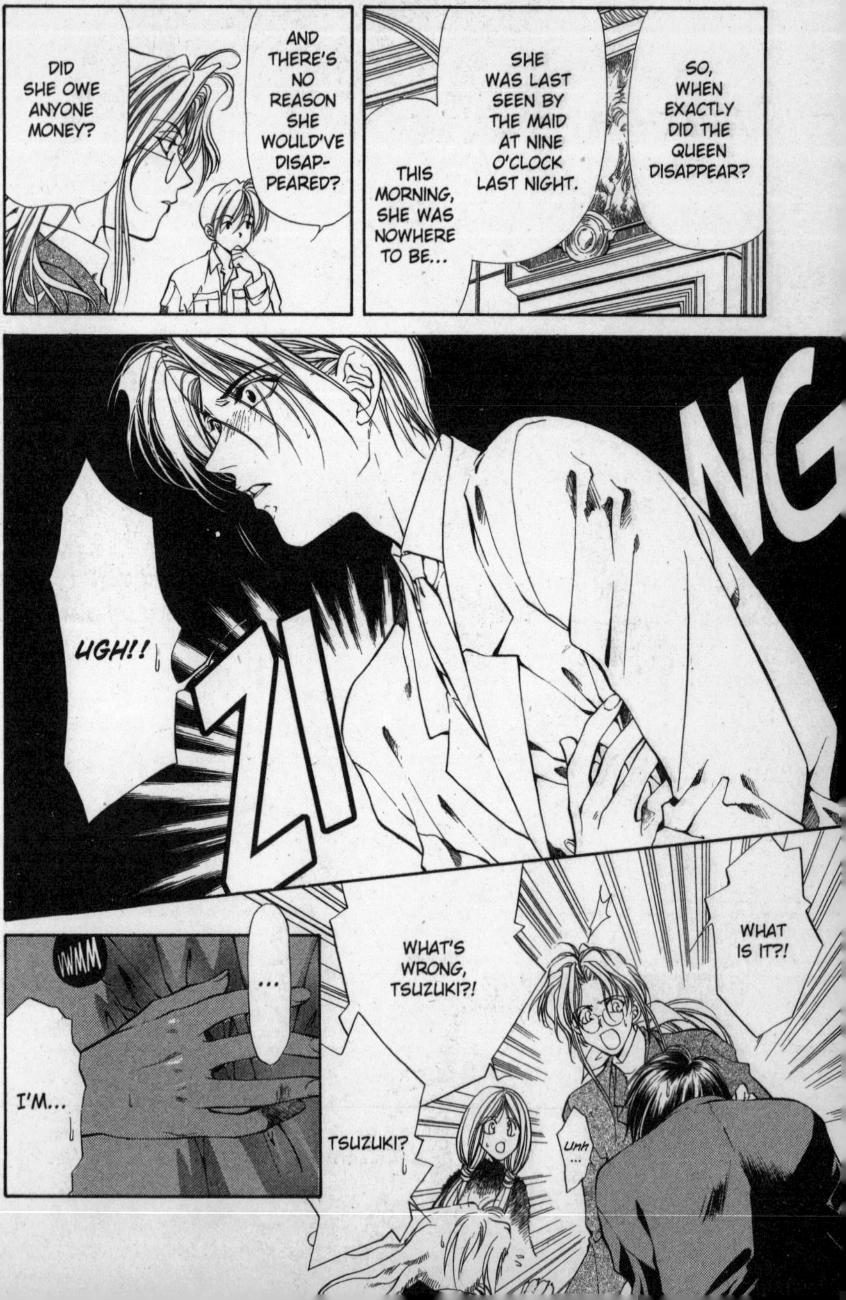
SO, WHEN EXACTLY DID THE QUEEN DISAPPEAR?
SHE WAS LAST SEEN BY THE MAID AT NINE O'CLOCK LAST NIGHT.
THIS MORNING, SHE WAS NOWHERE TO BE...
AND THERE'S NO REASON SHE WOULD'VE DISAP-PEARED?
DID SHE OWE ANYONE MONEY?
UGH!!
WHAT IS IT?!
WHAT'S WRONG, TSUZUKI?!
Umh ...
TSUZUKI?
...
I'M...
VWMM

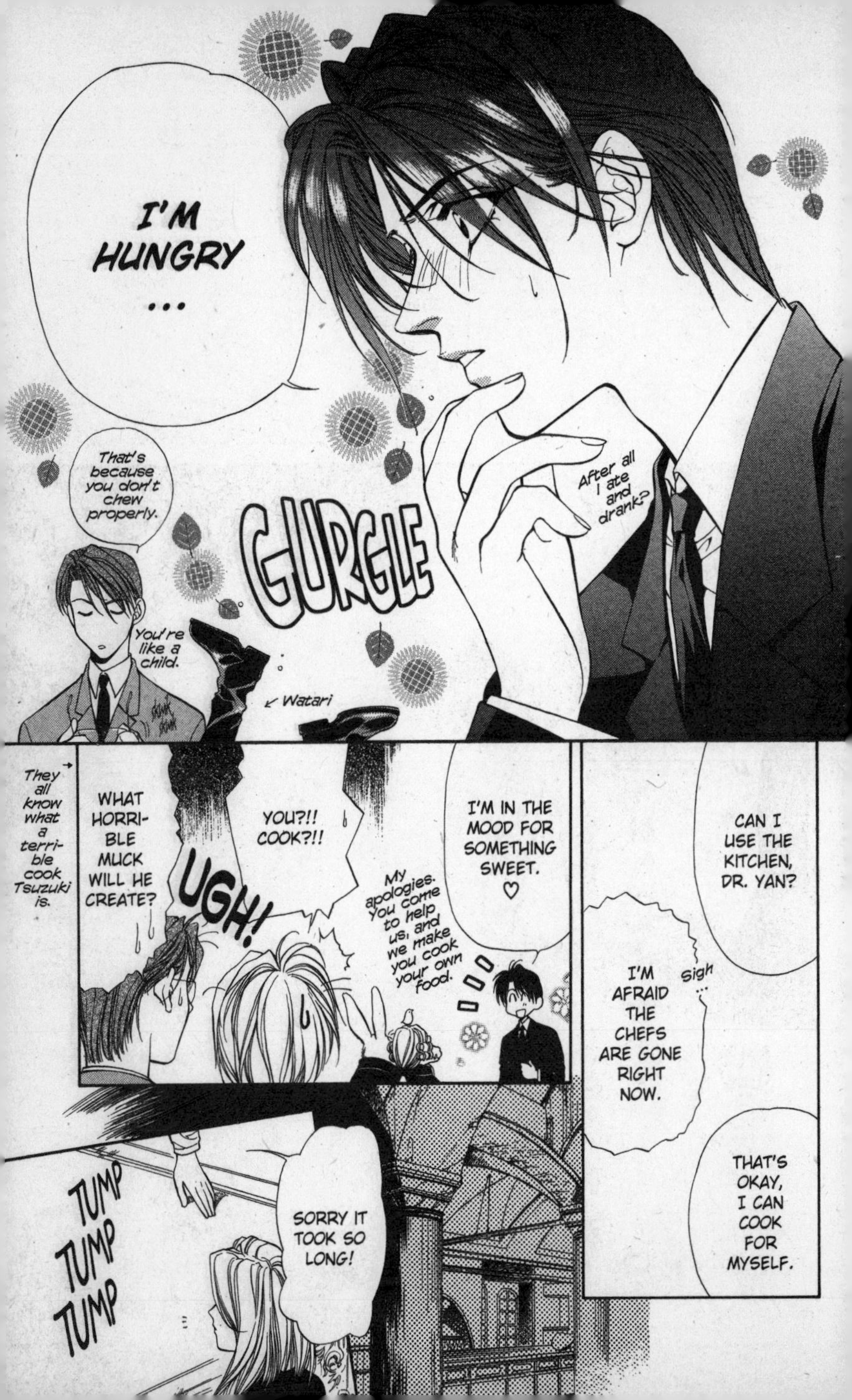
I'M HUNGRY ...
After all I ate and drank?
GURGLE
That's because you don't chew properly.
You're like a child.
← Watari
CAN I USE THE KITCHEN, DR. YAN?
Sigh...
I'M AFRAID THE CHEFS ARE GONE RIGHT NOW.
THAT'S OKAY, I CAN COOK FOR MYSELF.
I'M IN THE MOOD FOR SOMETHING SWEET. ♡
My apologies. You come to help us, and we make you cook your own food.
YOU?!! COOK?!!
UGH!
WHAT HORRIBLE MUCK WILL HE CREATE?
They all know what a terrible cook Tsuzuki is. →
SORRY IT TOOK SO LONG!
TUMP TUMP TUMP

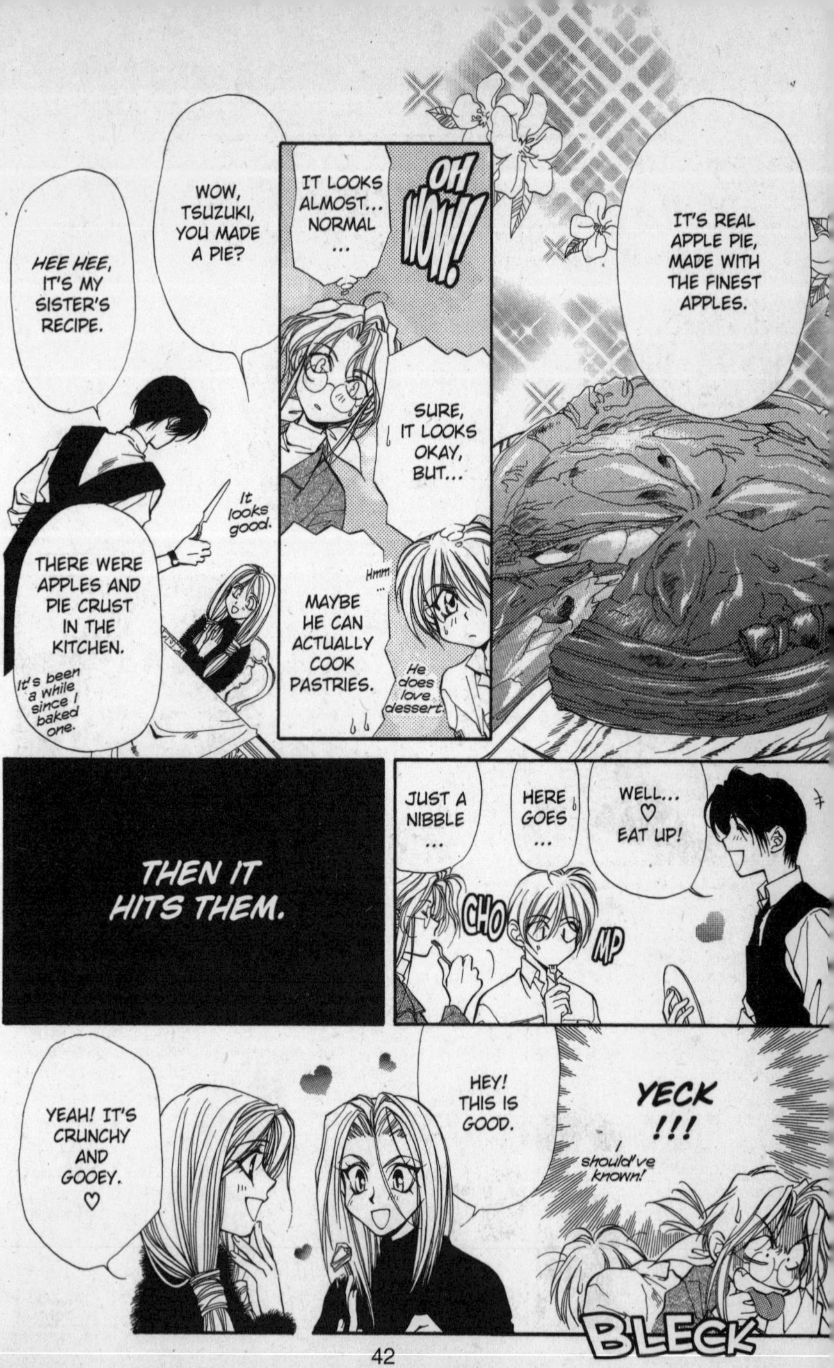
IT'S REAL APPLE PIE, MADE WITH THE FINEST APPLES.
OH WOW!!
IT LOOKS ALMOST... NORMAL ...
SURE, IT LOOKS OKAY, BUT...
Hmm ...
MAYBE HE CAN ACTUALLY COOK PASTRIES.
He does love dessert.
WOW, TSUZUKI, YOU MADE A PIE?
HEE HEE, IT'S MY SISTER'S RECIPE.
It looks good.
THERE WERE APPLES AND PIE CRUST IN THE KITCHEN.
It's been a while since I baked one.
WELL... ♡ EAT UP!
HERE GOES ...
JUST A NIBBLE ...
CHOMP
THEN IT HITS THEM.
YECK !!!
I should've known!
BLECK
HEY! THIS IS GOOD.
YEAH! IT'S CRUNCHY AND GOOEY. ♡

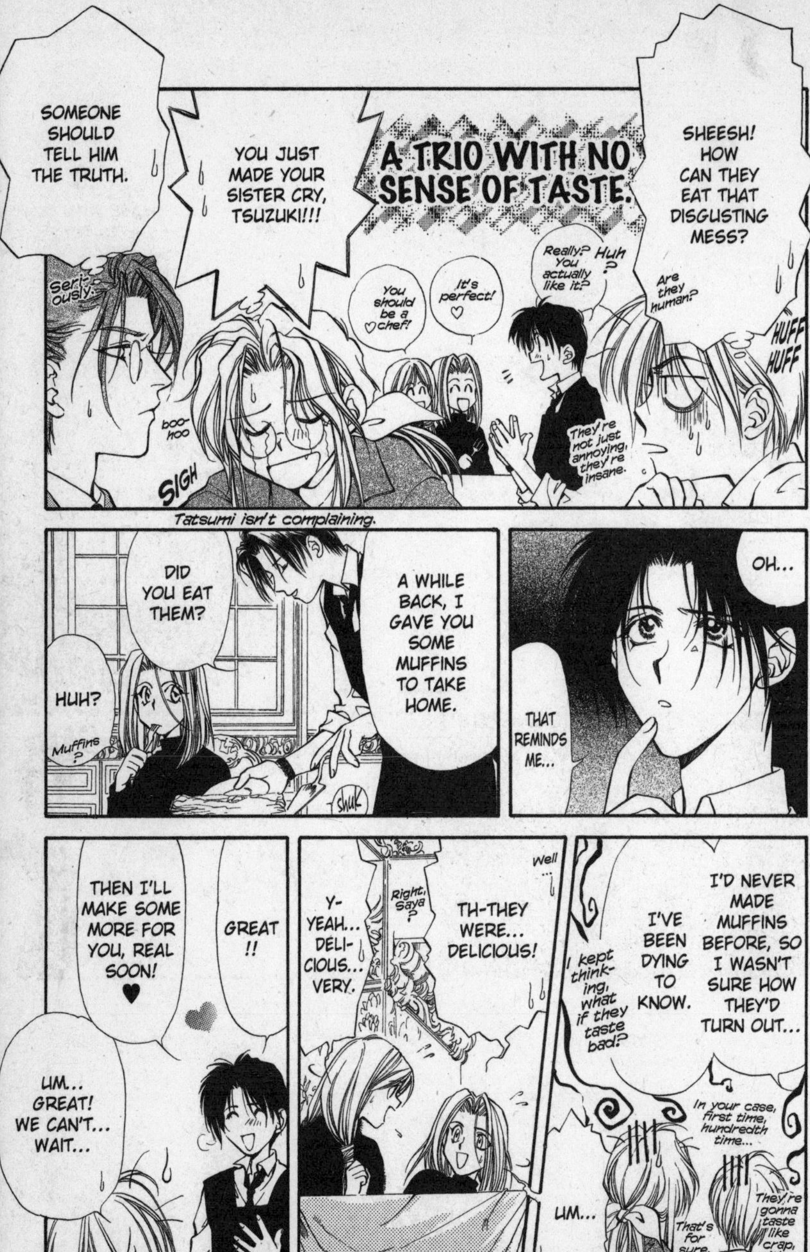
SHEESH! HOW CAN THEY EAT THAT DISGUSTING MESS?
Are they human?
HUFF HUFF
A TRIO WITH NO SENSE OF TASTE.
Huh?
Really? You actually like it?
They're not just annoying, they're insane.
It's perfect!
You should be a chef!
YOU JUST MADE YOUR SISTER CRY, TSUZUKI!!!
boo-hoo
SOMEONE SHOULD TELL HIM THE TRUTH.
Seri-ously.
SIGH
Tatsumi isn't complaining.
OH...
THAT REMINDS ME...
A WHILE BACK, I GAVE YOU SOME MUFFINS TO TAKE HOME.
DID YOU EAT THEM?
HUH?
Muffins?
shuk
I'D NEVER MADE MUFFINS BEFORE, SO I WASN'T SURE HOW THEY'D TURN OUT...
I'VE BEEN DYING TO KNOW.
I kept thinking, what if they taste bad?
In your case, first time, hundredth time...
They're gonna taste like crap, either way.
That's for sure.
UM...
Well...
TH-THEY WERE... DELICIOUS!
Right, Saya?
Y-YEAH... DELI-CIOUS... VERY.
GREAT!!
THEN I'LL MAKE SOME MORE FOR YOU, REAL SOON! ♥
UM... GREAT! WE CAN'T... WAIT...

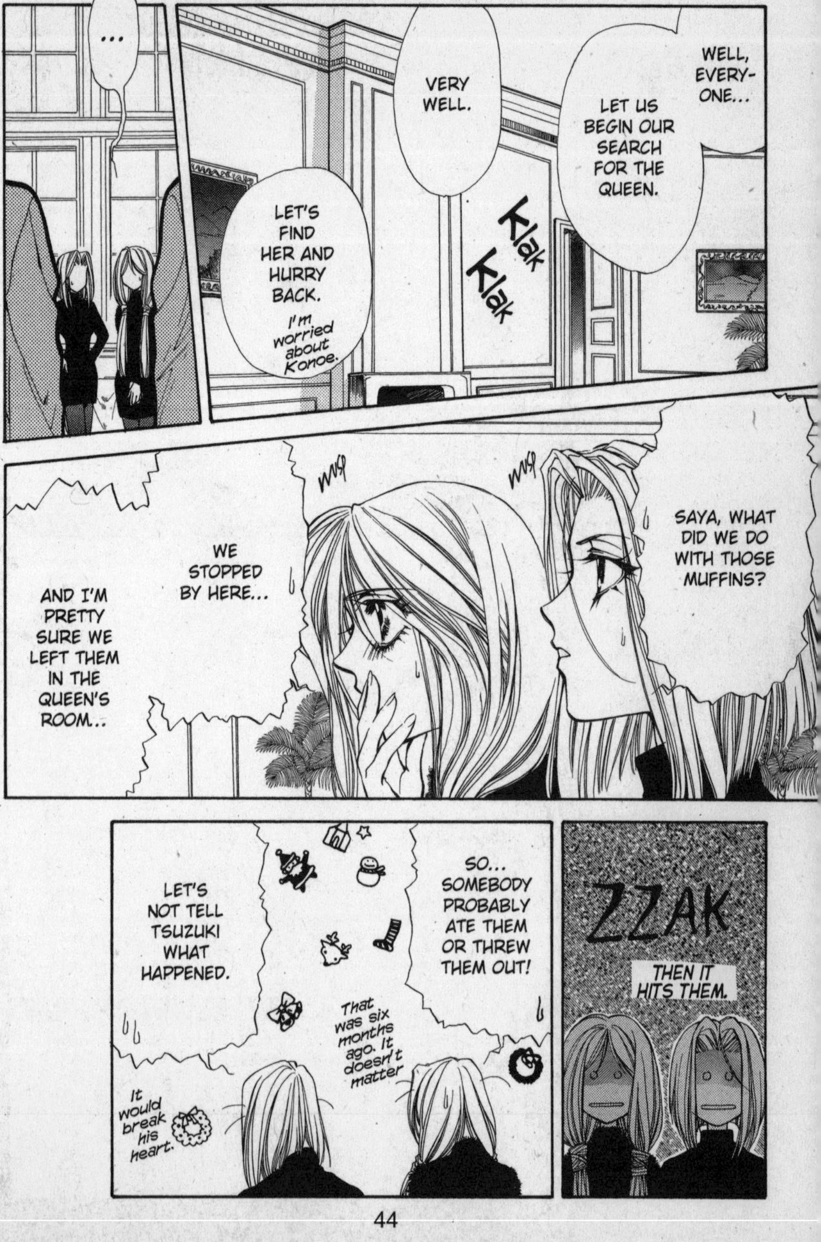
WELL, EVERY-ONE...
LET US BEGIN OUR SEARCH FOR THE QUEEN.
VERY WELL.
Klak Klak
LET'S FIND HER AND HURRY BACK.
I'm worried about Konoe.
...
wish
SAYA, WHAT DID WE DO WITH THOSE MUFFINS?
wish
WE STOPPED BY HERE...
AND I'M PRETTY SURE WE LEFT THEM IN THE QUEEN'S ROOM..
ZZAK
THEN IT HITS THEM.
SO... SOMEBODY PROBABLY ATE THEM OR THREW THEM OUT!
That was six months ago. It doesn't matter
LET'S NOT TELL TSUZUKI WHAT HAPPENED.
It would break his heart.

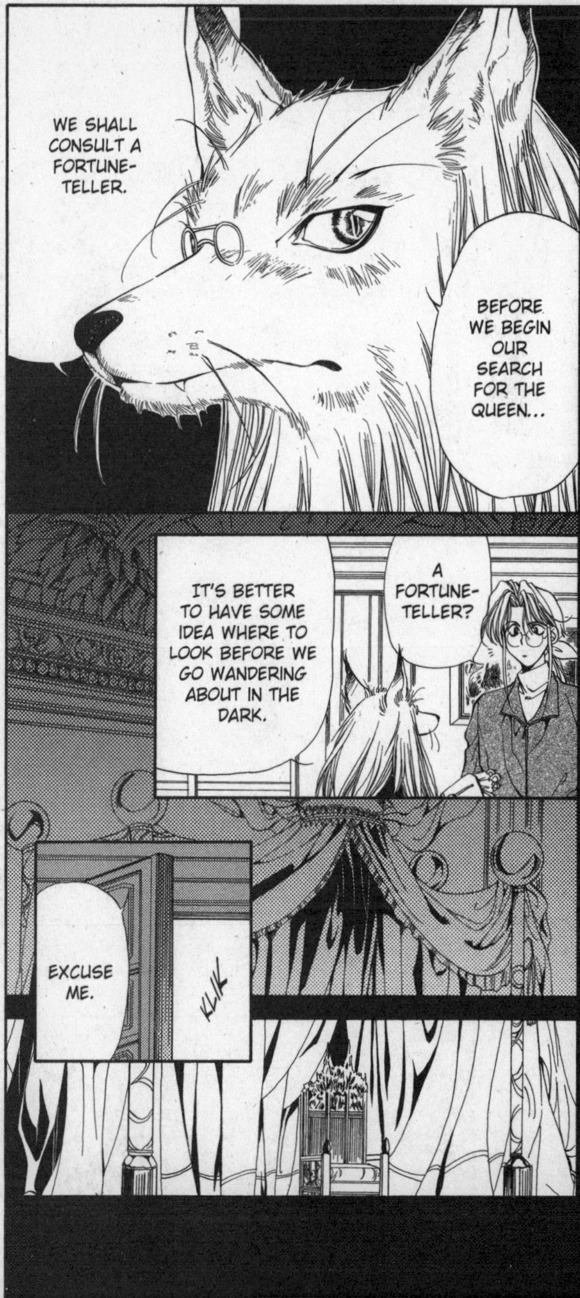
BEFORE WE BEGIN OUR SEARCH FOR THE QUEEN...
WE SHALL CONSULT A FORTUNE-TELLER.
A FORTUNE-TELLER?
IT'S BETTER TO HAVE SOME IDEA WHERE TO LOOK BEFORE WE GO WANDERING ABOUT IN THE DARK.
KLIK
EXCUSE ME.

Thanks for buying this book! (Hee!) Thank you!!

Hey there, this is volume four of Descendants of Darkness! This book contains three different two-part stories— which shows that, while long stories are hard to write, so are short ones! (Ha!) I don't have enough training... Oh, well. Anyway, the first half of this story is pretty strange. (Heh...) Everybody's stripping. Looking at it now, I'm surprised I could draw such scandalous illustrations. Now, about the character Ketto C—He's not just a rip-off from that video game! The name comes from a northern European fairy or spirit or something. (Ha!) Both characters were just inspired by the same creature, but if you want to think I copied it, I can't stop you. Actually, I'm a dog person, myself.

I want to go to Hokkaido.

But I do love Scottish Fold cats.

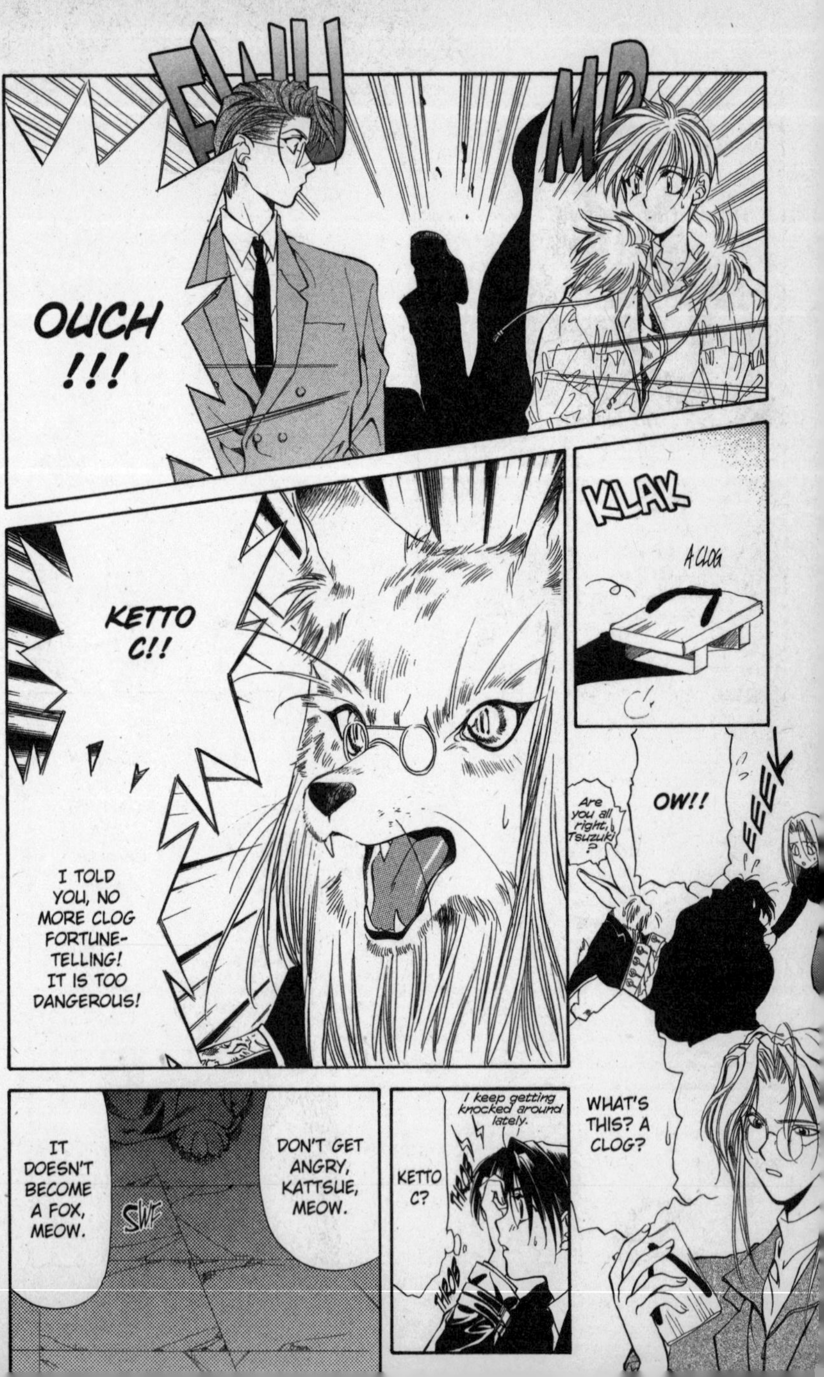
OUCH !!!
KLAK
A CLOG
KETTO C!!
I TOLD YOU, NO MORE CLOG FORTUNE-TELLING! IT IS TOO DANGEROUS!
OW!!
EEEK
Are you all right, Tsuzuki?
WHAT'S THIS? A CLOG?
I keep getting knocked around lately.
KETTO C?
THROB
THROB
DON'T GET ANGRY, KATTSUE, MEOW.
SWF
IT DOESN'T BECOME A FOX, MEOW.

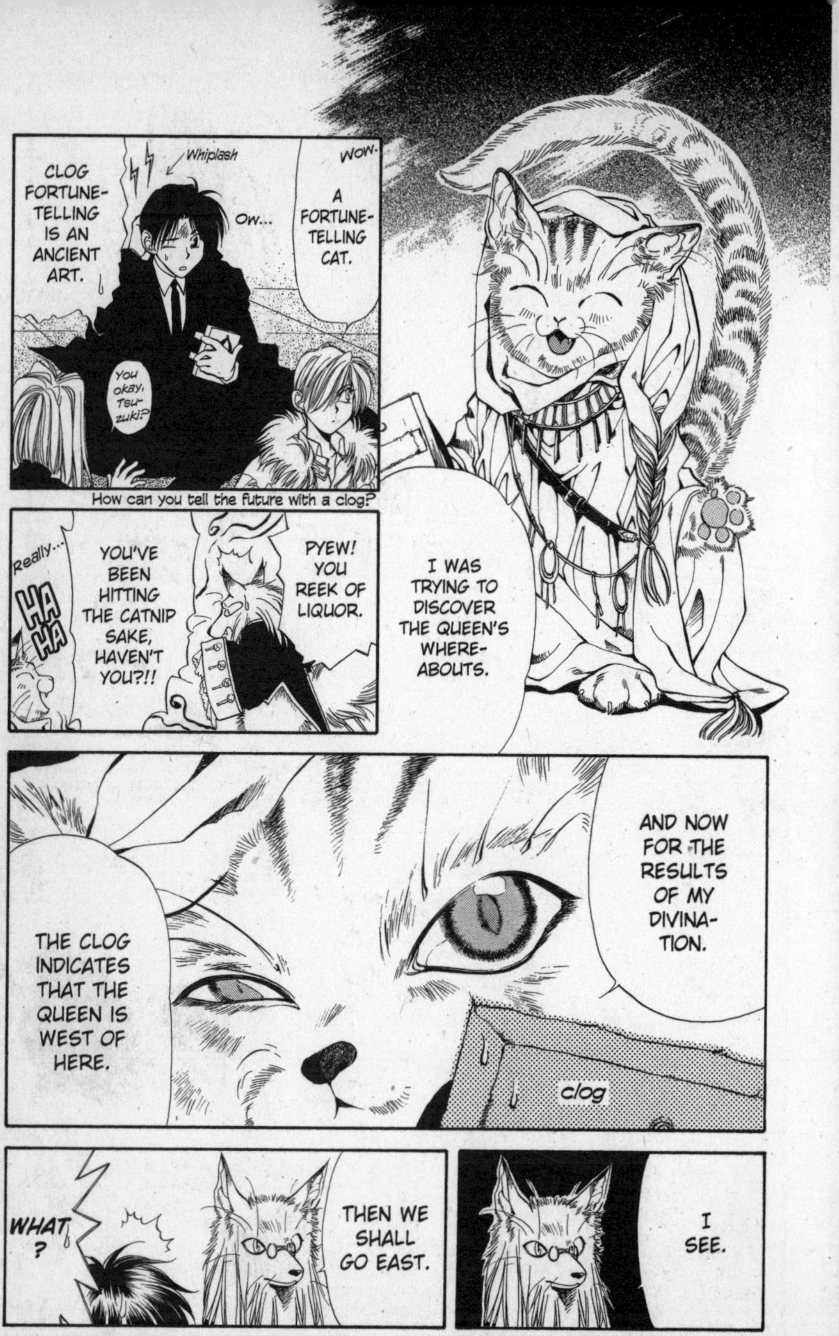
I WAS TRYING TO DISCOVER THE QUEEN'S WHEREABOUTS.
WOW.
A FORTUNE-TELLING CAT.
CLOG FORTUNE-TELLING IS AN ANCIENT ART.
Whiplash
Ow...
You okay, Tsuzuki?
How can you tell the future with a clog?
PYEW! YOU REEK OF LIQUOR.
YOU'VE BEEN HITTING THE CATNIP SAKE, HAVEN'T YOU?!!
HA HA
Really...
AND NOW FOR THE RESULTS OF MY DIVINATION.
THE CLOG INDICATES THAT THE QUEEN IS WEST OF HERE.
clog
I SEE.
THEN WE SHALL GO EAST.
WHAT?

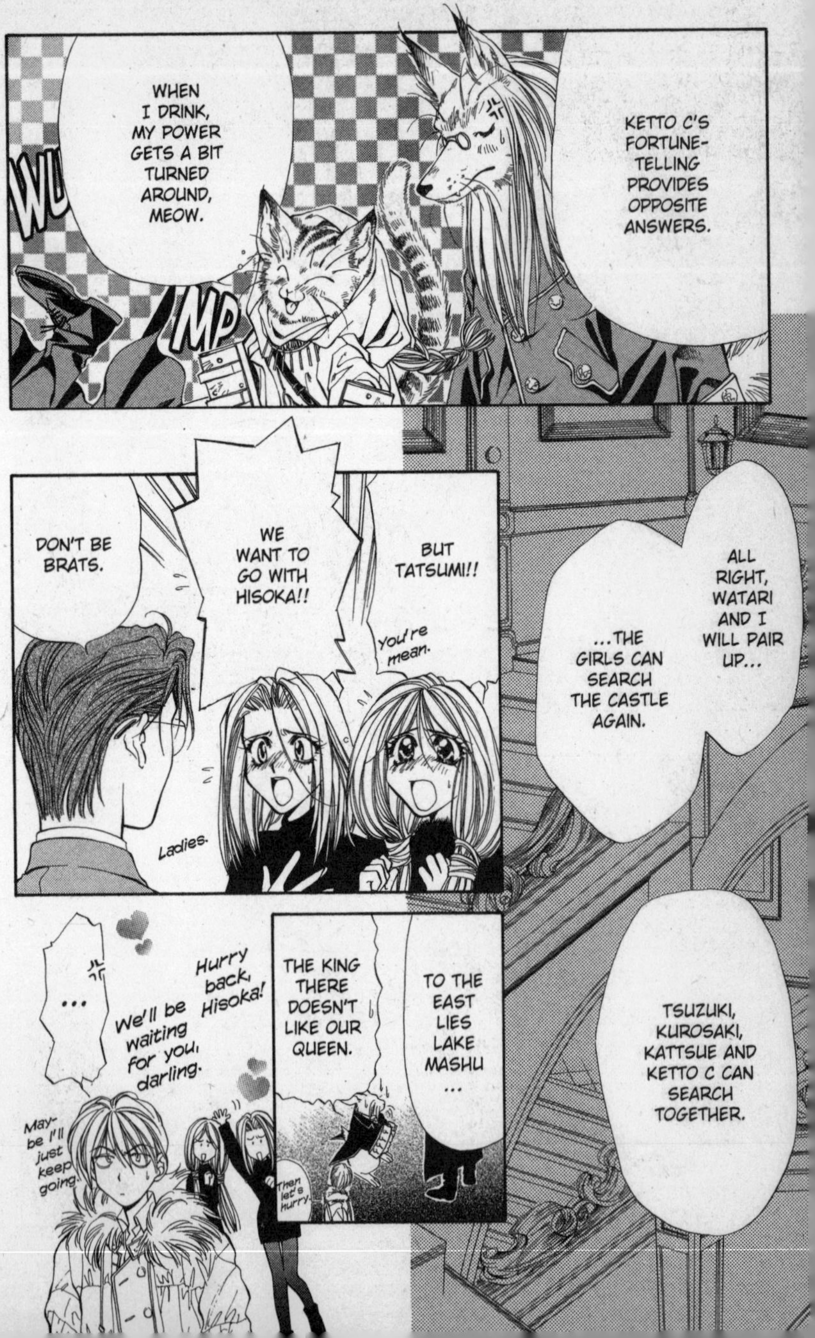
KETTO C'S FORTUNE-TELLING PROVIDES OPPOSITE ANSWERS.
WHEN I DRINK, MY POWER GETS A BIT TURNED AROUND, MEOW.
WUMP
ALL RIGHT, WATARI AND I WILL PAIR UP...
...THE GIRLS CAN SEARCH THE CASTLE AGAIN.
TSUZUKI, KUROSAKI, KATTSUE AND KETTO C CAN SEARCH TOGETHER.
BUT TATSUMI!!
You're mean.
WE WANT TO GO WITH HISOKA!!
DON'T BE BRATS.
Ladies.
TO THE EAST LIES LAKE MASHU...
THE KING THERE DOESN'T LIKE OUR QUEEN.
Then let's hurry.
Hurry back, Hisoka!
We'll be waiting for you, darling.
...
May-be I'll just keep going.

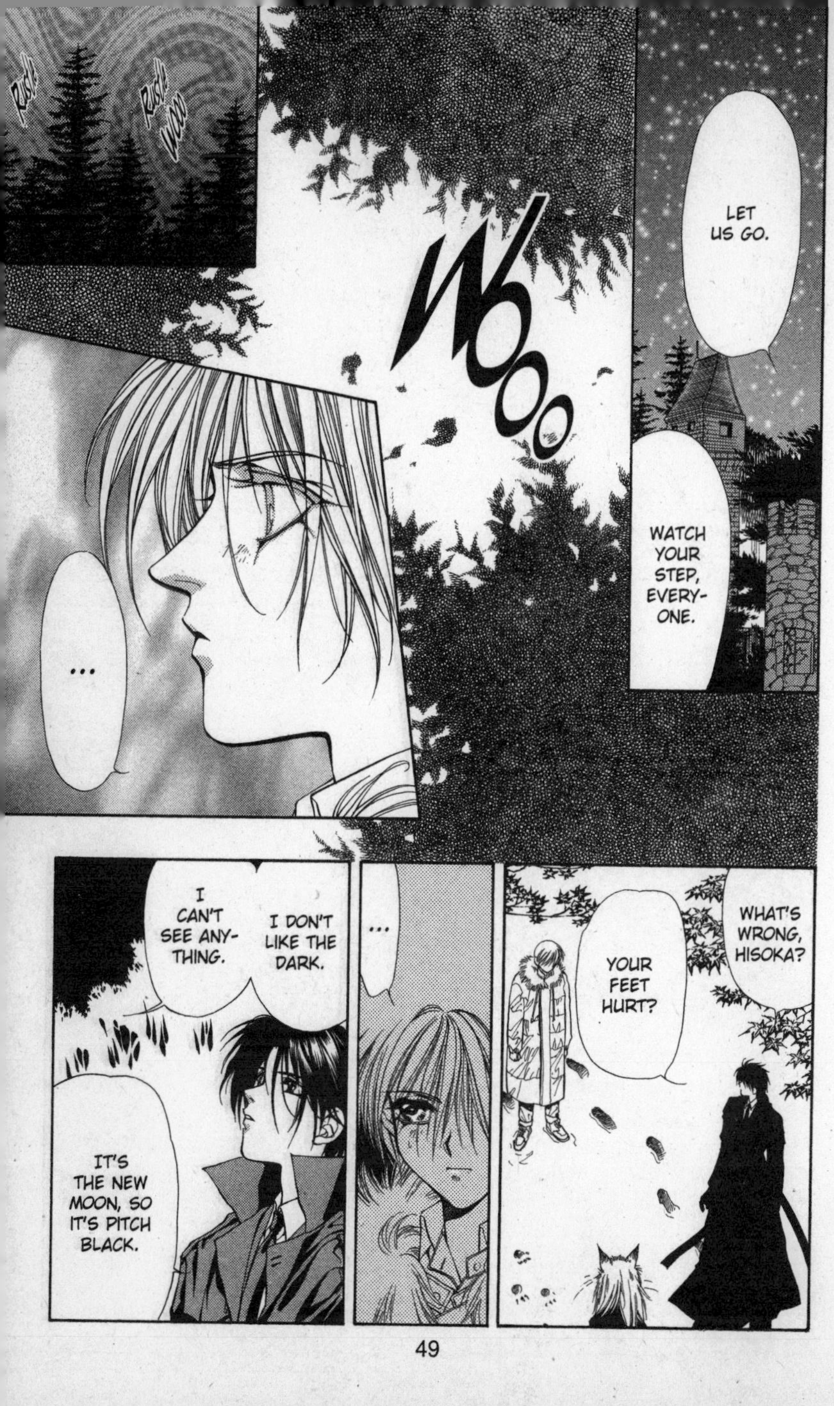
LET US GO.
WATCH YOUR STEP, EVERY-ONE.
WOOO
Rustle
Rustle Wooo
...
WHAT'S WRONG, HISOKA?
YOUR FEET HURT?
...
I DON'T LIKE THE DARK.
I CAN'T SEE ANY-THING.
IT'S THE NEW MOON, SO IT'S PITCH BLACK.

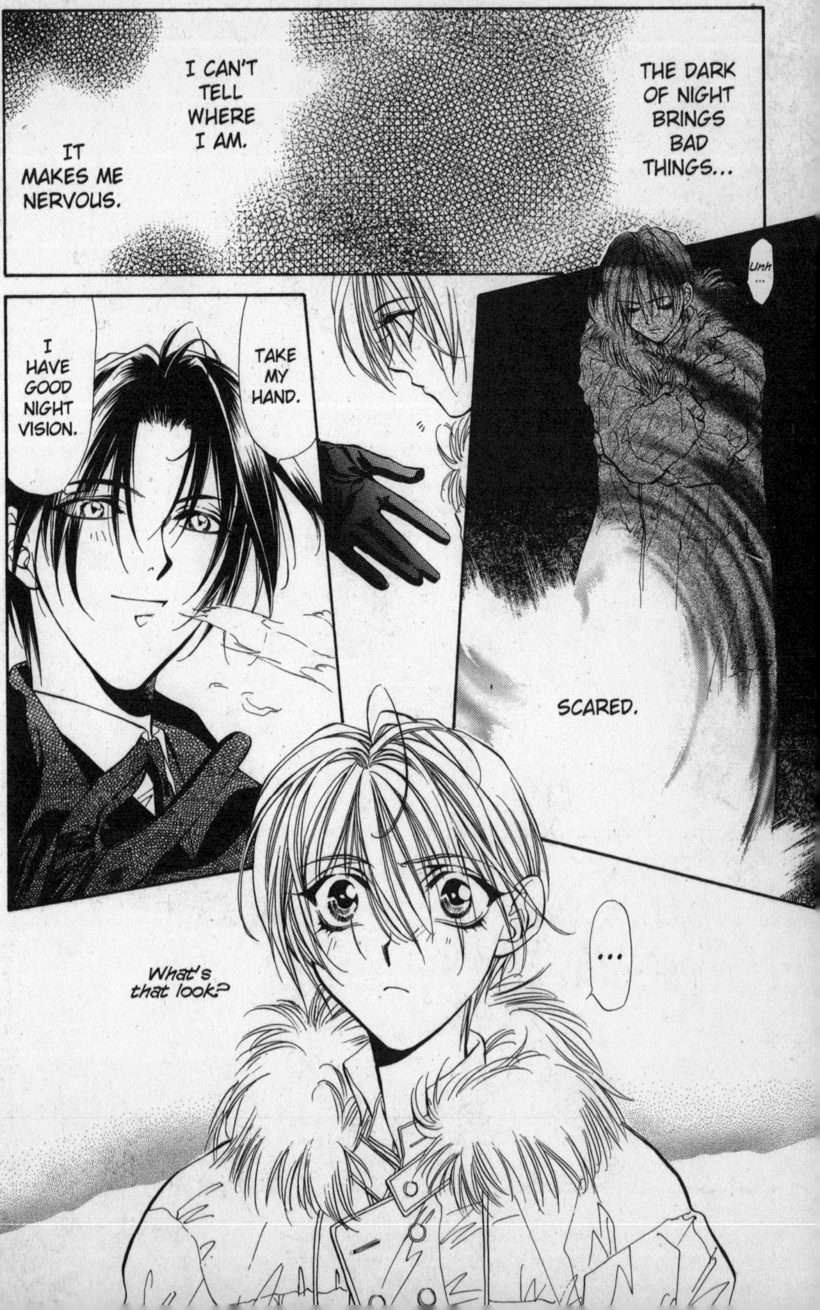
THE DARK OF NIGHT BRINGS BAD THINGS...
I CAN'T TELL WHERE I AM.
IT MAKES ME NERVOUS.
Unh ...
SCARED.
TAKE MY HAND.
I HAVE GOOD NIGHT VISION.
...
What's that look?

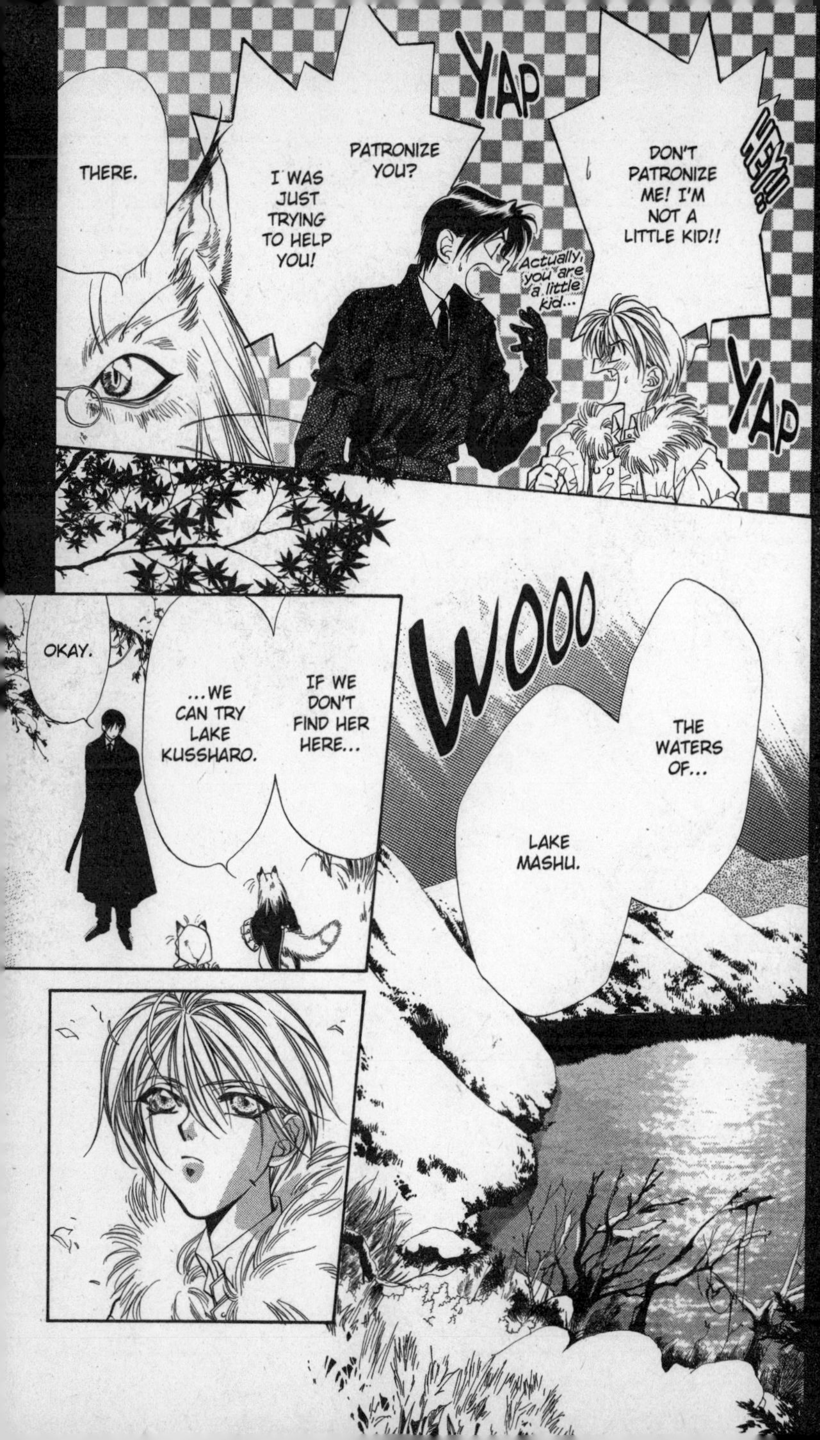
YAP
HEY!!
DON'T PATRONIZE ME! I'M NOT A LITTLE KID!!
YAP
Actually, you are a little kid...
PATRONIZE YOU?
I WAS JUST TRYING TO HELP YOU!
THERE.
WOOO
THE WATERS OF...
LAKE MASHU.
IF WE DON'T FIND HER HERE...
...WE CAN TRY LAKE KUSSHARO.
OKAY.

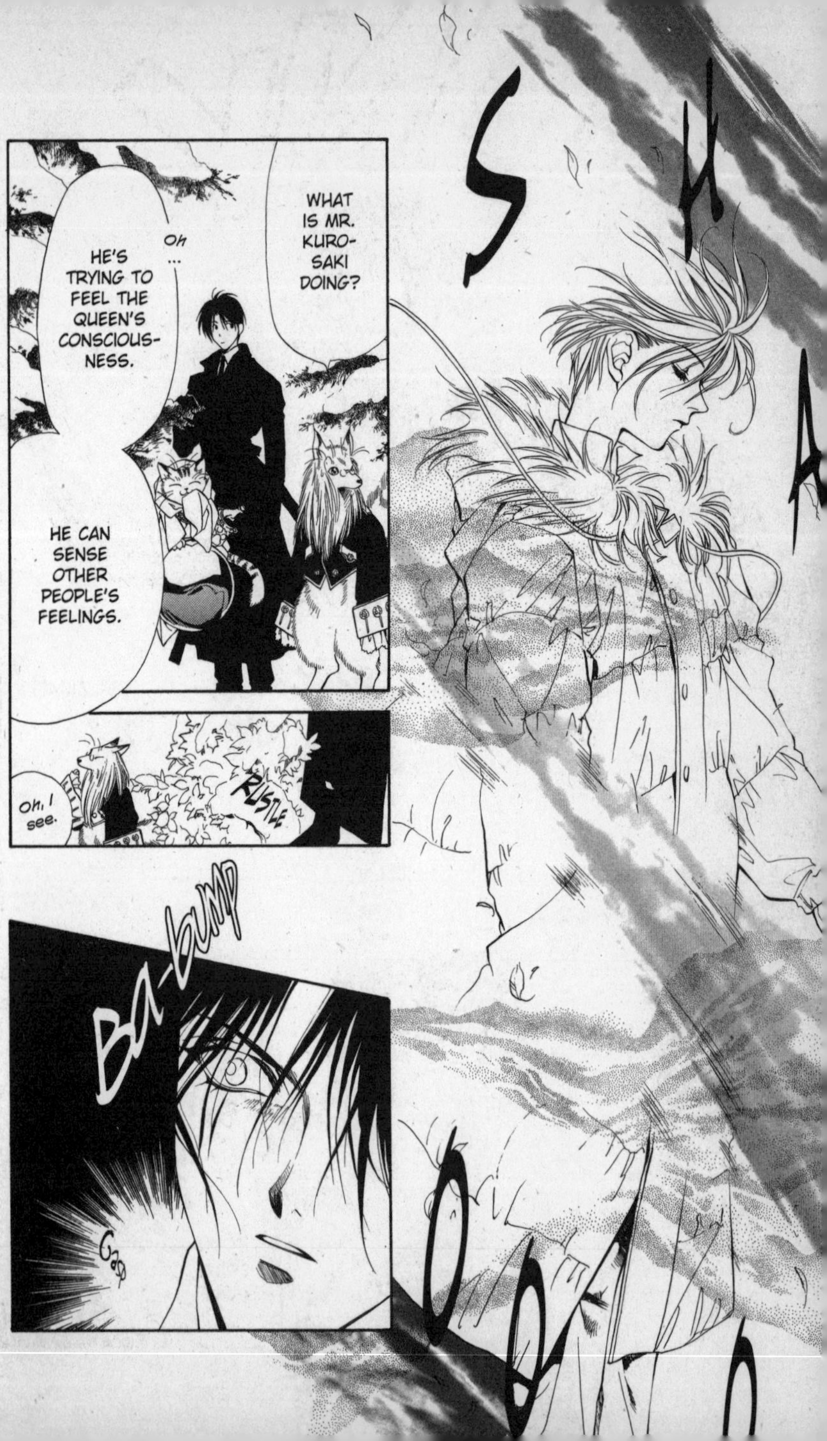
SHA
OOOO
WHAT IS MR. KURO-SAKI DOING?
Oh ...
HE'S TRYING TO FEEL THE QUEEN'S CONSCIOUS-NESS.
HE CAN SENSE OTHER PEOPLE'S FEELINGS.
RUSTLE
Oh, I see.
Ba-bump
Gasp

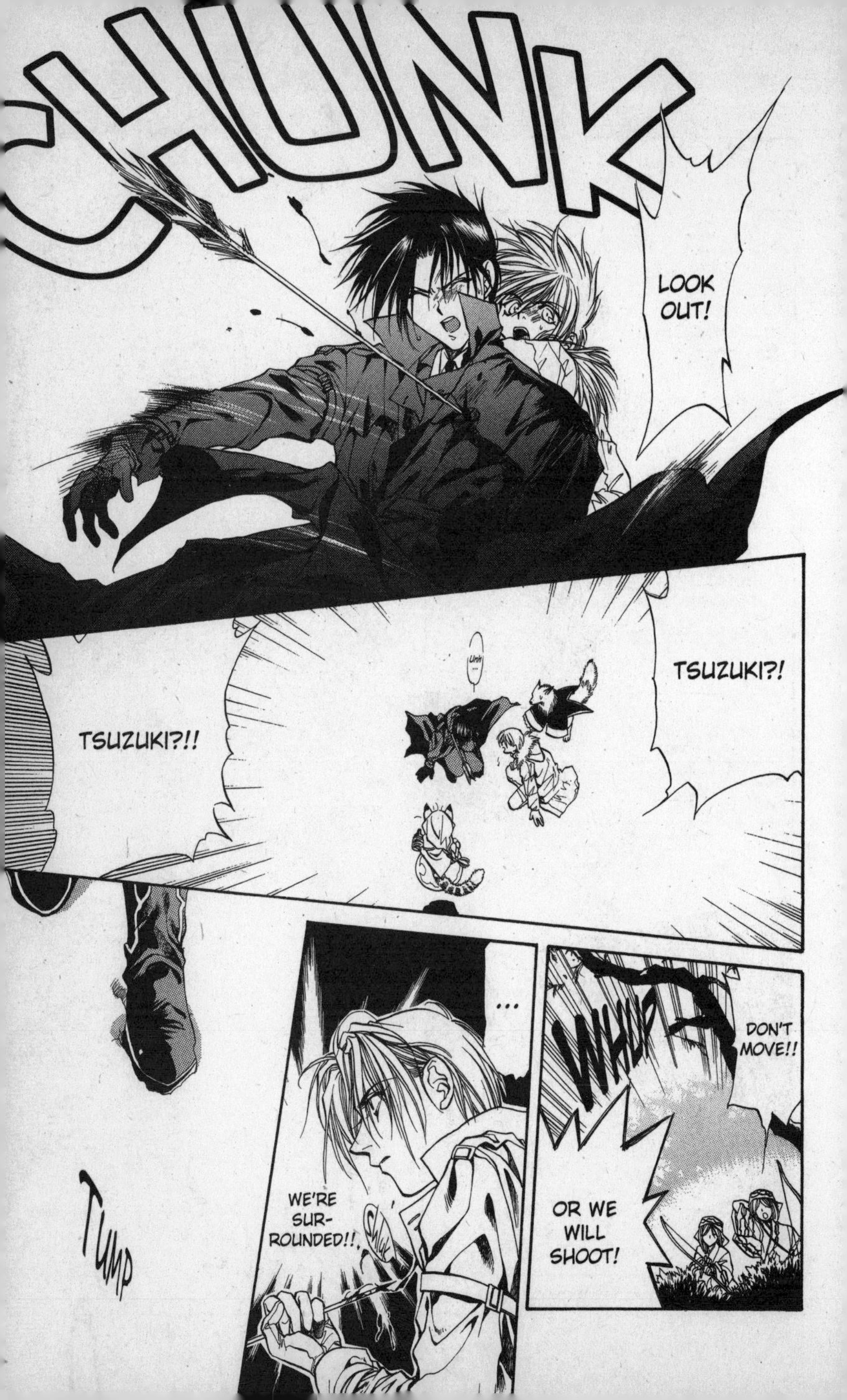
CHUNK
LOOK OUT!
TSUZUKI?!
Unh...
TSUZUKI?!!
DON'T MOVE!!
WHUP
OR WE WILL SHOOT!
...
WE'RE SUR- ROUNDED!!
TUMP

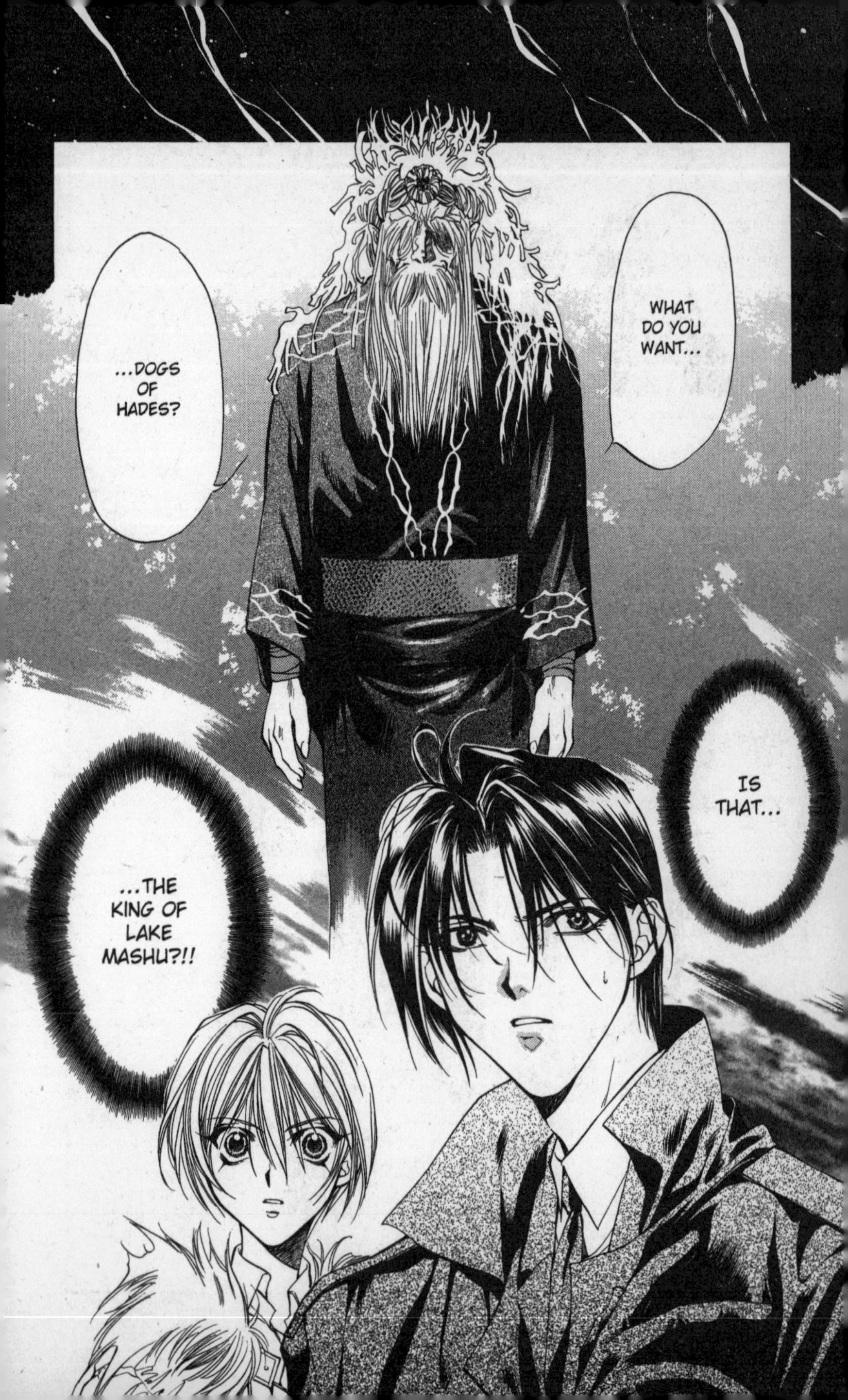
WHAT DO YOU WANT...
...DOGS OF HADES?
IS THAT...
...THE KING OF LAKE MASHU?!!

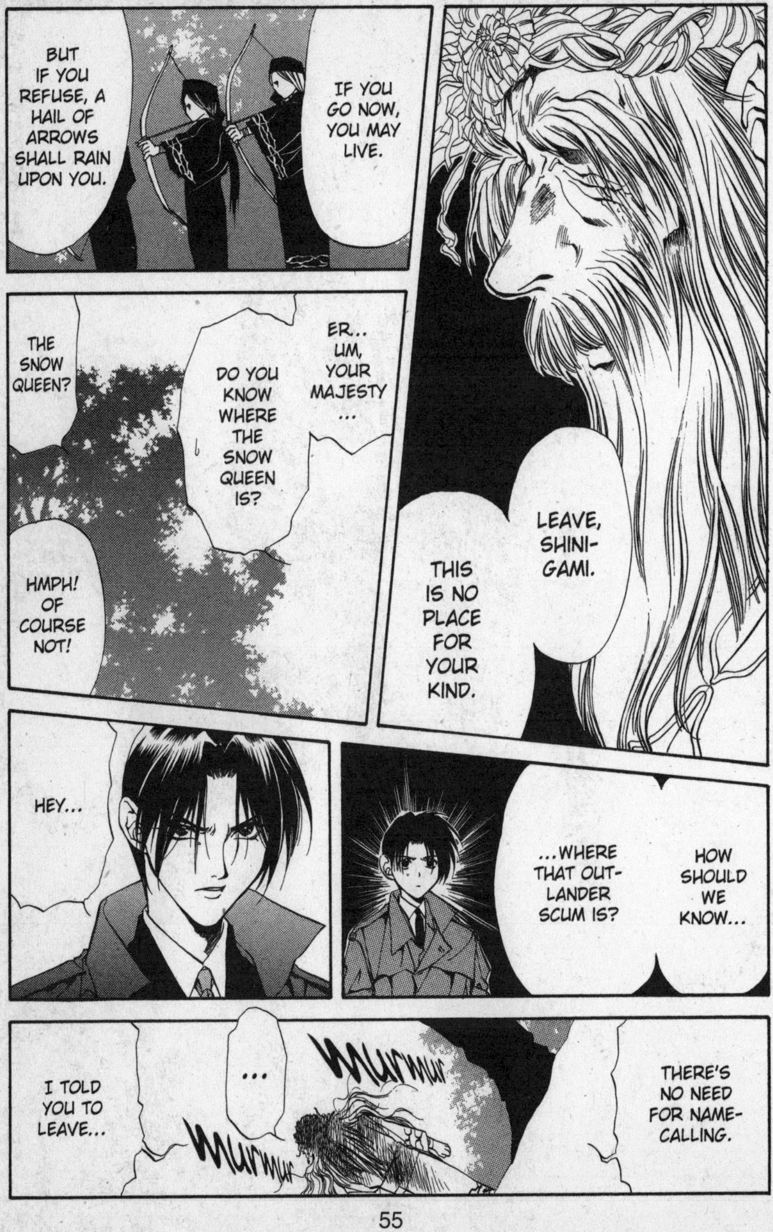
LEAVE, SHINIGAMI.
THIS IS NO PLACE FOR YOUR KIND.
IF YOU GO NOW, YOU MAY LIVE.
BUT IF YOU REFUSE, A HAIL OF ARROWS SHALL RAIN UPON YOU.
ER... UM, YOUR MAJESTY...
DO YOU KNOW WHERE THE SNOW QUEEN IS?
THE SNOW QUEEN?
HMPH! OF COURSE NOT!
HOW SHOULD WE KNOW...
...WHERE THAT OUT-LANDER SCUM IS?
HEY...
THERE'S NO NEED FOR NAME-CALLING.
Murmur
Murmur
...
I TOLD YOU TO LEAVE...

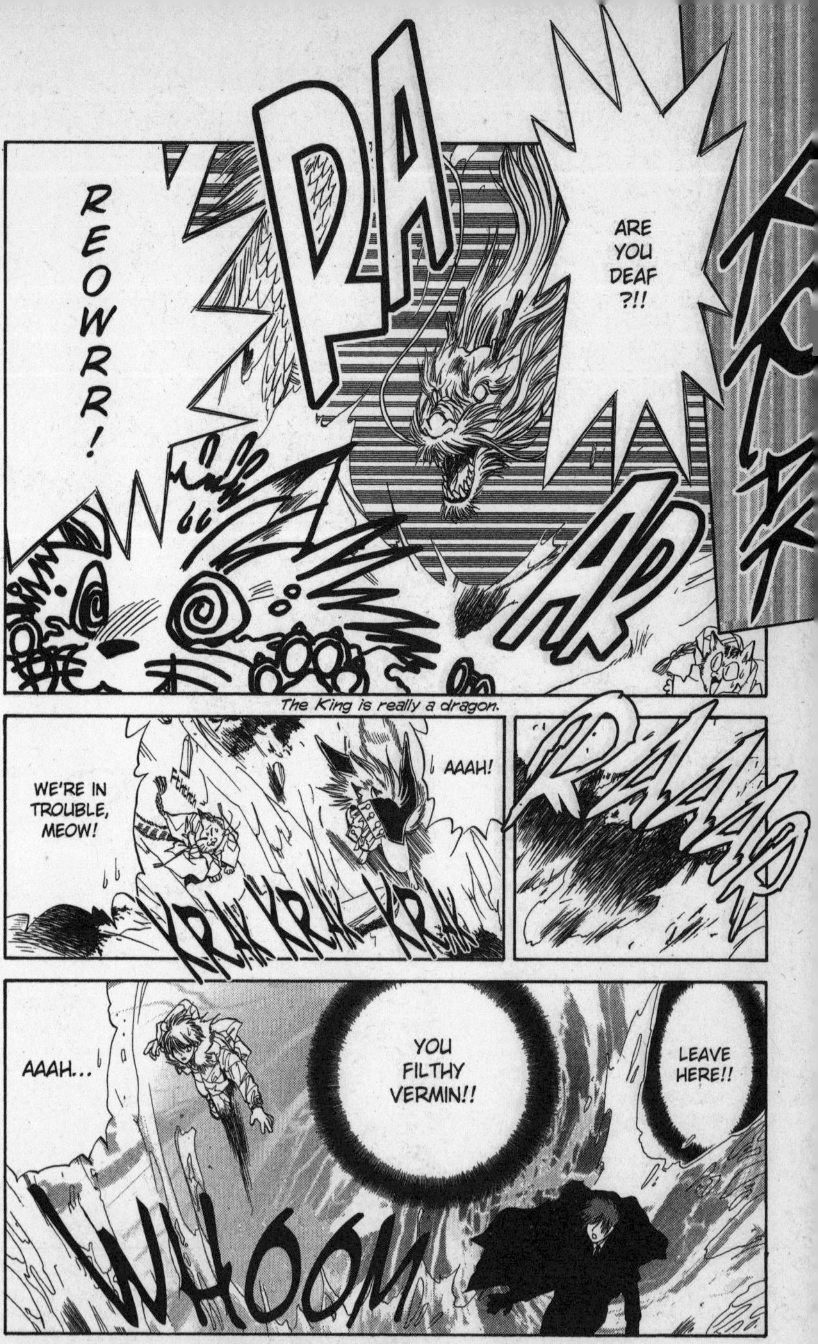
KRAK
ARE YOU DEAF ?!!
DA
AR
REOWRRR!
AAAH!
WE'RE IN TROUBLE, MEOW!
KRAK KRAK KRAK
LEAVE HERE!!
YOU FILTHY VERMIN!!
AAAH...
WHOOM
The King is really a dragon.

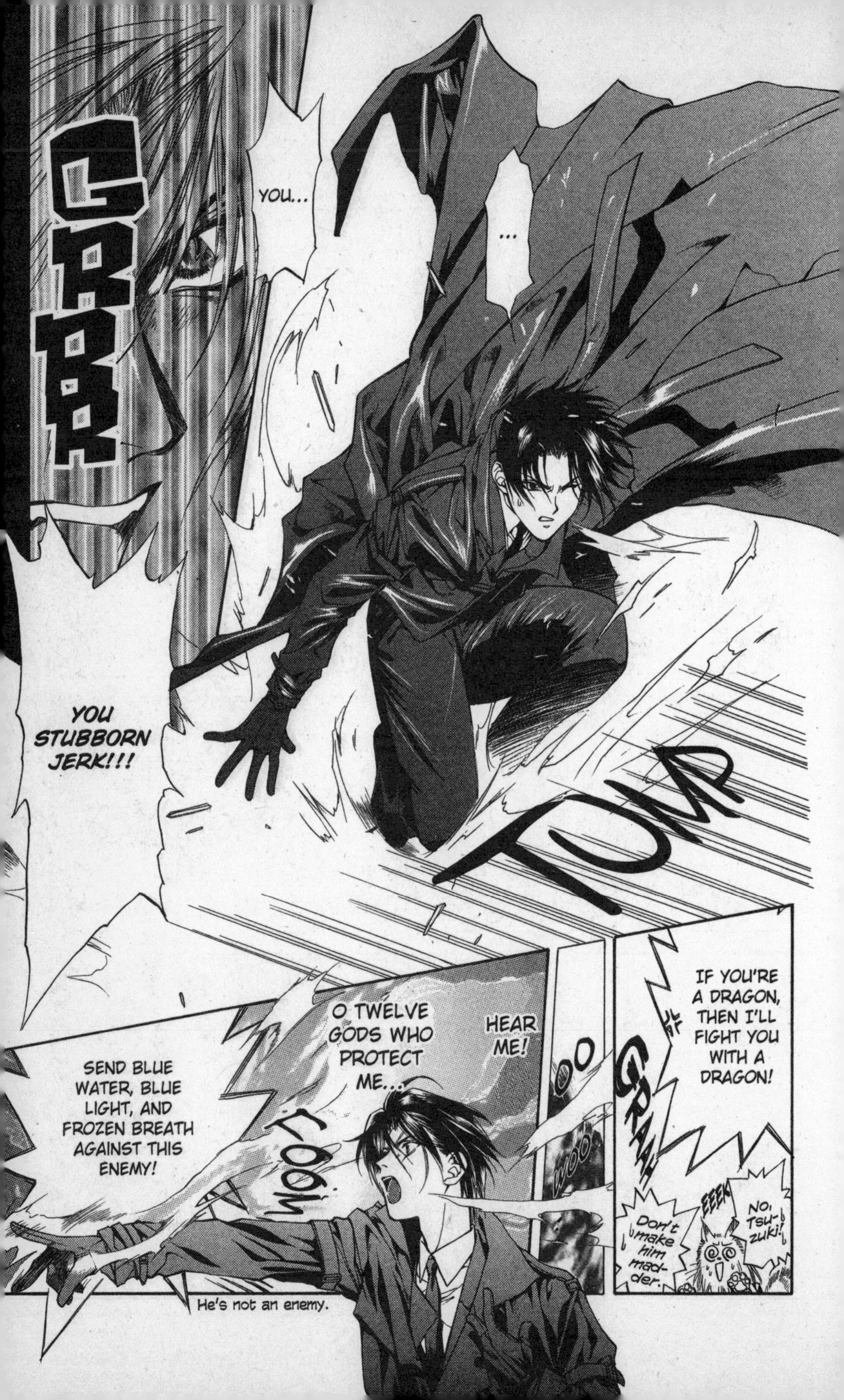
...
YOU...
GRRRR
YOU STUBBORN JERK!!!
TUMP
IF YOU'RE A DRAGON, THEN I'LL FIGHT YOU WITH A DRAGON!
GRAAH
NO, TSUZUKI!
EEEK
Don't make him madder.
HEAR ME!
O TWELVE GODS WHO PROTECT ME...
WOO
SEND BLUE WATER, BLUE LIGHT, AND FROZEN BREATH AGAINST THIS ENEMY!
FOOM
He's not an enemy.

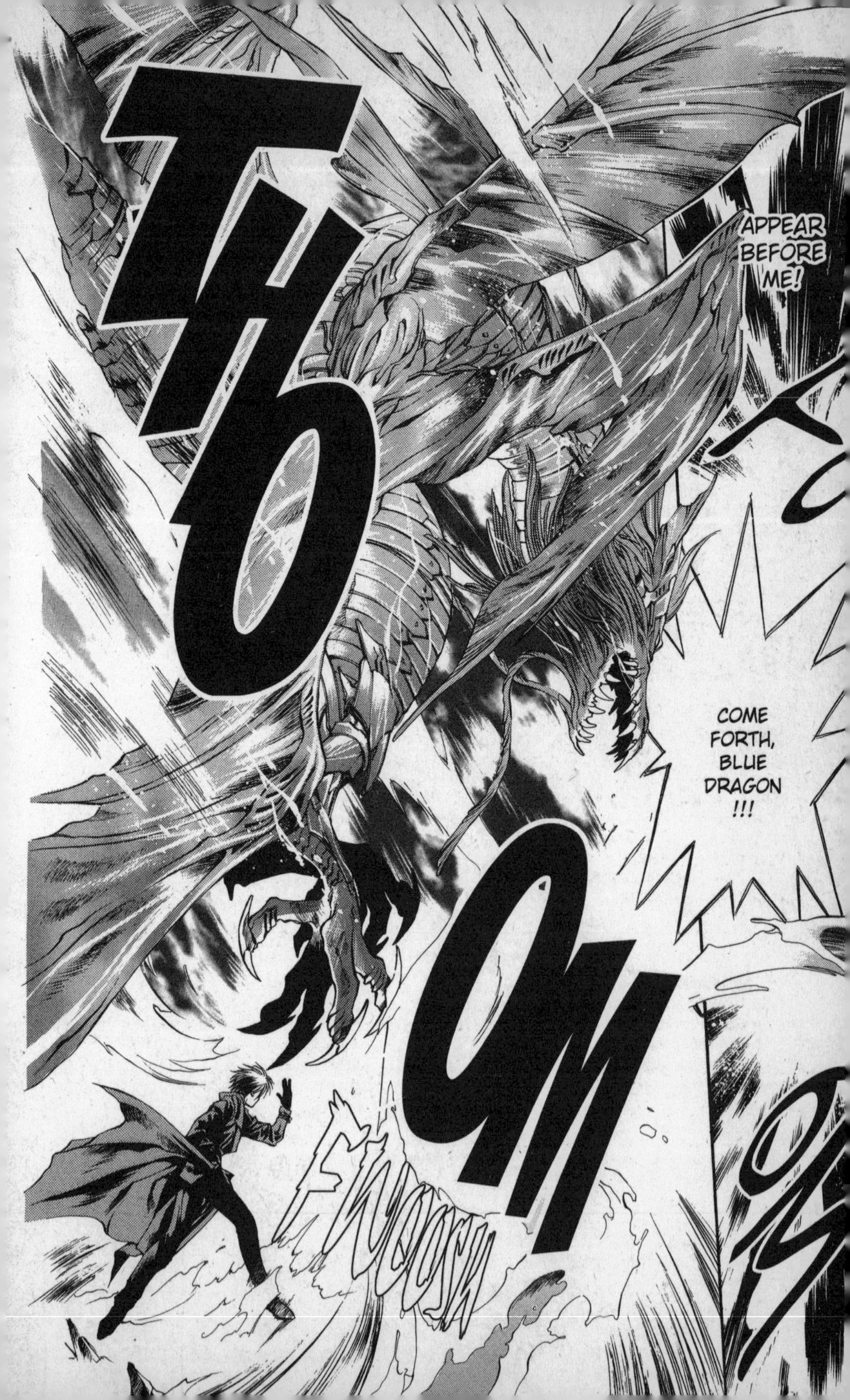
APPEAR BEFORE ME!
COME FORTH, BLUE DRAGON !!!

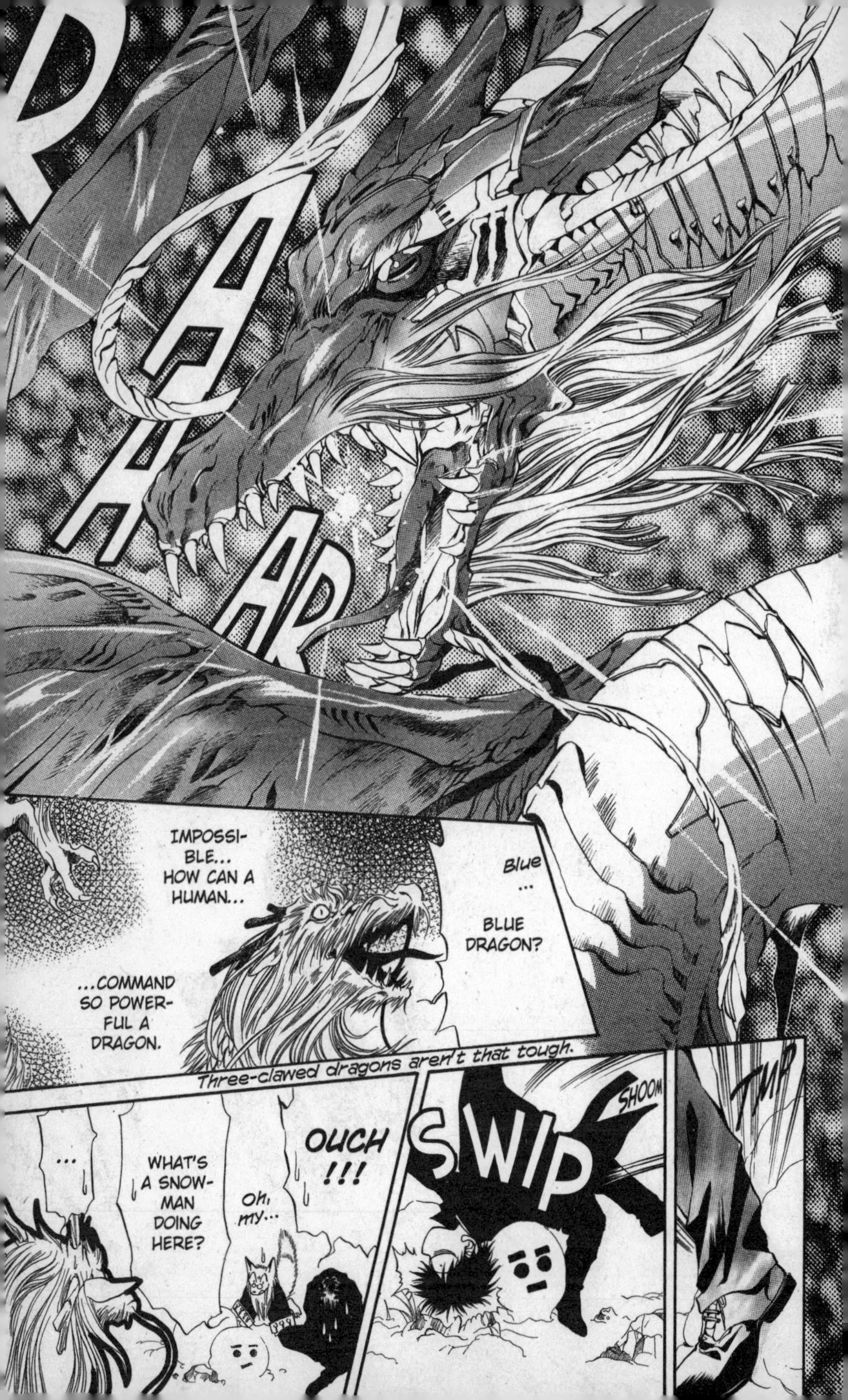
RAAAAR
Blue ... BLUE DRAGON?
IMPOSSIBLE... HOW CAN A HUMAN...
...COMMAND SO POWERFUL A DRAGON.
Three-clawed dragons aren't that tough.
TMP
SHOOM
SWIP
OUCH!!!
Oh, my...
WHAT'S A SNOWMAN DOING HERE?
...

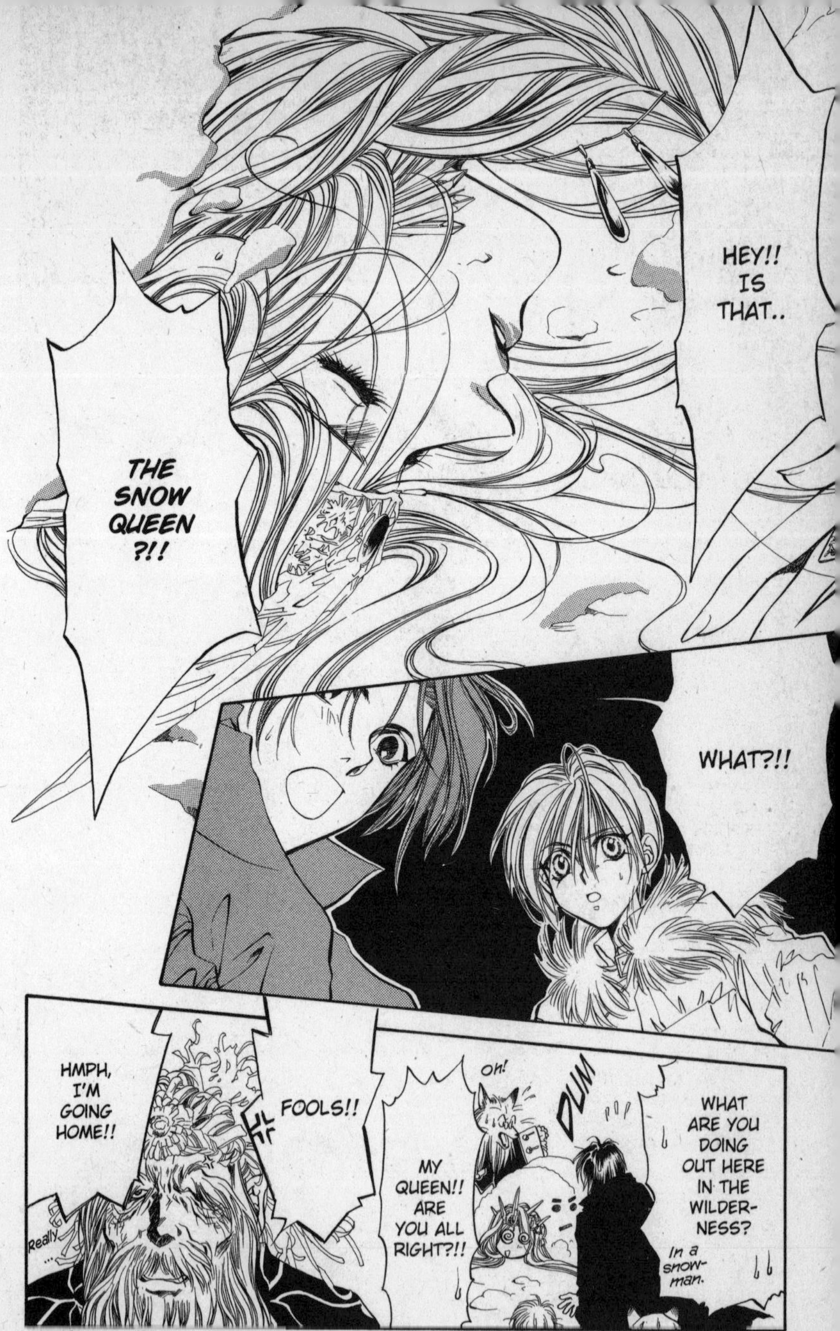
HEY!! IS THAT..
THE SNOW QUEEN ?!!
WHAT?!!
WHAT ARE YOU DOING OUT HERE IN THE WILDERNESS?
In a snowman.
DUM
Oh!
MY QUEEN!! ARE YOU ALL RIGHT?!!
FOOLS!!
HMPH, I'M GOING HOME!!
Really ...

I feel bad for the Blue Dragon.

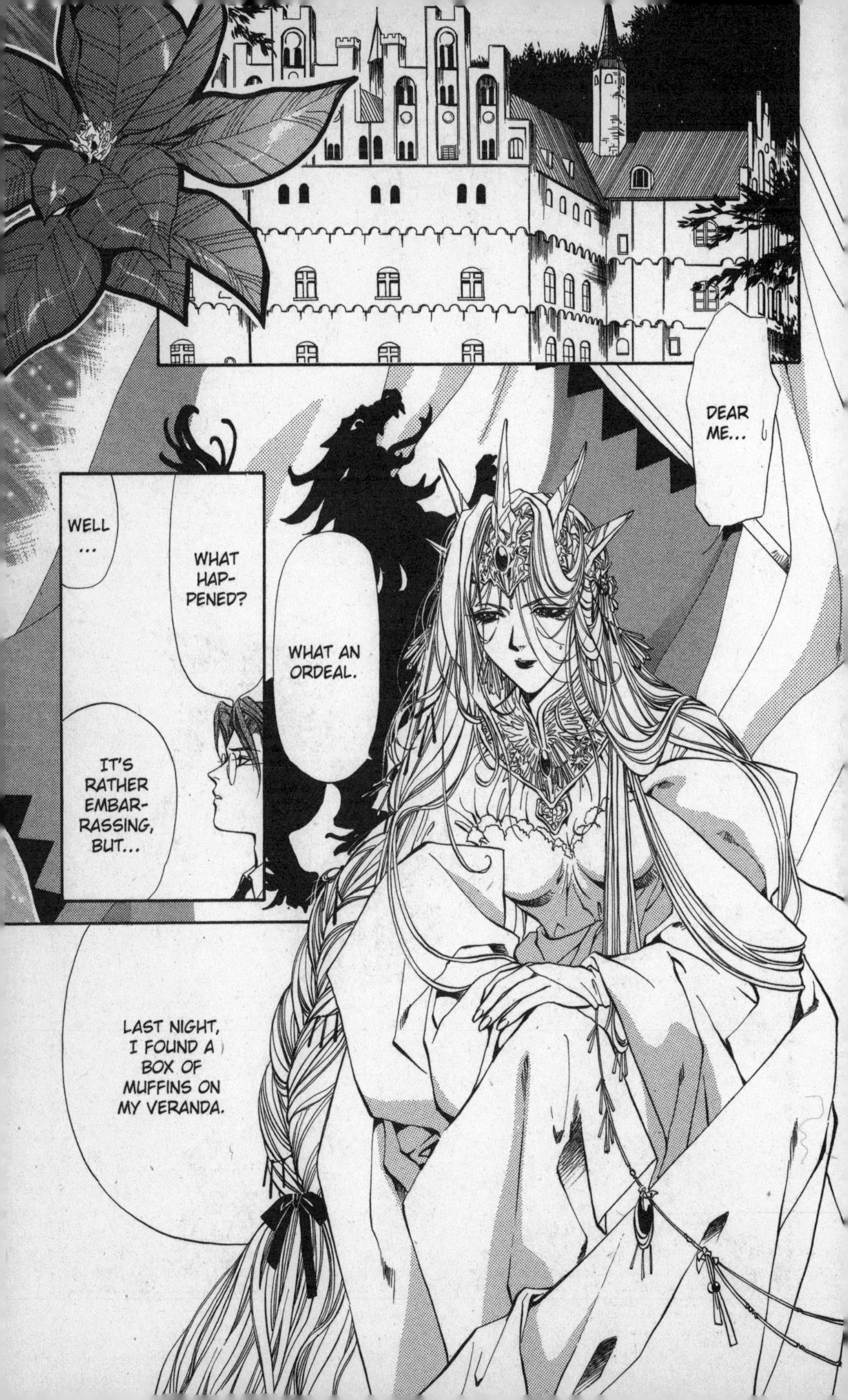
DEAR ME...
WHAT AN ORDEAL.
WHAT HAPPENED?
WELL...
IT'S RATHER EMBARRASSING, BUT...
LAST NIGHT, I FOUND A BOX OF MUFFINS ON MY VERANDA.

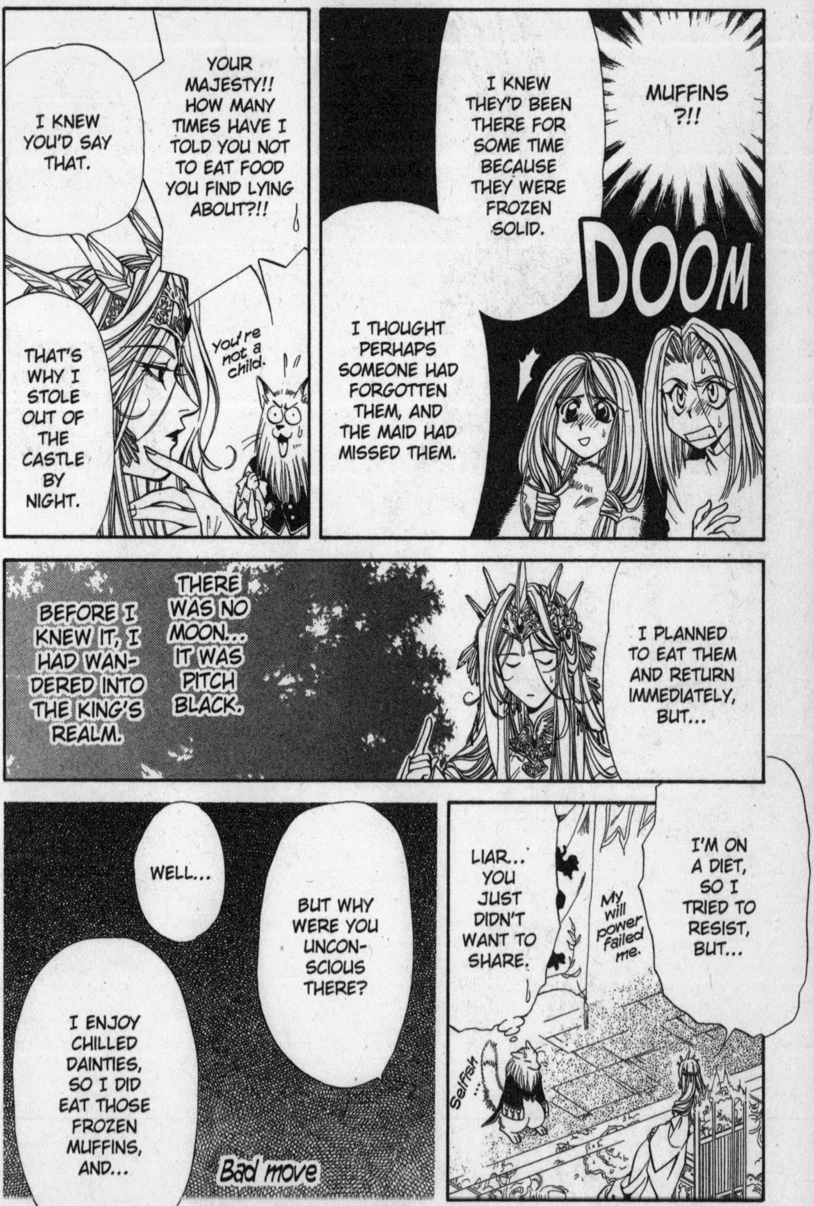
MUFFINS ?!!
DOOM
I KNEW THEY'D BEEN THERE FOR SOME TIME BECAUSE THEY WERE FROZEN SOLID.
I THOUGHT PERHAPS SOMEONE HAD FORGOTTEN THEM, AND THE MAID HAD MISSED THEM.
YOUR MAJESTY!! HOW MANY TIMES HAVE I TOLD YOU NOT TO EAT FOOD YOU FIND LYING ABOUT?!!
I KNEW YOU'D SAY THAT.
You're not a child.
THAT'S WHY I STOLE OUT OF THE CASTLE BY NIGHT.
I PLANNED TO EAT THEM AND RETURN IMMEDIATELY, BUT...
THERE WAS NO MOON... IT WAS PITCH BLACK.
BEFORE I KNEW IT, I HAD WAN-DERED INTO THE KING'S REALM.
I'M ON A DIET, SO I TRIED TO RESIST, BUT...
My will power failed me.
LIAR... YOU JUST DIDN'T WANT TO SHARE.
Selfish...
BUT WHY WERE YOU UNCON-SCIOUS THERE?
WELL...
I ENJOY CHILLED DAINTIES, SO I DID EAT THOSE FROZEN MUFFINS, AND...
Bad move

Even they've heard that Tsuzuki's cooking is bad. ↓

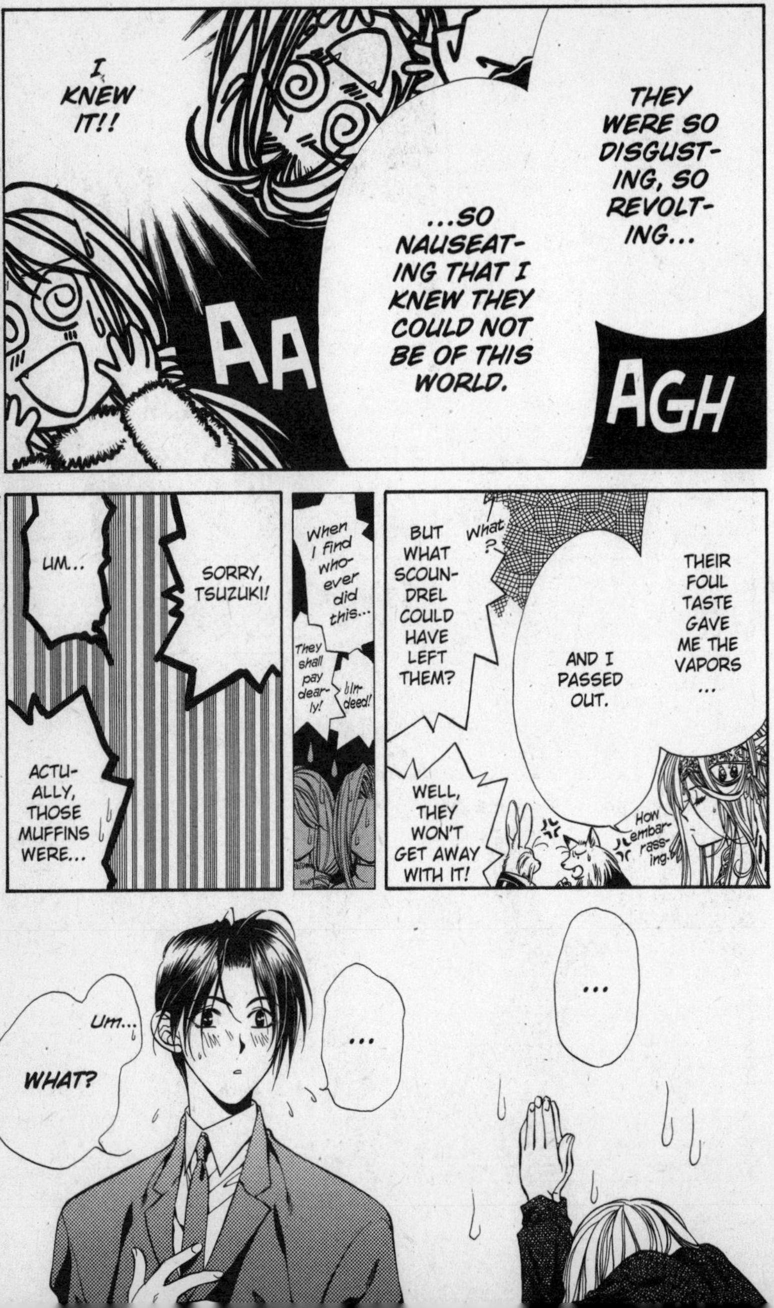

THEY WERE SO DISGUSTING, SO REVOLTING...
...SO NAUSEATING THAT I KNEW THEY COULD NOT BE OF THIS WORLD.
AAAGH
I KNEW IT!!
THEIR FOUL TASTE GAVE ME THE VAPORS...
AND I PASSED OUT.
How embarrassing.
What?
BUT WHAT SCOUNDREL COULD HAVE LEFT THEM?
WELL, THEY WON'T GET AWAY WITH IT!
When I find whoever did this...
They shall pay dearly!
Indeed!
SORRY, TSUZUKI!
UM...
ACTUALLY, THOSE MUFFINS WERE...
...
...
Um...
WHAT?

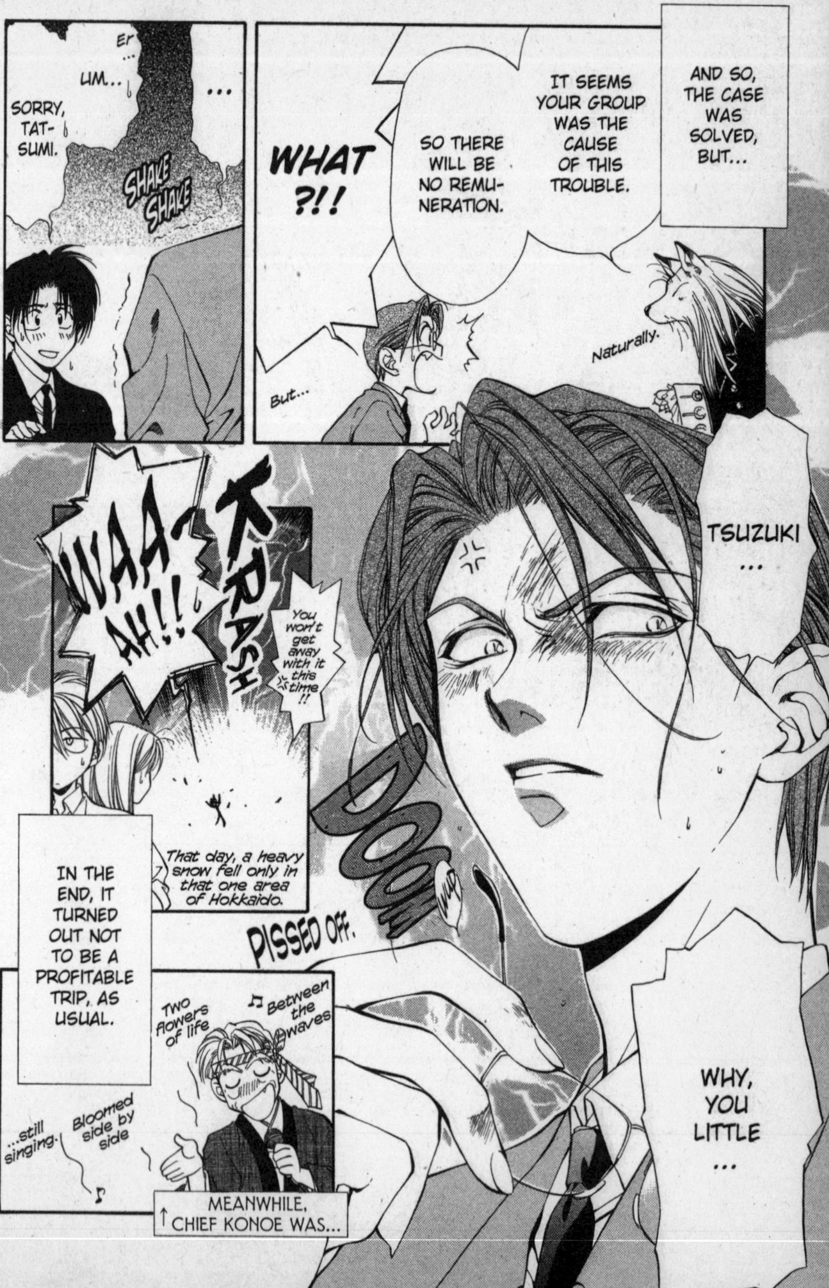
AND SO, THE CASE WAS SOLVED, BUT...
IT SEEMS YOUR GROUP WAS THE CAUSE OF THIS TROUBLE.
SO THERE WILL BE NO REMUNERATION.
Naturally.
WHAT ?!!
But...
...
Er ...
UM...
SORRY, TATSUMI.
SHAKE SHAKE
TSUZUKI ...
WHY, YOU LITTLE ...
DOOM
PISSED OFF.
KRASH
WAA-AH!!
You won't get away with it this time!!
That day, a heavy snow fell only in that one area of Hokkaido.
IN THE END, IT TURNED OUT NOT TO BE A PROFITABLE TRIP, AS USUAL.
Between the waves
Two flowers of life
Bloomed side by side
...still singing.
MEANWHILE, CHIEF KONOE WAS...

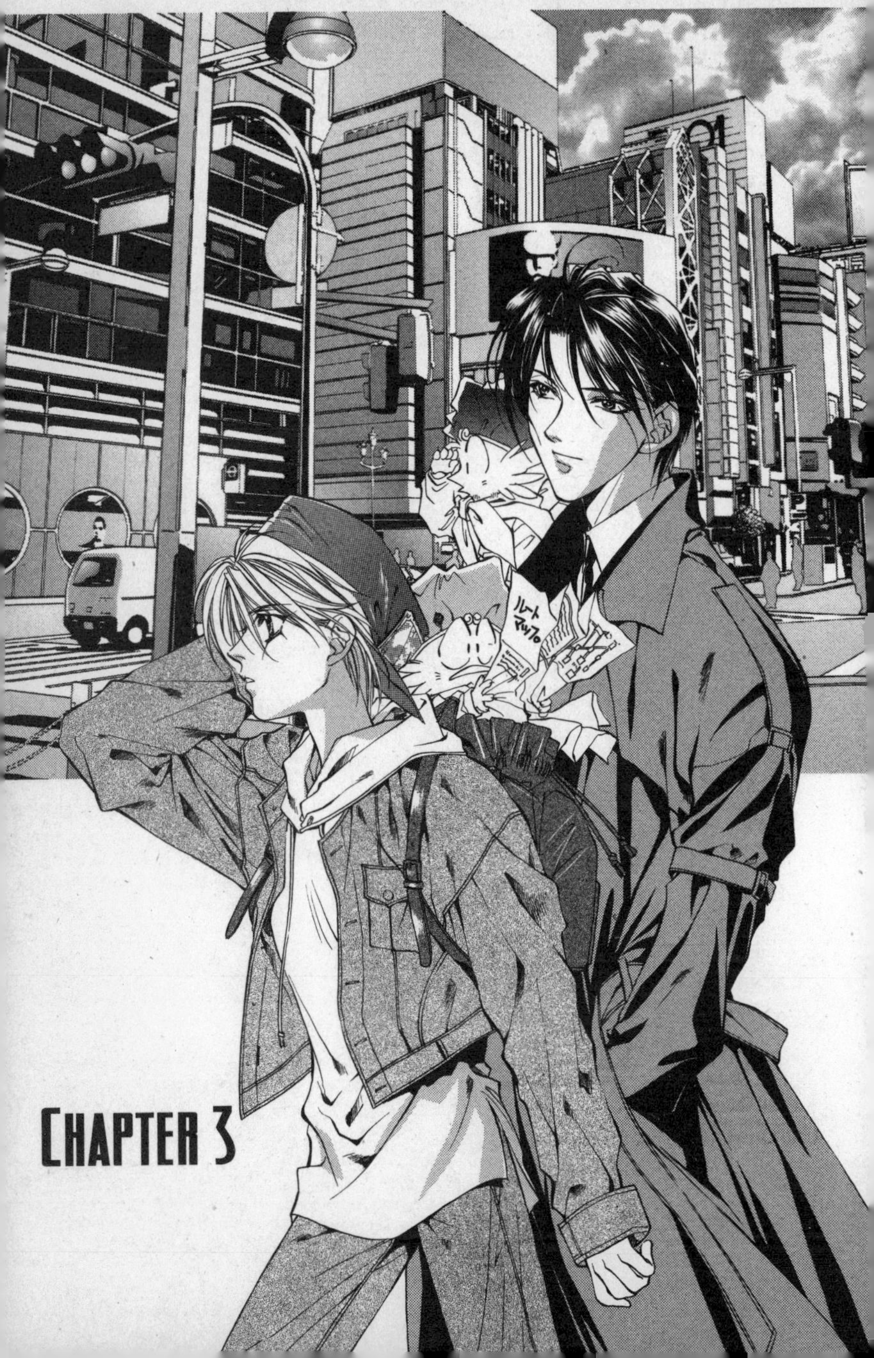
ルート
マップ
CHAPTER 3

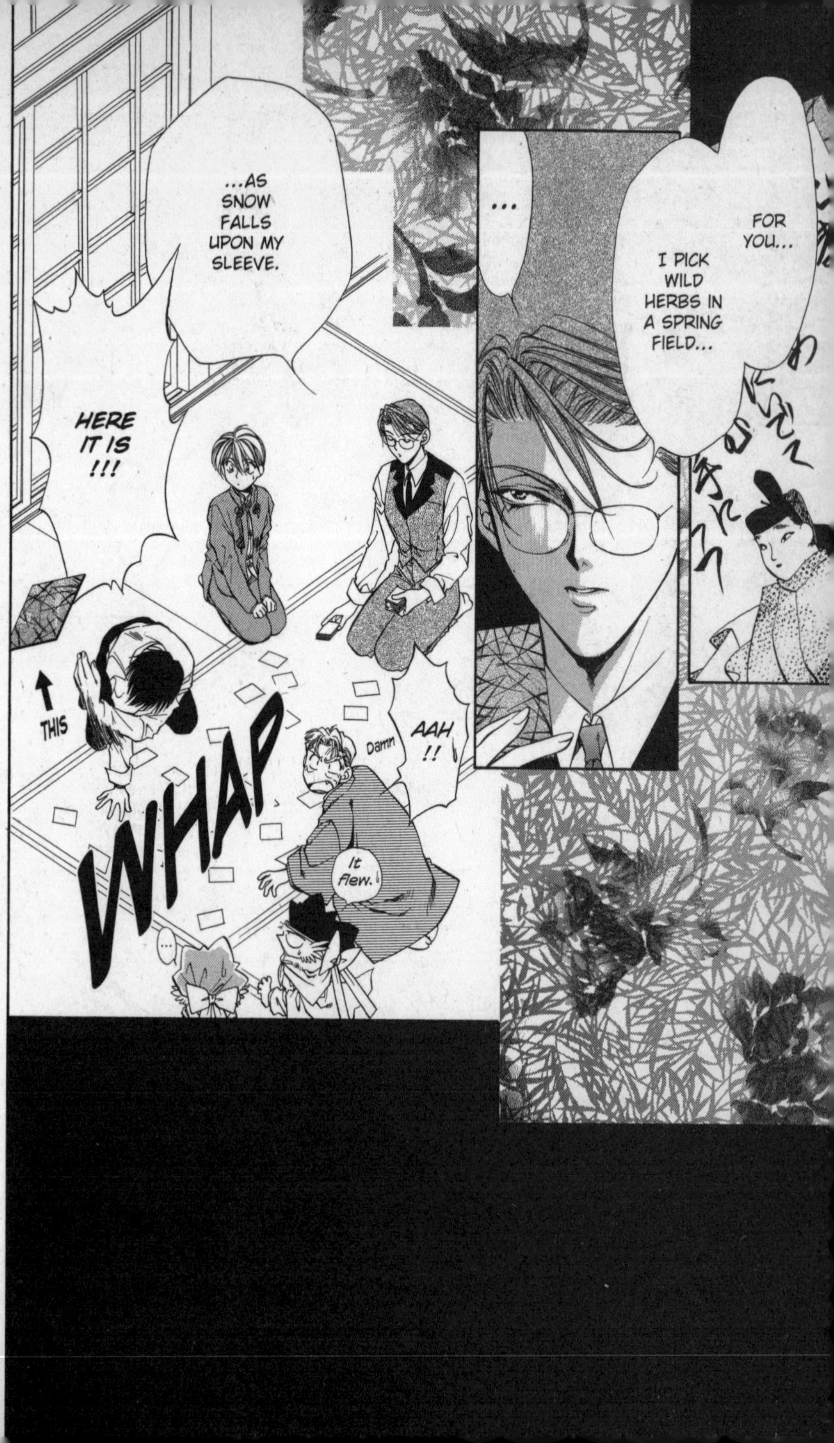
FOR YOU...
I PICK WILD HERBS IN A SPRING FIELD...
...
...AS SNOW FALLS UPON MY SLEEVE.
HERE IT IS !!!
THIS
AAH !!
Damn
WHAP
It flew.
...

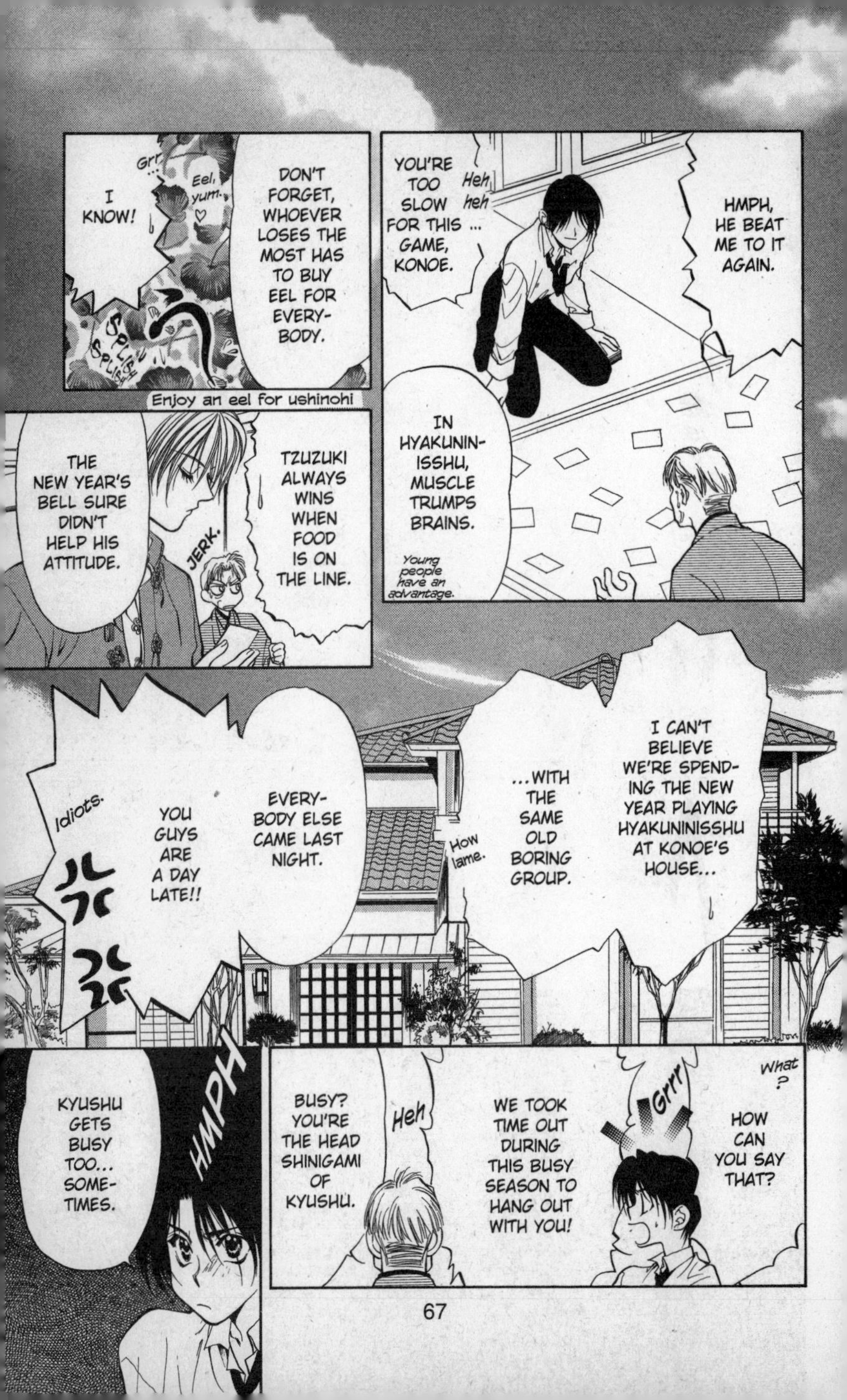
HMPH, HE BEAT ME TO IT AGAIN.
YOU'RE TOO SLOW FOR THIS ... GAME, KONOE.
Heh heh
IN HYAKUNIN-ISSHU, MUSCLE TRUMPS BRAINS.
Young people have an advantage.
DON'T FORGET, WHOEVER LOSES THE MOST HAS TO BUY EEL FOR EVERY-BODY.
Eel, yum. ♡
Grr...
I KNOW!
SPLISH SPLISH
Enjoy an eel for ushinohi
TZUZUKI ALWAYS WINS WHEN FOOD IS ON THE LINE.
JERK.
THE NEW YEAR'S BELL SURE DIDN'T HELP HIS ATTITUDE.
I CAN'T BELIEVE WE'RE SPEND-ING THE NEW YEAR PLAYING HYAKUNINISSHU AT KONOE'S HOUSE...
...WITH THE SAME OLD BORING GROUP.
How lame.
EVERY-BODY ELSE CAME LAST NIGHT.
YOU GUYS ARE A DAY LATE!!
Idiots.
What?
HOW CAN YOU SAY THAT?
Grrr
WE TOOK TIME OUT DURING THIS BUSY SEASON TO HANG OUT WITH YOU!
Heh
BUSY? YOU'RE THE HEAD SHINIGAMI OF KYUSHU.
HMPH
KYUSHU GETS BUSY TOO... SOME-TIMES.

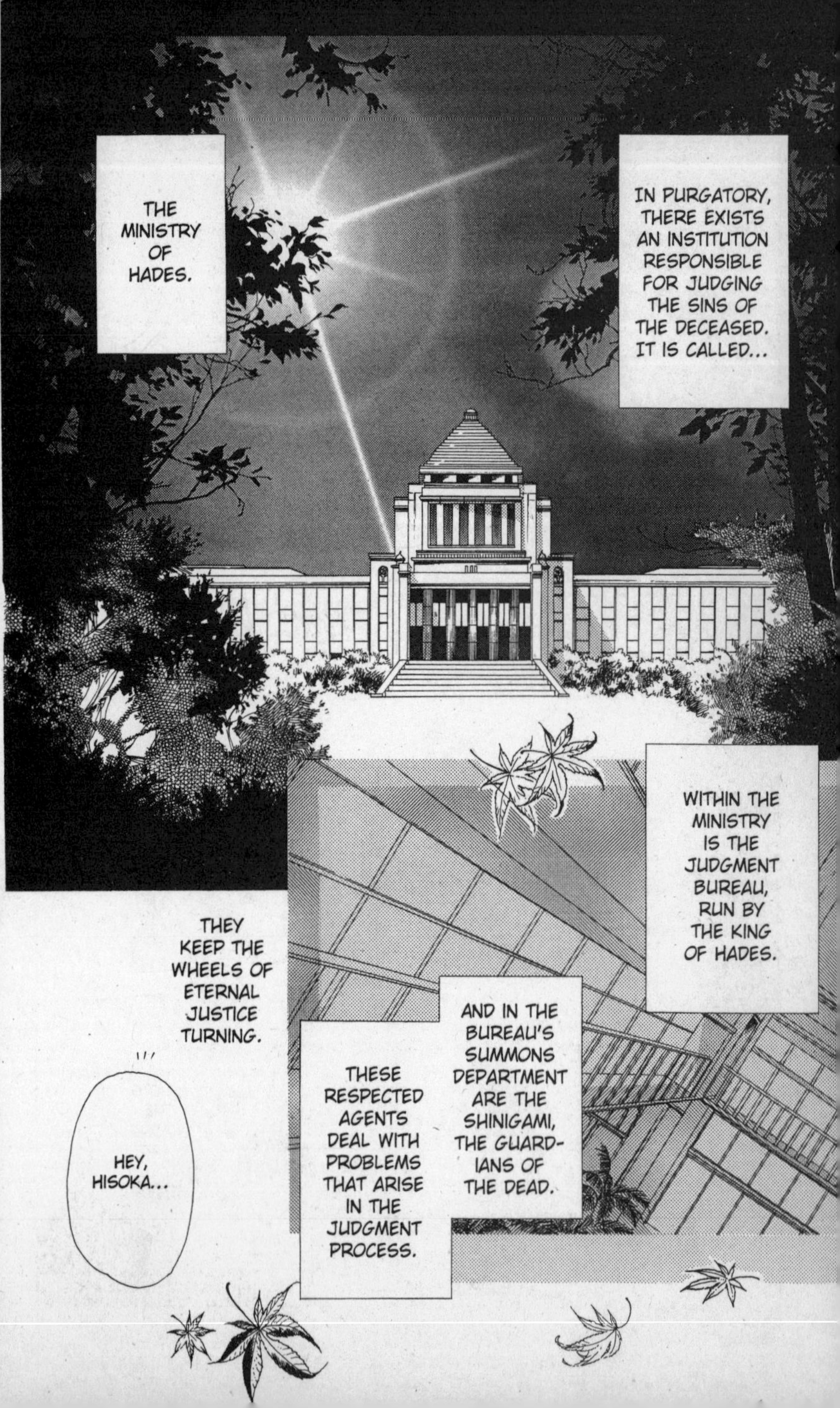
IN PURGATORY, THERE EXISTS AN INSTITUTION RESPONSIBLE FOR JUDGING THE SINS OF THE DECEASED. IT IS CALLED...
THE MINISTRY OF HADES.
WITHIN THE MINISTRY IS THE JUDGMENT BUREAU, RUN BY THE KING OF HADES.
AND IN THE BUREAU'S SUMMONS DEPARTMENT ARE THE SHINIGAMI, THE GUARDIANS OF THE DEAD.
THESE RESPECTED AGENTS DEAL WITH PROBLEMS THAT ARISE IN THE JUDGMENT PROCESS.
THEY KEEP THE WHEELS OF ETERNAL JUSTICE TURNING.
HEY, HISOKA...

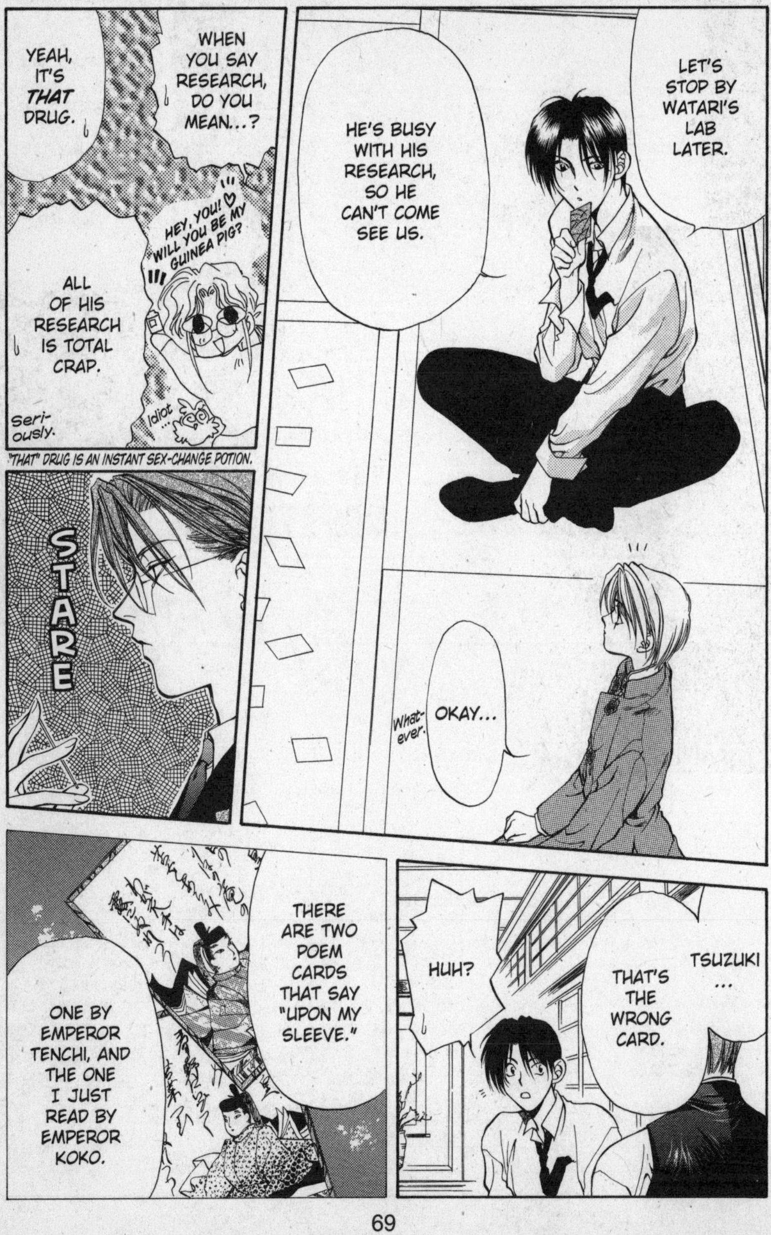
LET'S STOP BY WATARI'S LAB LATER.
HE'S BUSY WITH HIS RESEARCH, SO HE CAN'T COME SEE US.
OKAY...
Whatever.
WHEN YOU SAY RESEARCH, DO YOU MEAN...?
YEAH, IT'S *THAT* DRUG.
HEY, YOU! ♡ WILL YOU BE MY GUINEA PIG?
ALL OF HIS RESEARCH IS TOTAL CRAP.
Idiot...
Seriously.
"THAT" DRUG IS AN INSTANT SEX-CHANGE POTION.
STARE
TSUZUKI...
THAT'S THE WRONG CARD.
HUH?
THERE ARE TWO POEM CARDS THAT SAY "UPON MY SLEEVE."
ONE BY EMPEROR TENCHI, AND THE ONE I JUST READ BY EMPEROR KOKO.

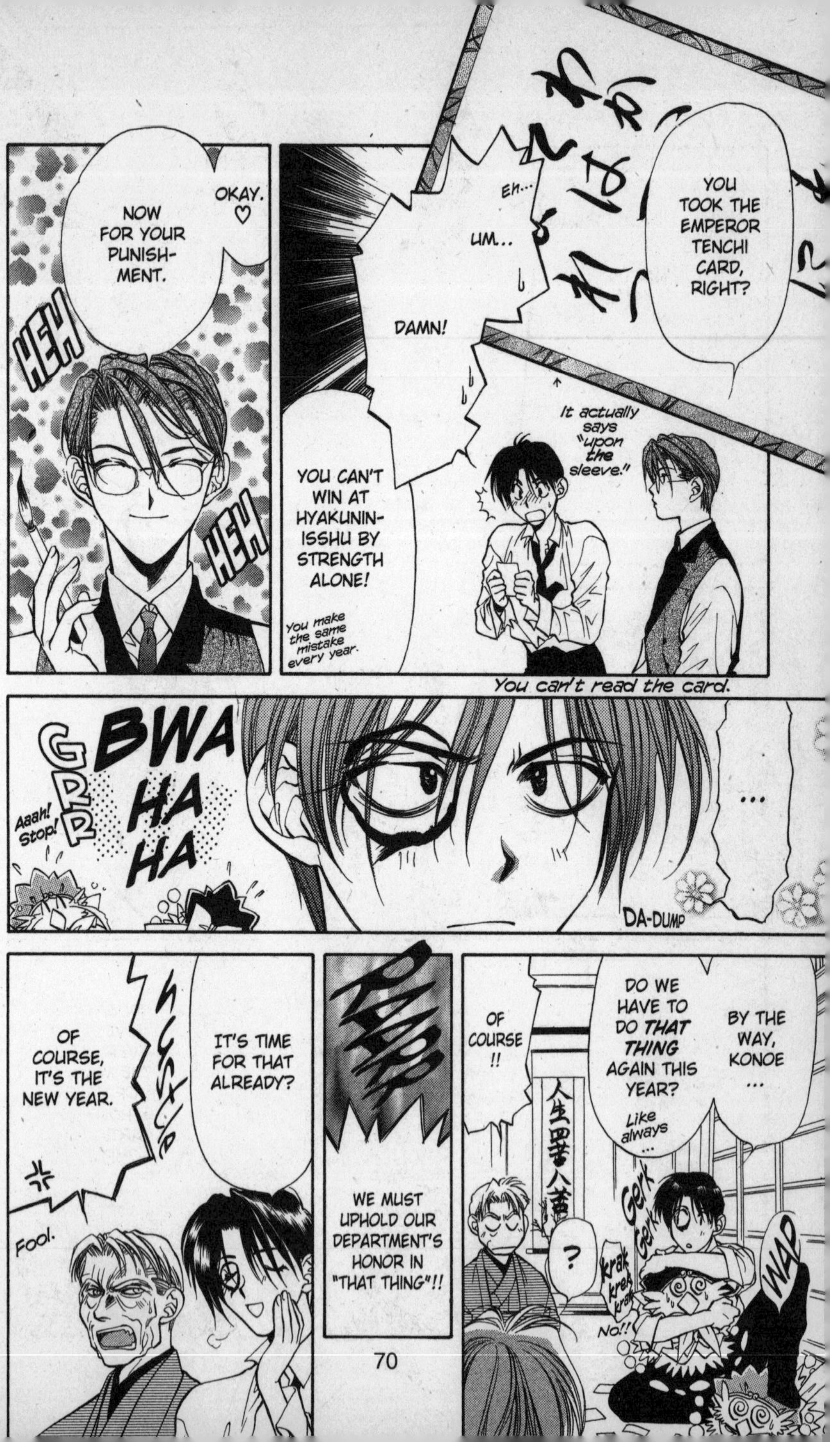

YOU TOOK THE EMPEROR TENCHI CARD, RIGHT?
Eh... UM..
It actually says "upon the sleeve."
DAMN!
YOU CAN'T WIN AT HYAKUNIN-ISSHU BY STRENGTH ALONE!
You make the same mistake every year.
You can't read the card.
OKAY. ♡
NOW FOR YOUR PUNISH-MENT.
HEH
HEH
...
DA-DUMP
BWA HA HA HA
GRR
Aaah! Stop!
BY THE WAY, KONOE...
DO WE HAVE TO DO THAT THING AGAIN THIS YEAR?
Like always...
OF COURSE!!
?
Gerk Gerk
krak krak krak
WAP
No!!
RAPP
WE MUST UPHOLD OUR DEPARTMENT'S HONOR IN "THAT THING"!!
IT'S TIME FOR THAT ALREADY?
rustle
OF COURSE, IT'S THE NEW YEAR.
Fool.

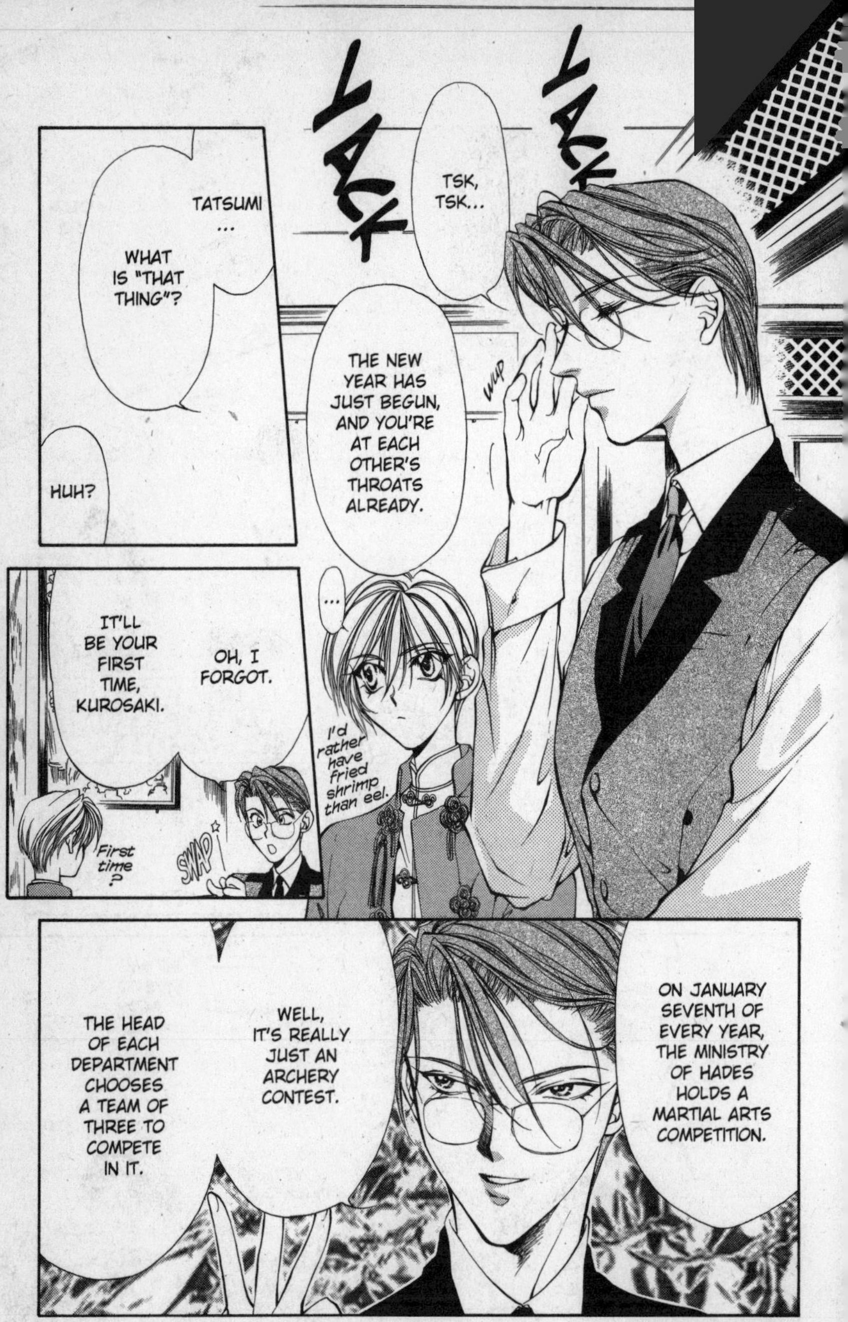

YACK
YACK
TSK, TSK...
WUP
THE NEW YEAR HAS JUST BEGUN, AND YOU'RE AT EACH OTHER'S THROATS ALREADY.
...
I'd rather have fried shrimp than eel.
TATSUMI...
WHAT IS "THAT THING"?
HUH?
OH, I FORGOT.
IT'LL BE YOUR FIRST TIME, KUROSAKI.
SWAP
First time?
ON JANUARY SEVENTH OF EVERY YEAR, THE MINISTRY OF HADES HOLDS A MARTIAL ARTS COMPETITION.
WELL, IT'S REALLY JUST AN ARCHERY CONTEST.
THE HEAD OF EACH DEPARTMENT CHOOSES A TEAM OF THREE TO COMPETE IN IT.

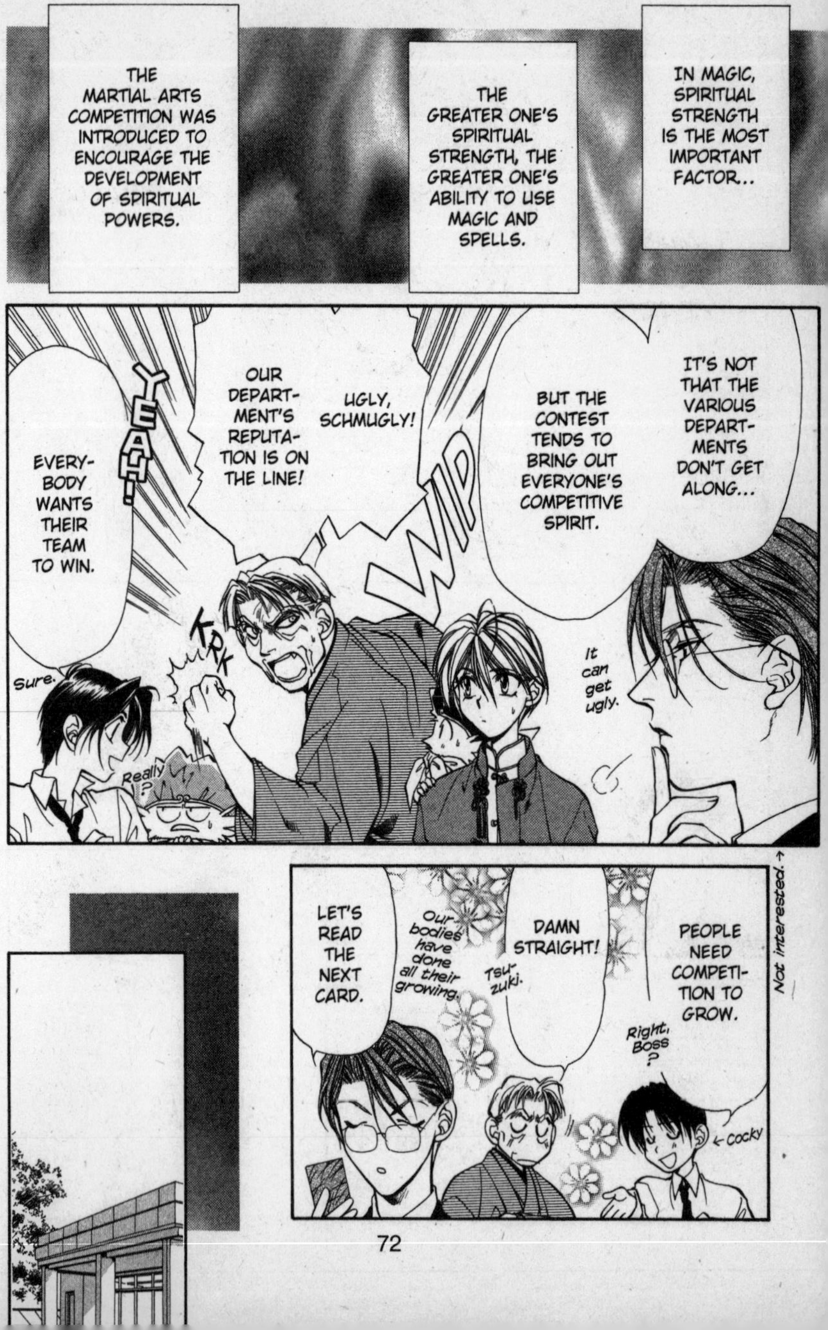
IN MAGIC, SPIRITUAL STRENGTH IS THE MOST IMPORTANT FACTOR...
THE GREATER ONE'S SPIRITUAL STRENGTH, THE GREATER ONE'S ABILITY TO USE MAGIC AND SPELLS.
THE MARTIAL ARTS COMPETITION WAS INTRODUCED TO ENCOURAGE THE DEVELOPMENT OF SPIRITUAL POWERS.
IT'S NOT THAT THE VARIOUS DEPART-MENTS DON'T GET ALONG...
BUT THE CONTEST TENDS TO BRING OUT EVERYONE'S COMPETITIVE SPIRIT.
WIP
It can get ugly.
UGLY, SCHMUGLY!
OUR DEPART-MENT'S REPUTA-TION IS ON THE LINE!
KRK
YEAH!
EVERY-BODY WANTS THEIR TEAM TO WIN.
Sure.
Really?
Not interested.
PEOPLE NEED COMPETI-TION TO GROW.
Right, Boss?
Cocky
DAMN STRAIGHT!
Tsu-zuki.
Our bodies have done all their growing.
LET'S READ THE NEXT CARD.

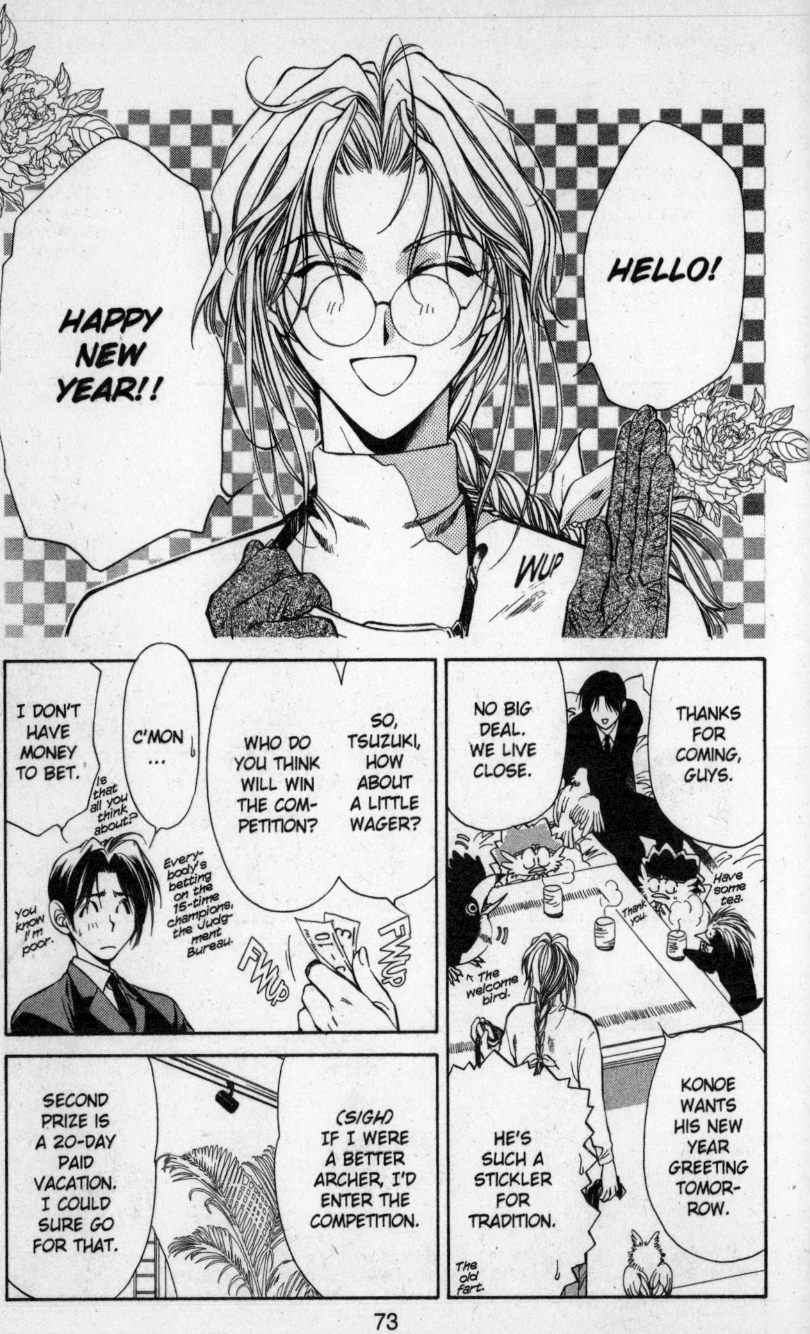
HELLO!
HAPPY NEW YEAR!!
WUP
THANKS FOR COMING, GUYS.
NO BIG DEAL. WE LIVE CLOSE.
Have some tea.
Thank you.
↖ The welcome bird.
KONOE WANTS HIS NEW YEAR GREETING TOMOR-ROW.
HE'S SUCH A STICKLER FOR TRADITION.
The old fart.
SO, TSUZUKI, HOW ABOUT A LITTLE WAGER?
WHO DO YOU THINK WILL WIN THE COM-PETITION?
FWUP
FWUP
Every-body's betting on the 15-time champions, the Judg-ment Bureau.
C'MON ...
Is that all you think about?
I DON'T HAVE MONEY TO BET.
You know I'm poor.
(SIGH) IF I WERE A BETTER ARCHER, I'D ENTER THE COMPETITION.
SECOND PRIZE IS A 20-DAY PAID VACATION. I COULD SURE GO FOR THAT.

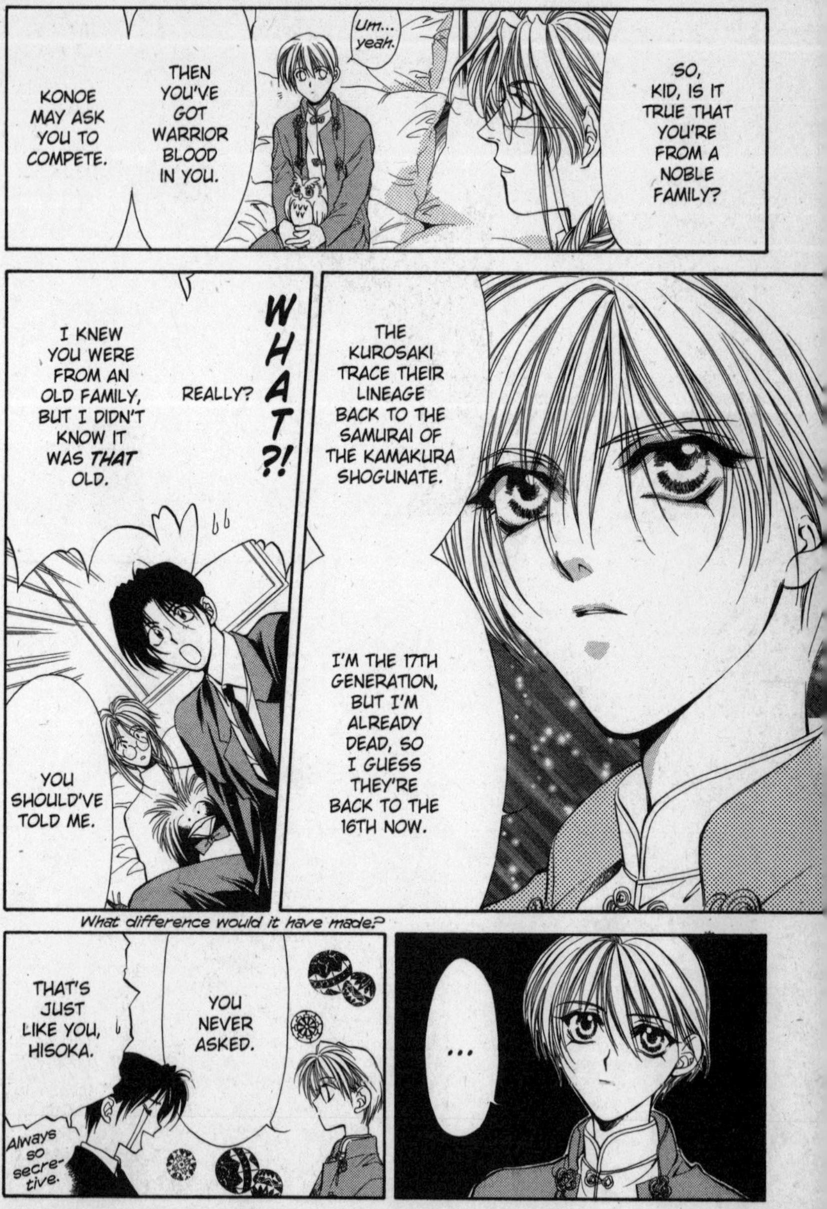

SO, KID, IS IT TRUE THAT YOU'RE FROM A NOBLE FAMILY?
Um... yeah.
THEN YOU'VE GOT WARRIOR BLOOD IN YOU.
KONOE MAY ASK YOU TO COMPETE.
THE KUROSAKI TRACE THEIR LINEAGE BACK TO THE SAMURAI OF THE KAMAKURA SHOGUNATE.
I'M THE 17TH GENERATION, BUT I'M ALREADY DEAD, SO I GUESS THEY'RE BACK TO THE 16TH NOW.
WHAT?!
REALLY?
I KNEW YOU WERE FROM AN OLD FAMILY, BUT I DIDN'T KNOW IT WAS *THAT* OLD.
YOU SHOULD'VE TOLD ME.
What difference would it have made?
...
YOU NEVER ASKED.
THAT'S JUST LIKE YOU, HISOKA.
Always so secretive.

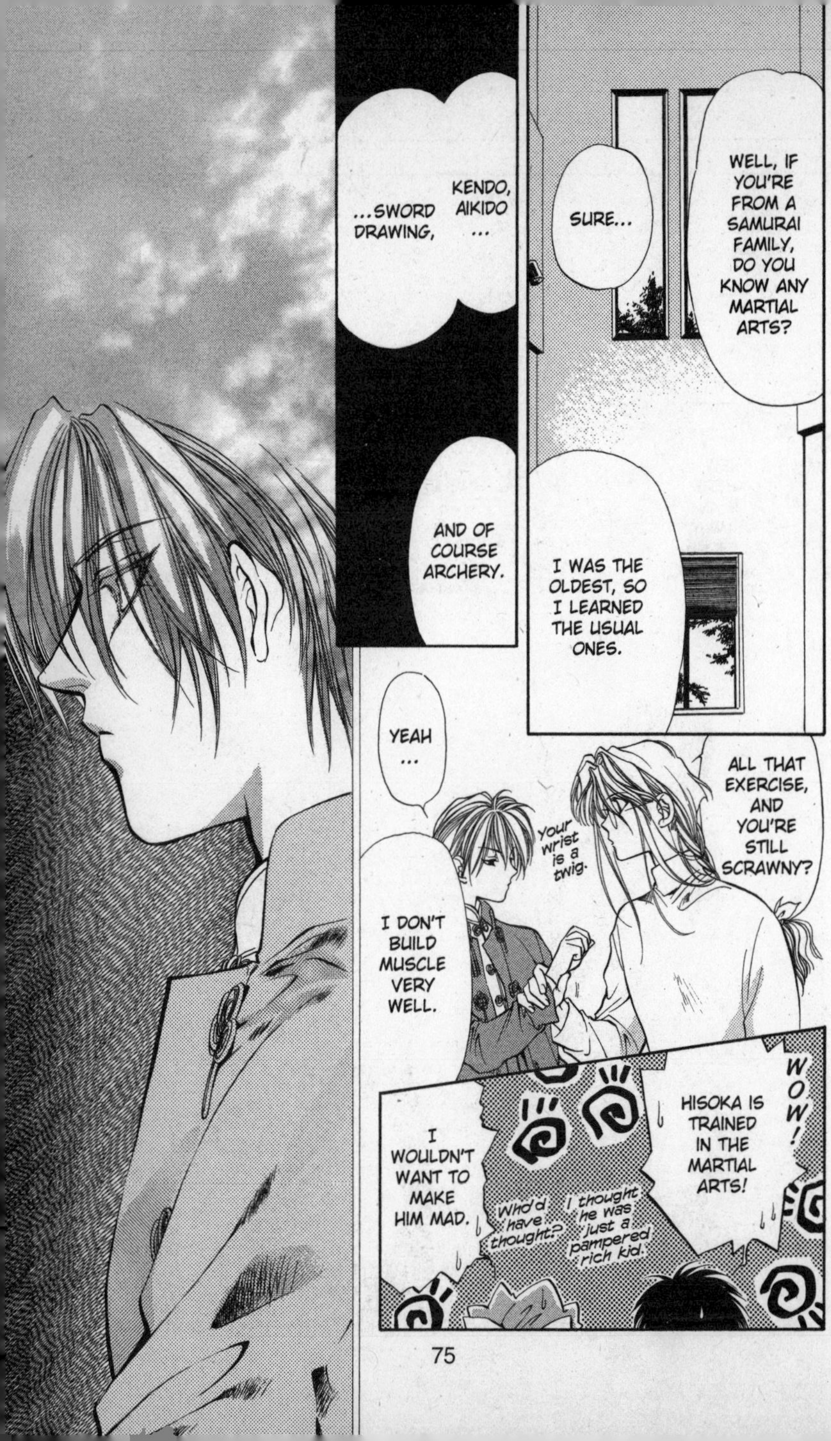
WELL, IF YOU'RE FROM A SAMURAI FAMILY, DO YOU KNOW ANY MARTIAL ARTS?
SURE...
KENDO, AIKIDO ...
...SWORD DRAWING,
I WAS THE OLDEST, SO I LEARNED THE USUAL ONES.
AND OF COURSE ARCHERY.
ALL THAT EXERCISE, AND YOU'RE STILL SCRAWNY?
Your wrist is a twig.
YEAH ...
I DON'T BUILD MUSCLE VERY WELL.
WOW!
HISOKA IS TRAINED IN THE MARTIAL ARTS!
I thought he was just a pampered rich kid.
Who'd have thought?
I WOULDN'T WANT TO MAKE HIM MAD.

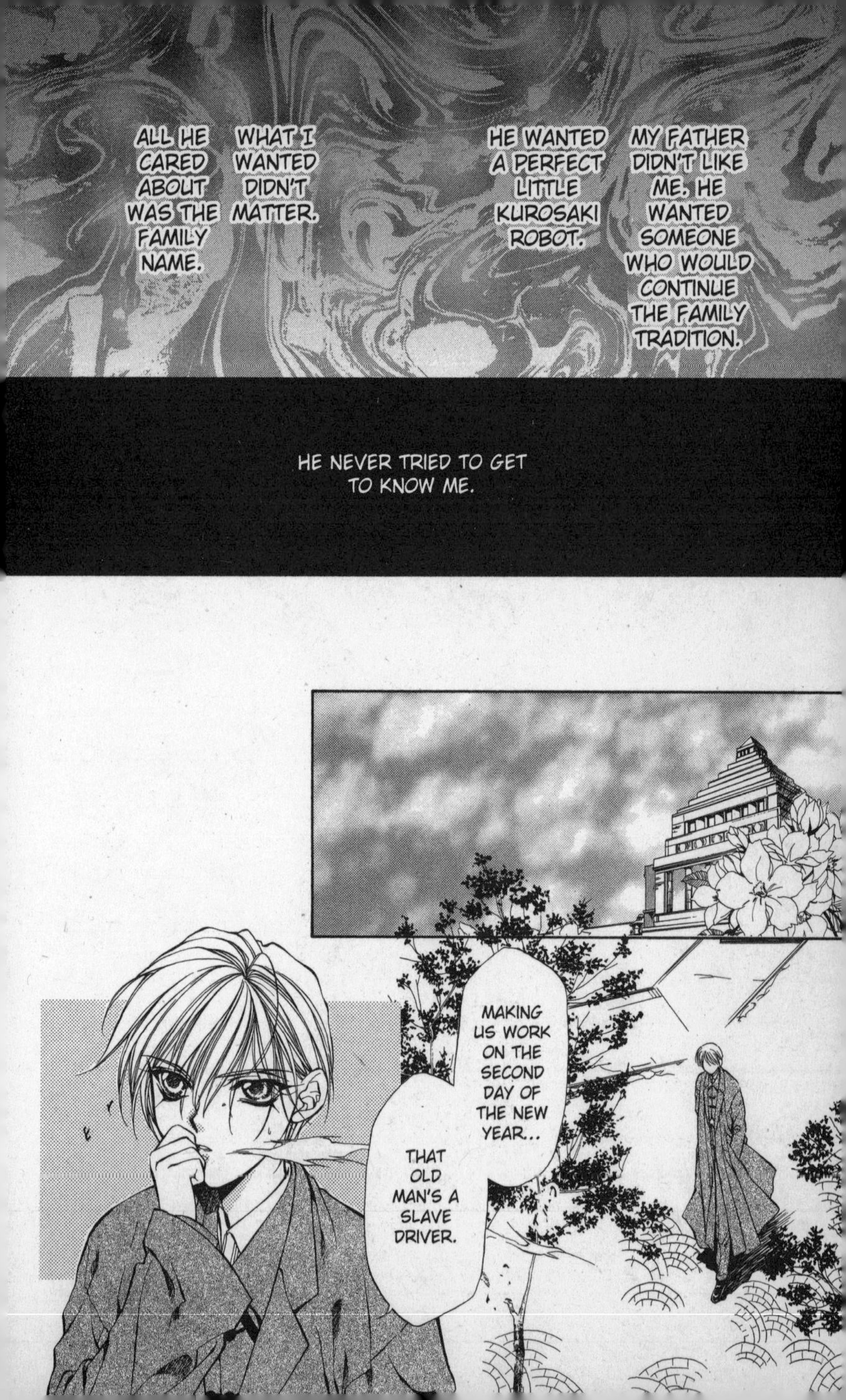
MY FATHER DIDN'T LIKE ME. HE WANTED SOMEONE WHO WOULD CONTINUE THE FAMILY TRADITION.
HE WANTED A PERFECT LITTLE KUROSAKI ROBOT.
WHAT I WANTED DIDN'T MATTER.
ALL HE CARED ABOUT WAS THE FAMILY NAME.
HE NEVER TRIED TO GET TO KNOW ME.
MAKING US WORK ON THE SECOND DAY OF THE NEW YEAR...
THAT OLD MAN'S A SLAVE DRIVER.

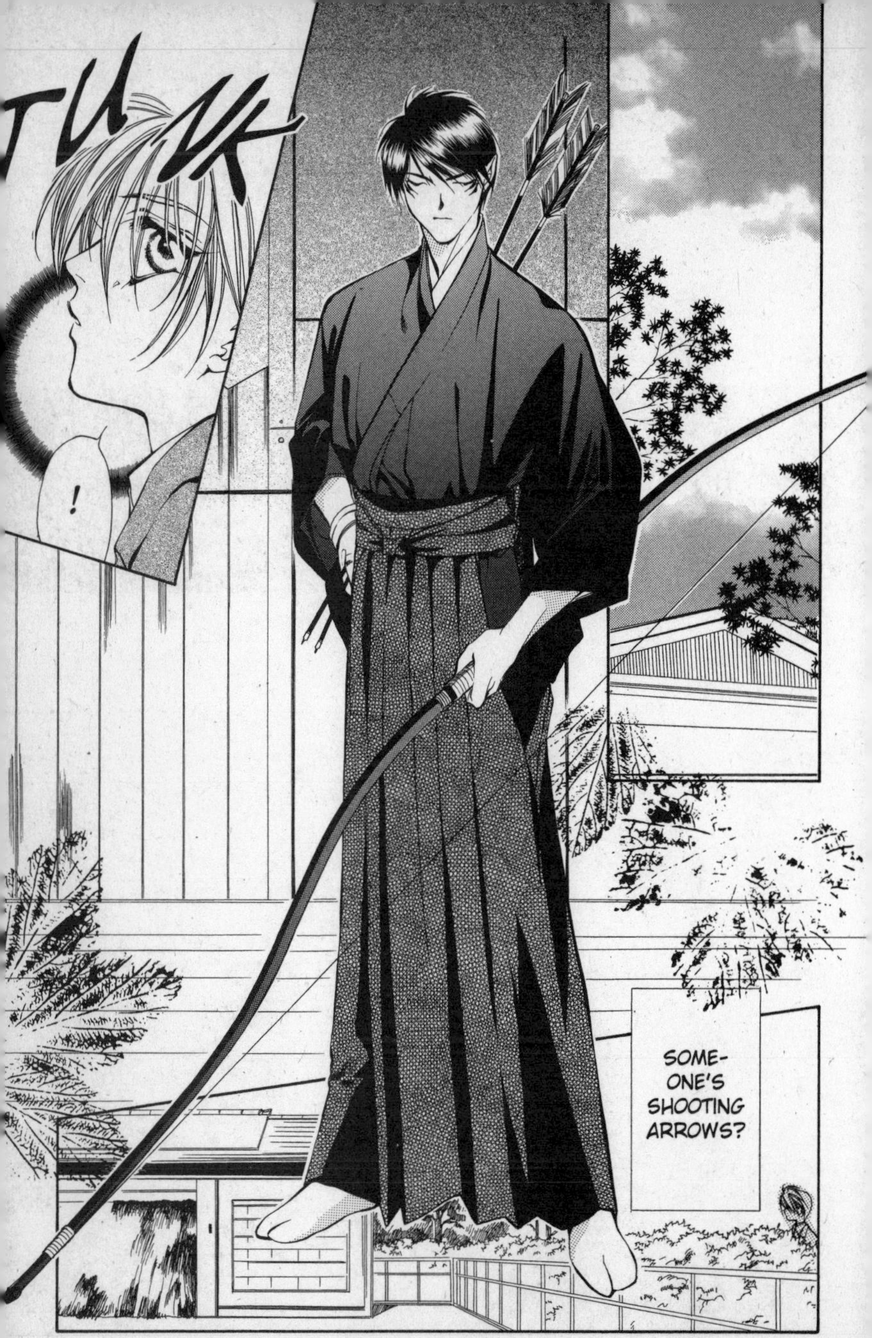
SOME-ONE'S SHOOTING ARROWS?
TUNK
!

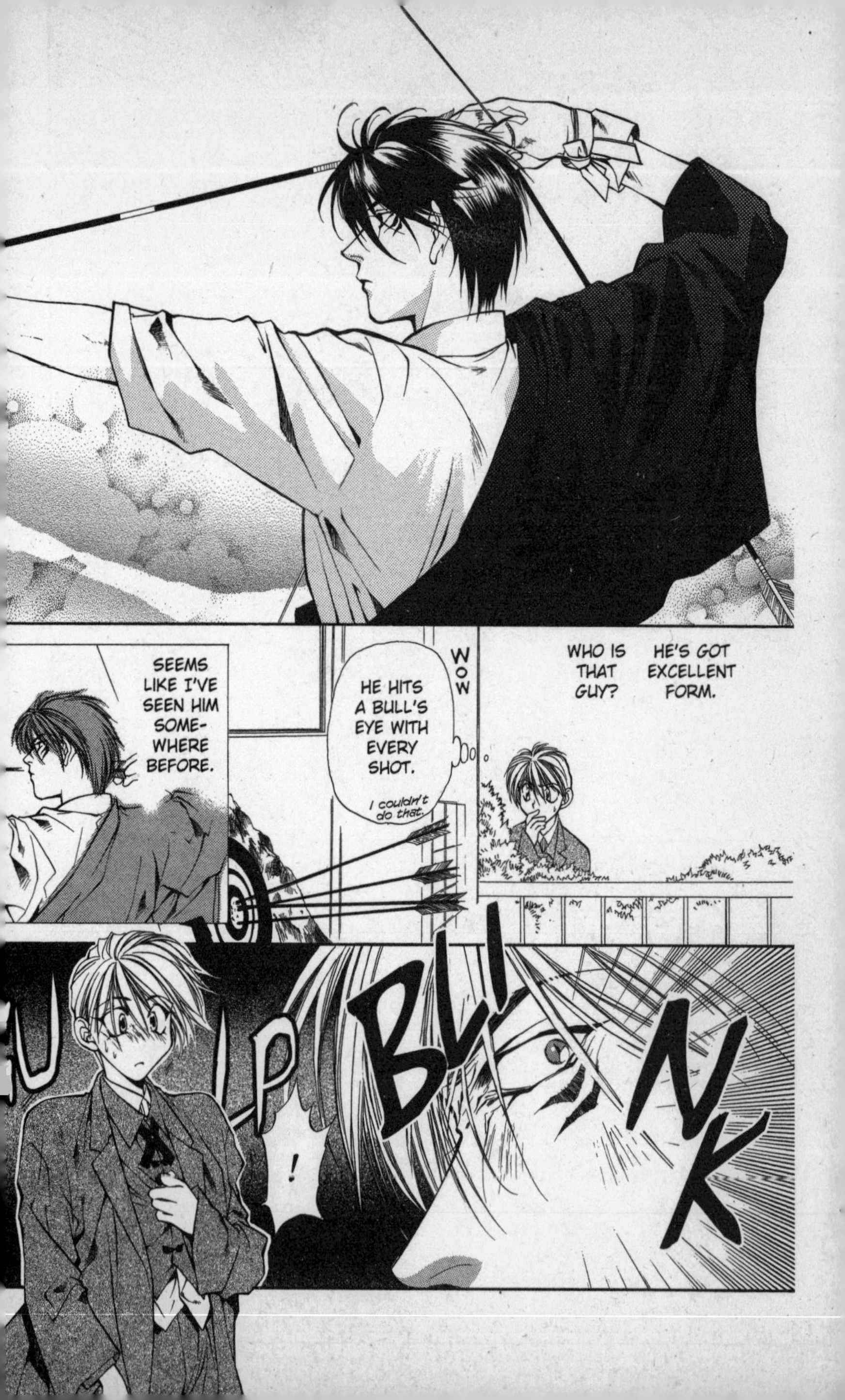
HE'S GOT EXCELLENT FORM.
WHO IS THAT GUY?
WOW
HE HITS A BULL'S EYE WITH EVERY SHOT.
I couldn't do that.
SEEMS LIKE I'VE SEEN HIM SOME-WHERE BEFORE.
BLINK
!
GULP

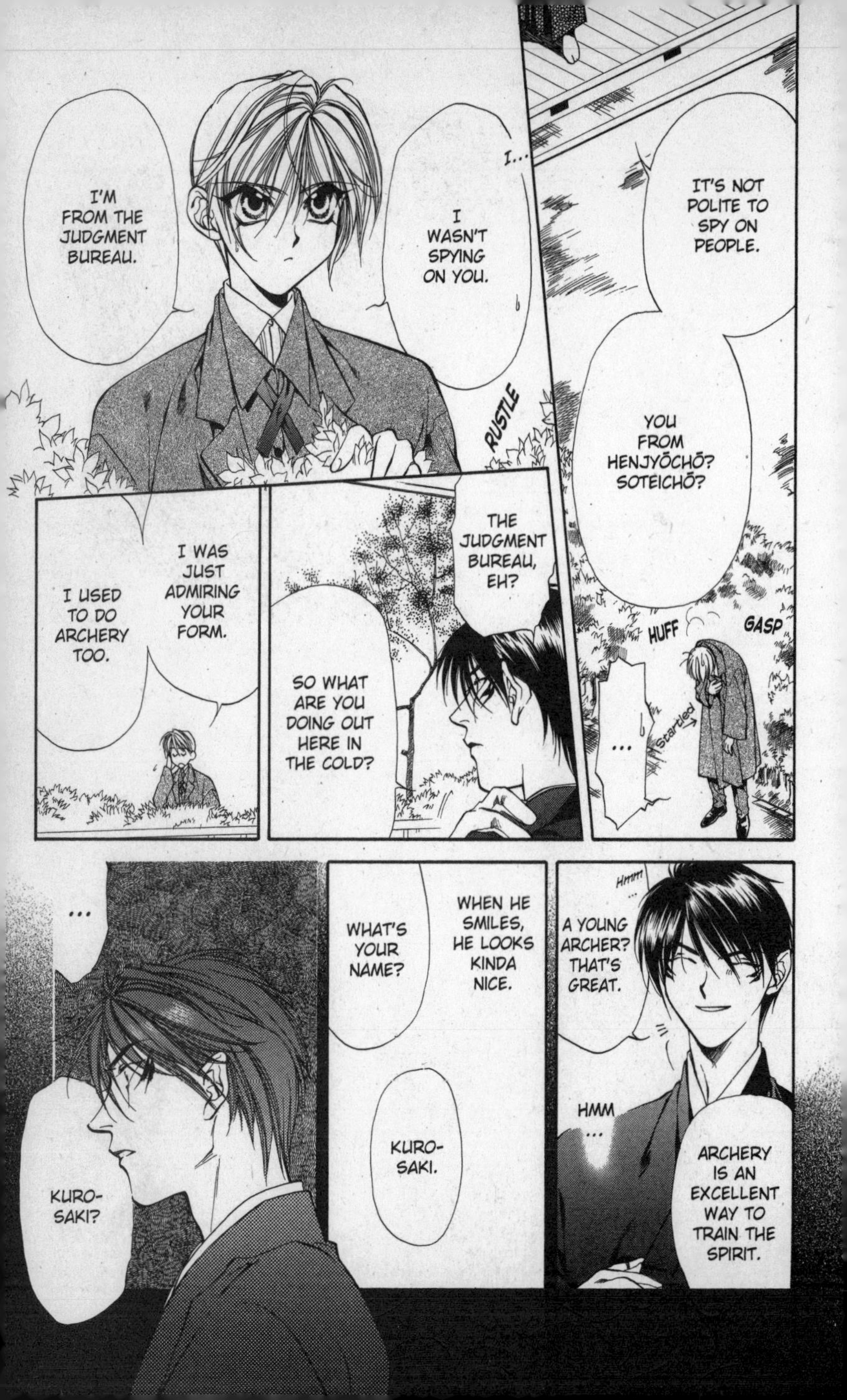
I...
IT'S NOT POLITE TO SPY ON PEOPLE.
YOU FROM HENJYŌCHŌ? SOTEICHŌ?
GASP
HUFF
Startled
...
I WASN'T SPYING ON YOU.
I'M FROM THE JUDGMENT BUREAU.
RUSTLE
THE JUDGMENT BUREAU, EH?
SO WHAT ARE YOU DOING OUT HERE IN THE COLD?
I WAS JUST ADMIRING YOUR FORM.
I USED TO DO ARCHERY TOO.
Hmm...
A YOUNG ARCHER? THAT'S GREAT.
HMM...
ARCHERY IS AN EXCELLENT WAY TO TRAIN THE SPIRIT.
WHEN HE SMILES, HE LOOKS KINDA NICE.
WHAT'S YOUR NAME?
KURO-SAKI.
...
KURO-SAKI?

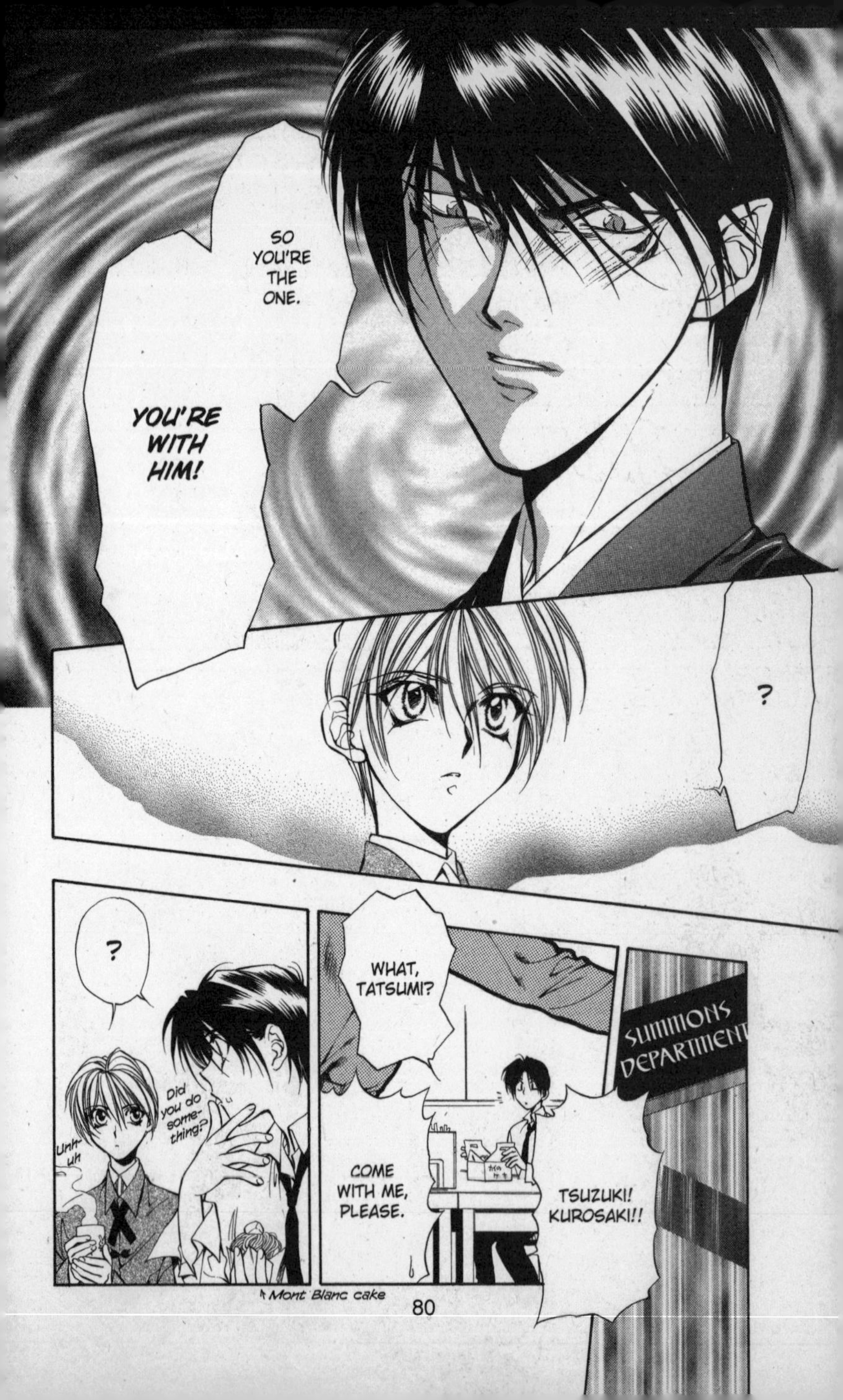
SO YOU'RE THE ONE.
YOU'RE WITH HIM!
?
SUMMONS DEPARTMENT
TSUZUKI! KUROSAKI!!
COME WITH ME, PLEASE.
WHAT, TATSUMI?
?
Did you do something?
Unh-uh
Mont Blanc cake

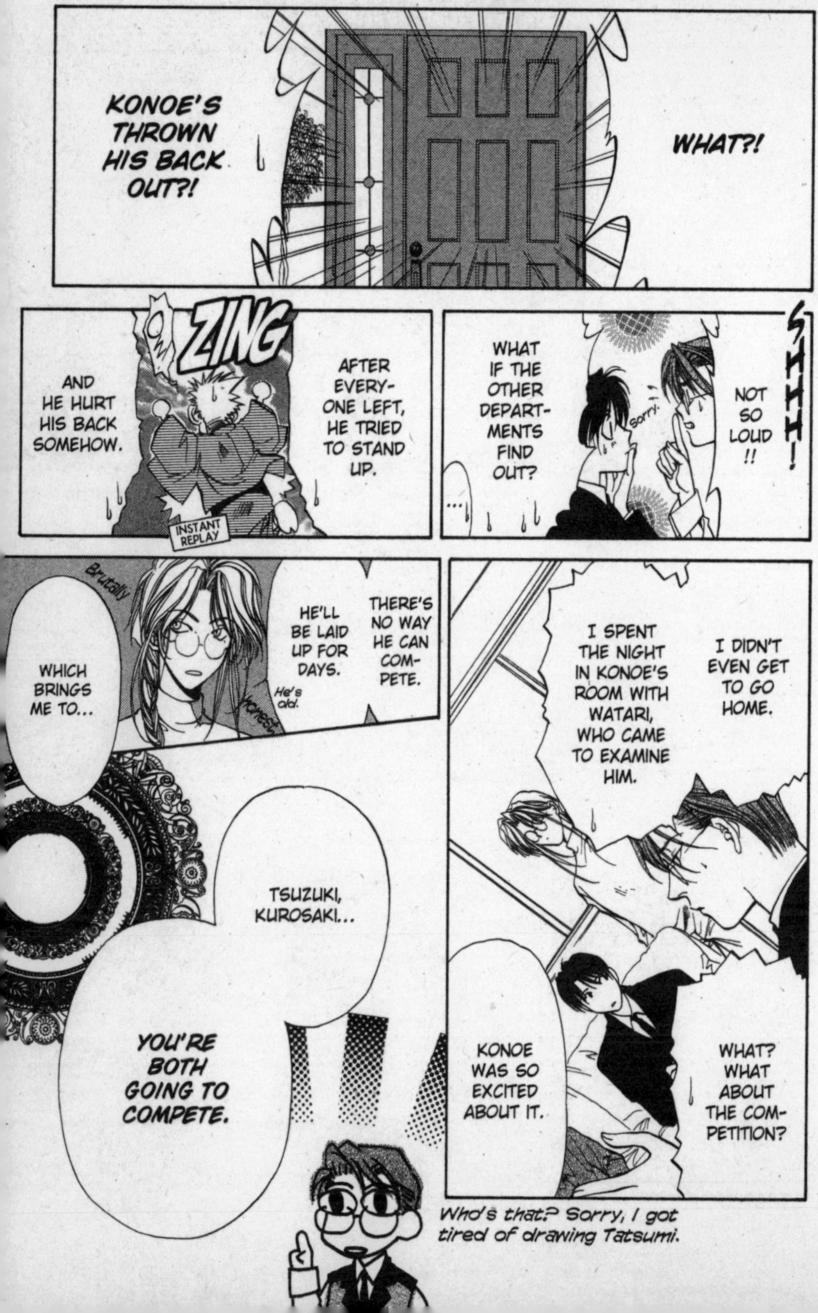
WHAT?!
KONOE'S THROWN HIS BACK OUT?!
NOT SO LOUD!!
SHHH!
Sorry.
WHAT IF THE OTHER DEPARTMENTS FIND OUT?
...
AFTER EVERYONE LEFT, HE TRIED TO STAND UP.
ZING
AND HE HURT HIS BACK SOMEHOW.
INSTANT REPLAY
I DIDN'T EVEN GET TO GO HOME.
I SPENT THE NIGHT IN KONOE'S ROOM WITH WATARI, WHO CAME TO EXAMINE HIM.
WHAT? WHAT ABOUT THE COMPETITION?
KONOE WAS SO EXCITED ABOUT IT.
THERE'S NO WAY HE CAN COMPETE.
HE'LL BE LAID UP FOR DAYS.
He's old.
Brutally
Honest
WHICH BRINGS ME TO...
TSUZUKI, KUROSAKI...
YOU'RE BOTH GOING TO COMPETE.
Who's that? Sorry, I got tired of drawing Tatsumi.

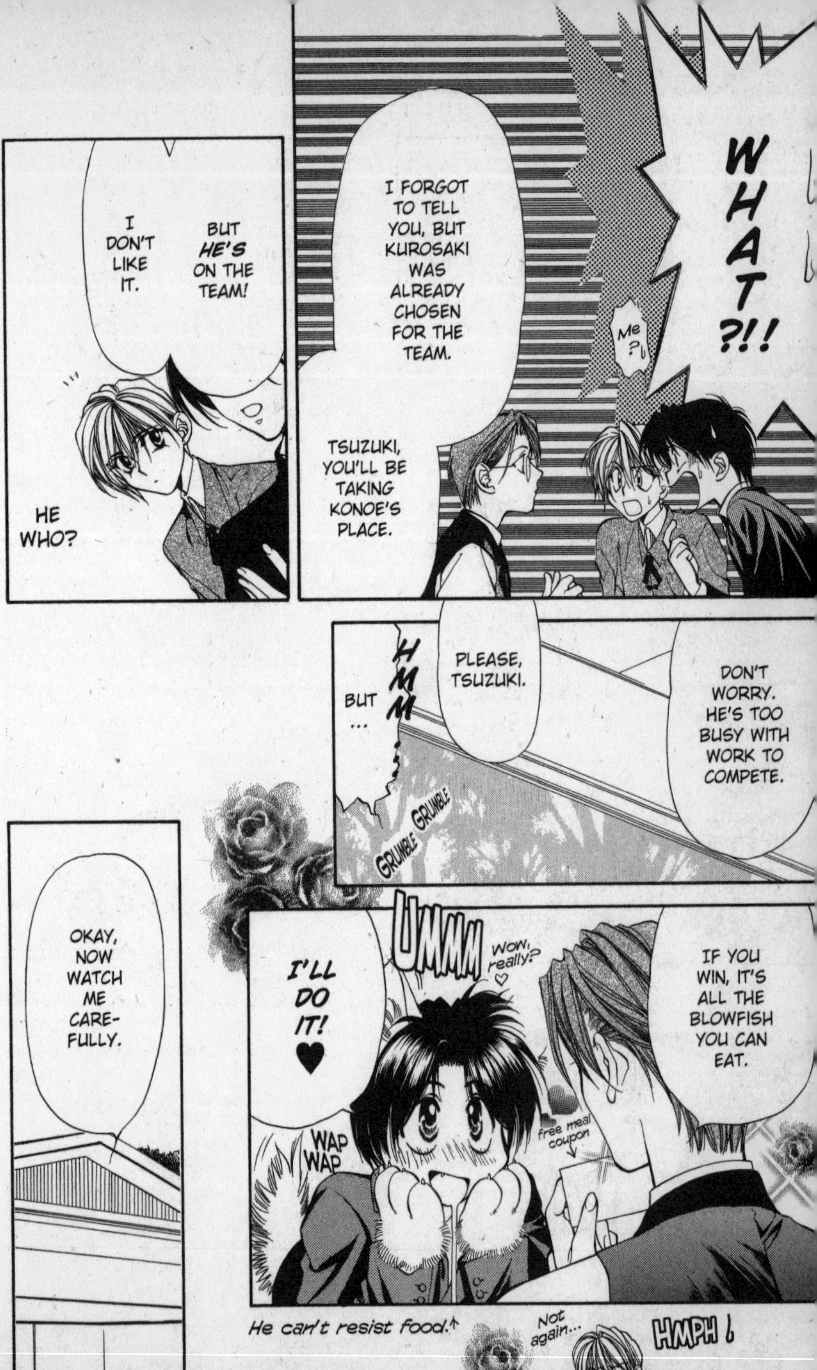
WHAT?!!
Me?
I FORGOT TO TELL YOU, BUT KUROSAKI WAS ALREADY CHOSEN FOR THE TEAM.
TSUZUKI, YOU'LL BE TAKING KONOE'S PLACE.
BUT HE'S ON THE TEAM!
I DON'T LIKE IT.
HE WHO?
DON'T WORRY. HE'S TOO BUSY WITH WORK TO COMPETE.
PLEASE, TSUZUKI.
HMM...
BUT ...
GRUMBLE GRUMBLE
IF YOU WIN, IT'S ALL THE BLOWFISH YOU CAN EAT.
Wow, really? ♥
UMMM
I'LL DO IT! ♥
free meal coupon
WAP WAP
HMPH
Not again...
He can't resist food.
OKAY, NOW WATCH ME CARE-FULLY.

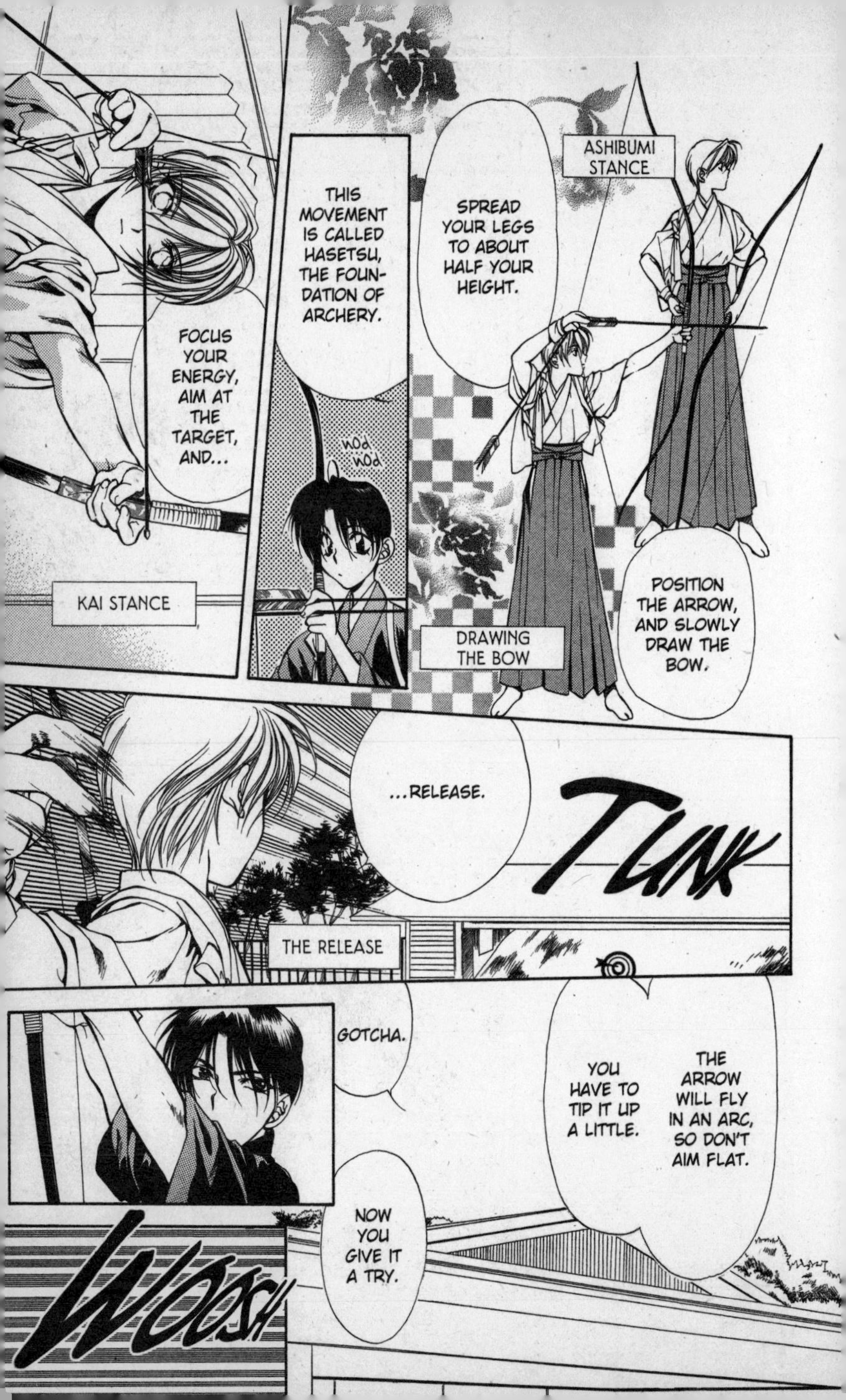
ASHIBUMI STANCE
SPREAD YOUR LEGS TO ABOUT HALF YOUR HEIGHT.
DRAWING THE BOW
POSITION THE ARROW, AND SLOWLY DRAW THE BOW.
THIS MOVEMENT IS CALLED HASETSU, THE FOUN-DATION OF ARCHERY.
FOCUS YOUR ENERGY, AIM AT THE TARGET, AND...
KAI STANCE
...RELEASE.
TUNK
THE RELEASE
THE ARROW WILL FLY IN AN ARC, SO DON'T AIM FLAT.
YOU HAVE TO TIP IT UP A LITTLE.
GOTCHA.
NOW YOU GIVE IT A TRY.
WOOSH

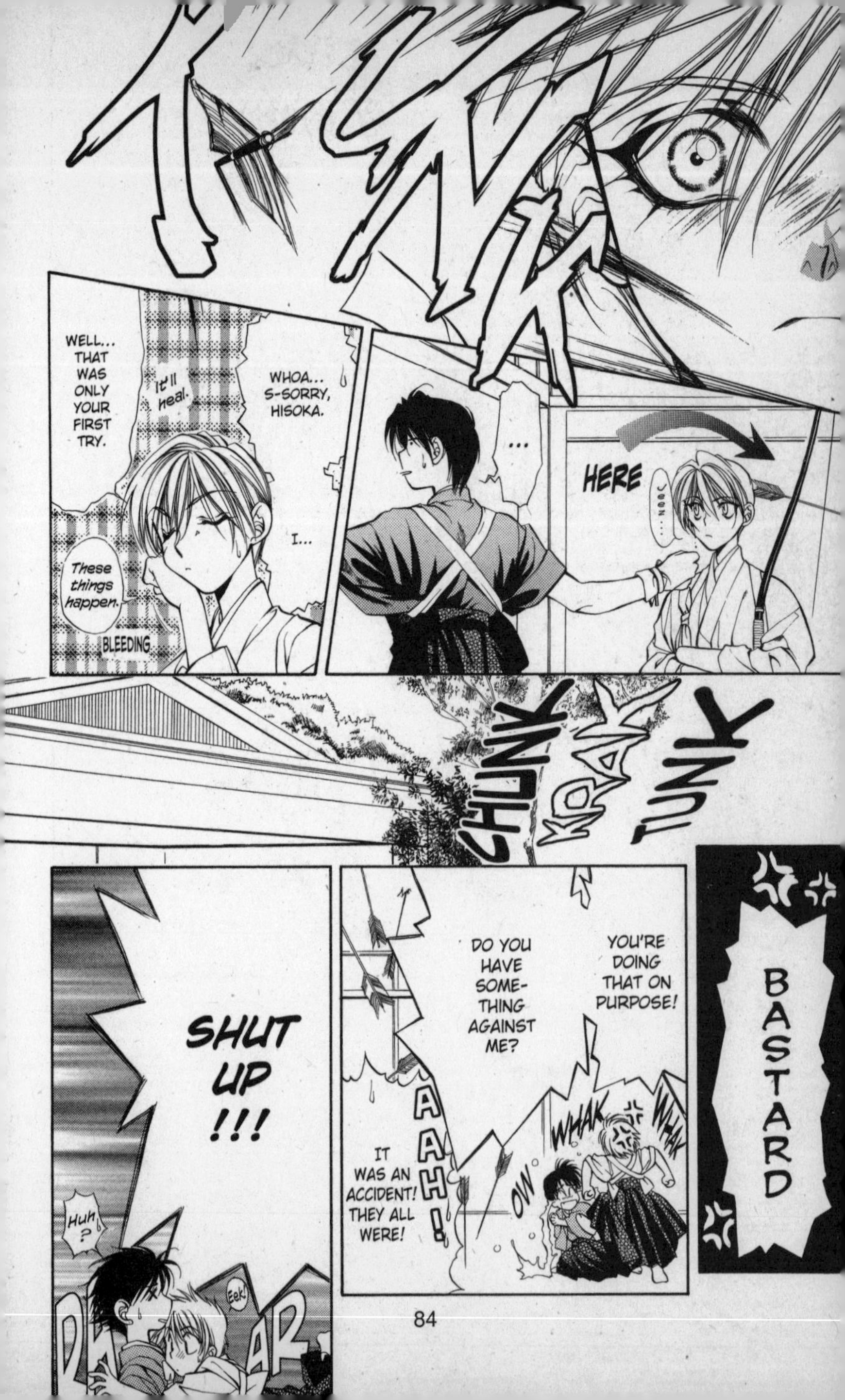
HERE
Jeez...
...
WHOA... S-SORRY, HISOKA.
I...
WELL... THAT WAS ONLY YOUR FIRST TRY.
It'll heal.
These things happen.
BLEEDING
CHUNK
BASTARD
YOU'RE DOING THAT ON PURPOSE!
DO YOU HAVE SOME-THING AGAINST ME?
WHAK
WHAK
OW
AAAH!
IT WAS AN ACCIDENT! THEY ALL WERE!
SHUT UP!!!
Huh?
Eek!

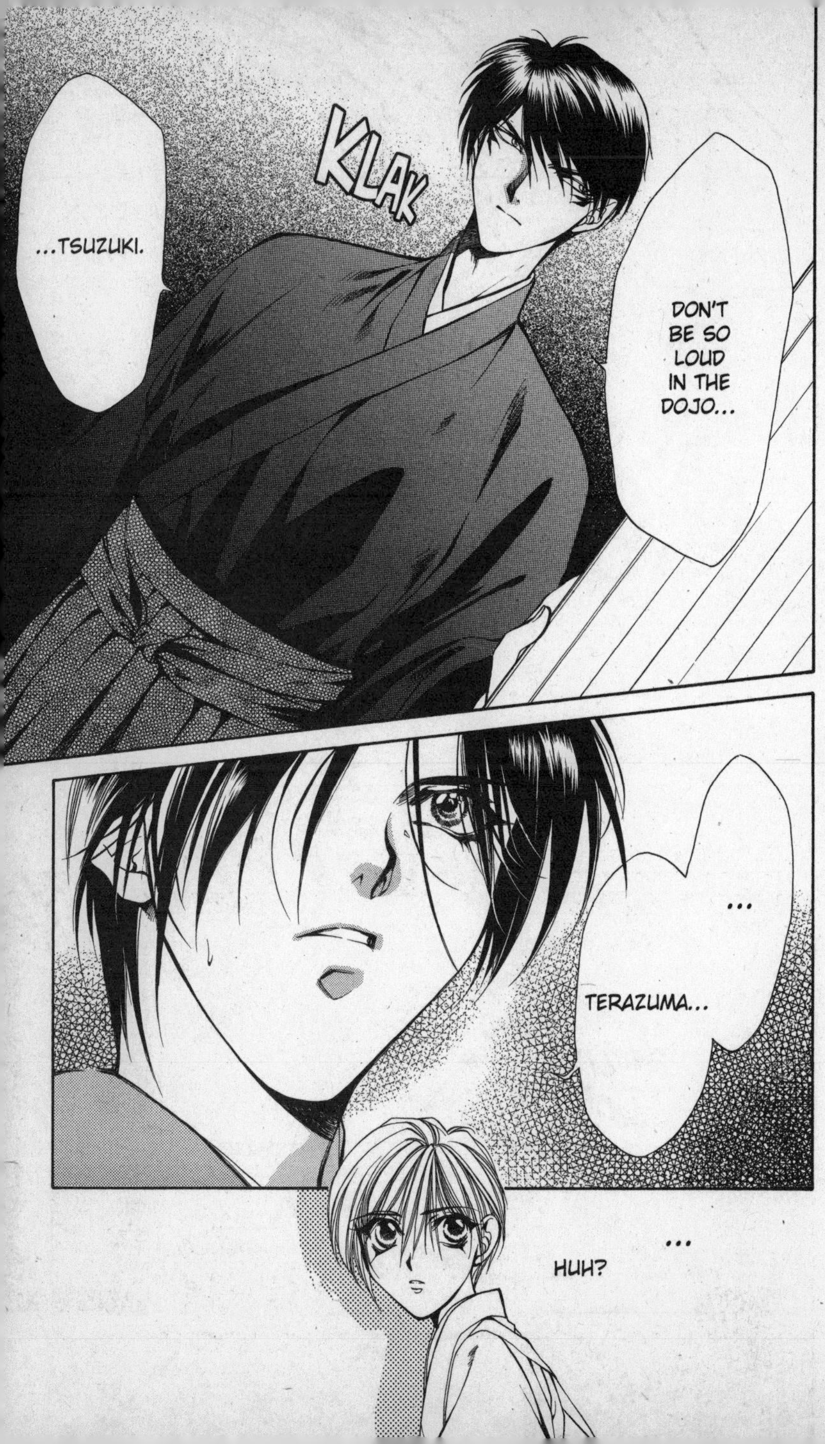
DON'T BE SO LOUD IN THE DOJO...
KLAK
...TSUZUKI.
...
TERAZUMA...
...
HUH?

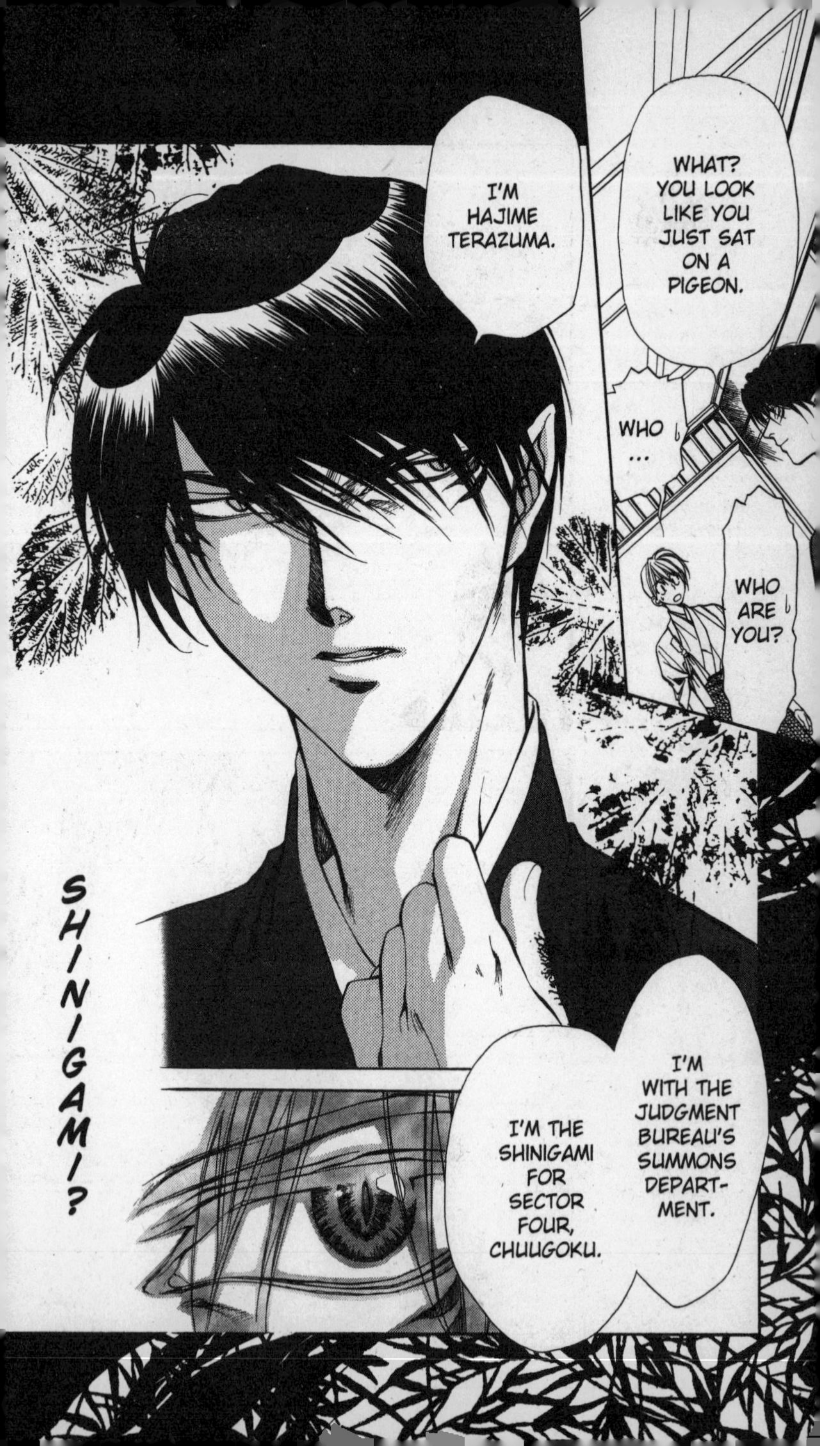
WHAT? YOU LOOK LIKE YOU JUST SAT ON A PIGEON.
WHO ...
WHO ARE YOU?
I'M HAJIME TERAZUMA.
I'M WITH THE JUDGMENT BUREAU'S SUMMONS DEPART-MENT.
I'M THE SHINIGAMI FOR SECTOR FOUR, CHUUGOKU.
SHINIGAMI?

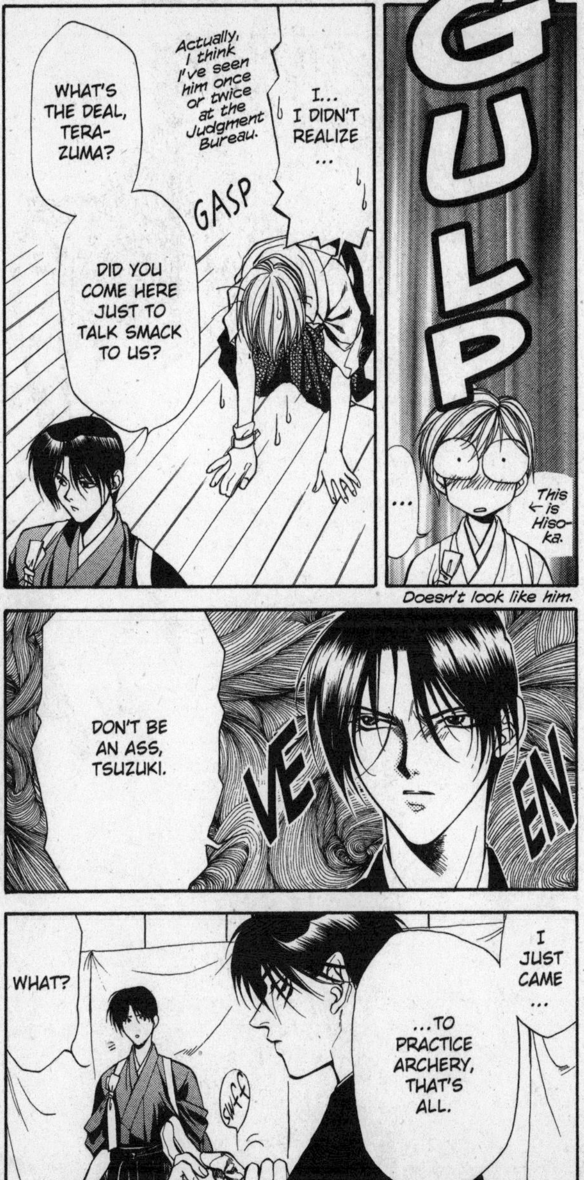
GULP
...
This ← is Hisoka.
I... I DIDN'T REALIZE ...
Actually, I think I've seen him once or twice at the Judgment Bureau.
WHAT'S THE DEAL, TERA-ZUMA?
GASP
DID YOU COME HERE JUST TO TALK SMACK TO US?
Doesn't look like him.
EN
VE
DON'T BE AN ASS, TSUZUKI.
I JUST CAME ...
...TO PRACTICE ARCHERY, THAT'S ALL.
WHAT?

▲ Yugake—A glove that protects the thumb when shooting arrows.

Short stories make it easier to introduce new characters. In the Hokkaido story, there were Yuma and Saya. And in this New Year's archery competition story, we meet Hajime Terazuma and Wakaba. (Ha!) He looks so much like Tsuzuki. His hair's even black. I resisted introducing him because I had a hard time coming up with ideas. (Why don't I like him? It's too hard to draw him when he changes form.) Then, when I was struggling over what to do with him, my editor said, "Put him in a *hakama." It was a tough story, really tough. It fell apart in the end. (Ha) But then, this is **cosplay manga... so I guess it's okay.

I like a man who looks good in a hakama!

*Hakama—a man's traditional skirt.
**Cosplay—costume play. Don't worry, it's not something perverted.

When did this become a cosplay manga?

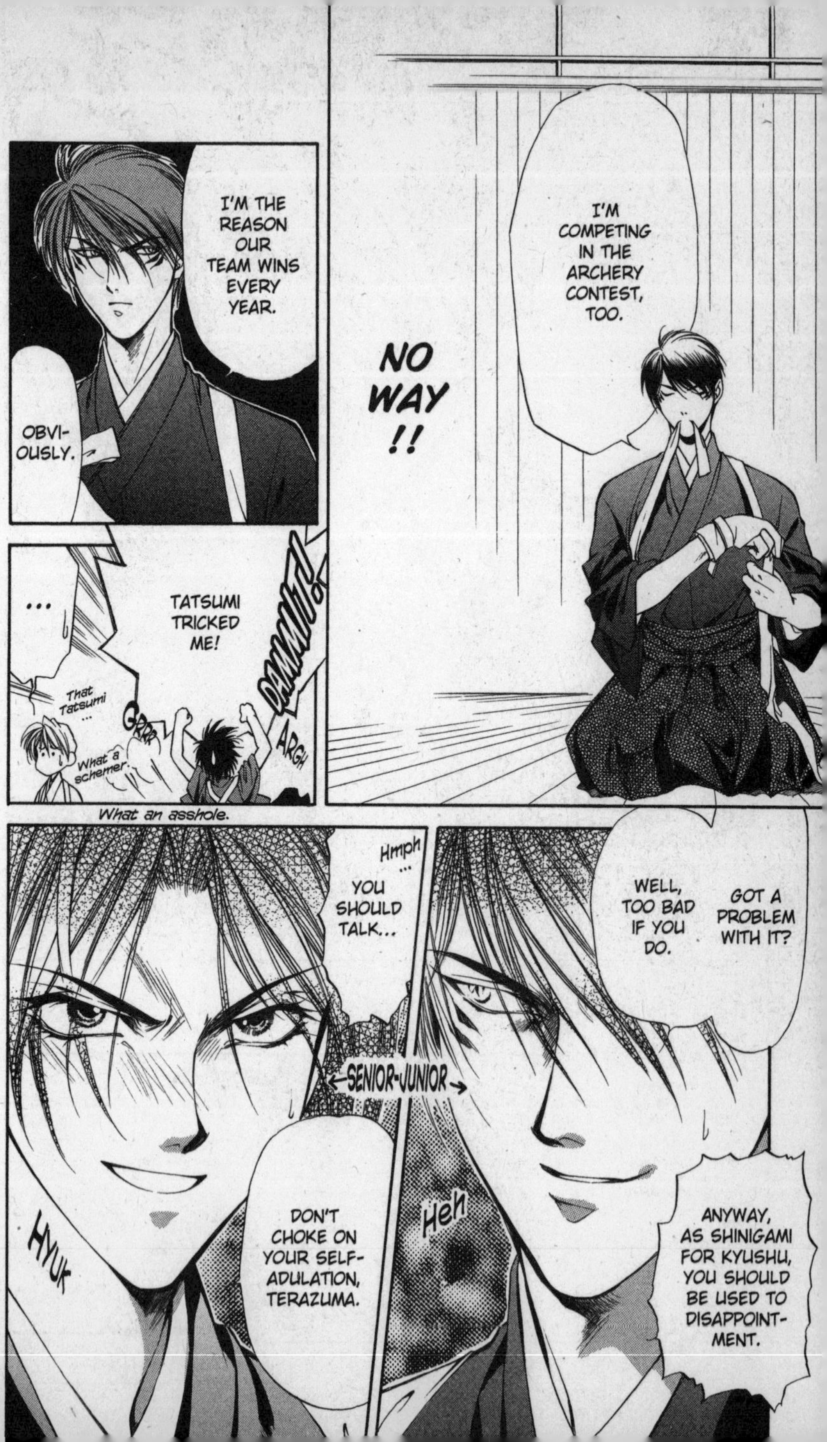
I'M COMPETING IN THE ARCHERY CONTEST, TOO.
NO WAY!!
I'M THE REASON OUR TEAM WINS EVERY YEAR.
OBVIOUSLY.
TATSUMI TRICKED ME!
...
GRRR
ARGH
That Tatsumi ...
What a schemer.
What an asshole.
GOT A PROBLEM WITH IT?
WELL, TOO BAD IF YOU DO.
ANYWAY, AS SHINIGAMI FOR KYUSHU, YOU SHOULD BE USED TO DISAPPOINTMENT.
Heh
←SENIOR-JUNIOR→
Hmph ...
YOU SHOULD TALK...
DON'T CHOKE ON YOUR SELF-ADULATION, TERAZUMA.
HYUK

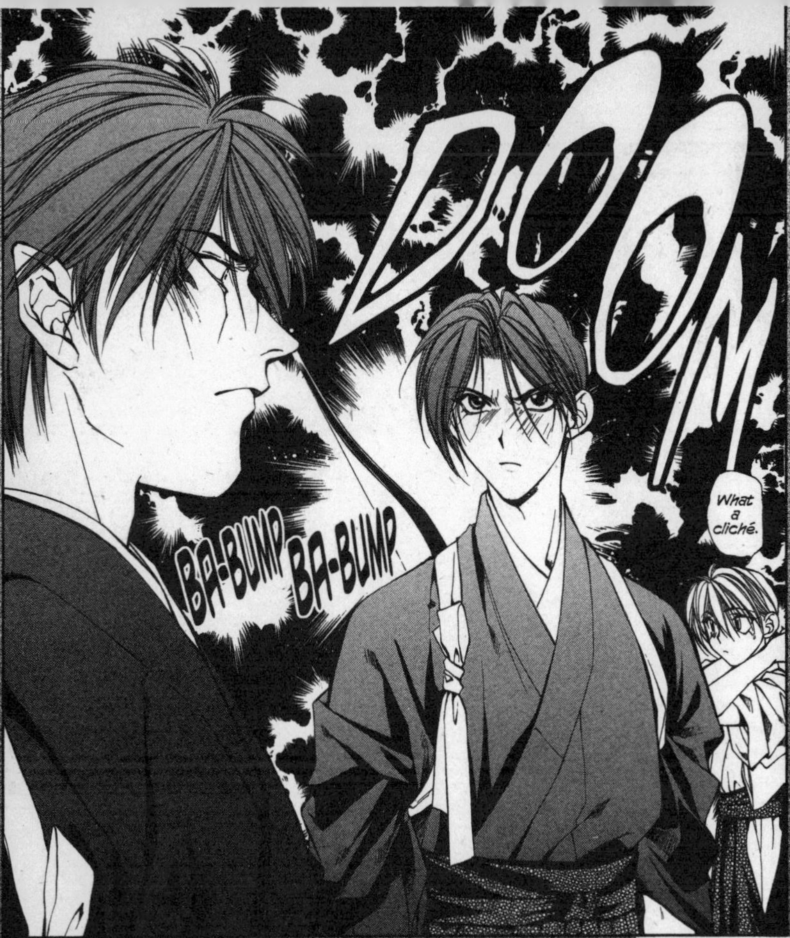
DOOM
BA-BUMP BA-BUMP
What a cliché.

☆ Shut up, Hisoka.

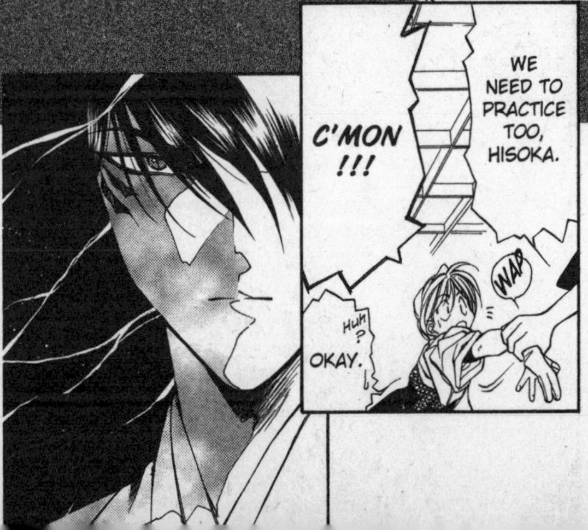
WE NEED TO PRACTICE TOO, HISOKA.
C'MON !!!
WAP
Huh?
OKAY.

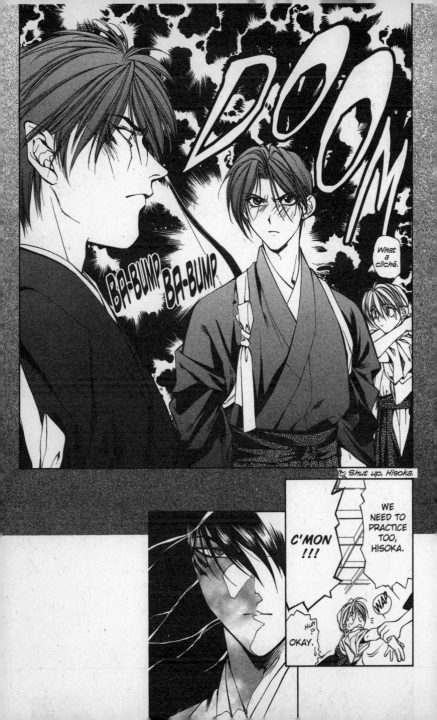

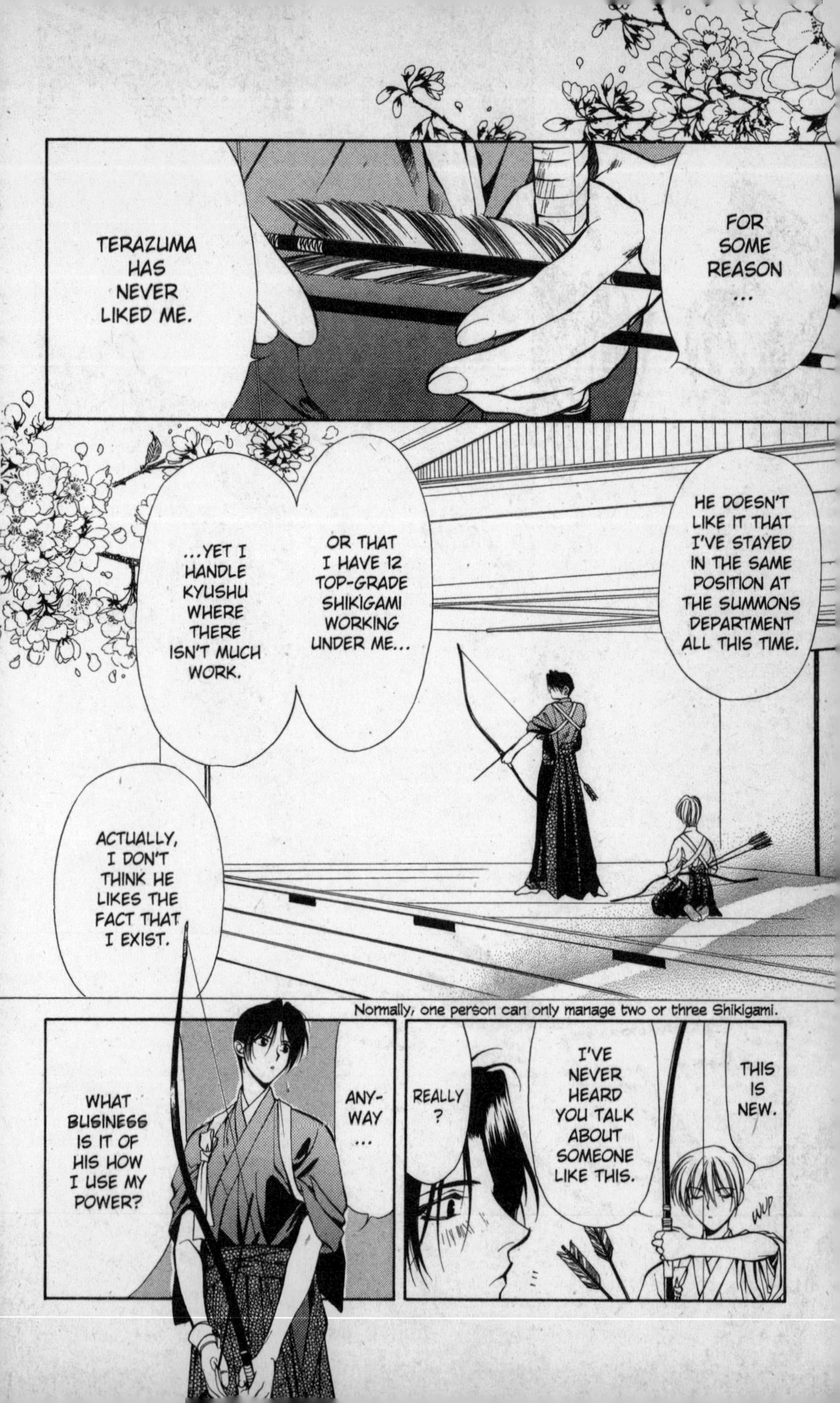
FOR SOME REASON...
TERAZUMA HAS NEVER LIKED ME.
HE DOESN'T LIKE IT THAT I'VE STAYED IN THE SAME POSITION AT THE SUMMONS DEPARTMENT ALL THIS TIME.
OR THAT I HAVE 12 TOP-GRADE SHIKIGAMI WORKING UNDER ME...
...YET I HANDLE KYUSHU WHERE THERE ISN'T MUCH WORK.
ACTUALLY, I DON'T THINK HE LIKES THE FACT THAT I EXIST.
Normally, one person can only manage two or three Shikigami.
THIS IS NEW.
I'VE NEVER HEARD YOU TALK ABOUT SOMEONE LIKE THIS.
REALLY?
WUP
ANY-WAY...
WHAT BUSINESS IS IT OF HIS HOW I USE MY POWER?

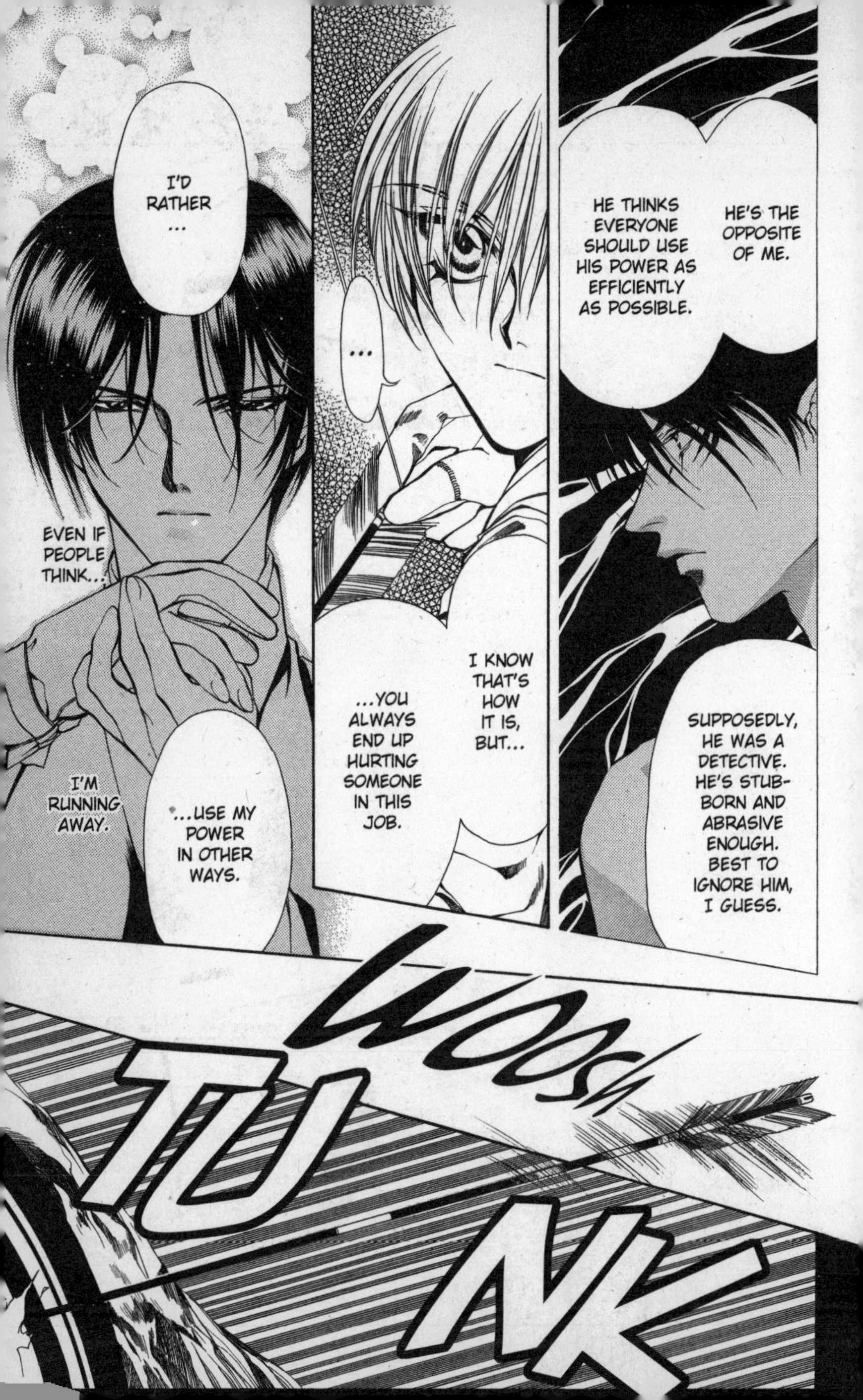
HE'S THE OPPOSITE OF ME.
HE THINKS EVERYONE SHOULD USE HIS POWER AS EFFICIENTLY AS POSSIBLE.
SUPPOSEDLY, HE WAS A DETECTIVE. HE'S STUB-BORN AND ABRASIVE ENOUGH. BEST TO IGNORE HIM, I GUESS.
...
I KNOW THAT'S HOW IT IS, BUT...
...YOU ALWAYS END UP HURTING SOMEONE IN THIS JOB.
I'D RATHER ...
...USE MY POWER IN OTHER WAYS.
EVEN IF PEOPLE THINK...
I'M RUNNING AWAY.
WOOSH
TUNK

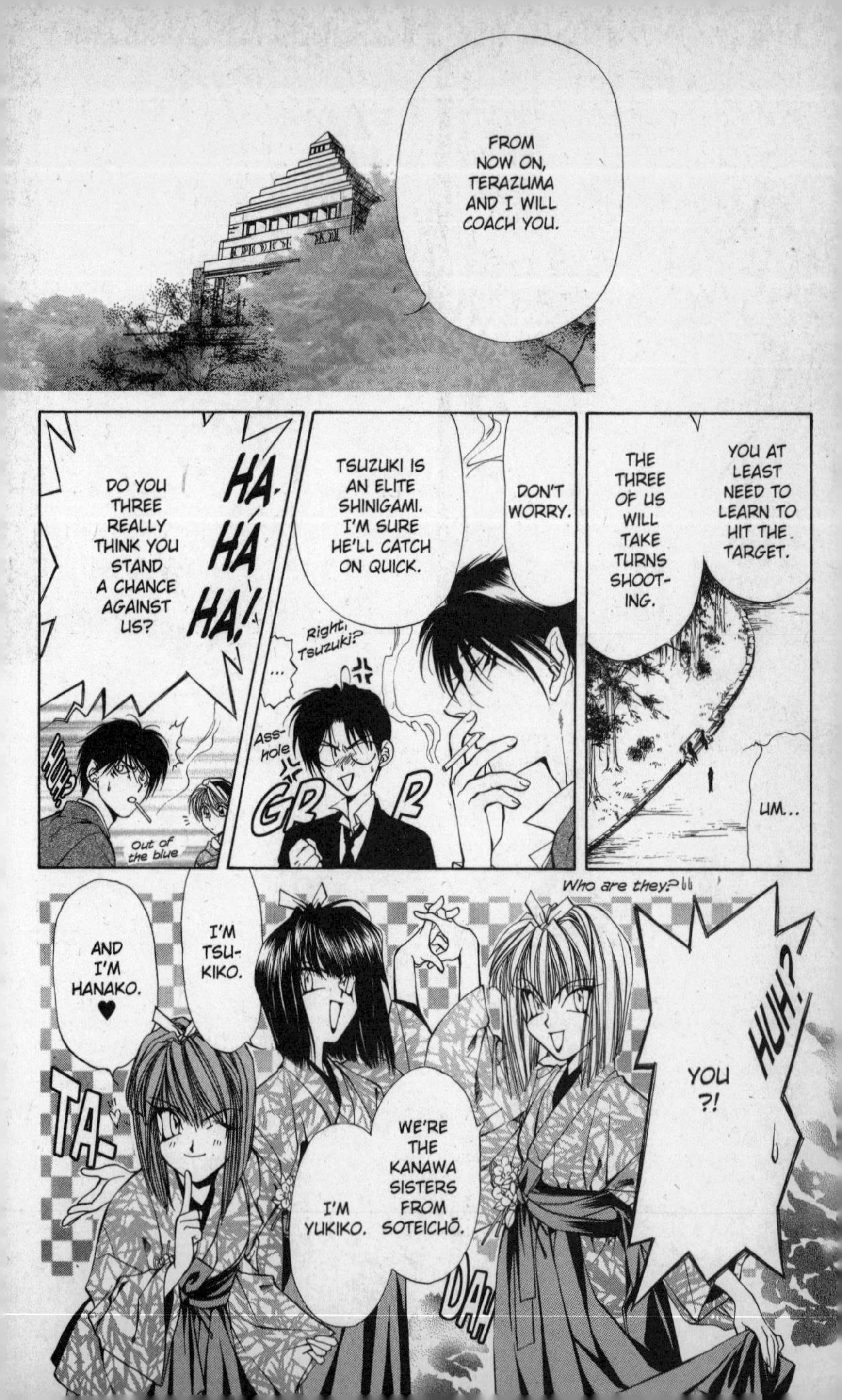
FROM NOW ON, TERAZUMA AND I WILL COACH YOU.
YOU AT LEAST NEED TO LEARN TO HIT THE TARGET.
THE THREE OF US WILL TAKE TURNS SHOOTING.
UM...
DON'T WORRY.
TSUZUKI IS AN ELITE SHINIGAMI. I'M SURE HE'LL CATCH ON QUICK.
Right, Tsuzuki?
...
Asshole
GRR
HA HA HA!
DO YOU THREE REALLY THINK YOU STAND A CHANCE AGAINST US?
HUH?
Out of the blue
Who are they?
HUH?
YOU ?!
WE'RE THE KANAWA SISTERS FROM SOTEICHŌ.
I'M YUKIKO.
I'M TSUKIKO.
AND I'M HANAKO. ♥
TA-DAH

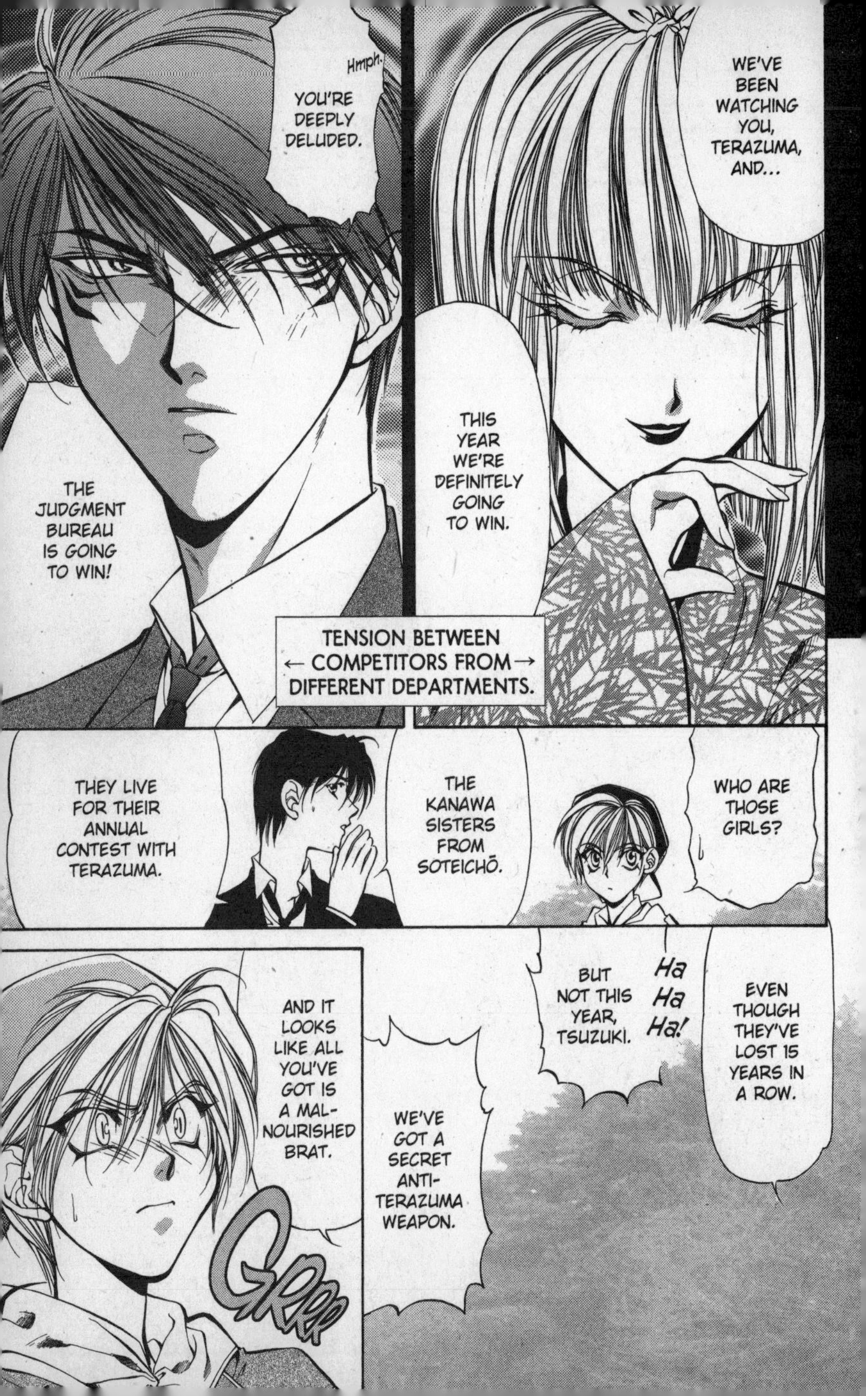
WE'VE BEEN WATCHING YOU, TERAZUMA, AND...
THIS YEAR WE'RE DEFINITELY GOING TO WIN.
Hmph.
YOU'RE DEEPLY DELUDED.
THE JUDGMENT BUREAU IS GOING TO WIN!
TENSION BETWEEN ← COMPETITORS FROM → DIFFERENT DEPARTMENTS.
WHO ARE THOSE GIRLS?
THE KANAWA SISTERS FROM SOTEICHŌ.
THEY LIVE FOR THEIR ANNUAL CONTEST WITH TERAZUMA.
EVEN THOUGH THEY'VE LOST 15 YEARS IN A ROW.
Ha Ha Ha!
BUT NOT THIS YEAR, TSUZUKI.
WE'VE GOT A SECRET ANTI-TERAZUMA WEAPON.
AND IT LOOKS LIKE ALL YOU'VE GOT IS A MAL-NOURISHED BRAT.
GRRR

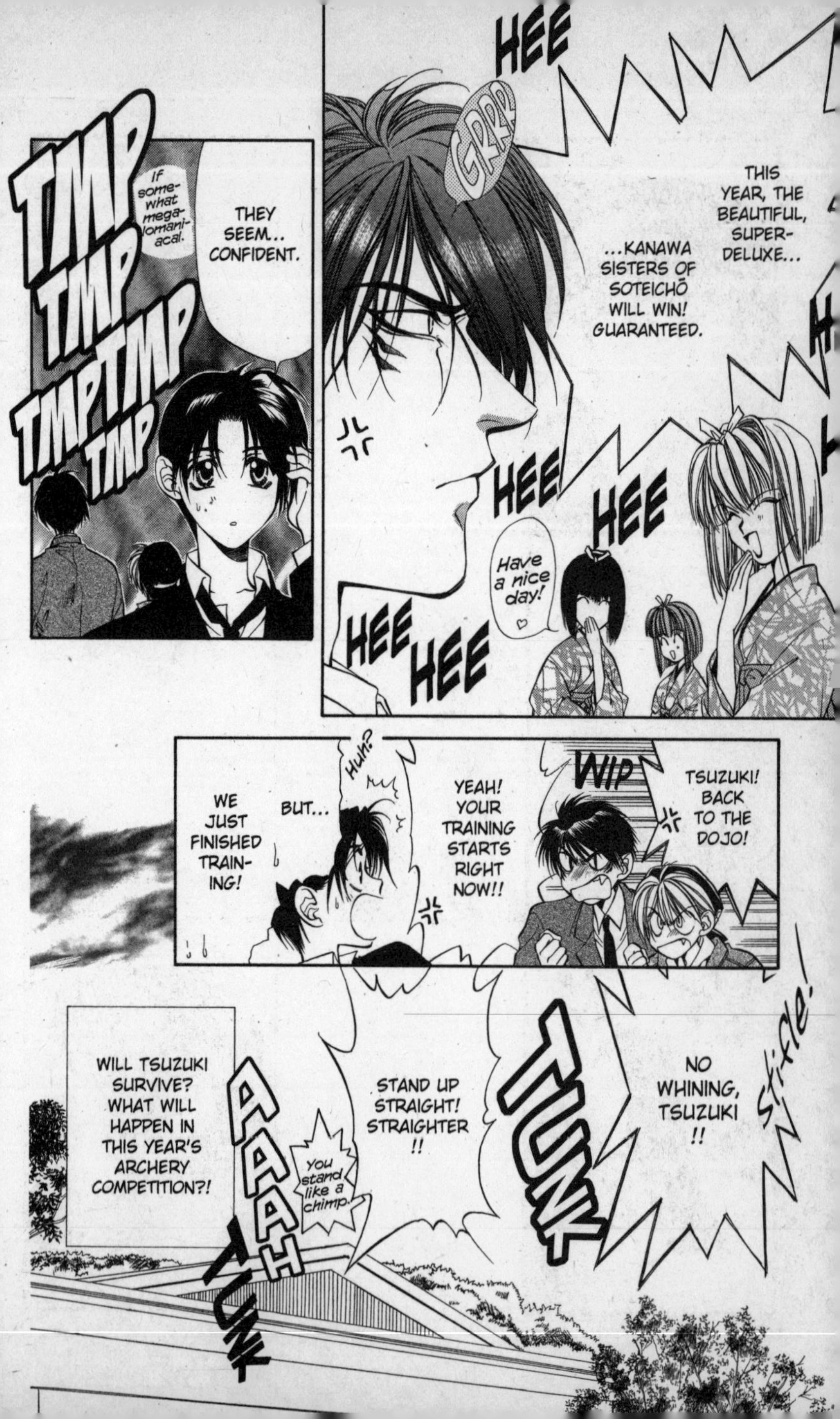
HEE
GRR
THIS YEAR, THE BEAUTIFUL, SUPER-DELUXE...
...KANAWA SISTERS OF SOTEICHŌ WILL WIN! GUARANTEED.
HEE
HEE
Have a nice day! ♡
HEE HEE
TMP TMP TMPTMP TMP
THEY SEEM... CONFIDENT.
If some-what mega-lomani-acal.
TSUZUKI! BACK TO THE DOJO!
WIP
YEAH! YOUR TRAINING STARTS RIGHT NOW!!
Huh?
BUT...
WE JUST FINISHED TRAIN-ING!
Stifle!
NO WHINING, TSUZUKI !!
TUNK
STAND UP STRAIGHT! STRAIGHTER !!
You stand like a chimp.
AAAAH
TUNK
WILL TSUZUKI SURVIVE? WHAT WILL HAPPEN IN THIS YEAR'S ARCHERY COMPETITION?!

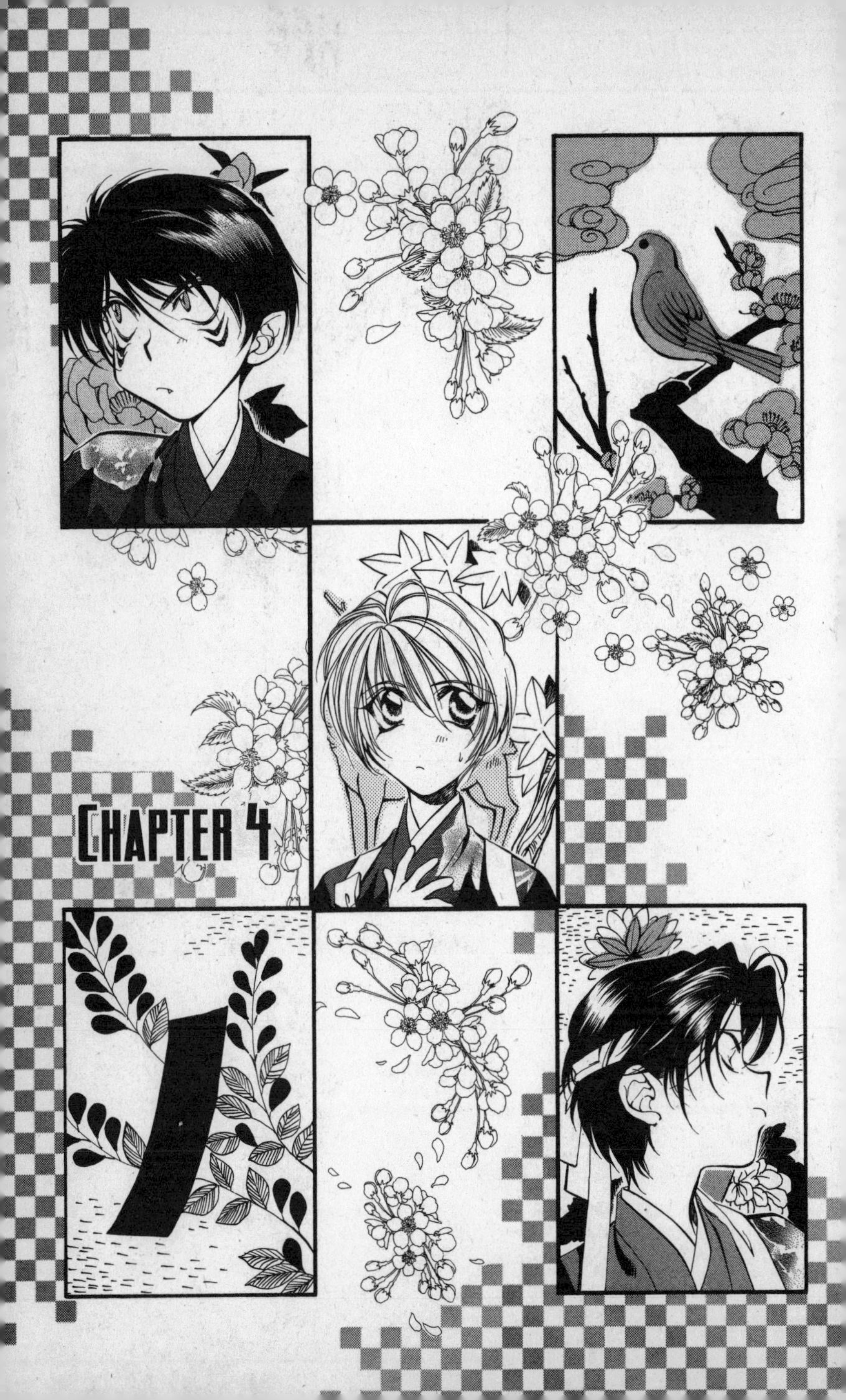
CHAPTER 4

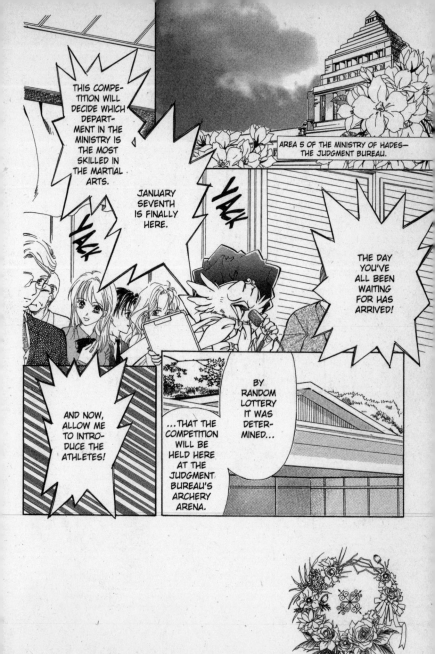

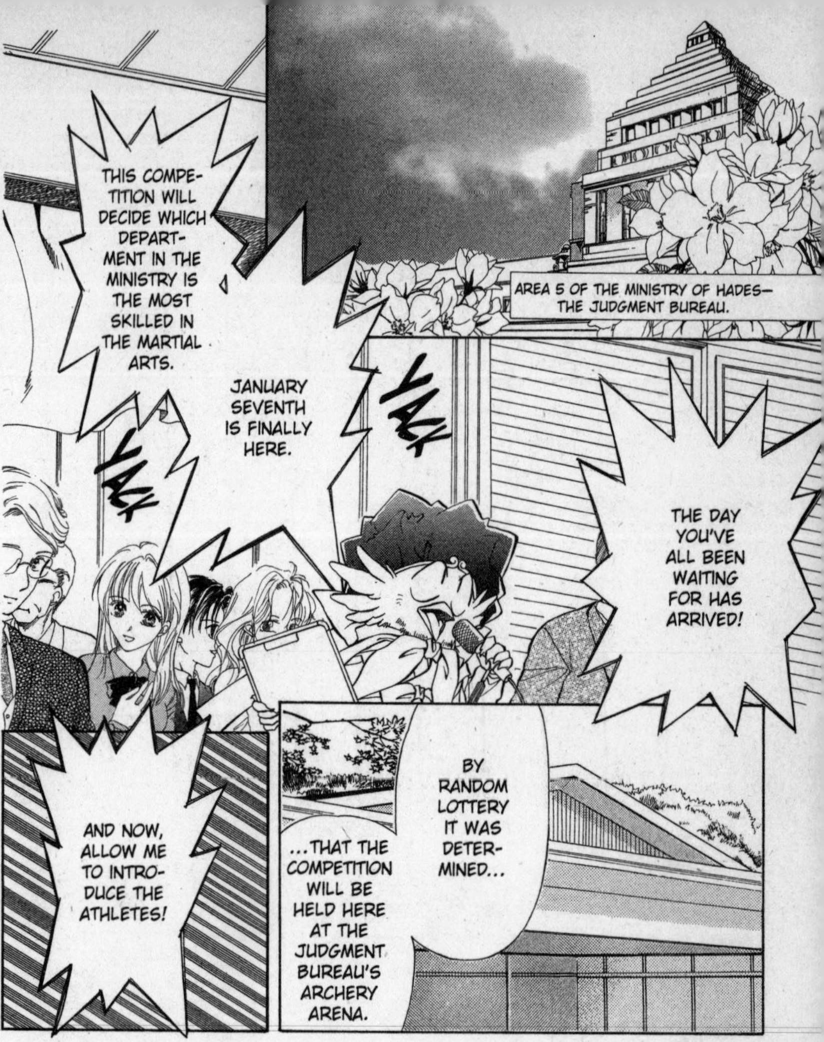
AREA 5 OF THE MINISTRY OF HADES—THE JUDGMENT BUREAU.
THE DAY YOU'VE ALL BEEN WAITING FOR HAS ARRIVED!
JANUARY SEVENTH IS FINALLY HERE.
YACK
THIS COMPETITION WILL DECIDE WHICH DEPARTMENT IN THE MINISTRY IS THE MOST SKILLED IN THE MARTIAL ARTS.
YACK
BY RANDOM LOTTERY IT WAS DETERMINED...
...THAT THE COMPETITION WILL BE HELD HERE AT THE JUDGMENT BUREAU'S ARCHERY ARENA.
AND NOW, ALLOW ME TO INTRODUCE THE ATHLETES!

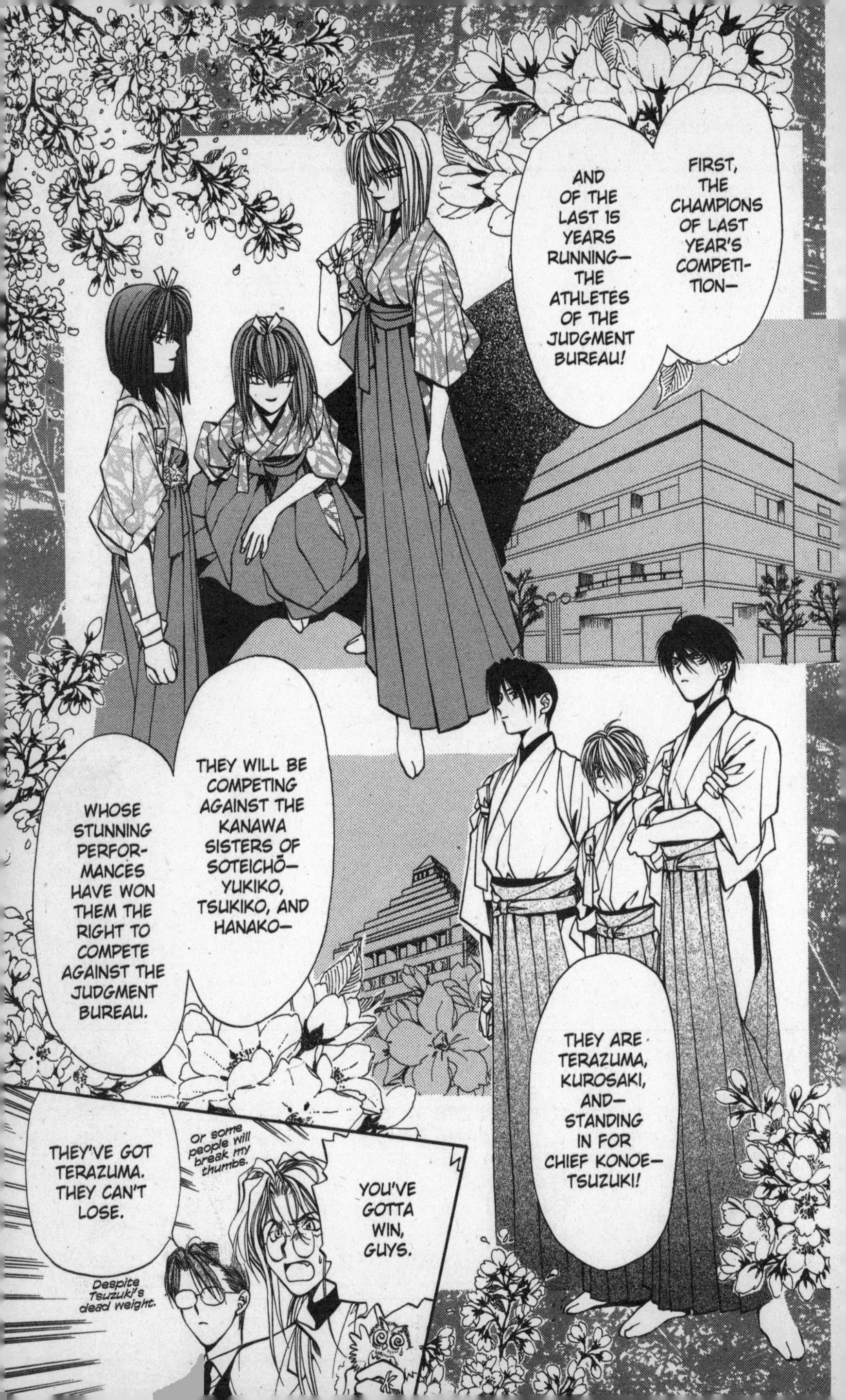
FIRST, THE CHAMPIONS OF LAST YEAR'S COMPETI-TION—
AND OF THE LAST 15 YEARS RUNNING—THE ATHLETES OF THE JUDGMENT BUREAU!
THEY ARE TERAZUMA, KUROSAKI, AND—STANDING IN FOR CHIEF KONOE—TSUZUKI!
THEY WILL BE COMPETING AGAINST THE KANAWA SISTERS OF SOTEICHŌ—YUKIKO, TSUKIKO, AND HANAKO—
WHOSE STUNNING PERFOR-MANCES HAVE WON THEM THE RIGHT TO COMPETE AGAINST THE JUDGMENT BUREAU.
YOU'VE GOTTA WIN, GUYS.
Or some people will break my thumbs.
THEY'VE GOT TERAZUMA. THEY CAN'T LOSE.
Despite Tsuzuki's dead weight.

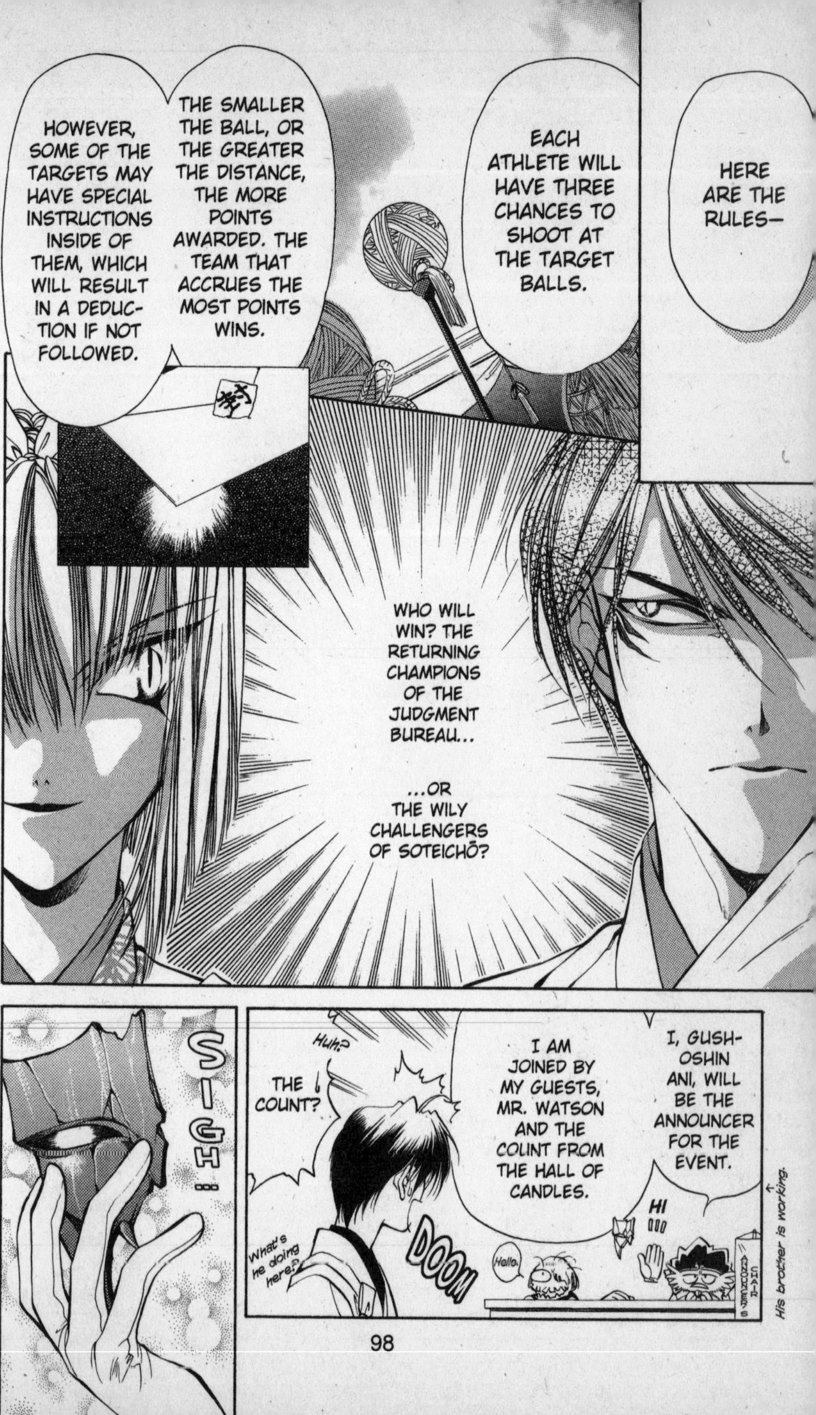
HERE ARE THE RULES—
EACH ATHLETE WILL HAVE THREE CHANCES TO SHOOT AT THE TARGET BALLS.
THE SMALLER THE BALL, OR THE GREATER THE DISTANCE, THE MORE POINTS AWARDED. THE TEAM THAT ACCRUES THE MOST POINTS WINS.
HOWEVER, SOME OF THE TARGETS MAY HAVE SPECIAL INSTRUCTIONS INSIDE OF THEM, WHICH WILL RESULT IN A DEDUCTION IF NOT FOLLOWED.
WHO WILL WIN? THE RETURNING CHAMPIONS OF THE JUDGMENT BUREAU...
...OR THE WILY CHALLENGERS OF SOTEICHŌ?
His brother is working.
I, GUSHOSHIN ANI, WILL BE THE ANNOUNCER FOR THE EVENT.
ANNOUNCER'S CHAIR
HI!!!
I AM JOINED BY MY GUESTS, MR. WATSON AND THE COUNT FROM THE HALL OF CANDLES.
Hello.
Huh?
THE COUNT?
DOOM
What's he doing here?
SIGH...

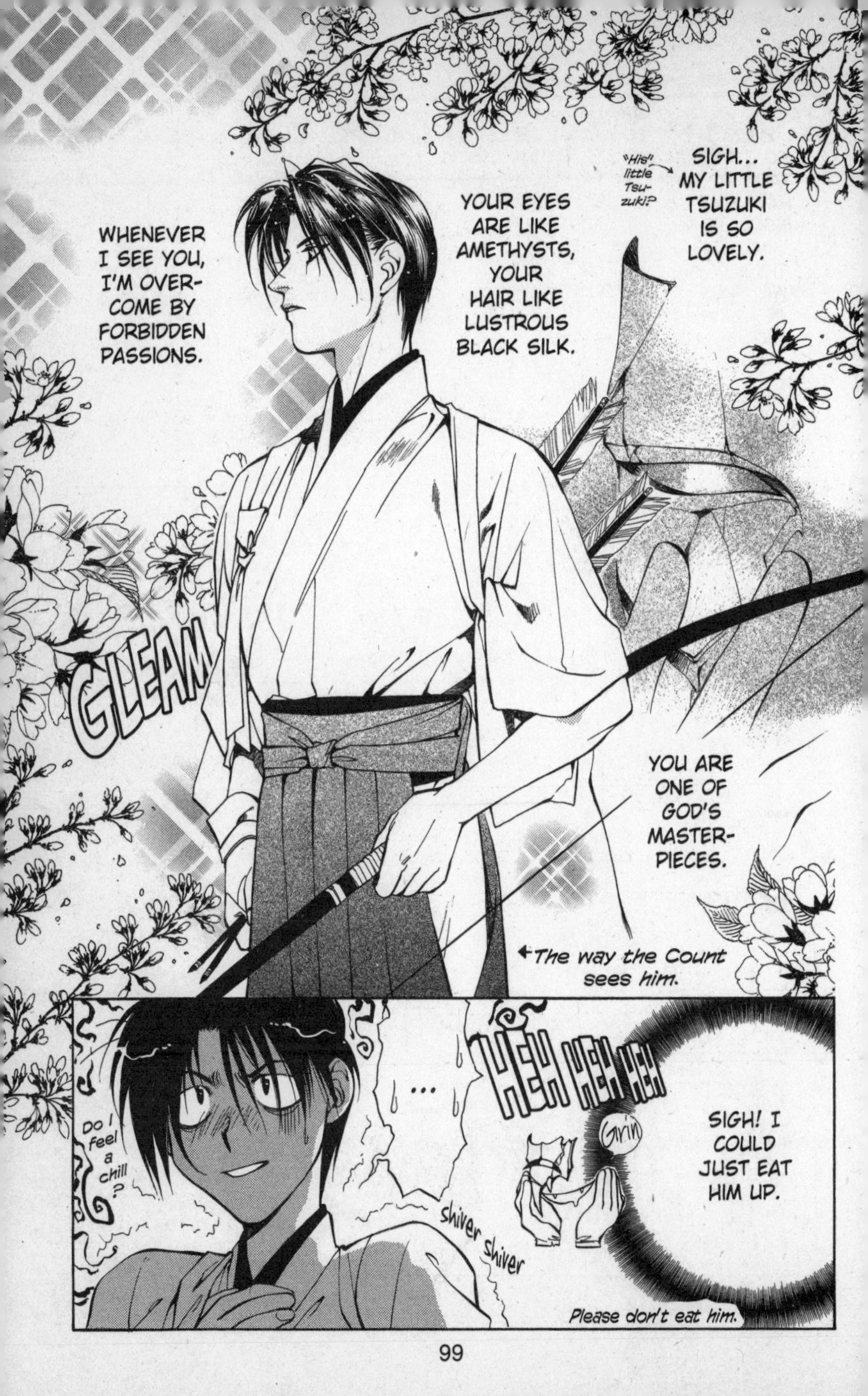

SIGH... MY LITTLE TSUZUKI IS SO LOVELY.
"His" little Tsuzuki?
YOUR EYES ARE LIKE AMETHYSTS, YOUR HAIR LIKE LUSTROUS BLACK SILK.
WHENEVER I SEE YOU, I'M OVER-COME BY FORBIDDEN PASSIONS.
YOU ARE ONE OF GOD'S MASTER-PIECES.
GLEAM
The way the Count sees him.
SIGH! I COULD JUST EAT HIM UP.
Grin
HEH HEH HEH
Please don't eat him.
...
shiver shiver
Do I feel a chill?

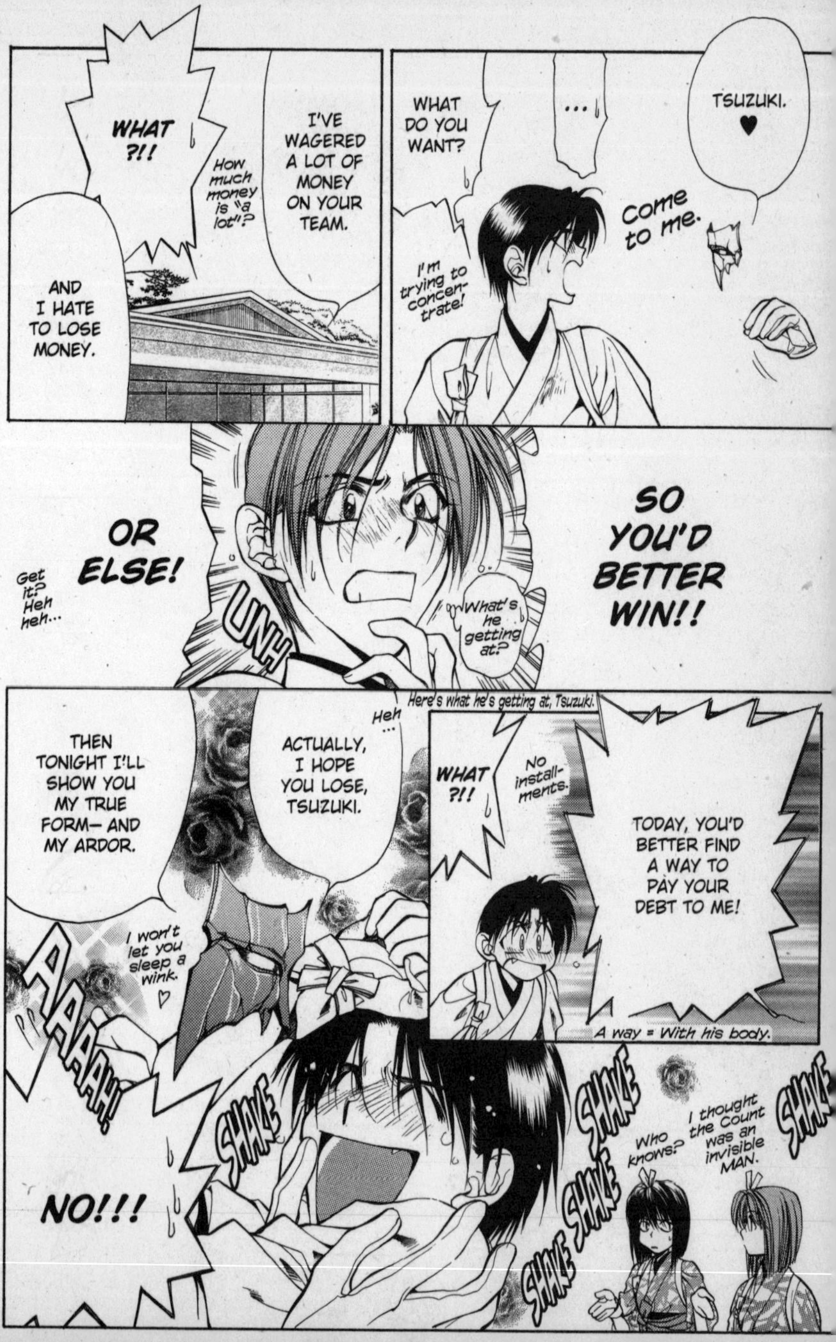
TSUZUKI. ♥
Come to me.
...
WHAT DO YOU WANT?
I'm trying to concentrate!
I'VE WAGERED A LOT OF MONEY ON YOUR TEAM.
How much money is "a lot"?
WHAT ?!!
AND I HATE TO LOSE MONEY.
SO YOU'D BETTER WIN!!
What's he getting at?
UNH
OR ELSE!
Get it? Heh heh...
Here's what he's getting at, Tsuzuki.
TODAY, YOU'D BETTER FIND A WAY TO PAY YOUR DEBT TO ME!
No installments.
WHAT ?!!
A way = With his body.
Heh...
ACTUALLY, I HOPE YOU LOSE, TSUZUKI.
THEN TONIGHT I'LL SHOW YOU MY TRUE FORM— AND MY ARDOR.
I won't let you sleep a wink. ♥
AAAAH!
SHAKE SHAKE
SHAKE SHAKE SHAKE SHAKE
I thought the Count was an invisible MAN.
Who knows?
NO!!!

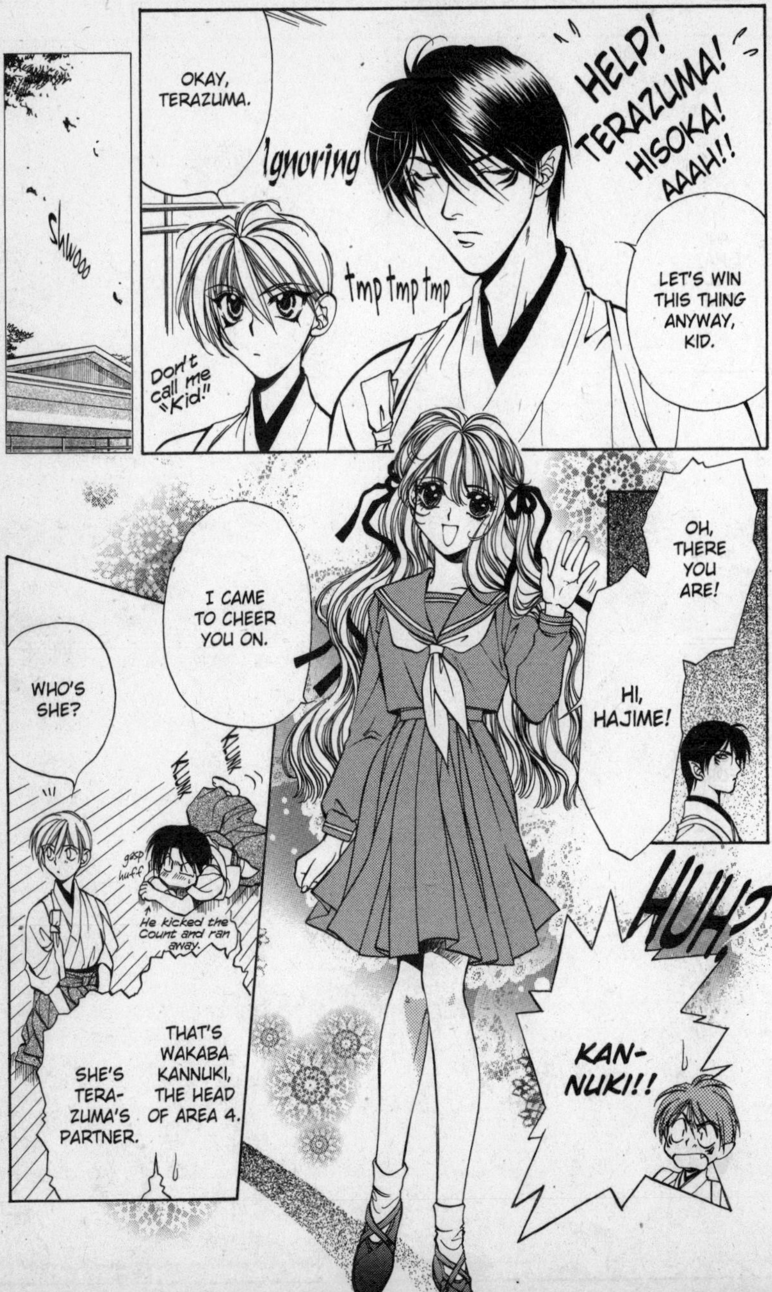
HELP! TERAZUMA! HISOKA! AAAH!!
OKAY, TERAZUMA.
Ignoring
LET'S WIN THIS THING ANYWAY, KID.
tmp tmp tmp
Don't call me "Kid!"
shwooo
OH, THERE YOU ARE!
HI, HAJIME!
I CAME TO CHEER YOU ON.
HUH?
KAN-NUKI!!
WHO'S SHE?
KLUNK
KLUNK
gasp huff
He kicked the Count and ran away.
THAT'S WAKABA KANNUKI, THE HEAD OF AREA 4.
SHE'S TERA-ZUMA'S PARTNER.

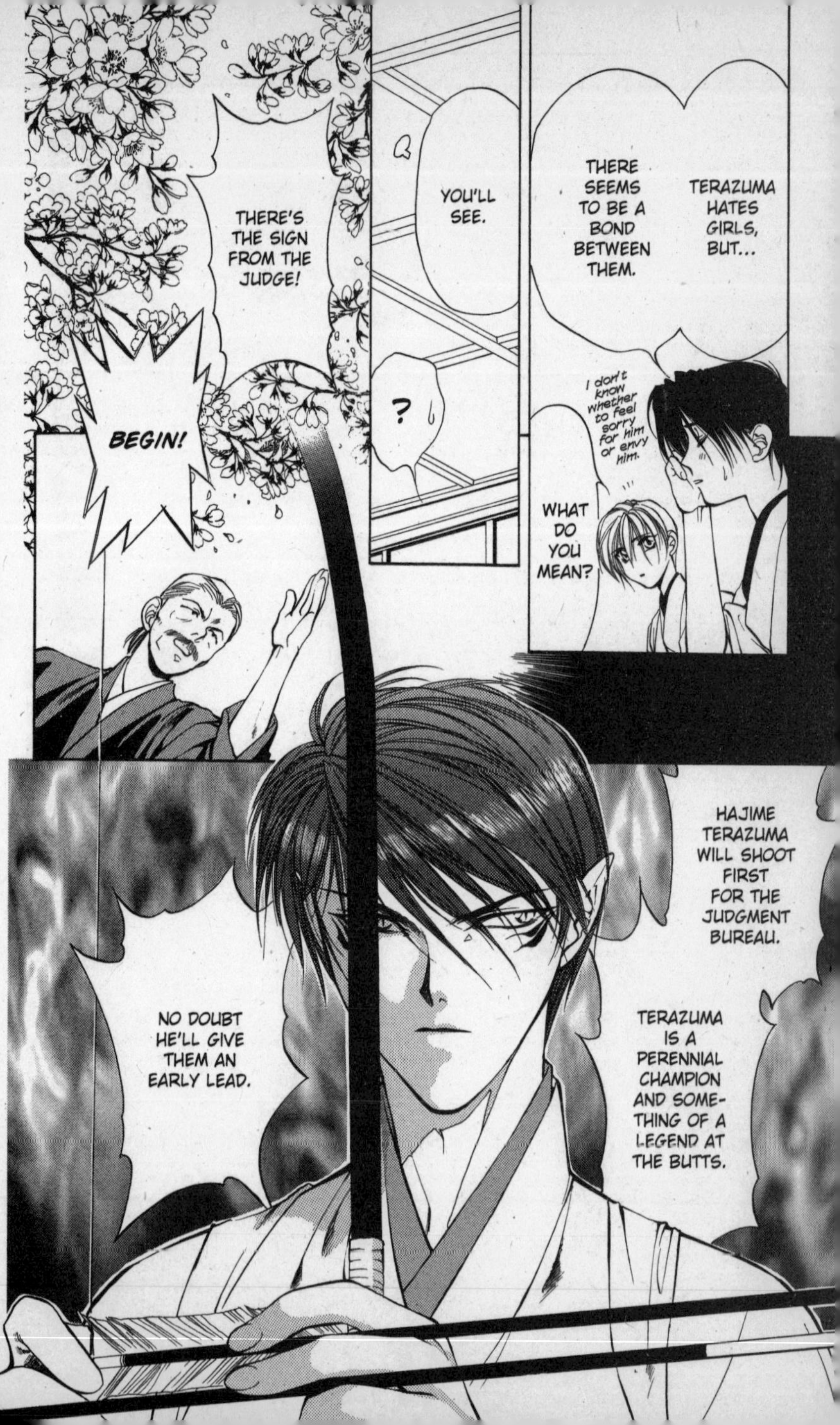
TERAZUMA HATES GIRLS, BUT...
THERE SEEMS TO BE A BOND BETWEEN THEM.
I don't know whether to feel sorry for him or envy him.
WHAT DO YOU MEAN?
YOU'LL SEE.
?
THERE'S THE SIGN FROM THE JUDGE!
BEGIN!
HAJIME TERAZUMA WILL SHOOT FIRST FOR THE JUDGMENT BUREAU.
TERAZUMA IS A PERENNIAL CHAMPION AND SOME-THING OF A LEGEND AT THE BUTTS.
NO DOUBT HE'LL GIVE THEM AN EARLY LEAD.

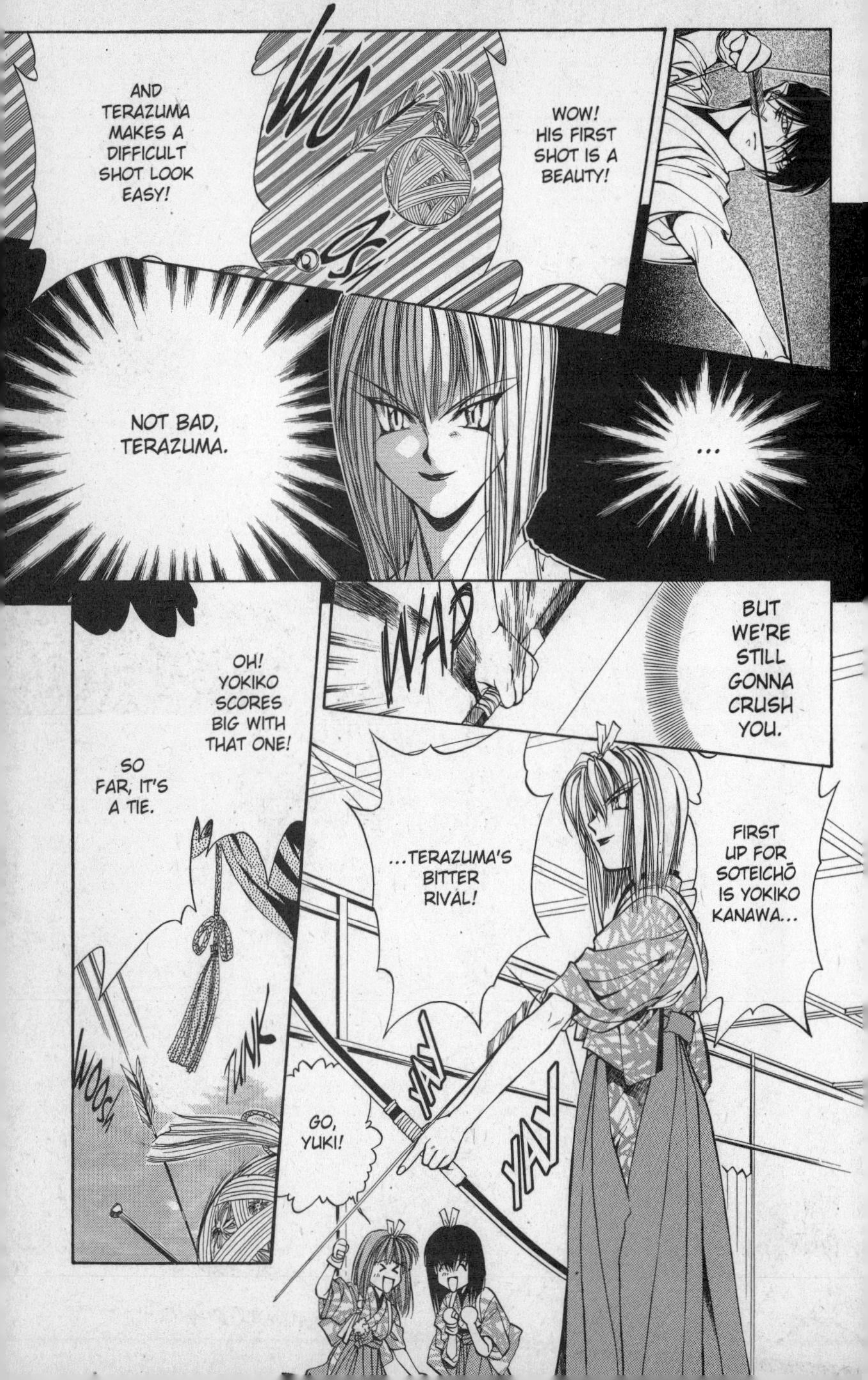
WOW! HIS FIRST SHOT IS A BEAUTY!
WOOSH
AND TERAZUMA MAKES A DIFFICULT SHOT LOOK EASY!
...
NOT BAD, TERAZUMA.
WAP
BUT WE'RE STILL GONNA CRUSH YOU.
FIRST UP FOR SOTEICHŌ IS YOKIKO KANAWA...
...TERAZUMA'S BITTER RIVAL!
YAY
YAY
GO, YUKI!
OH! YOKIKO SCORES BIG WITH THAT ONE!
SO FAR, IT'S A TIE.
ZUNK
WOOSH

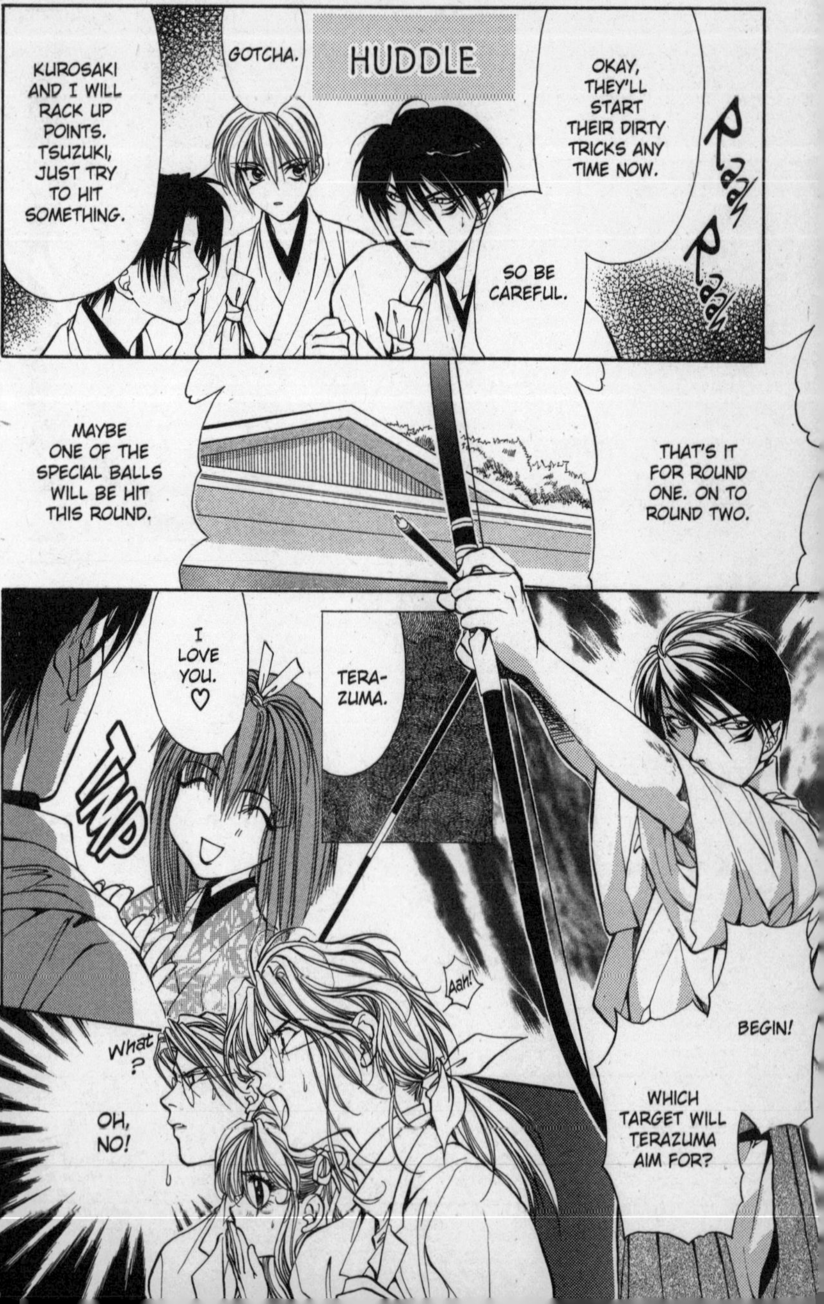
Raah Raah
OKAY, THEY'LL START THEIR DIRTY TRICKS ANY TIME NOW.
SO BE CAREFUL.
HUDDLE
KUROSAKI AND I WILL RACK UP POINTS. TSUZUKI, JUST TRY TO HIT SOMETHING.
GOTCHA.
THAT'S IT FOR ROUND ONE. ON TO ROUND TWO.
MAYBE ONE OF THE SPECIAL BALLS WILL BE HIT THIS ROUND.
TERA-ZUMA.
I LOVE YOU. ♡
TIMP
BEGIN!
WHICH TARGET WILL TERAZUMA AIM FOR?
Aah!
What?
OH, NO!

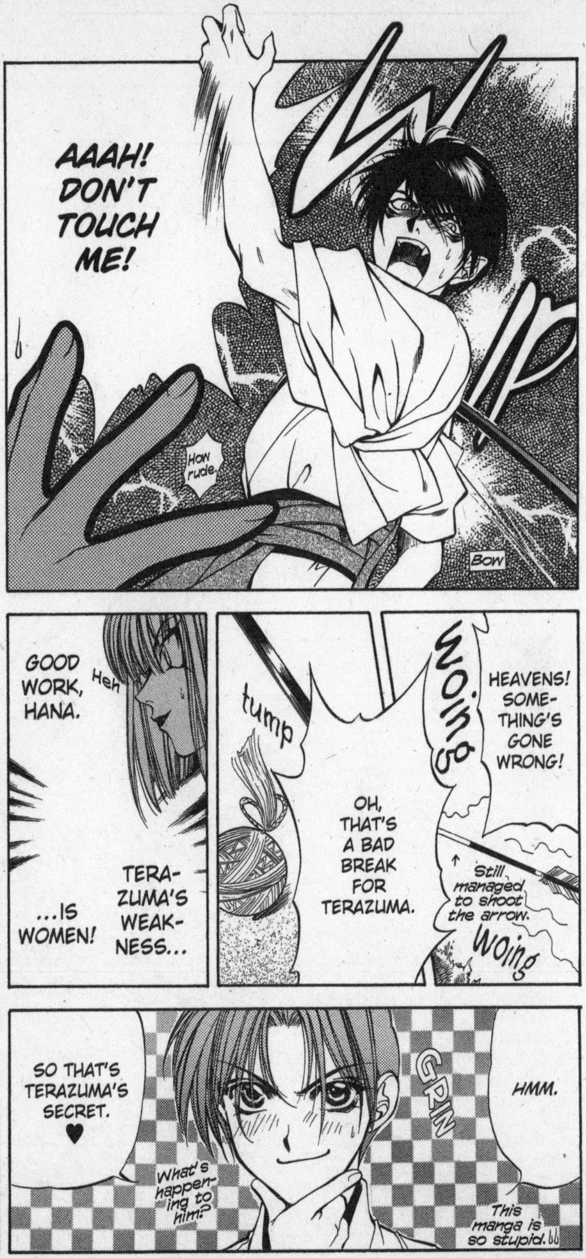
AAAH! DON'T TOUCH ME!
How rude.
Bow
Woing
HEAVENS! SOMETHING'S GONE WRONG!
tump
OH, THAT'S A BAD BREAK FOR TERAZUMA.
Still managed to shoot the arrow.
Woing
Heh
GOOD WORK, HANA.
TERA-ZUMA'S WEAK-NESS...
...IS WOMEN!
HMM.
GRIN
SO THAT'S TERAZUMA'S SECRET. ♥
What's happen-ing to him?
This manga is so stupid.

Uh-oh... It fell apart.

That's right, it fell apart! This time, the whole thing fell apart. (Ha!) Even Hajime and Tatsumi fell apart. They all fell apart. I fell apart, too. I can't even write clearly. I'm really sleepy, but I have a job to do. I'm the goddess of sleep deprivation, I guess. Okay, new subject. In this manga, I often refer to Kyushu as being in the country. I mean that as a compliment. I hate cities. I hate crowded places like Tokyo. I'd rather die than live in a place where the water tastes bad. So I think of the country as a wonderful place that would be nice to live in. I hope you people in Kyushu won't get mad at me. (Ahem) I like places where you can be close to nature. Is that weird?

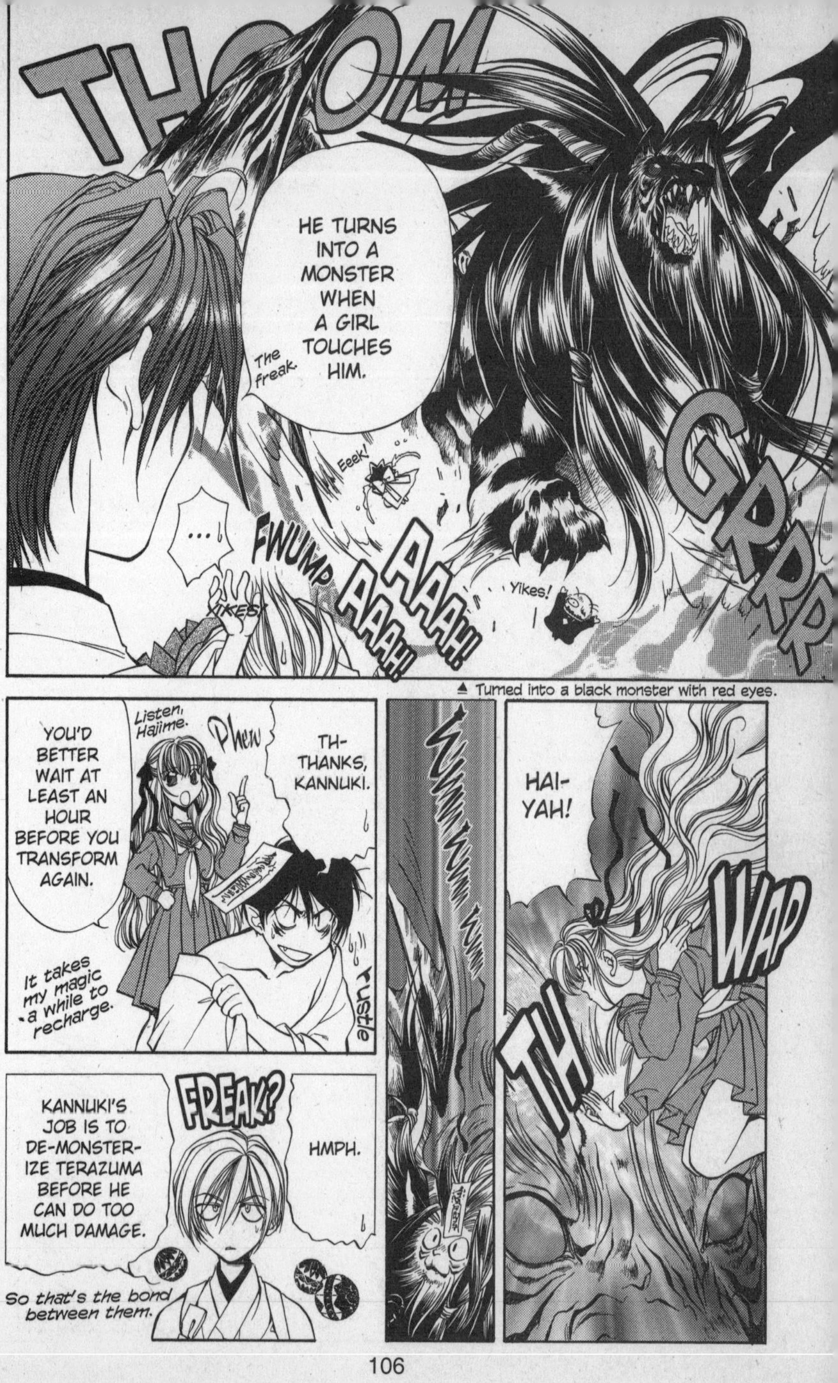
THOOM
HE TURNS INTO A MONSTER WHEN A GIRL TOUCHES HIM.
The freak.
GRRR
Eeek!
Yikes!
AAAH! AAAH!
FWUMP
...!
YIKES!
HAI-YAH!
WAP
TH
WMMM
TH-THANKS, KANNUKI.
Phew
Listen, Hajime.
YOU'D BETTER WAIT AT LEAST AN HOUR BEFORE YOU TRANSFORM AGAIN.
rustle
It takes my magic a while to recharge.
HMPH.
FREAK?
KANNUKI'S JOB IS TO DE-MONSTER-IZE TERAZUMA BEFORE HE CAN DO TOO MUCH DAMAGE.
So that's the bond between them.
▲ Turned into a black monster with red eyes.

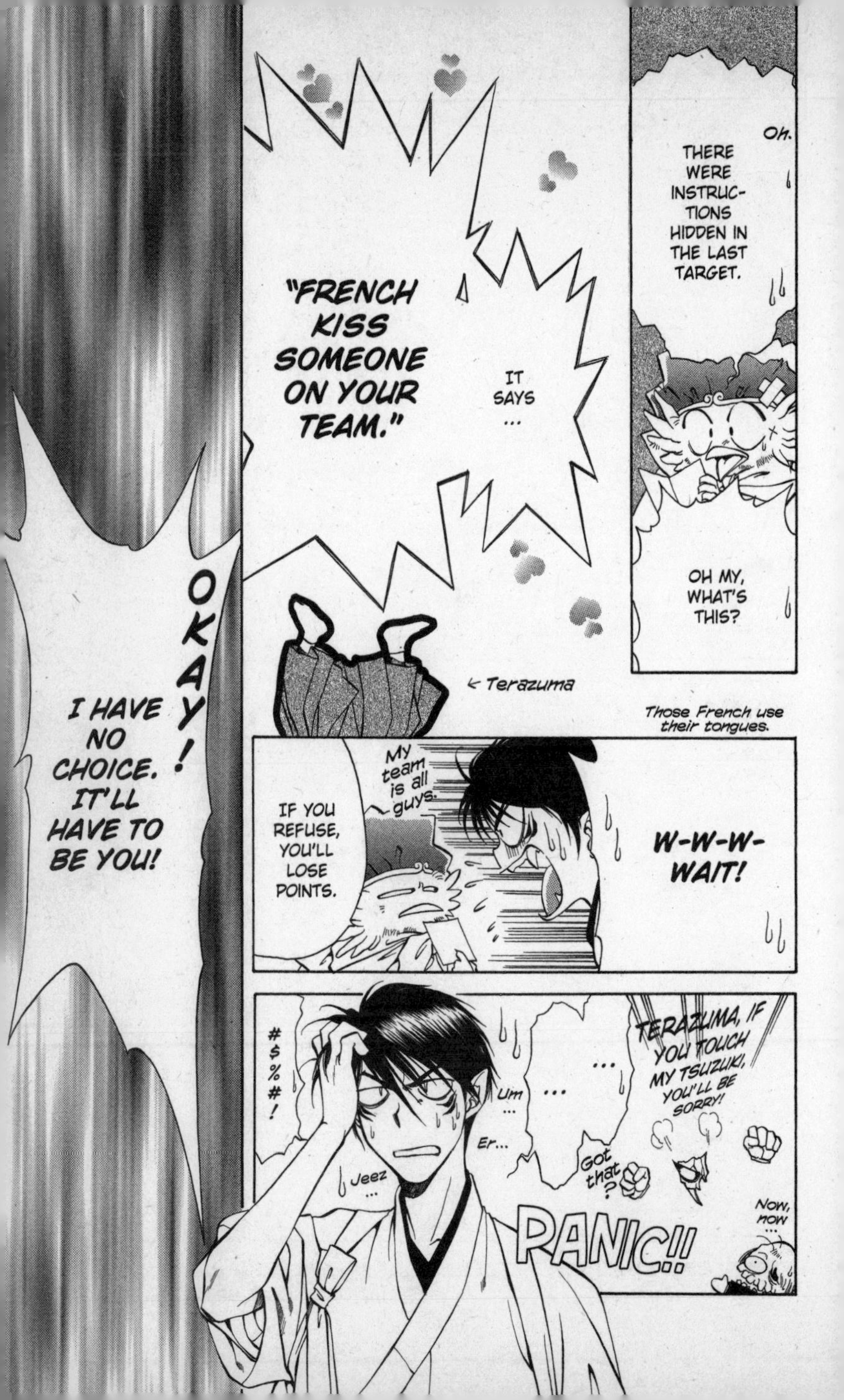
Oh.
THERE WERE INSTRUCTIONS HIDDEN IN THE LAST TARGET.
OH MY, WHAT'S THIS?
IT SAYS ...
"FRENCH KISS SOMEONE ON YOUR TEAM."
← Terazuma
Those French use their tongues.
W-W-W-WAIT!
My team is all guys.
IF YOU REFUSE, YOU'LL LOSE POINTS.
TERAZUMA, IF YOU TOUCH MY TSUZUKI, YOU'LL BE SORRY!
Got that?
Now, now ...
...
...
Um ...
Er...
#$%#!
Jeez ...
PANIC!!
OKAY!
I HAVE NO CHOICE. IT'LL HAVE TO BE YOU!

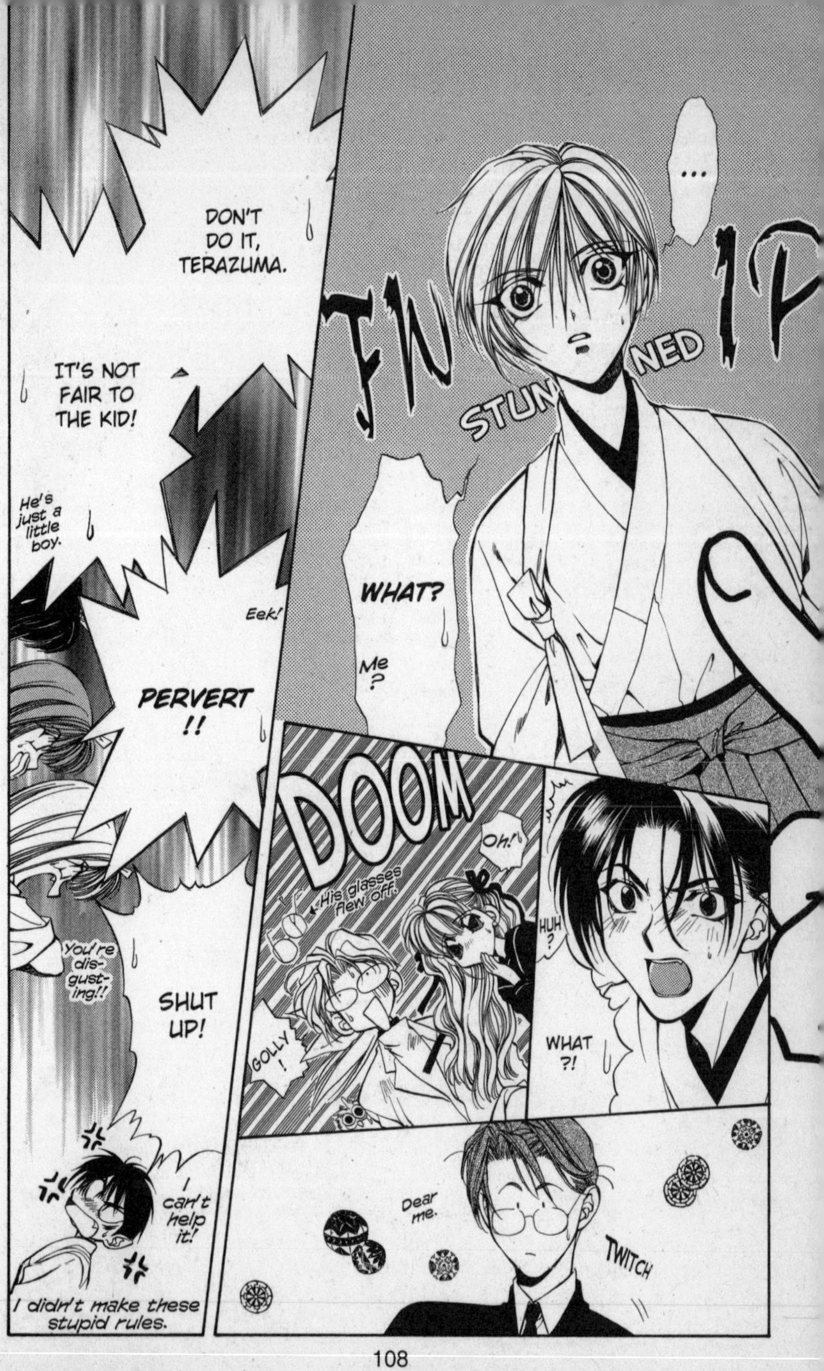
...
STUNNED
WHAT?
Me ?
HUH ?
WHAT ?!
DOOM
Oh!
His glasses flew off.
GOLLY !
Dear me.
TWITCH
DON'T DO IT, TERAZUMA.
IT'S NOT FAIR TO THE KID!
He's just a little boy.
Eek!
PERVERT !!
You're disgusting!!
SHUT UP!
I can't help it!
I didn't make these stupid rules.

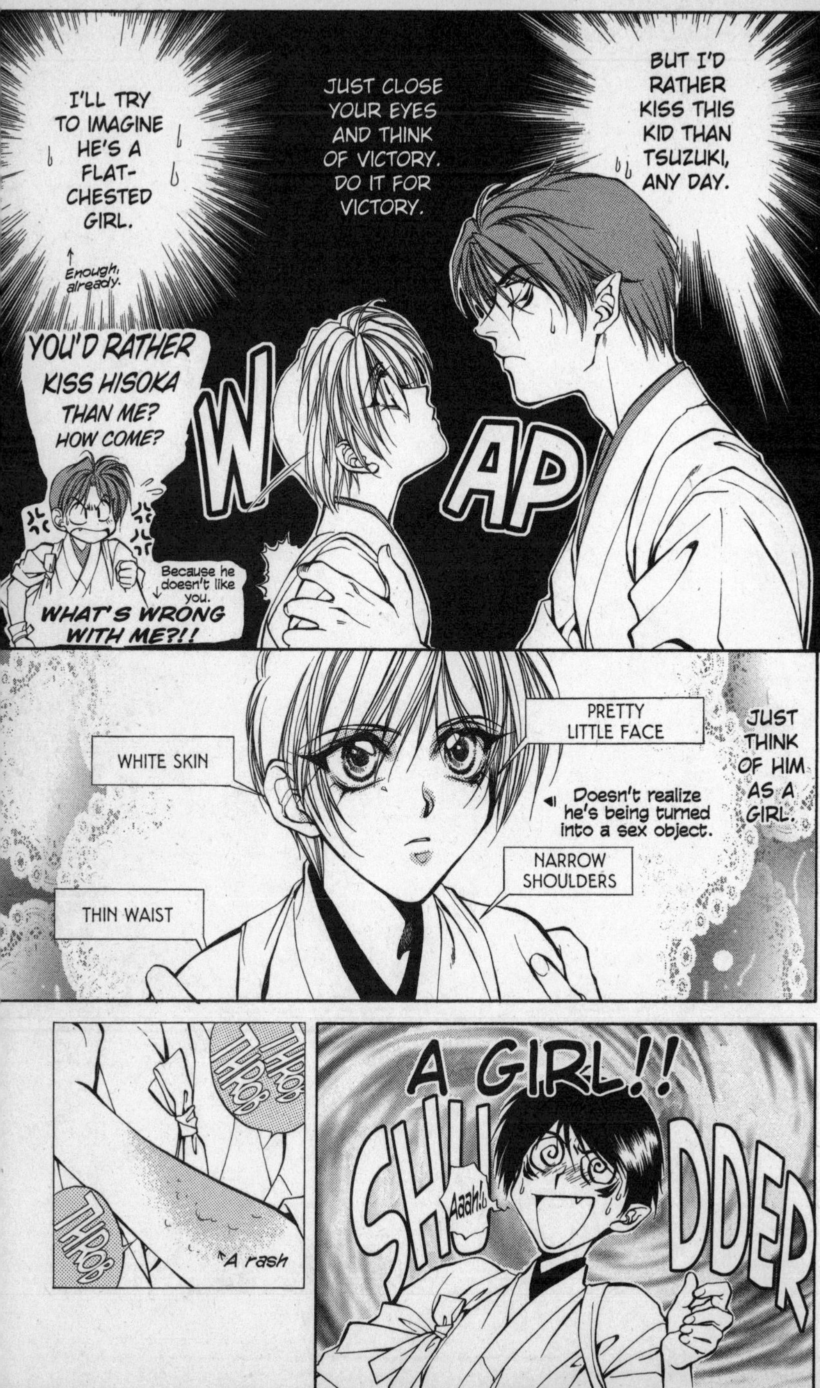

BUT I'D RATHER KISS THIS KID THAN TSUZUKI, ANY DAY.
JUST CLOSE YOUR EYES AND THINK OF VICTORY. DO IT FOR VICTORY.
I'LL TRY TO IMAGINE HE'S A FLAT-CHESTED GIRL.
Enough, already.
WAP
YOU'D RATHER KISS HISOKA THAN ME? HOW COME?
Because he doesn't like you.
WHAT'S WRONG WITH ME?!!
JUST THINK OF HIM AS A GIRL.
PRETTY LITTLE FACE
WHITE SKIN
Doesn't realize he's being turned into a sex object.
NARROW SHOULDERS
THIN WAIST
A GIRL!!
SHUDDER
Aaah!
THROB
THROB
A rash

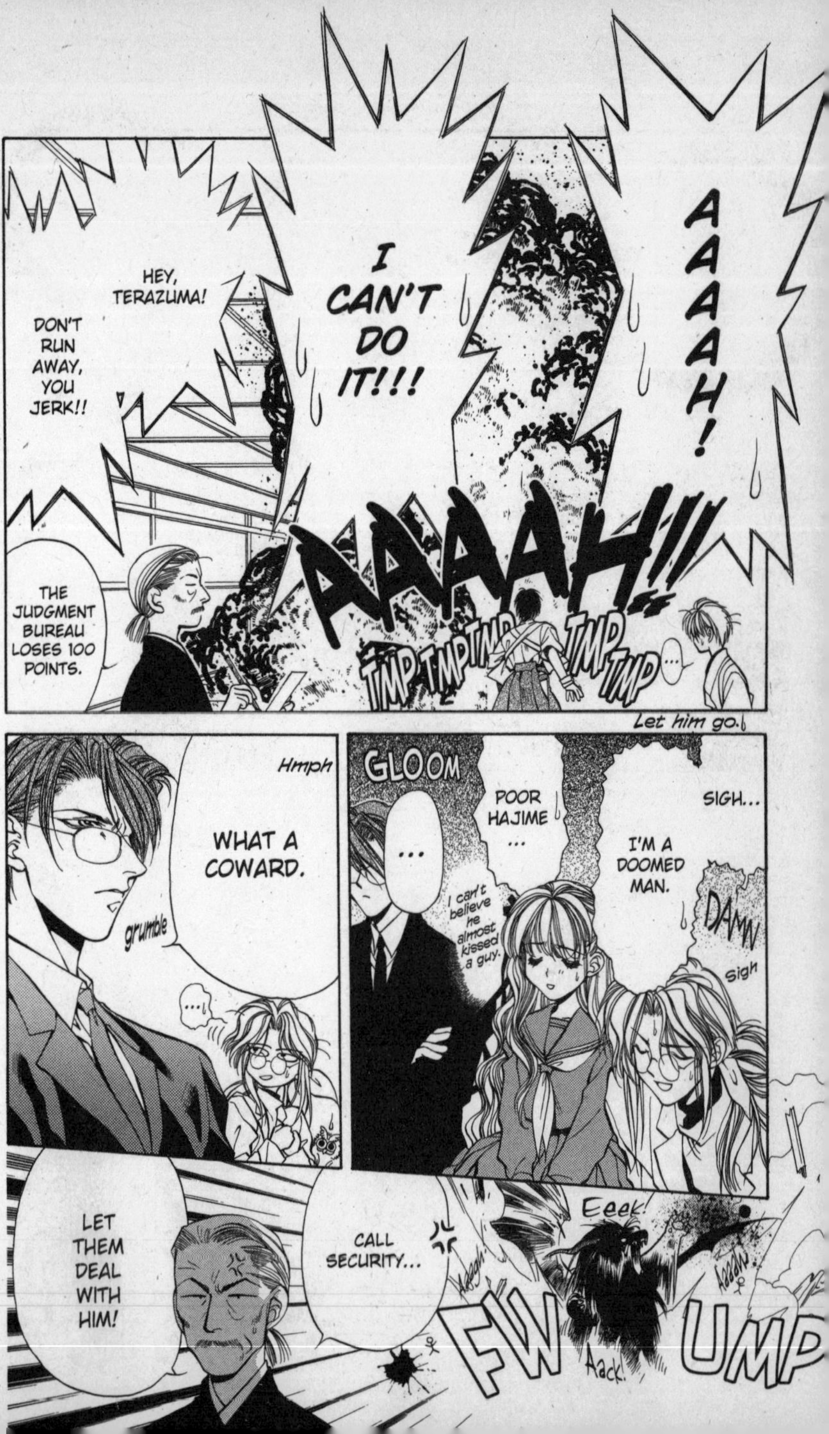
AAAAAH!
I CAN'T DO IT!!!
AAAAH!!
TMP TMP TMP
TMP TMP
...
Let him go.
HEY, TERAZUMA!
DON'T RUN AWAY, YOU JERK!!
THE JUDGMENT BUREAU LOSES 100 POINTS.
SIGH...
I'M A DOOMED MAN.
DAMN
Sigh
POOR HAJIME ...
I can't believe he almost kissed a guy.
GLOOM
...
Hmph
WHAT A COWARD.
grumble
...!
Eeek!
Aaagh!
Aaagh!
FWUMP
Aack!
CALL SECURITY...
LET THEM DEAL WITH HIM!

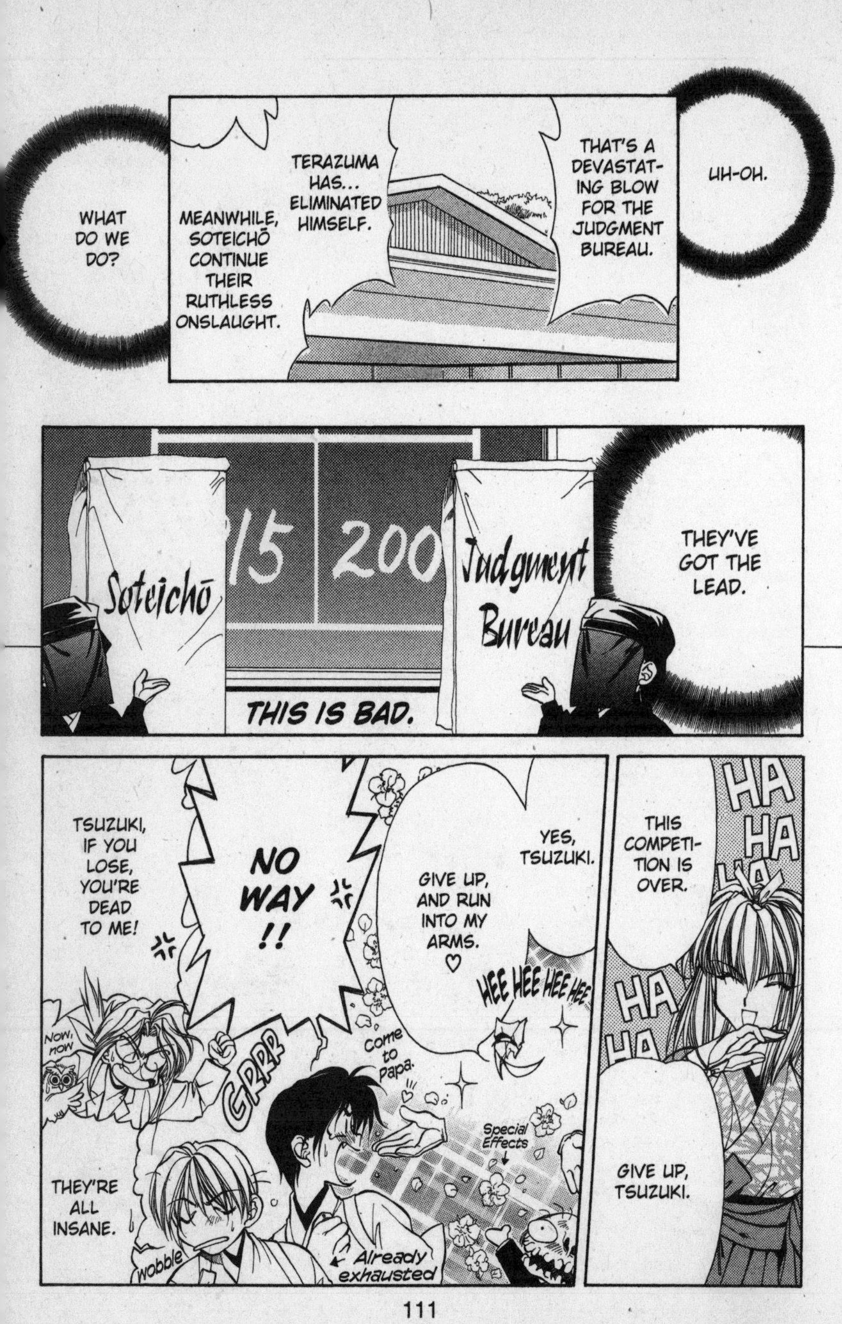

UH-OH.
THAT'S A DEVASTATING BLOW FOR THE JUDGMENT BUREAU.
TERAZUMA HAS... ELIMINATED HIMSELF.
MEANWHILE, SOTEICHŌ CONTINUE THEIR RUTHLESS ONSLAUGHT.
WHAT DO WE DO?
THEY'VE GOT THE LEAD.
Judgment Bureau
200
15
Soteichō
THIS IS BAD.
HA HA HA
THIS COMPETITION IS OVER.
HA HA
GIVE UP, TSUZUKI.
YES, TSUZUKI.
GIVE UP, AND RUN INTO MY ARMS. ♡
HEE HEE HEE HEE
NO WAY!!
TSUZUKI, IF YOU LOSE, YOU'RE DEAD TO ME!
Come to Papa.
GRRR
Now, now
Special Effects
THEY'RE ALL INSANE.
Already exhausted
wobble

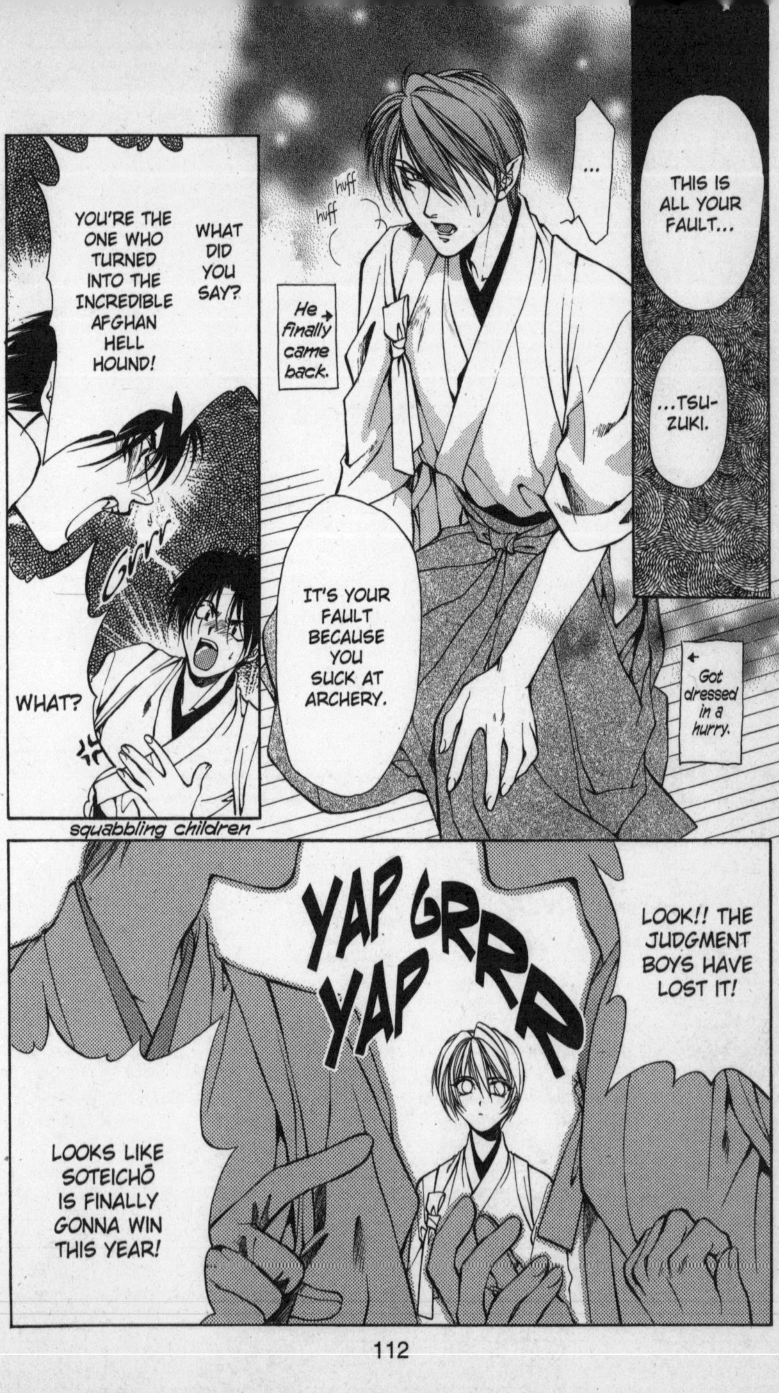
THIS IS ALL YOUR FAULT...
...TSU-ZUKI.
...
huff huff
He finally came back.
Got dressed in a hurry.
IT'S YOUR FAULT BECAUSE YOU SUCK AT ARCHERY.
WHAT DID YOU SAY?
YOU'RE THE ONE WHO TURNED INTO THE INCREDIBLE AFGHAN HELL HOUND!
Grrr
WHAT?
squabbling children
LOOK!! THE JUDGMENT BOYS HAVE LOST IT!
YAP GRRR YAP
LOOKS LIKE SOTEICHŌ IS FINALLY GONNA WIN THIS YEAR!

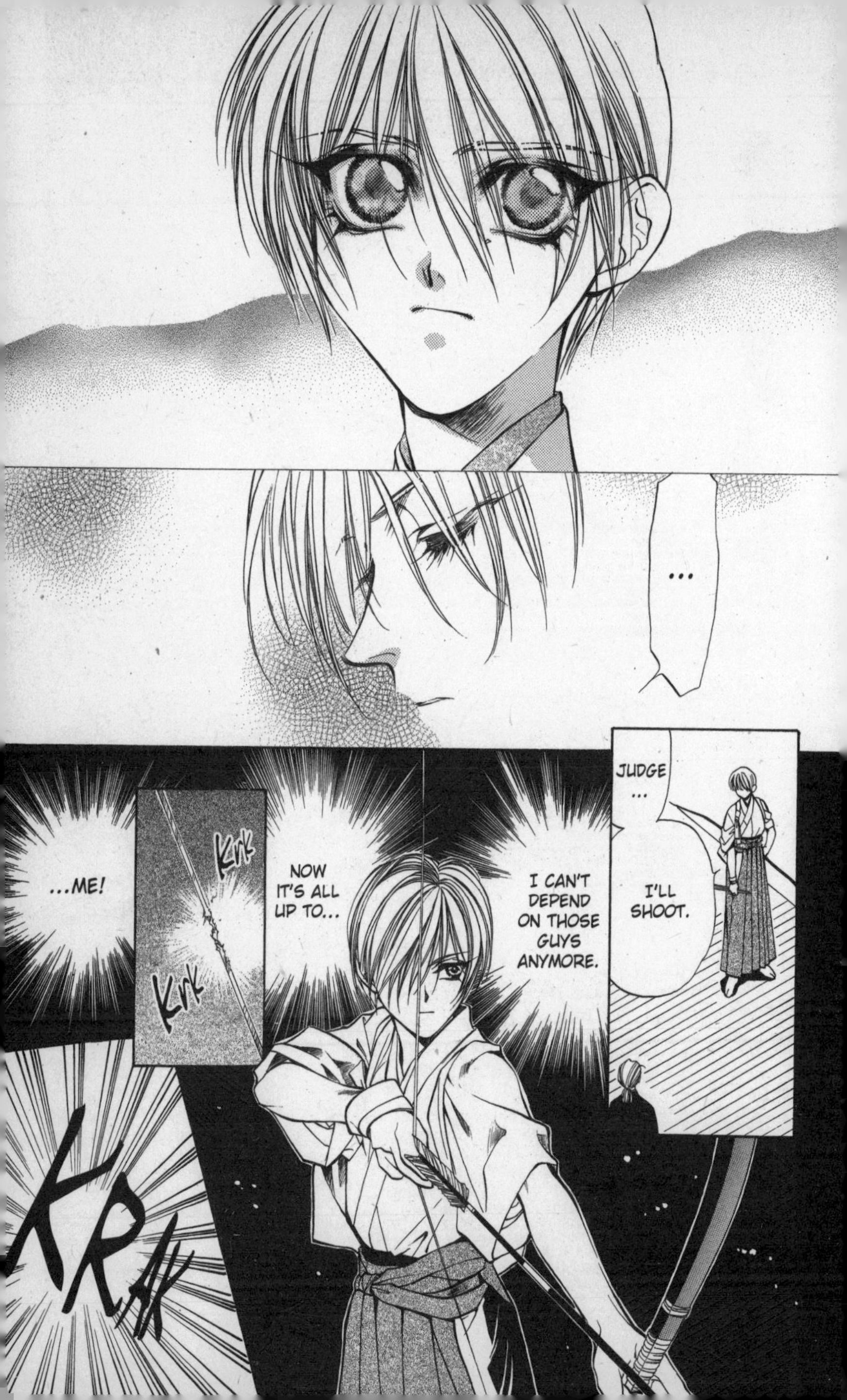
...
JUDGE...
I'LL SHOOT.
I CAN'T DEPEND ON THOSE GUYS ANYMORE.
NOW IT'S ALL UP TO...
Krik
Krik
...ME!
KRAK

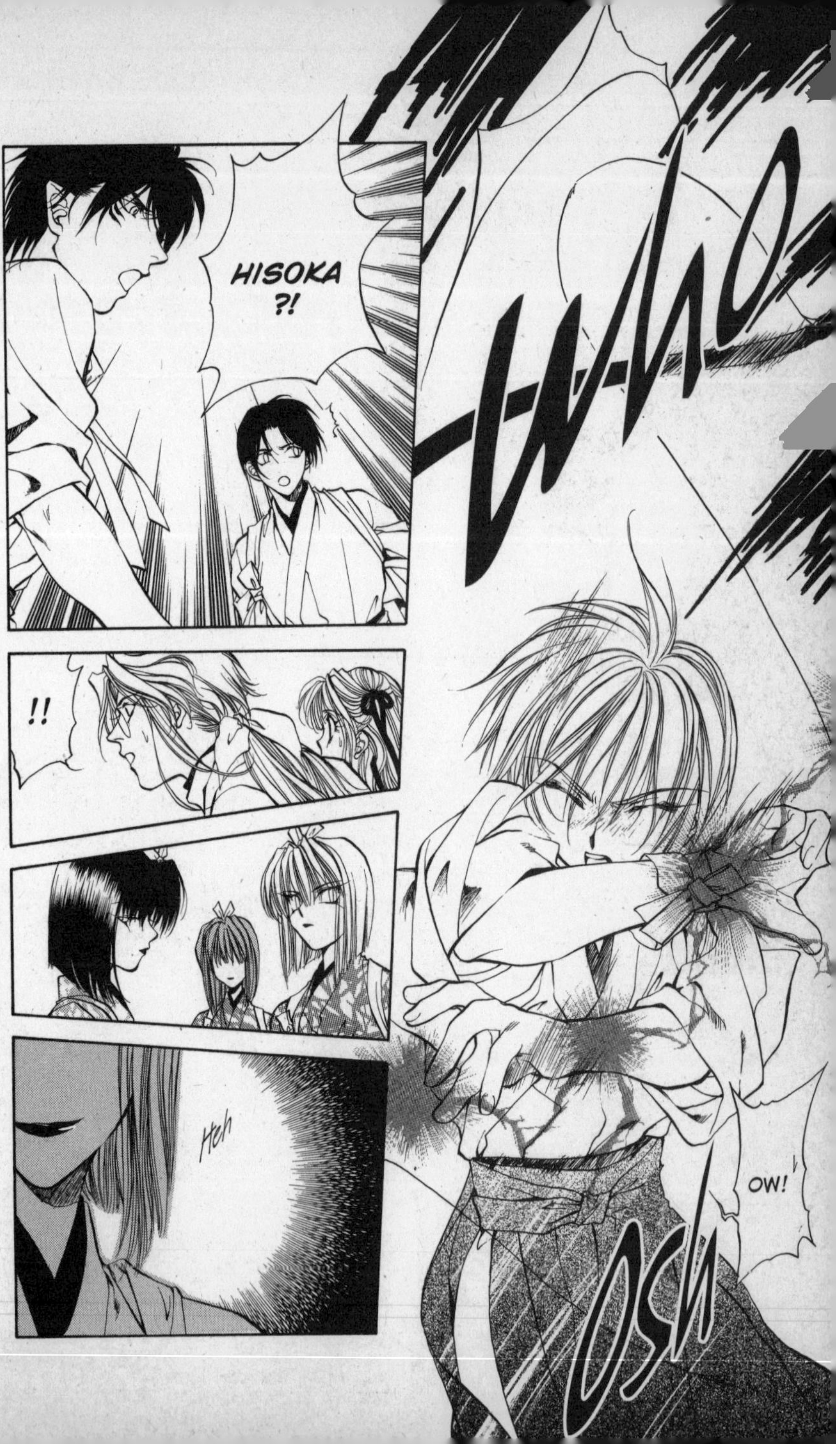

W-h-o
OW!
osh
HISOKA ?!
!!
Heh

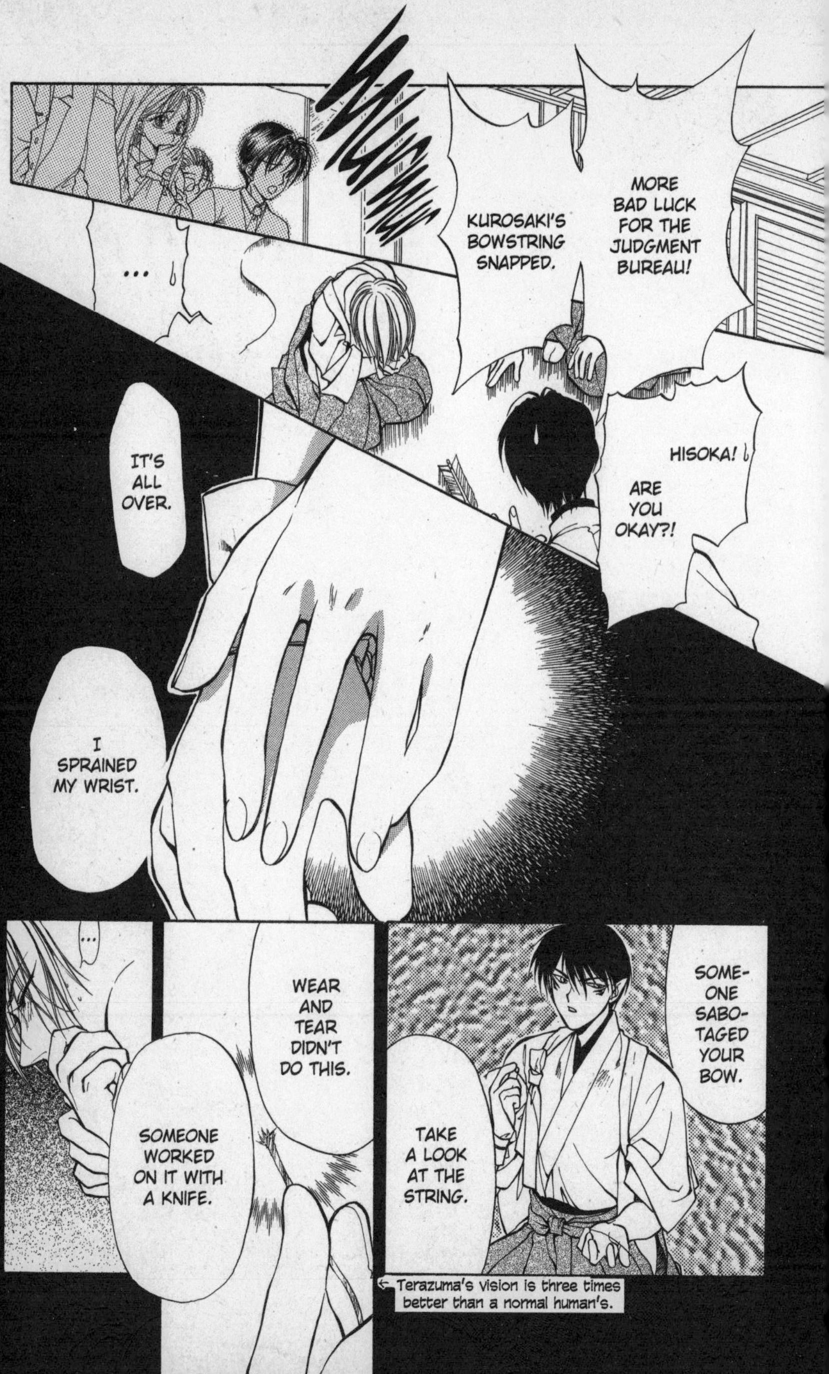
MORE BAD LUCK FOR THE JUDGMENT BUREAU!
KUROSAKI'S BOWSTRING SNAPPED.
...
HISOKA!
ARE YOU OKAY?!
IT'S ALL OVER.
I SPRAINED MY WRIST.
SOME-ONE SABO-TAGED YOUR BOW.
TAKE A LOOK AT THE STRING.
← Terazuma's vision is three times better than a normal human's.
WEAR AND TEAR DIDN'T DO THIS.
SOMEONE WORKED ON IT WITH A KNIFE.
...

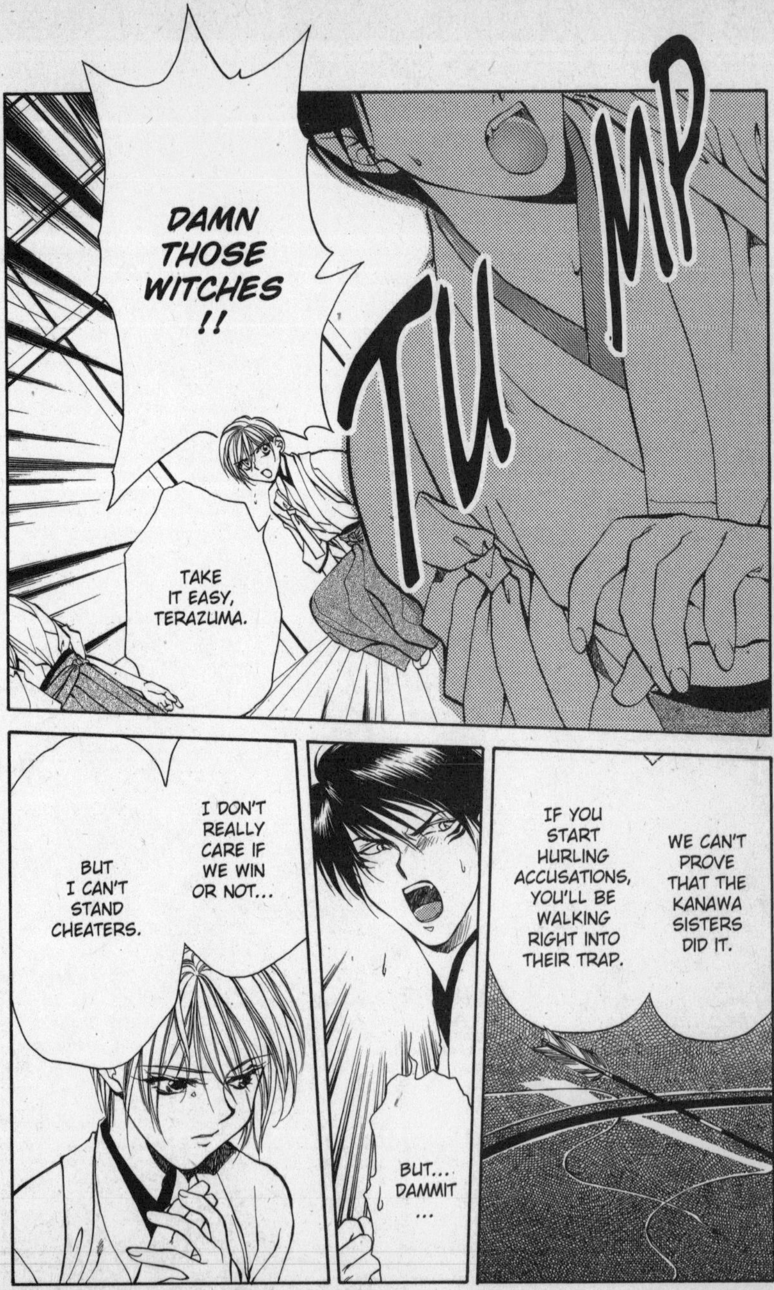
TUMP
DAMN THOSE WITCHES !!
TAKE IT EASY, TERAZUMA.
WE CAN'T PROVE THAT THE KANAWA SISTERS DID IT.
IF YOU START HURLING ACCUSATIONS, YOU'LL BE WALKING RIGHT INTO THEIR TRAP.
BUT... DAMMIT ...
I DON'T REALLY CARE IF WE WIN OR NOT...
BUT I CAN'T STAND CHEATERS.

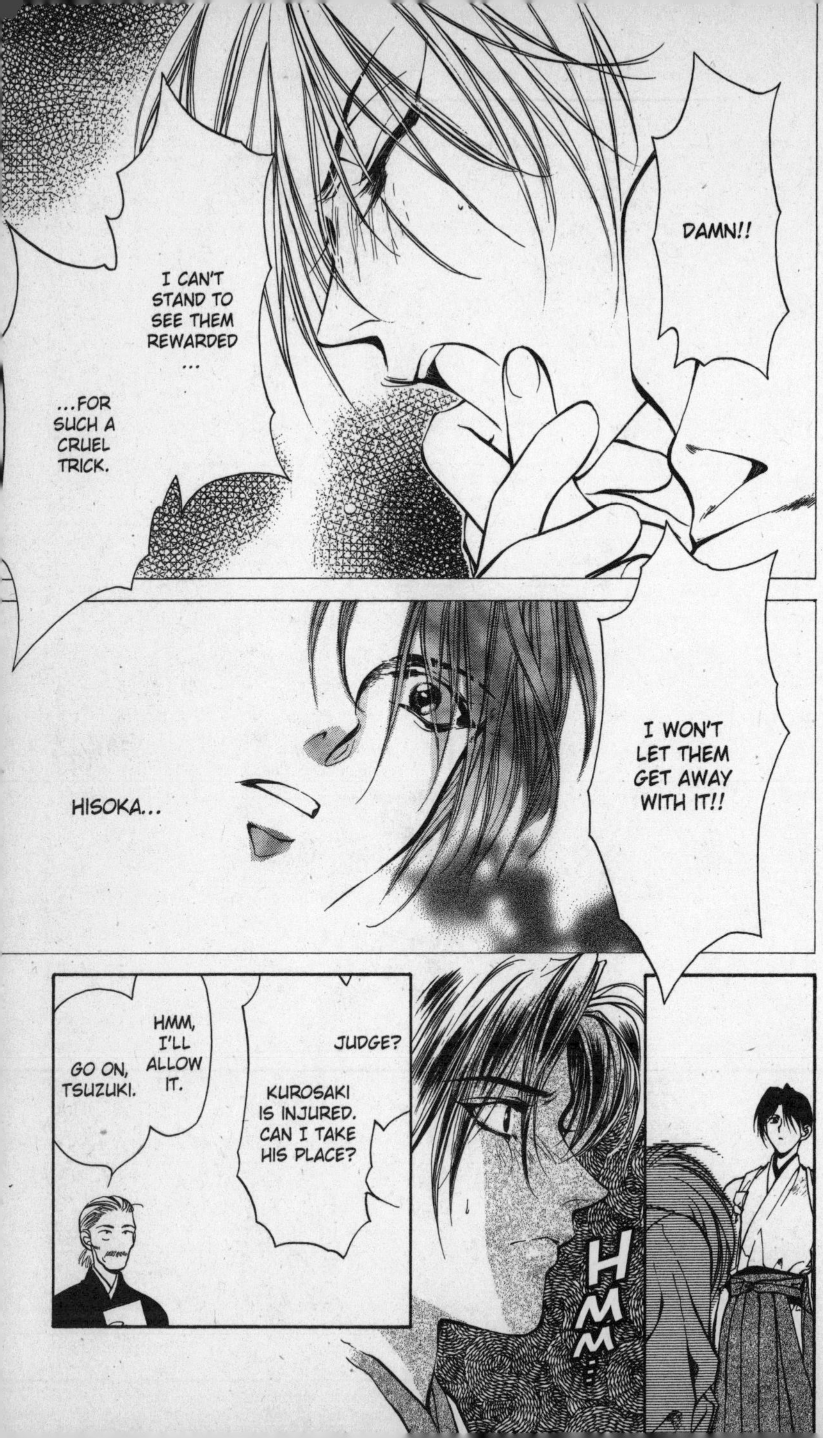
DAMN!!
I CAN'T STAND TO SEE THEM REWARDED ...
...FOR SUCH A CRUEL TRICK.
I WON'T LET THEM GET AWAY WITH IT!!
HISOKA...
HMM...
JUDGE?
KUROSAKI IS INJURED. CAN I TAKE HIS PLACE?
HMM, I'LL ALLOW IT.
GO ON, TSUZUKI.

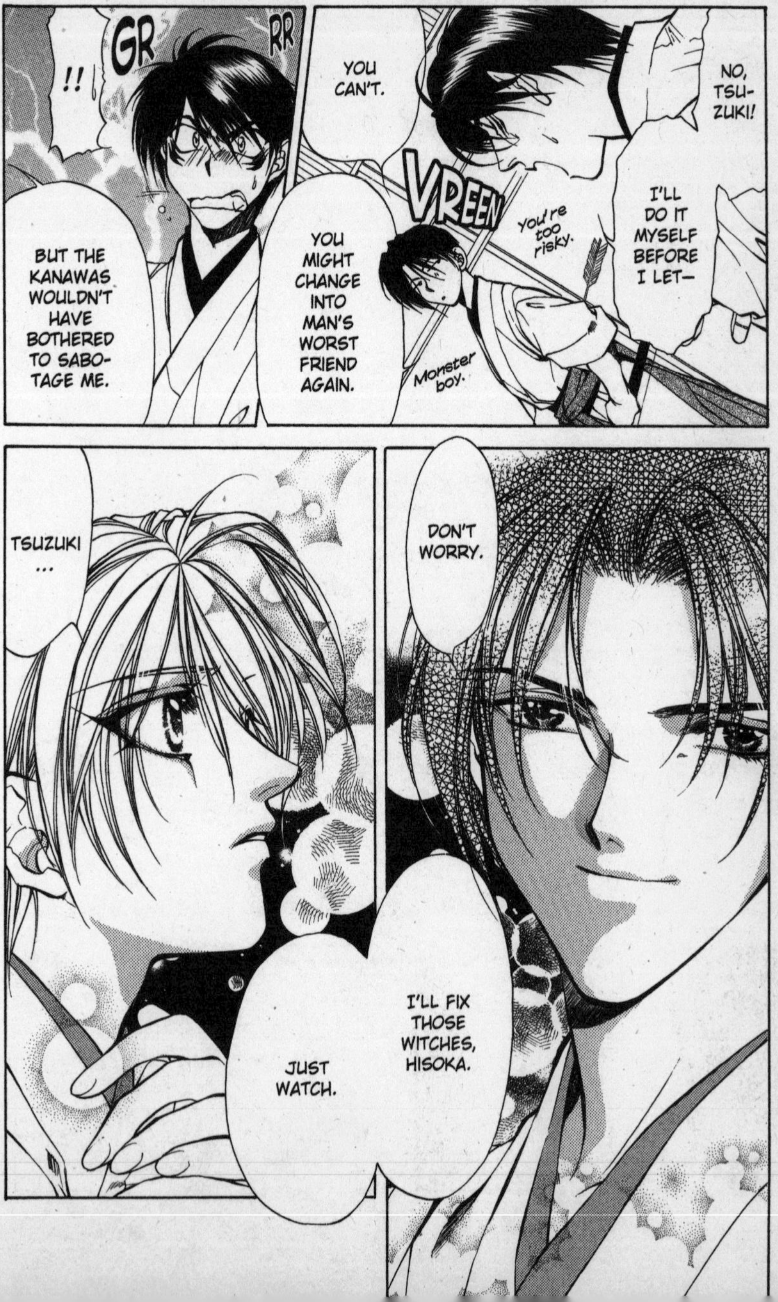
NO, TSU-ZUKI!
I'LL DO IT MYSELF BEFORE I LET—
YOU CAN'T.
VREEN
You're too risky.
YOU MIGHT CHANGE INTO MAN'S WORST FRIEND AGAIN.
Monster boy.
GR RR
!!
BUT THE KANAWAS WOULDN'T HAVE BOTHERED TO SABO-TAGE ME.
DON'T WORRY.
I'LL FIX THOSE WITCHES, HISOKA.
JUST WATCH.
TSUZUKI ...

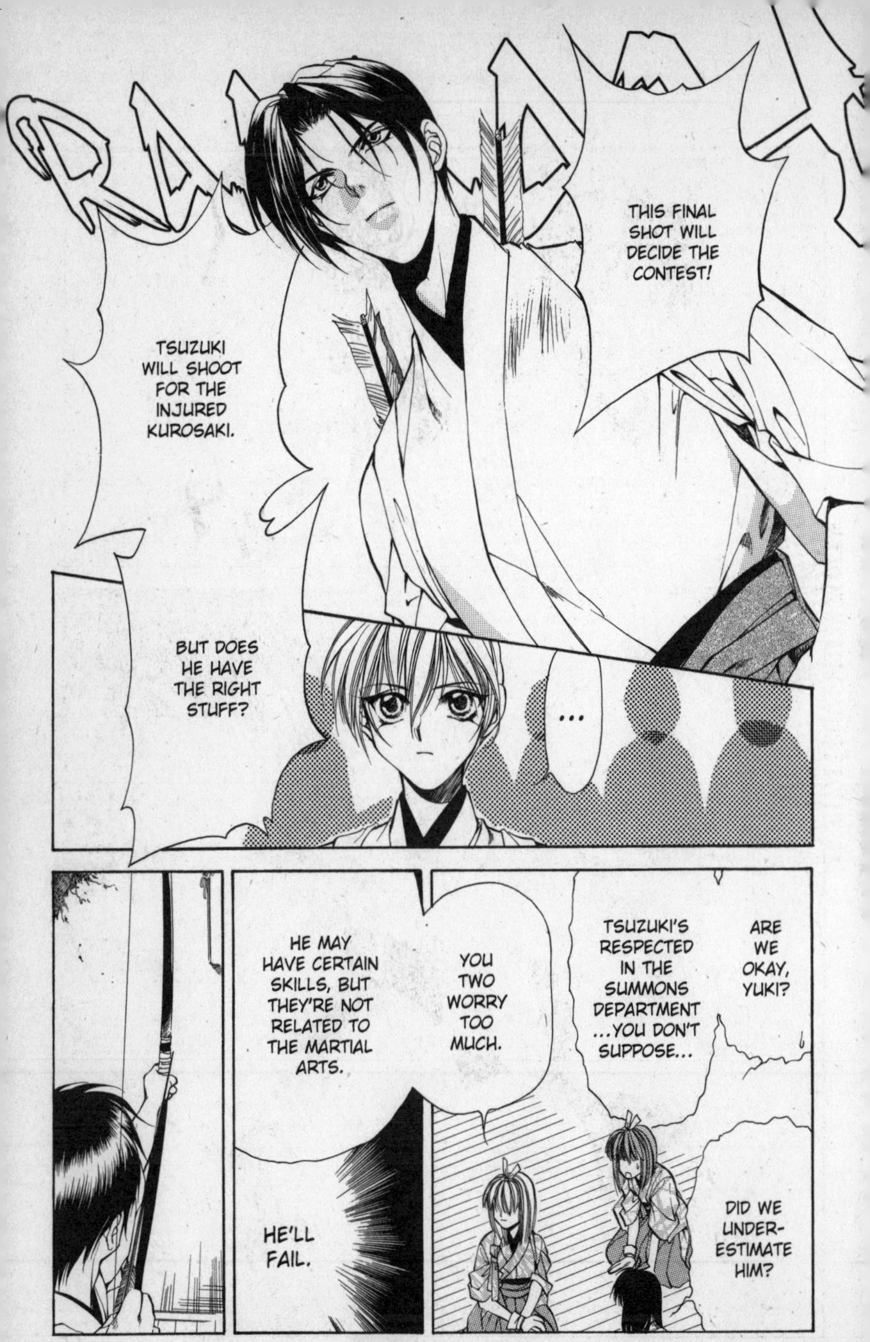
THIS FINAL SHOT WILL DECIDE THE CONTEST!
TSUZUKI WILL SHOOT FOR THE INJURED KUROSAKI.
BUT DOES HE HAVE THE RIGHT STUFF?
...
ARE WE OKAY, YUKI?
TSUZUKI'S RESPECTED IN THE SUMMONS DEPARTMENT ...YOU DON'T SUPPOSE...
DID WE UNDER-ESTIMATE HIM?
YOU TWO WORRY TOO MUCH.
HE MAY HAVE CERTAIN SKILLS, BUT THEY'RE NOT RELATED TO THE MARTIAL ARTS.
HE'LL FAIL.

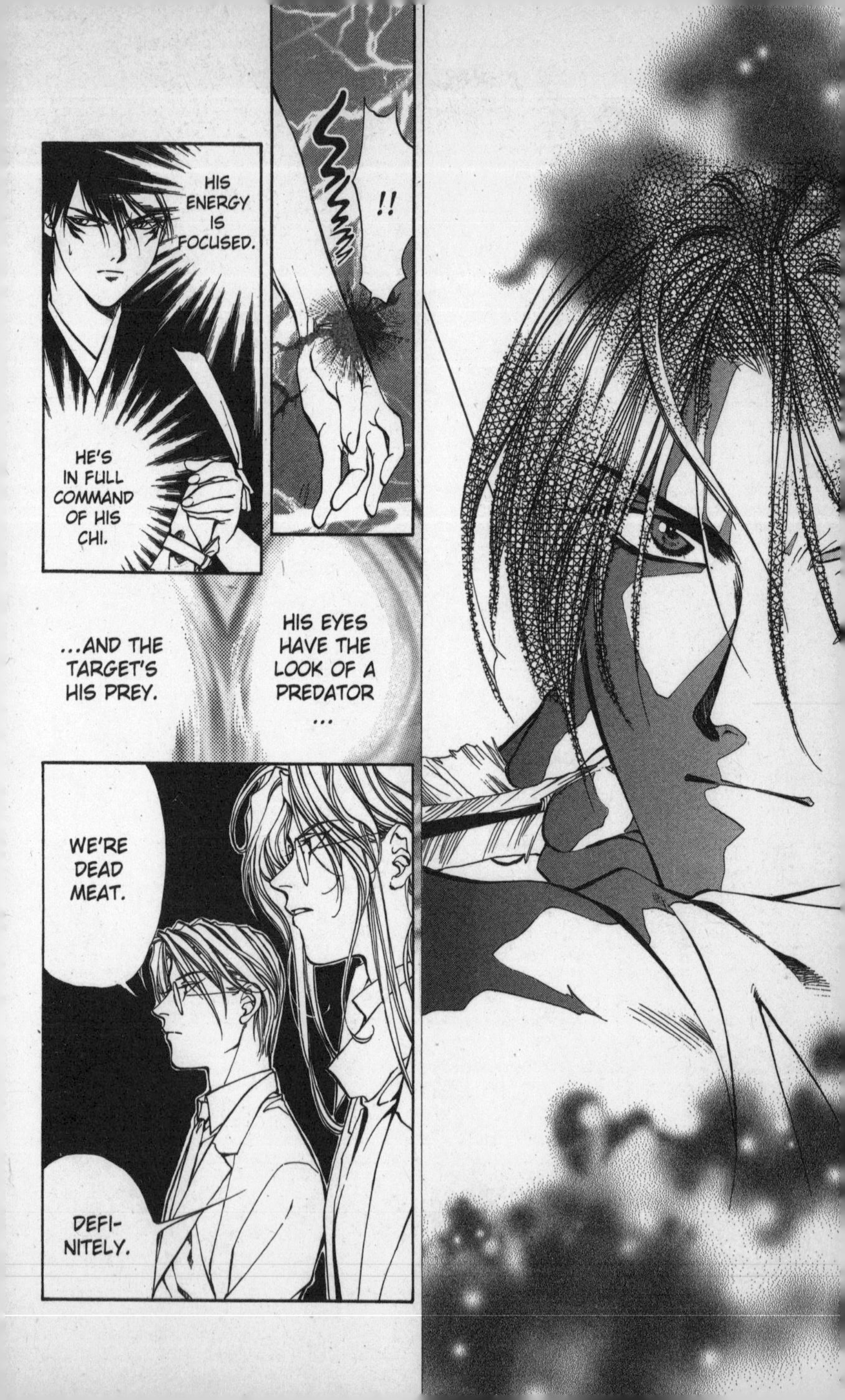
!!
HIS ENERGY IS FOCUSED.
HE'S IN FULL COMMAND OF HIS CHI.
HIS EYES HAVE THE LOOK OF A PREDATOR...
...AND THE TARGET'S HIS PREY.
WE'RE DEAD MEAT.
DEFI-NITELY.

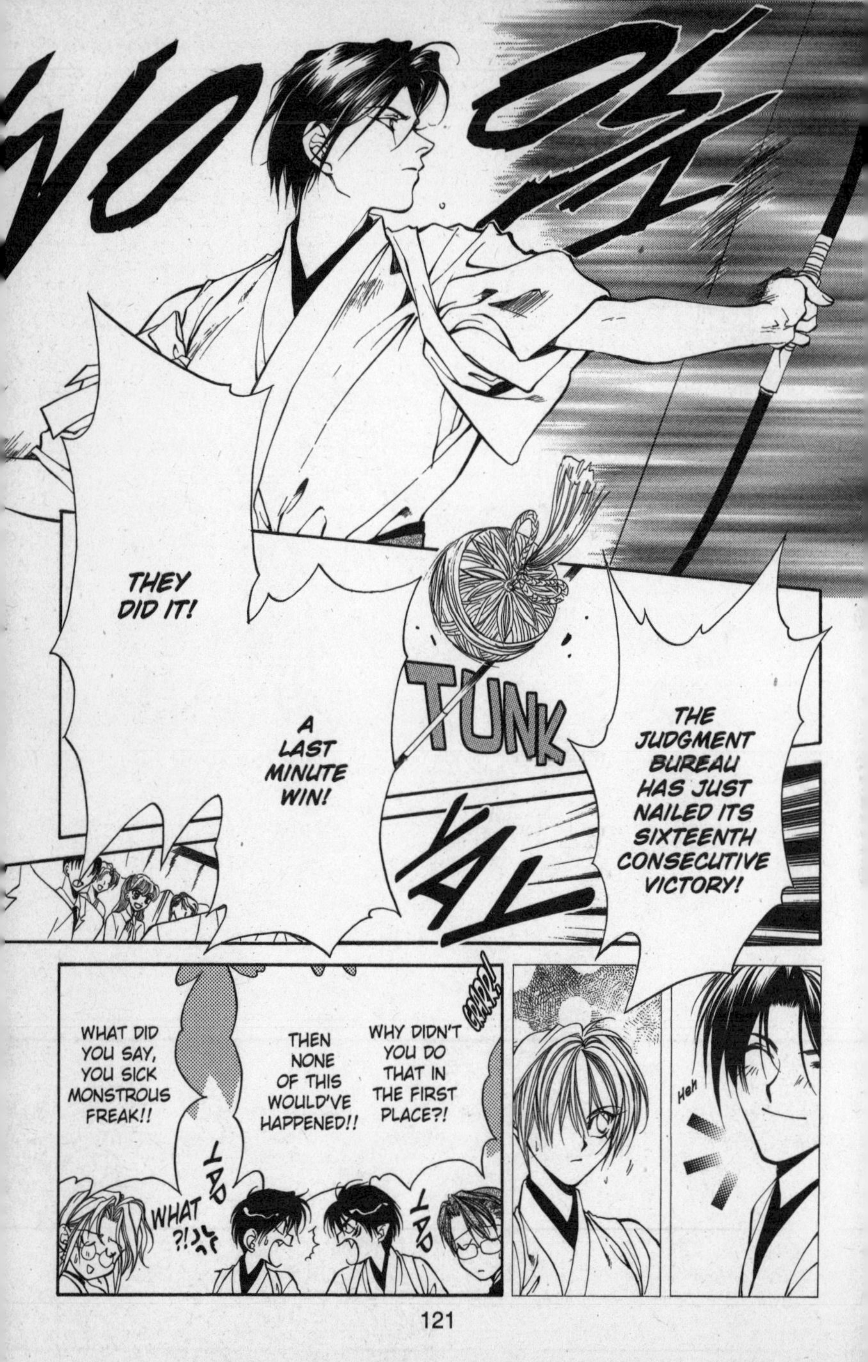
THE JUDGMENT BUREAU HAS JUST NAILED ITS SIXTEENTH CONSECUTIVE VICTORY!
TUNK
A LAST MINUTE WIN!
YAY
THEY DID IT!
Heh
WHY DIDN'T YOU DO THAT IN THE FIRST PLACE?!
THEN NONE OF THIS WOULD'VE HAPPENED!!
YAP
WHAT DID YOU SAY, YOU SICK MONSTROUS FREAK!!
YAP
WHAT ?!

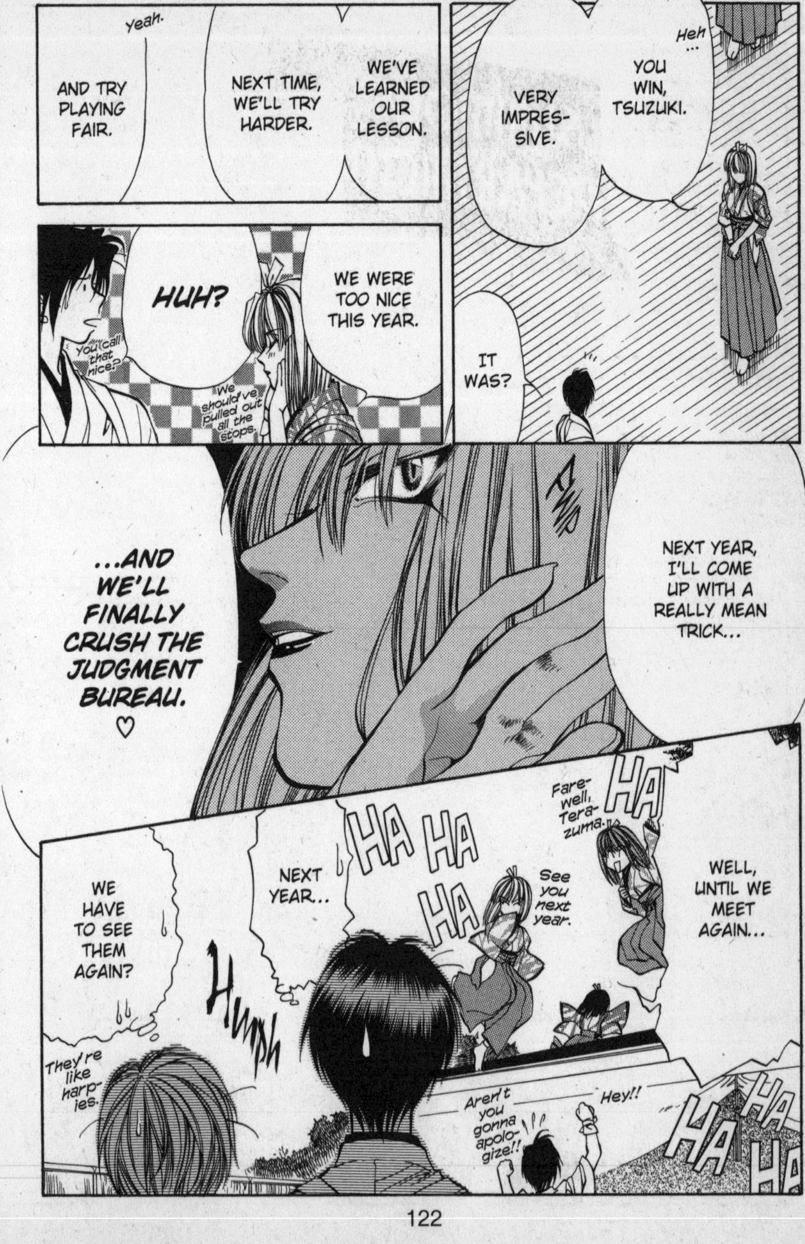
Heh...
YOU WIN, TSUZUKI.
VERY IMPRES-SIVE.
IT WAS?
WE'VE LEARNED OUR LESSON.
NEXT TIME, WE'LL TRY HARDER.
AND TRY PLAYING FAIR.
Yeah.
WE WERE TOO NICE THIS YEAR.
HUH?
We should've pulled out all the stops.
You call that nice?
NEXT YEAR, I'LL COME UP WITH A REALLY MEAN TRICK...
...AND WE'LL FINALLY CRUSH THE JUDGMENT BUREAU. ♡
HA
WELL, UNTIL WE MEET AGAIN...
Fare-well, Tera-zuma.
See you next year.
HA HA HA
NEXT YEAR...
WE HAVE TO SEE THEM AGAIN?
Humph
They're like harpies.
Hey!!
Aren't you gonna apolo-gize!!
HA HA HA HA

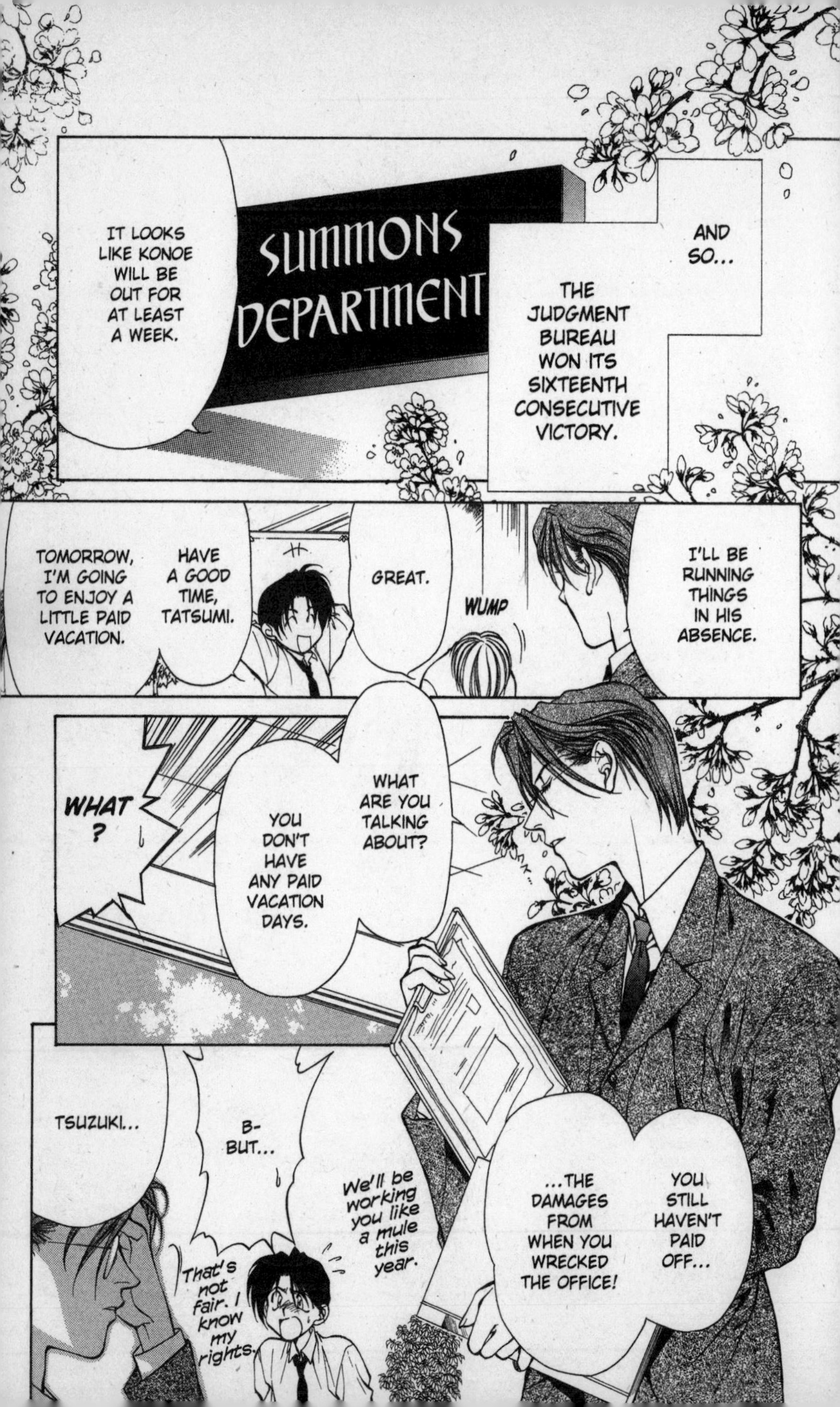
AND SO...
THE JUDGMENT BUREAU WON ITS SIXTEENTH CONSECUTIVE VICTORY.
SUMMONS DEPARTMENT
IT LOOKS LIKE KONOE WILL BE OUT FOR AT LEAST A WEEK.
I'LL BE RUNNING THINGS IN HIS ABSENCE.
WUMP
GREAT.
HAVE A GOOD TIME, TATSUMI.
TOMORROW, I'M GOING TO ENJOY A LITTLE PAID VACATION.
WHAT ARE YOU TALKING ABOUT?
YOU DON'T HAVE ANY PAID VACATION DAYS.
WHAT?
YOU STILL HAVEN'T PAID OFF...
...THE DAMAGES FROM WHEN YOU WRECKED THE OFFICE!
We'll be working you like a mule this year.
B-BUT...
That's not fair. I know my rights.
TSUZUKI...

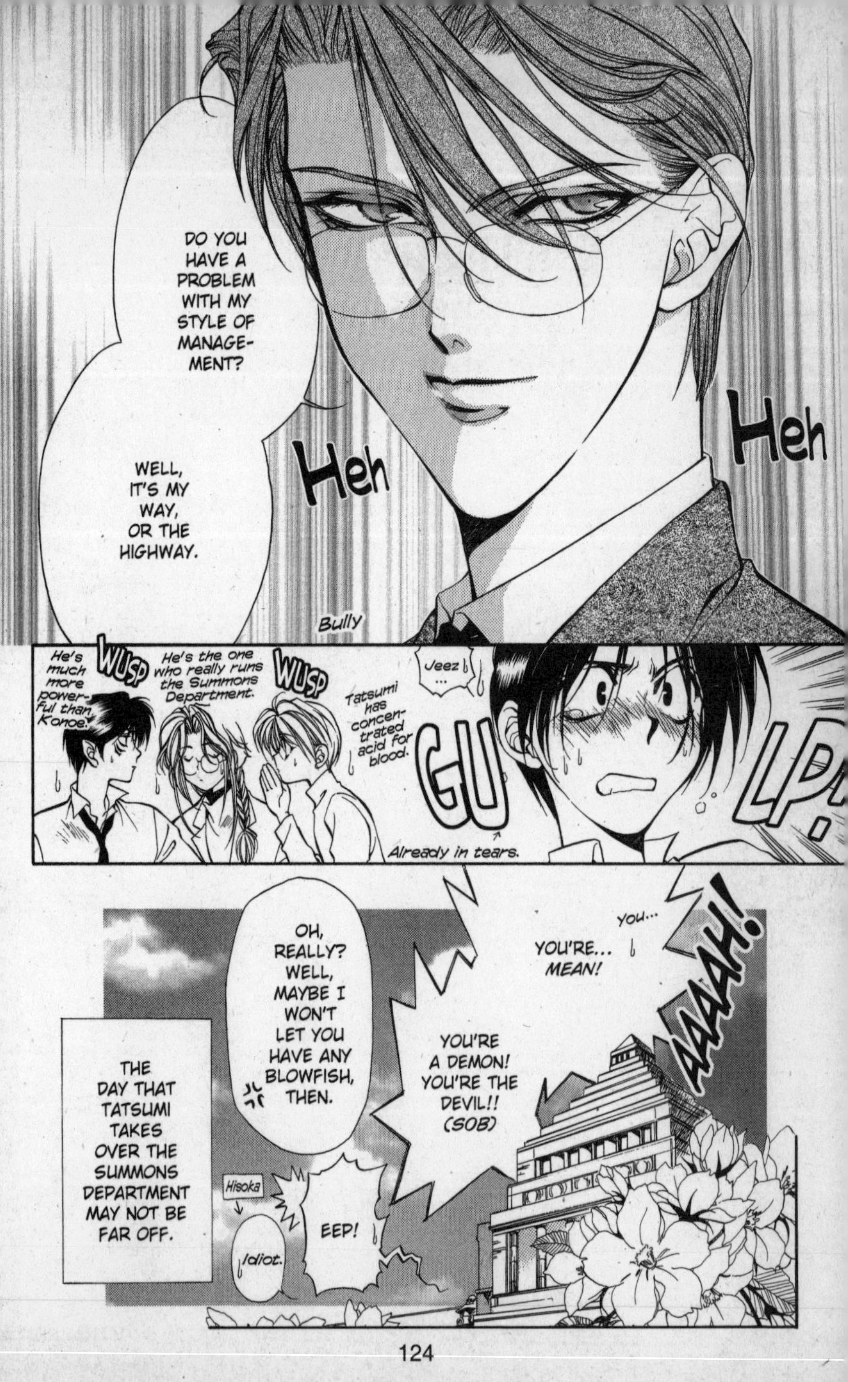

Heh
DO YOU HAVE A PROBLEM WITH MY STYLE OF MANAGE-MENT?
WELL, IT'S MY WAY, OR THE HIGHWAY.
Heh
Bully
GULP!
Jeez...
Already in tears.
Tatsumi has concen-trated acid for blood.
WUSP
He's the one who really runs the Summons Department.
WUSP
He's much more power-ful than Konoe.
AAAAH!
You...
YOU'RE... MEAN!
YOU'RE A DEMON! YOU'RE THE DEVIL!! (SOB)
OH, REALLY? WELL, MAYBE I WON'T LET YOU HAVE ANY BLOWFISH, THEN.
EEP!
Hisoka
Idiot.
THE DAY THAT TATSUMI TAKES OVER THE SUMMONS DEPARTMENT MAY NOT BE FAR OFF.

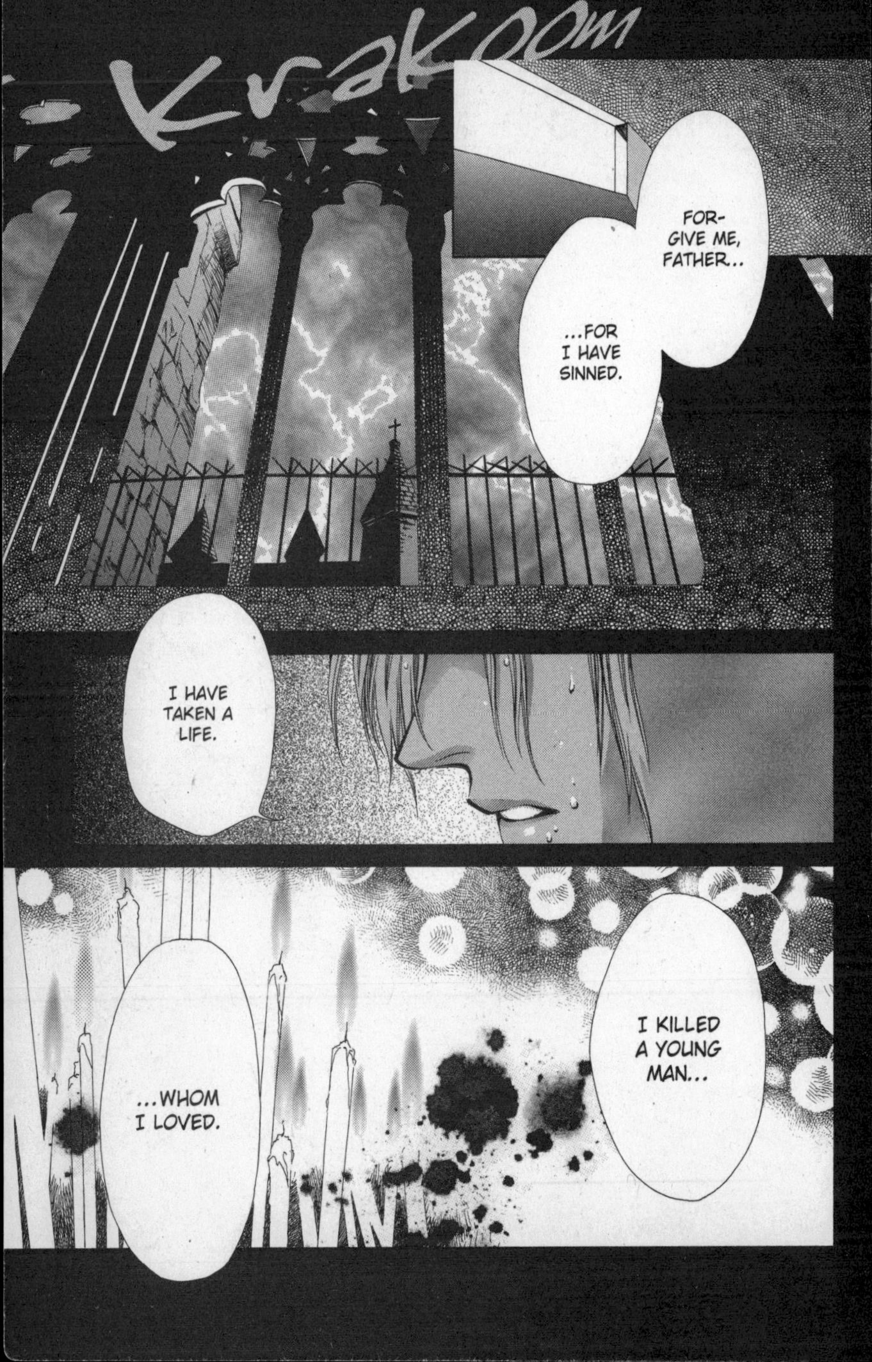
KRAKOOM
FOR-GIVE ME, FATHER...
...FOR I HAVE SINNED.
I HAVE TAKEN A LIFE.
I KILLED A YOUNG MAN...
...WHOM I LOVED.

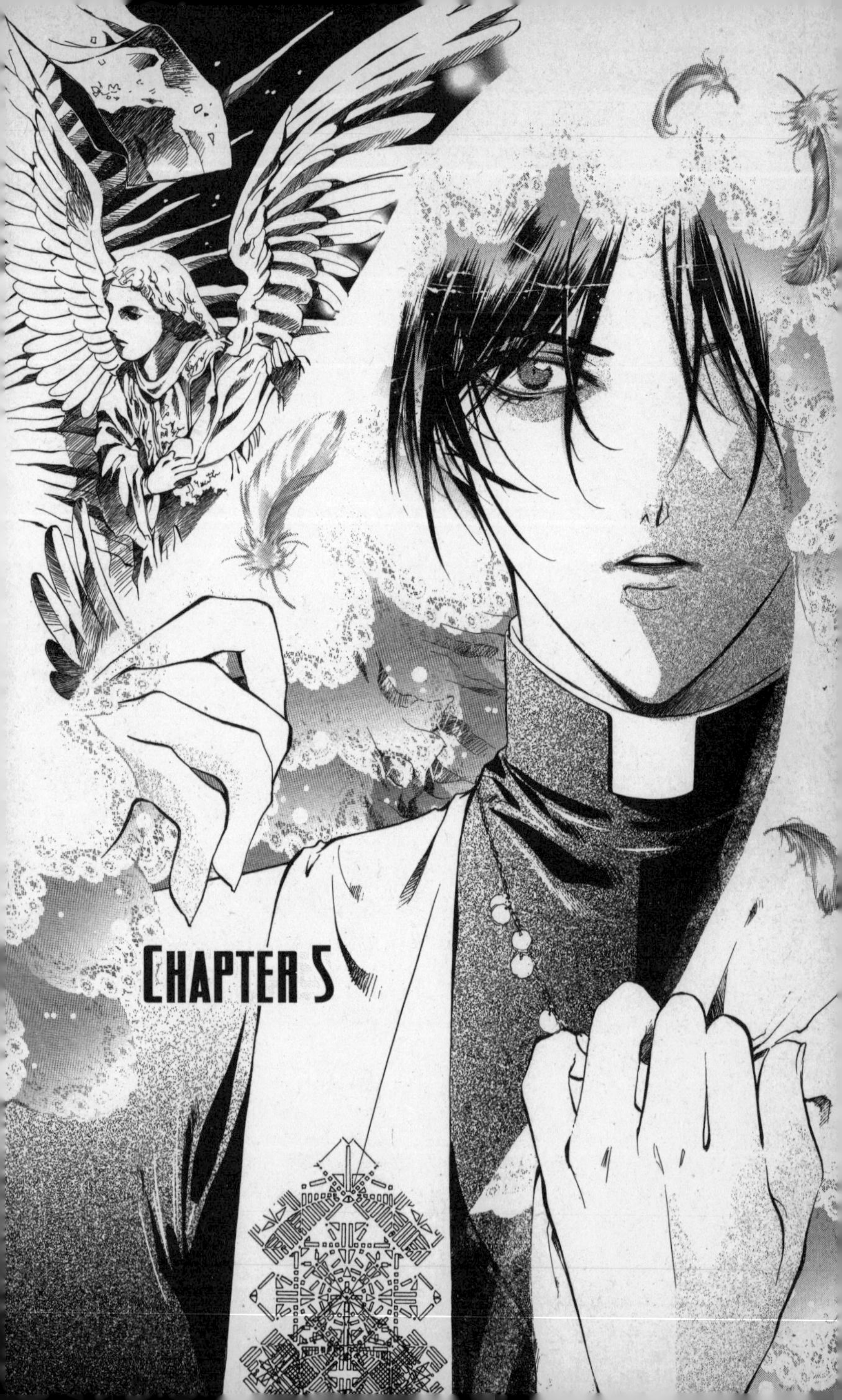
CHAPTER 5

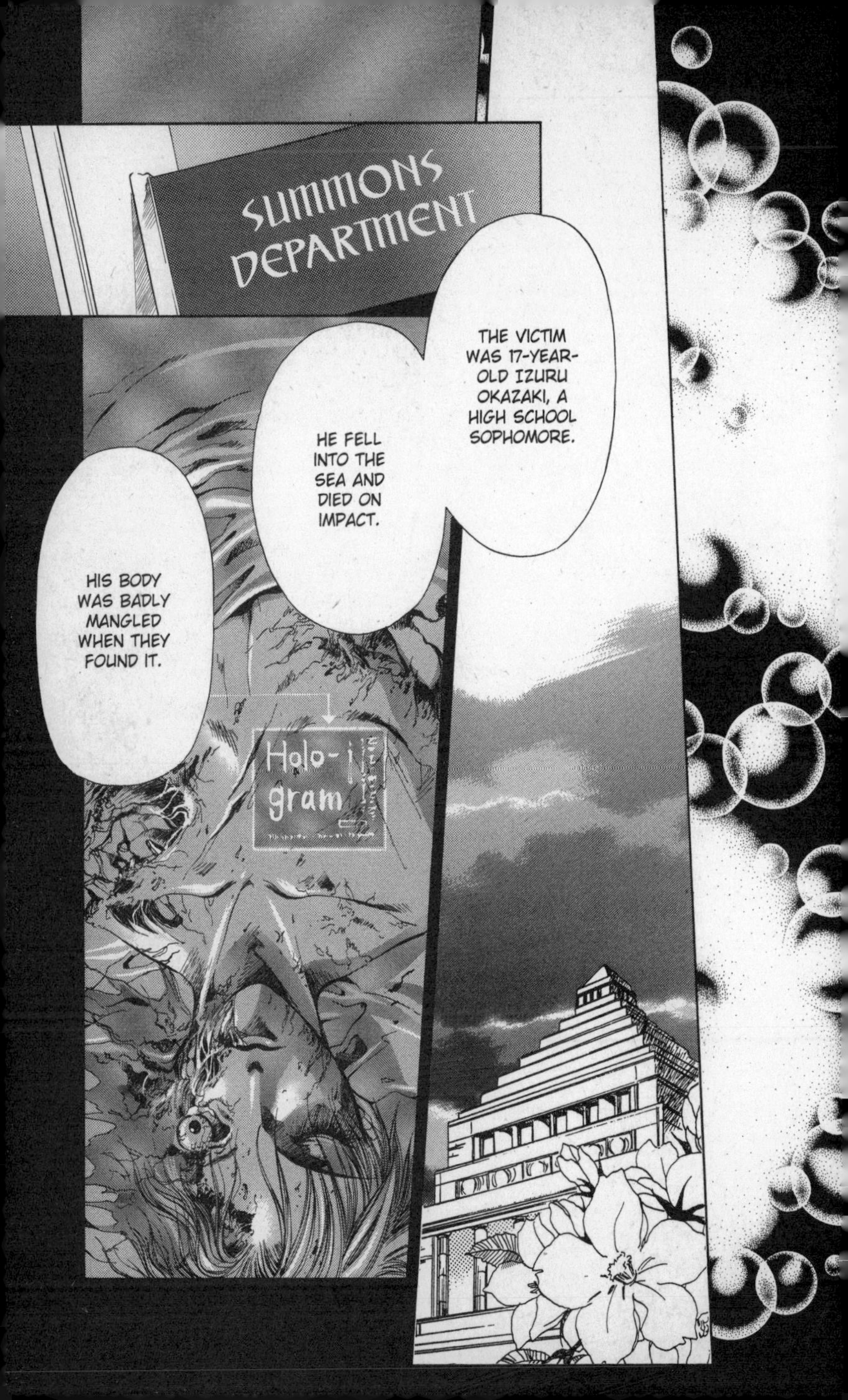
SUMMONS DEPARTMENT
THE VICTIM WAS 17-YEAR-OLD IZURU OKAZAKI, A HIGH SCHOOL SOPHOMORE.
HE FELL INTO THE SEA AND DIED ON IMPACT.
HIS BODY WAS BADLY MANGLED WHEN THEY FOUND IT.
Holo-gram

THE FISHERMAN WHO DISCOVERED HIS CORPSE SAID THAT IT WAS BLOATED AND WATERLOGGED. FISH HAD BEEN NIBBLING AT IT, AND THE SKIN HAD TURNED TO SLIME.

...
Yeck...

HUH? IS SOMETHING WRONG?

I-IT'S NOTHING. PROCEED, TATSUMI.

blink

MYSTERIES?

THE POLICE HAVE BEEN DILIGENTLY INVESTIGATING THE CASE, BUT IT'S PLAGUED WITH MYSTERIES.

THEY DON'T EVEN HAVE A SUSPECT YET.

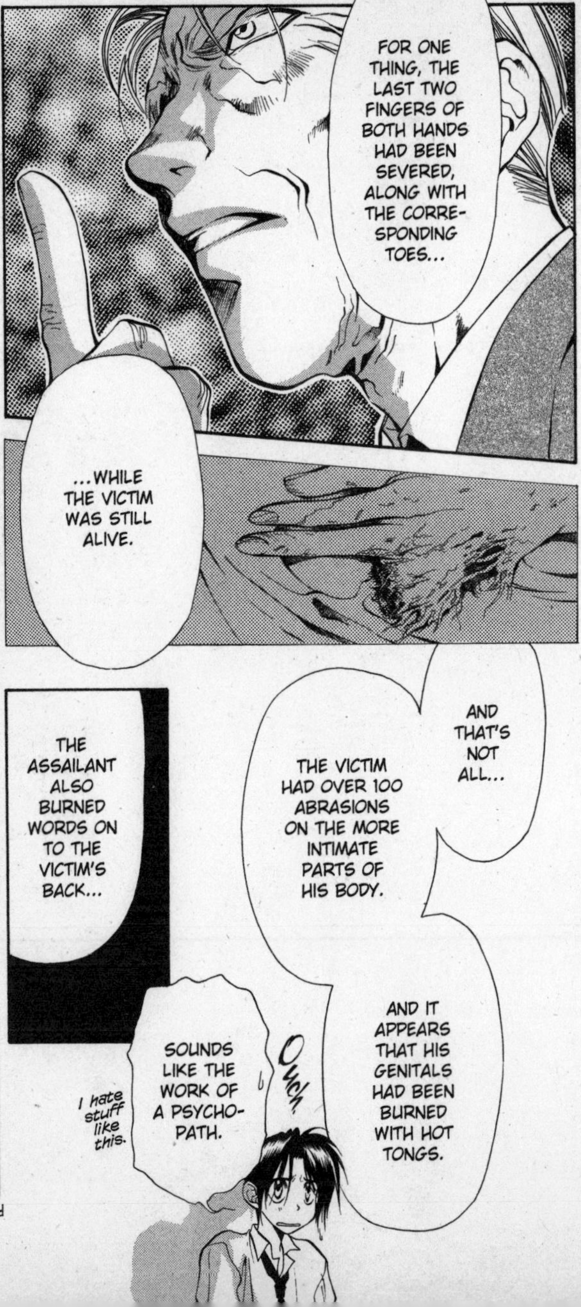
FOR ONE THING, THE LAST TWO FINGERS OF BOTH HANDS HAD BEEN SEVERED, ALONG WITH THE CORRESPONDING TOES...
...WHILE THE VICTIM WAS STILL ALIVE.
AND THAT'S NOT ALL...
THE VICTIM HAD OVER 100 ABRASIONS ON THE MORE INTIMATE PARTS OF HIS BODY.
AND IT APPEARS THAT HIS GENITALS HAD BEEN BURNED WITH HOT TONGS.
THE ASSAILANT ALSO BURNED WORDS ON TO THE VICTIM'S BACK...
Ouch.
SOUNDS LIKE THE WORK OF A PSYCHOPATH.
I hate stuff like this.

Yeah... it's hard.

That's right. This story has finally made it into graphic novel form. This could be bad, couldn't it? I bet there are a lot of readers saying "I'll never read Descendants of Darkness again!" (Ha!) Well, I don't care. There are plenty of manga in the world, so go read something else. I just draw what I want to draw! If you don't like it, then don't read it. You can never please everybody. I do it the way I want. (Sorry if I sound arrogant.) Now I'm going to explain something.

The Name of the Rose

This is the name of a book by Umberto Eco. It's a murder mystery set in a monastery (I think). I saw the film adaptation on TV a while back, so I don't really remember. I think Sean Connery was in it. I know there were these two fat gay monks that were kind of lame.

Homosexuality is permitted in Buddhism. What a strange religion...

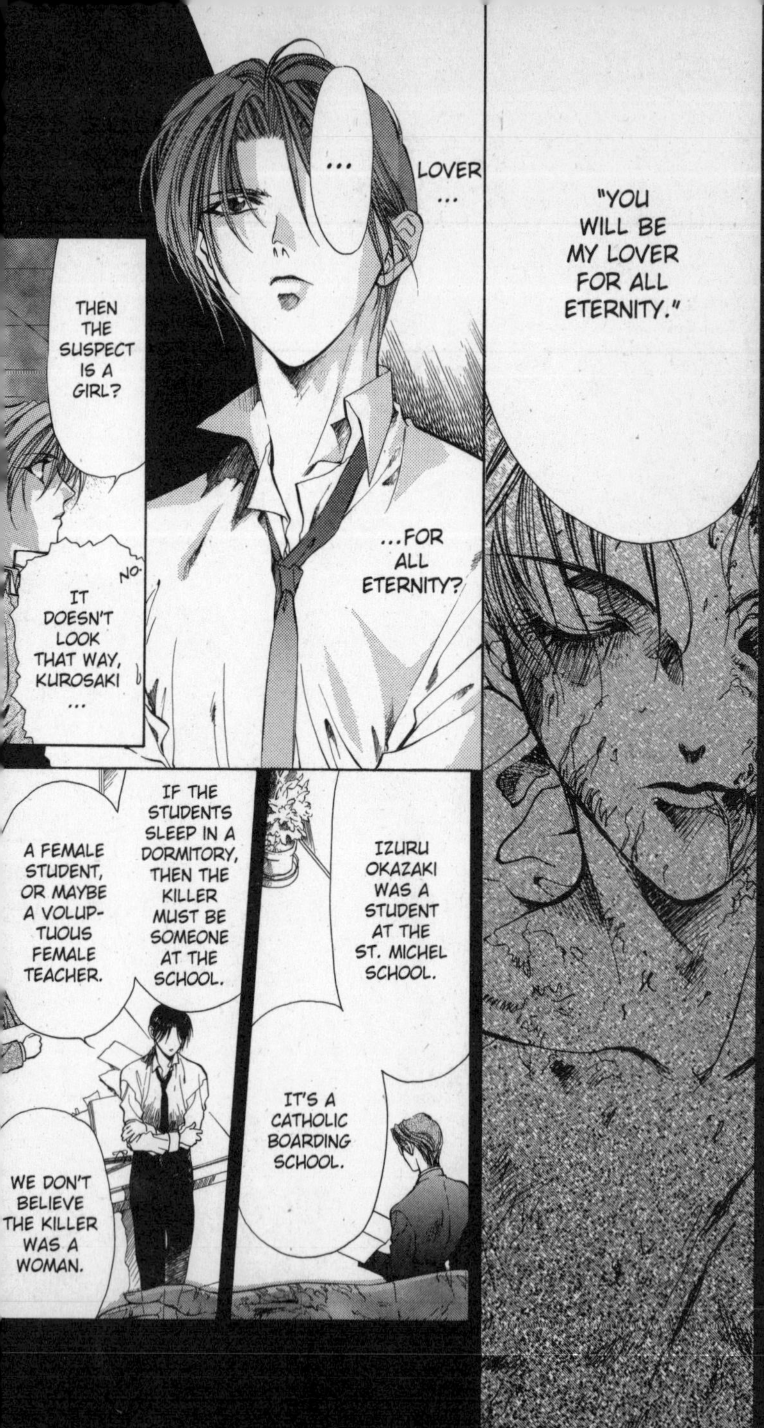
"YOU WILL BE MY LOVER FOR ALL ETERNITY."
... LOVER ...
...FOR ALL ETERNITY?
THEN THE SUSPECT IS A GIRL?
NO.
IT DOESN'T LOOK THAT WAY, KUROSAKI ...
IZURU OKAZAKI WAS A STUDENT AT THE ST. MICHEL SCHOOL.
IT'S A CATHOLIC BOARDING SCHOOL.
IF THE STUDENTS SLEEP IN A DORMITORY, THEN THE KILLER MUST BE SOMEONE AT THE SCHOOL.
A FEMALE STUDENT, OR MAYBE A VOLUP-TUOUS FEMALE TEACHER.
WE DON'T BELIEVE THE KILLER WAS A WOMAN.

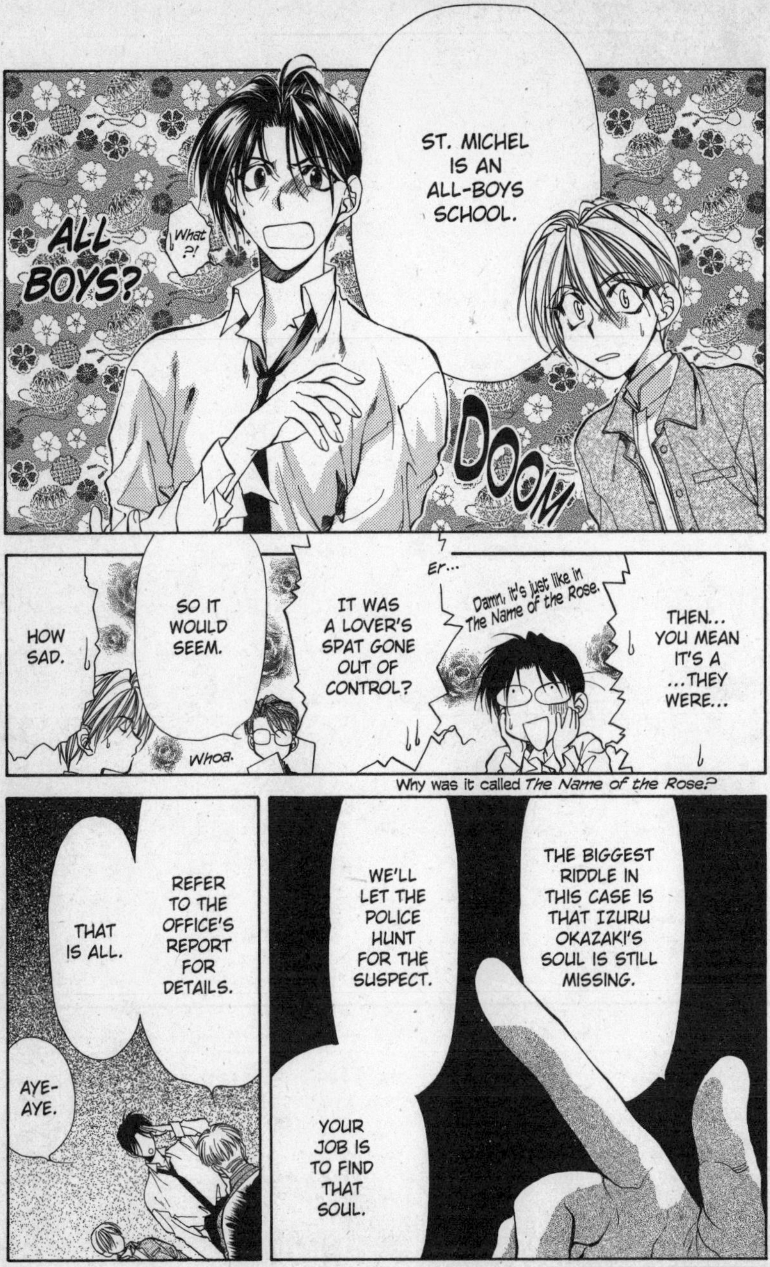
ST. MICHEL IS AN ALL-BOYS SCHOOL.
DOOM
What ?!
ALL BOYS?
THEN... YOU MEAN IT'S A ...THEY WERE...
Damn, it's just like in The Name of the Rose.
Er...
IT WAS A LOVER'S SPAT GONE OUT OF CONTROL?
SO IT WOULD SEEM.
Whoa.
HOW SAD.
Why was it called *The Name of the Rose?*
THE BIGGEST RIDDLE IN THIS CASE IS THAT IZURU OKAZAKI'S SOUL IS STILL MISSING.
WE'LL LET THE POLICE HUNT FOR THE SUSPECT.
YOUR JOB IS TO FIND THAT SOUL.
REFER TO THE OFFICE'S REPORT FOR DETAILS.
THAT IS ALL.
AYE-AYE.

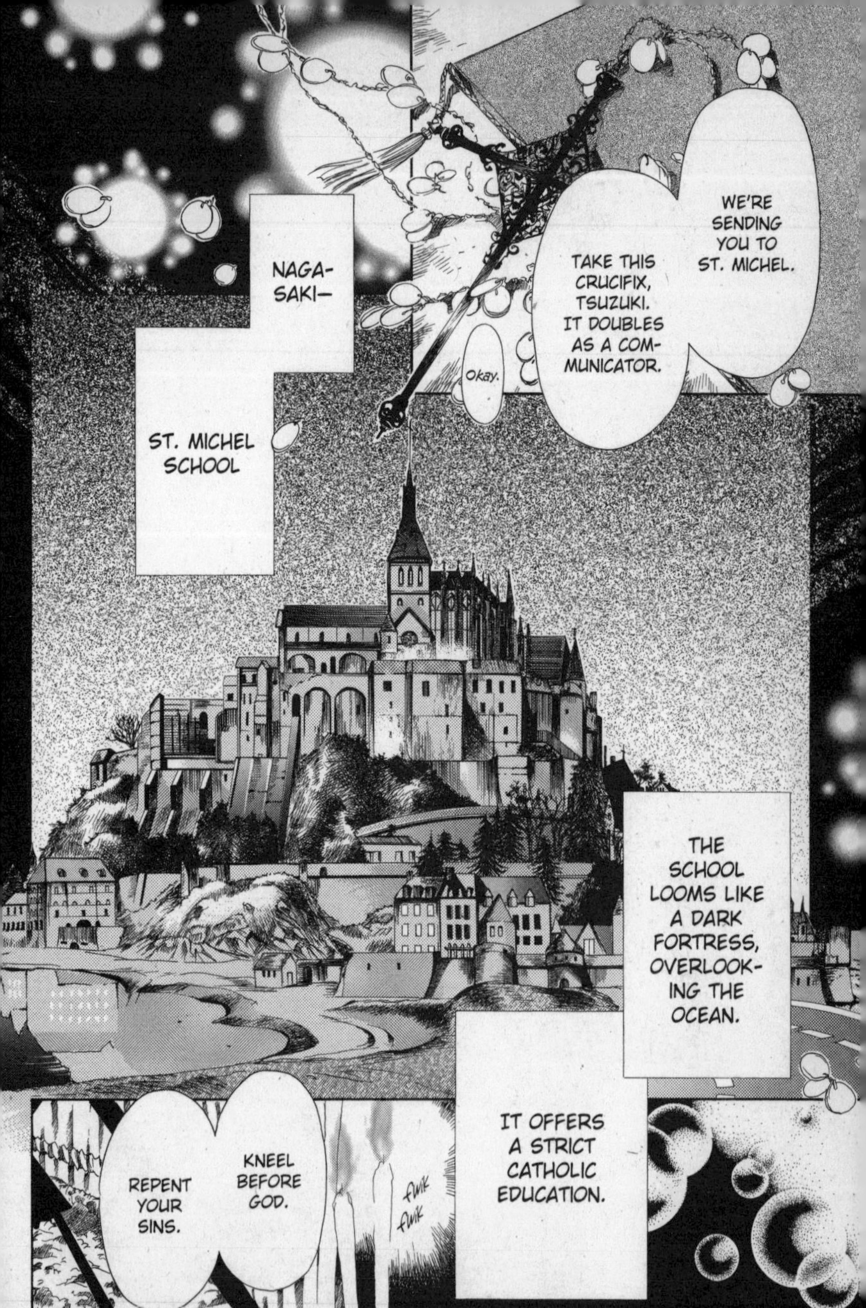
WE'RE SENDING YOU TO ST. MICHEL.
TAKE THIS CRUCIFIX, TSUZUKI. IT DOUBLES AS A COM-MUNICATOR.
Okay.
NAGA-SAKI—
ST. MICHEL SCHOOL
THE SCHOOL LOOMS LIKE A DARK FORTRESS, OVERLOOK-ING THE OCEAN.
IT OFFERS A STRICT CATHOLIC EDUCATION.
fwik fwik
KNEEL BEFORE GOD.
REPENT YOUR SINS.

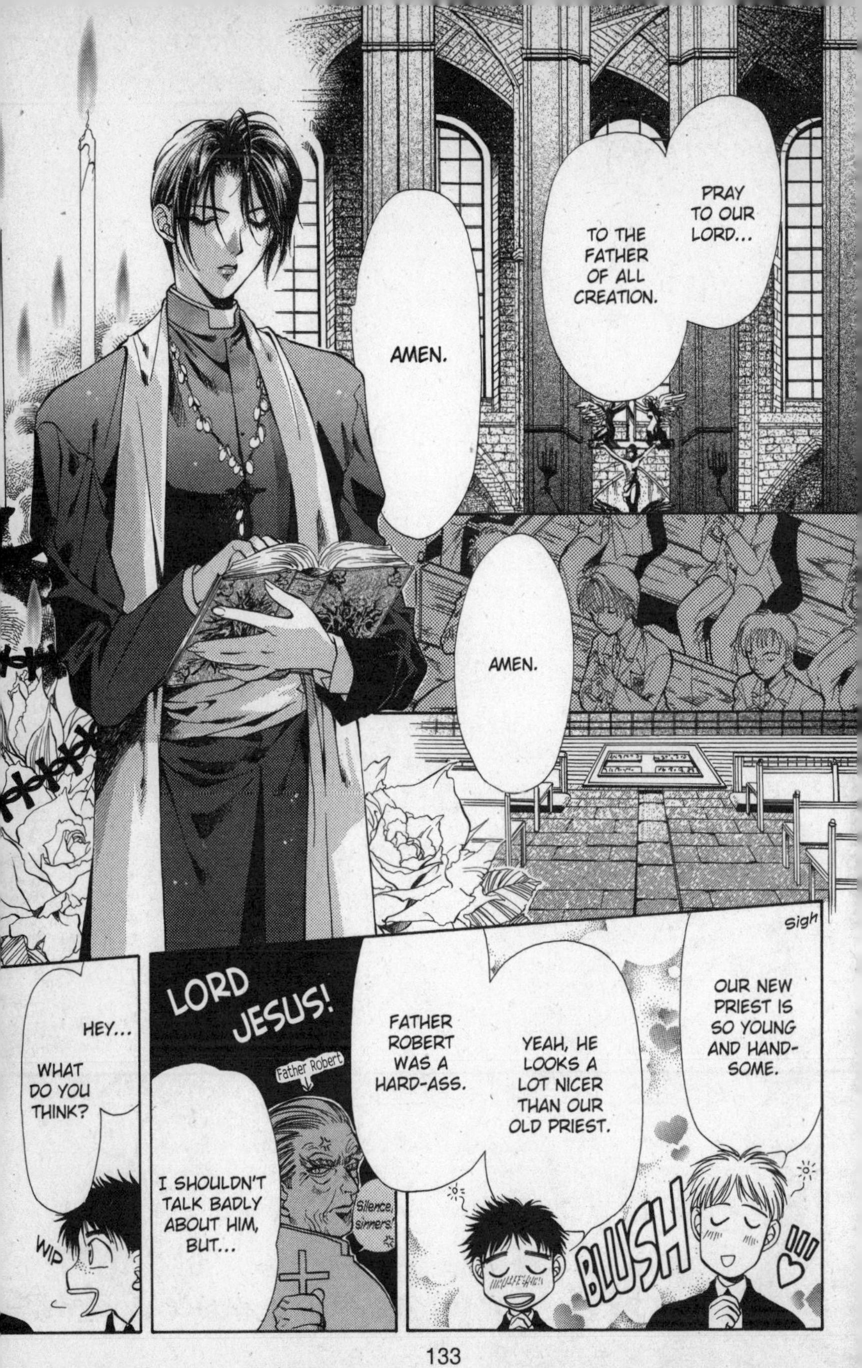

PRAY TO OUR LORD...
TO THE FATHER OF ALL CREATION.
AMEN.
AMEN.
Sigh
OUR NEW PRIEST IS SO YOUNG AND HAND-SOME.
YEAH, HE LOOKS A LOT NICER THAN OUR OLD PRIEST.
BLUSH
FATHER ROBERT WAS A HARD-ASS.
LORD JESUS!
Father Robert
Silence, sinners!
I SHOULDN'T TALK BADLY ABOUT HIM, BUT...
HEY...
WHAT DO YOU THINK?
WIP

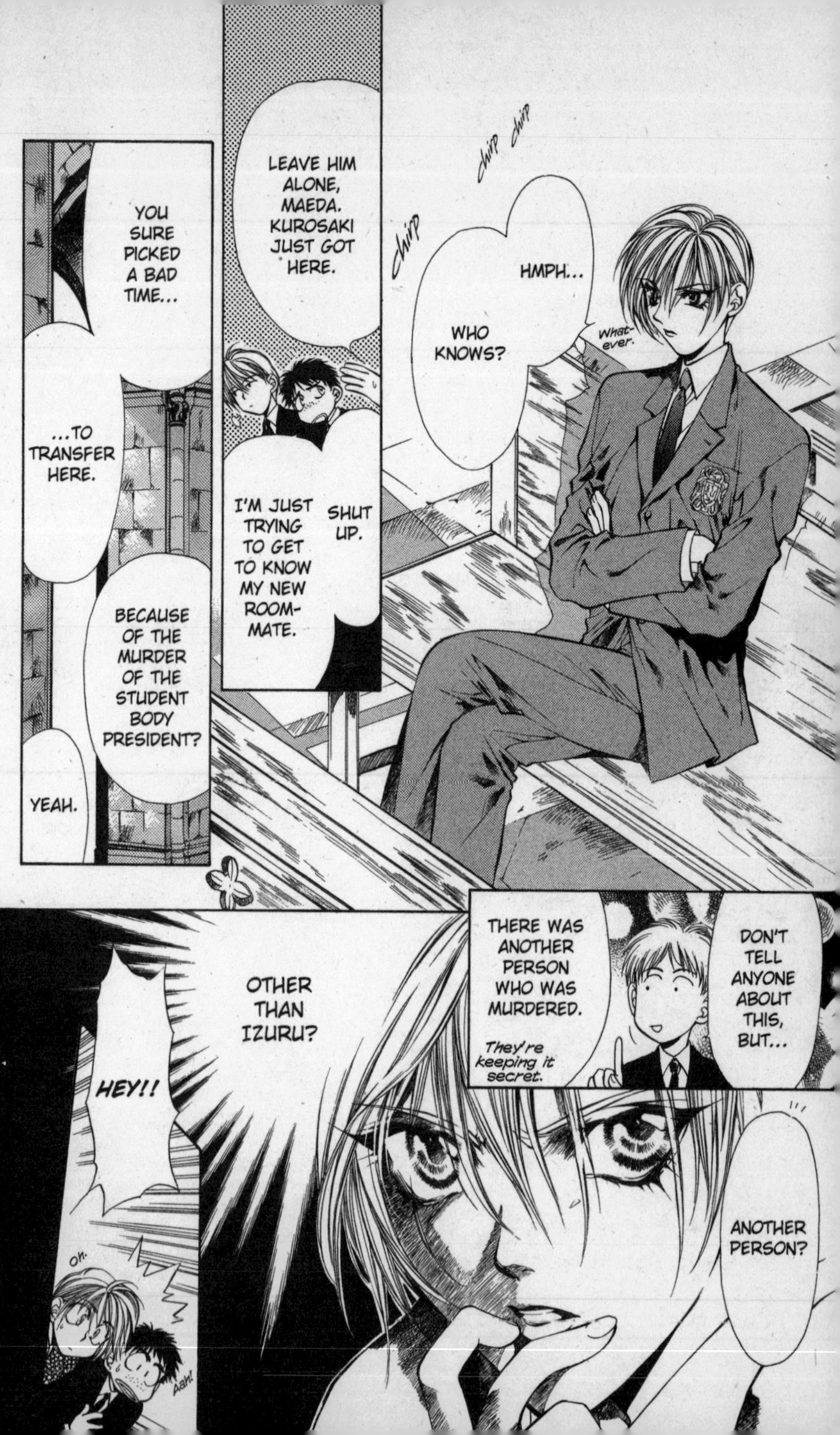
chirp chirp
chirp
HMPH...
WHO KNOWS?
What-ever.
LEAVE HIM ALONE, MAEDA. KUROSAKI JUST GOT HERE.
SHUT UP.
I'M JUST TRYING TO GET TO KNOW MY NEW ROOM-MATE.
YOU SURE PICKED A BAD TIME...
...TO TRANSFER HERE.
BECAUSE OF THE MURDER OF THE STUDENT BODY PRESIDENT?
YEAH.
DON'T TELL ANYONE ABOUT THIS, BUT...
THERE WAS ANOTHER PERSON WHO WAS MURDERED.
They're keeping it secret.
ANOTHER PERSON?
OTHER THAN IZURU?
HEY!!
Oh.
Aah!

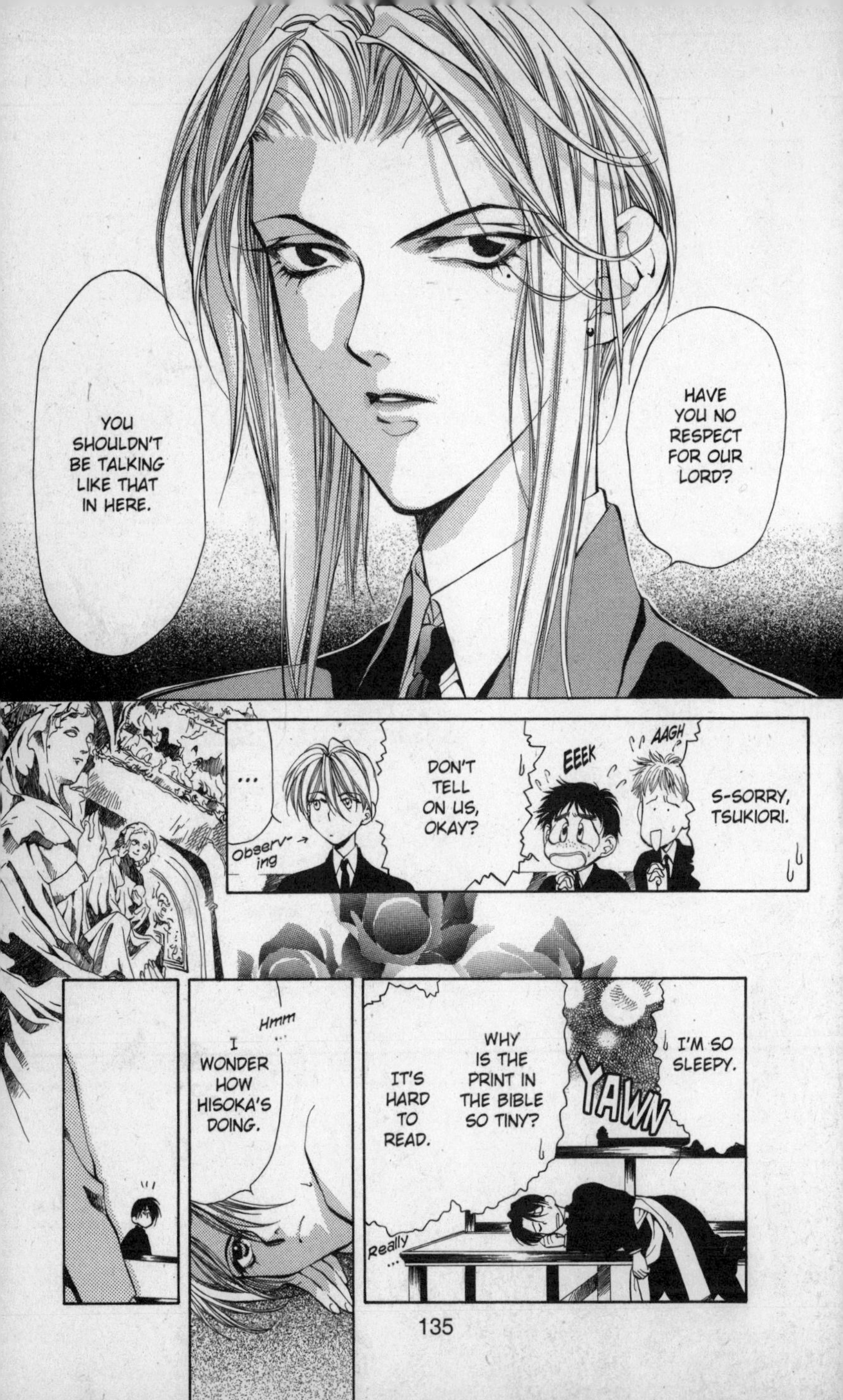
HAVE YOU NO RESPECT FOR OUR LORD?
YOU SHOULDN'T BE TALKING LIKE THAT IN HERE.
AAGH
EEEK
S-SORRY, TSUKIORI.
DON'T TELL ON US, OKAY?
...
Observing
I'M SO SLEEPY.
YAWN
WHY IS THE PRINT IN THE BIBLE SO TINY?
IT'S HARD TO READ.
Really...
Hmm...
I WONDER HOW HISOKA'S DOING.

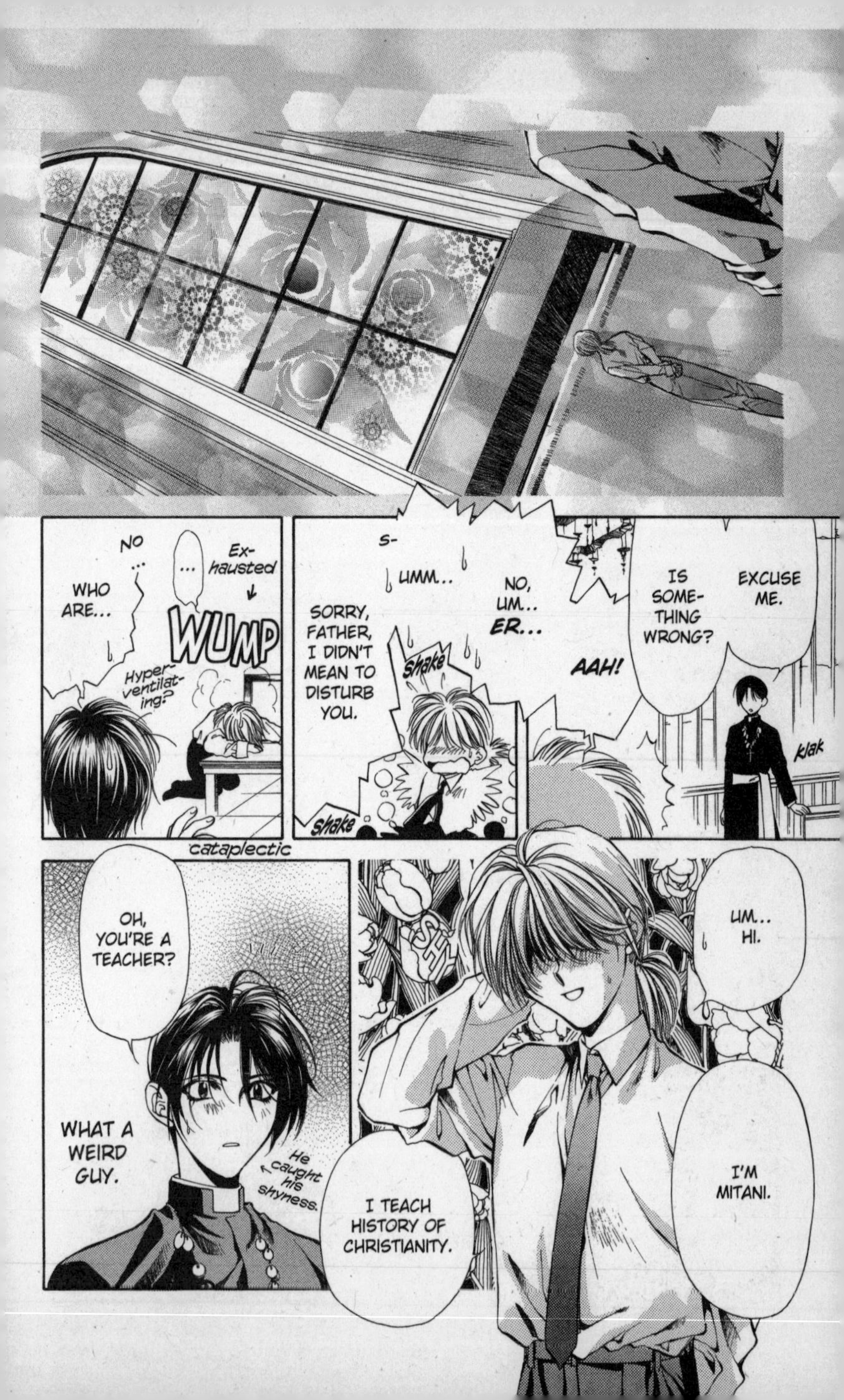
EXCUSE ME.
IS SOMETHING WRONG?
klak
AAH!
S-
UMM...
NO, UM... ER...
SORRY, FATHER, I DIDN'T MEAN TO DISTURB YOU.
Shake
shake
Ex-hausted
WUMP
...
NO ...
WHO ARE...
Hyper-ventilating?
cataplectic
UM... HI.
I'M MITANI.
I TEACH HISTORY OF CHRISTIANITY.
OH, YOU'RE A TEACHER?
WHAT A WEIRD GUY.
He caught his shyness.

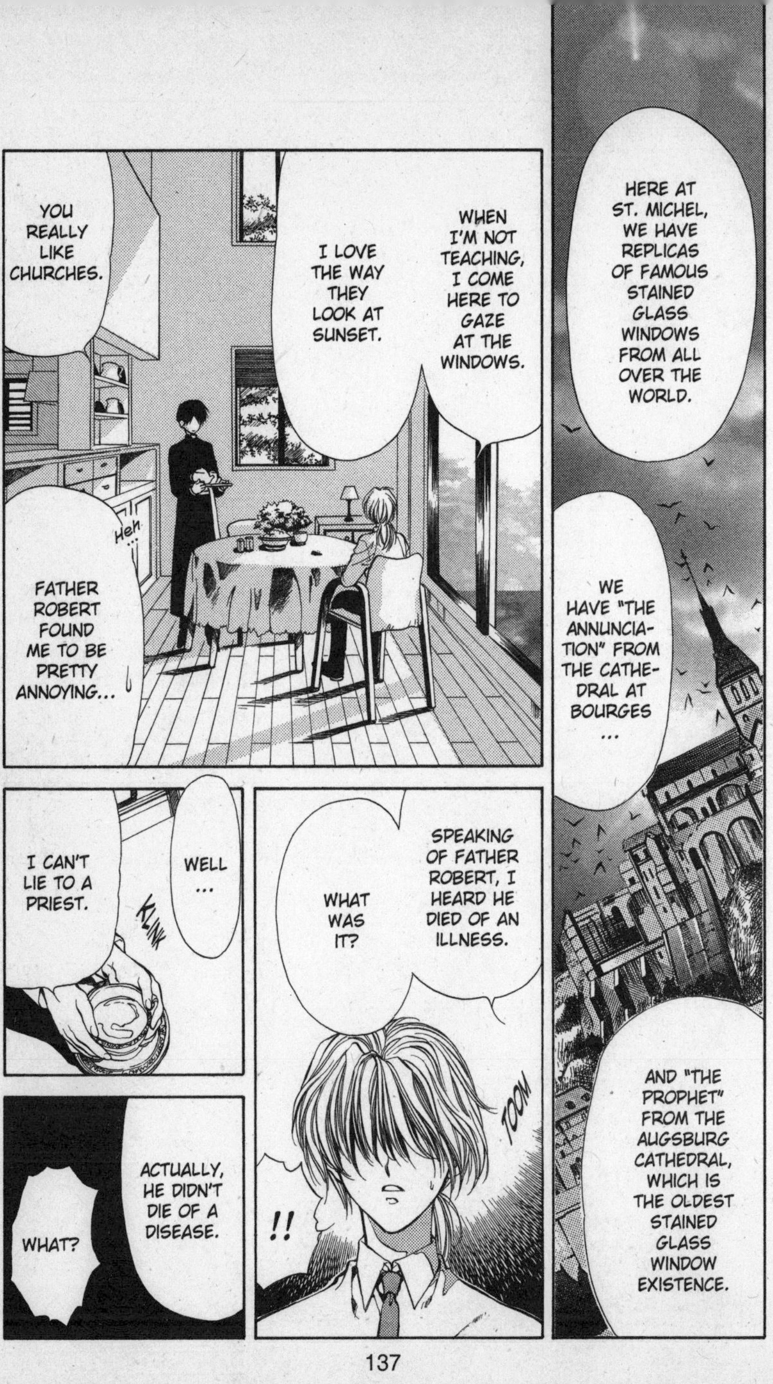
HERE AT ST. MICHEL, WE HAVE REPLICAS OF FAMOUS STAINED GLASS WINDOWS FROM ALL OVER THE WORLD.
WE HAVE "THE ANNUNCIATION" FROM THE CATHEDRAL AT BOURGES ...
AND "THE PROPHET" FROM THE AUGSBURG CATHEDRAL, WHICH IS THE OLDEST STAINED GLASS WINDOW EXISTENCE.
WHEN I'M NOT TEACHING, I COME HERE TO GAZE AT THE WINDOWS.
I LOVE THE WAY THEY LOOK AT SUNSET.
YOU REALLY LIKE CHURCHES.
Heh ...
FATHER ROBERT FOUND ME TO BE PRETTY ANNOYING...
SPEAKING OF FATHER ROBERT, I HEARD HE DIED OF AN ILLNESS.
WHAT WAS IT?
TOOM
!!
WELL ...
I CAN'T LIE TO A PRIEST.
KLINK
ACTUALLY, HE DIDN'T DIE OF A DISEASE.
WHAT?

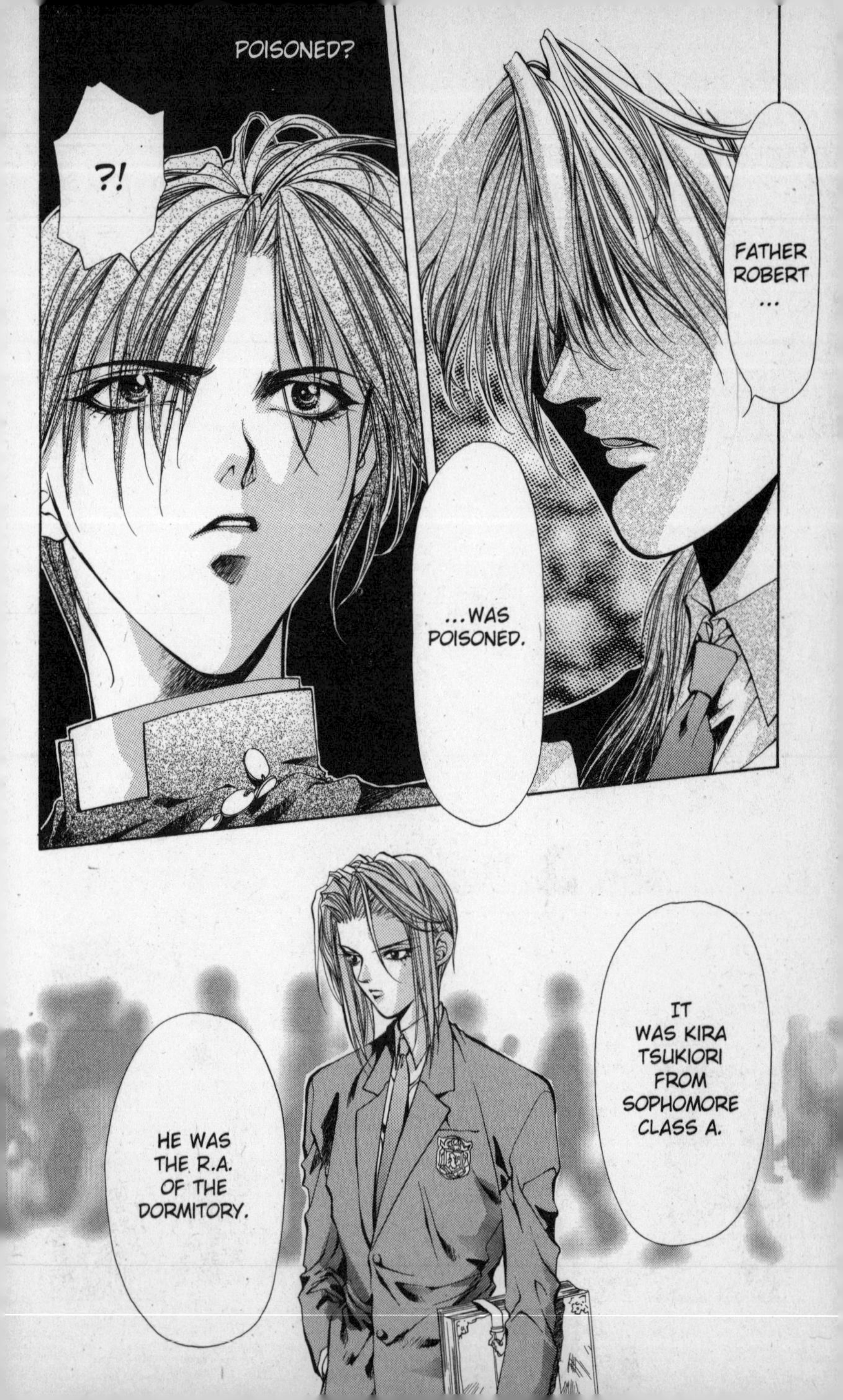
FATHER ROBERT ...
...WAS POISONED.
POISONED?
?!
IT WAS KIRA TSUKIORI FROM SOPHOMORE CLASS A.
HE WAS THE R.A. OF THE DORMITORY.

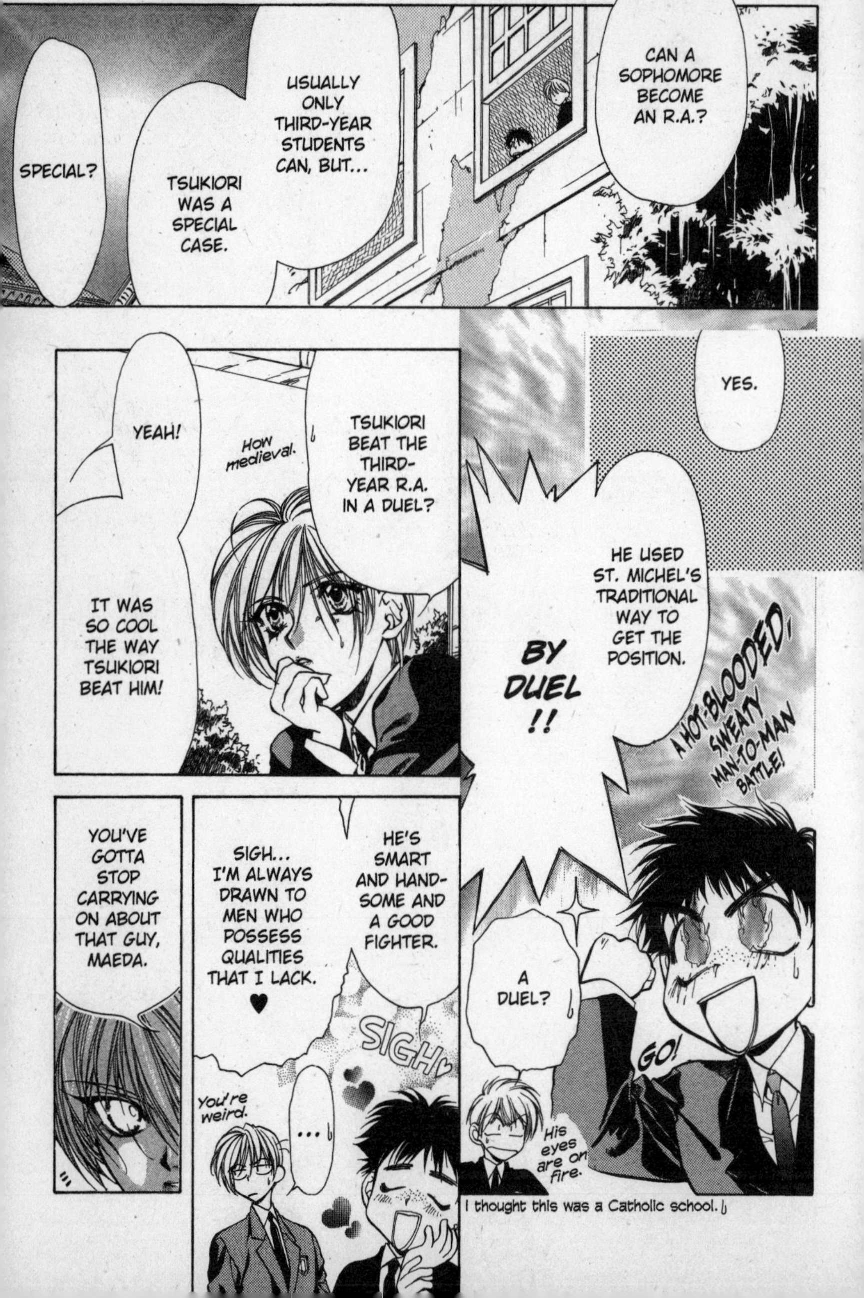

CAN A SOPHOMORE BECOME AN R.A.?
USUALLY ONLY THIRD-YEAR STUDENTS CAN, BUT...
TSUKIORI WAS A SPECIAL CASE.
SPECIAL?
YES.
HE USED ST. MICHEL'S TRADITIONAL WAY TO GET THE POSITION.
BY DUEL !!
A HOT-BLOODED, SWEATY MAN-TO-MAN BATTLE!
A DUEL?
GO!
His eyes are on fire.
I thought this was a Catholic school.
TSUKIORI BEAT THE THIRD-YEAR R.A. IN A DUEL?
How medieval.
YEAH!
IT WAS SO COOL THE WAY TSUKIORI BEAT HIM!
HE'S SMART AND HANDSOME AND A GOOD FIGHTER.
SIGH... I'M ALWAYS DRAWN TO MEN WHO POSSESS QUALITIES THAT I LACK. ♥
SIGH♥
...
You're weird.
YOU'VE GOTTA STOP CARRYING ON ABOUT THAT GUY, MAEDA.

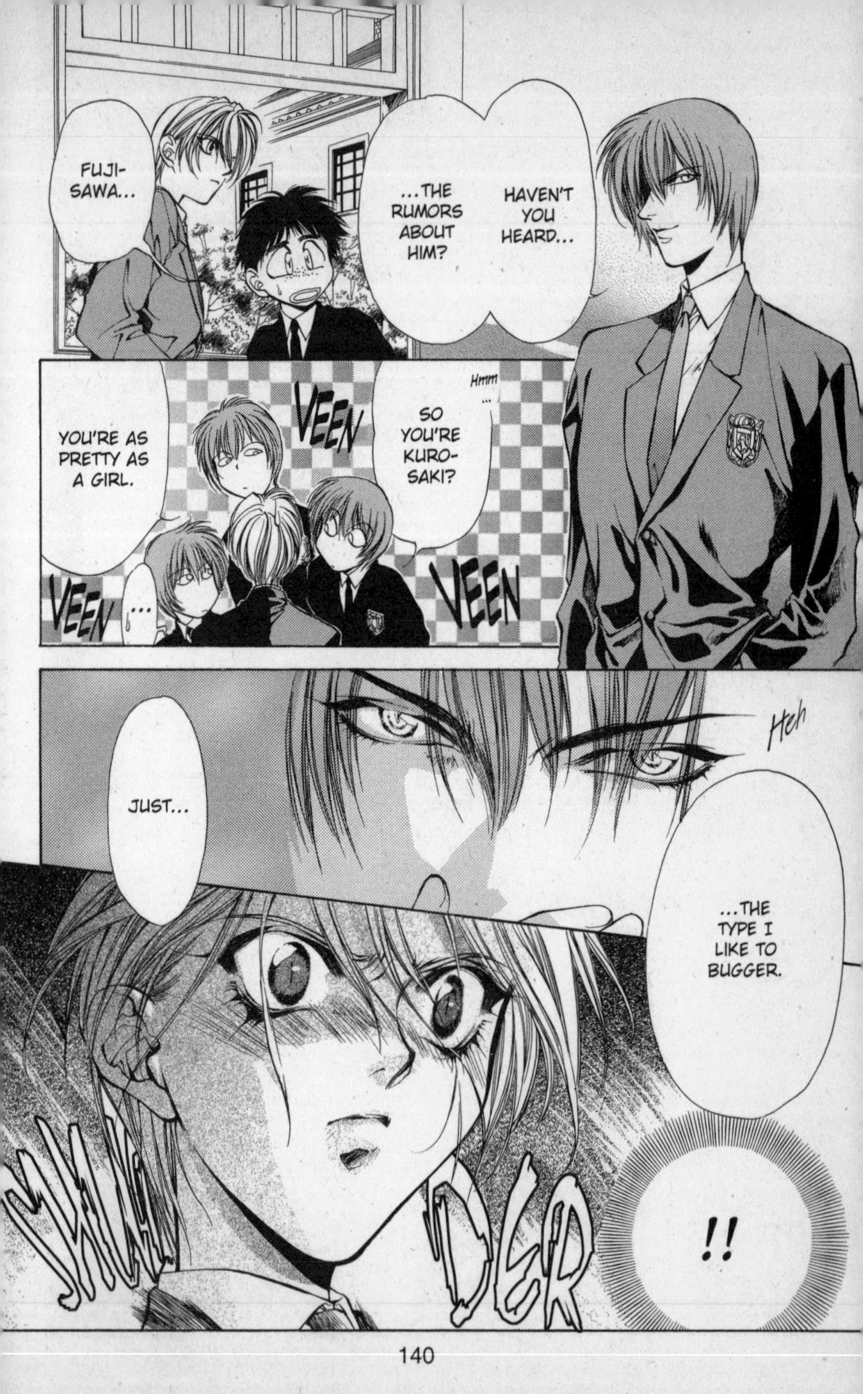
HAVEN'T YOU HEARD...
...THE RUMORS ABOUT HIM?
FUJI-SAWA...
Hmm ...
SO YOU'RE KURO-SAKI?
VEEN
VEEN
VEEN
YOU'RE AS PRETTY AS A GIRL.
...
Heh
JUST...
...THE TYPE I LIKE TO BUGGER.
!!
SHUDDER

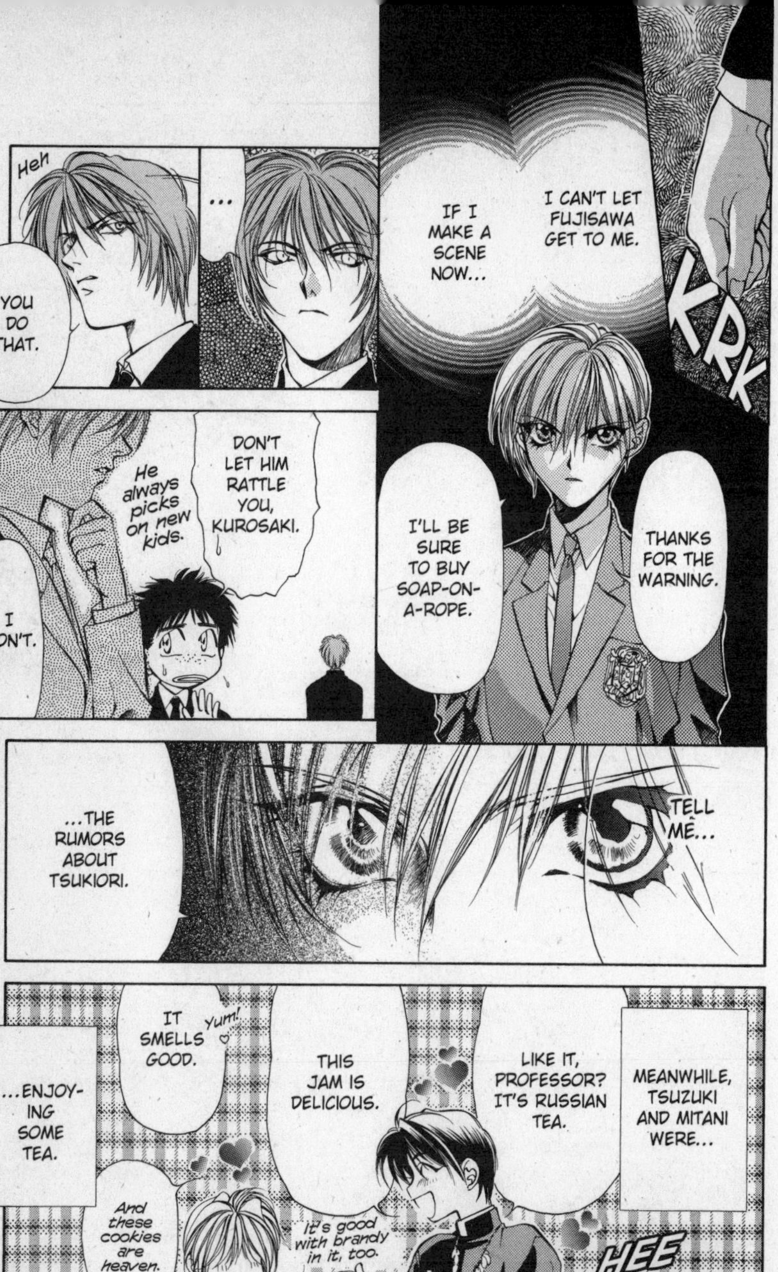
KRK
I CAN'T LET FUJISAWA GET TO ME.
IF I MAKE A SCENE NOW...
THANKS FOR THE WARNING.
I'LL BE SURE TO BUY SOAP-ON-A-ROPE.
...
Heh
YOU DO THAT.
DON'T LET HIM RATTLE YOU, KUROSAKI.
He always picks on new kids.
I WON'T.
TELL ME...
...THE RUMORS ABOUT TSUKIORI.
MEANWHILE, TSUZUKI AND MITANI WERE...
LIKE IT, PROFESSOR? IT'S RUSSIAN TEA.
It's good with brandy in it, too.
HEE HEE
THIS JAM IS DELICIOUS.
IT SMELLS GOOD.
Yum!
And these cookies are heaven.
...ENJOY-ING SOME TEA.

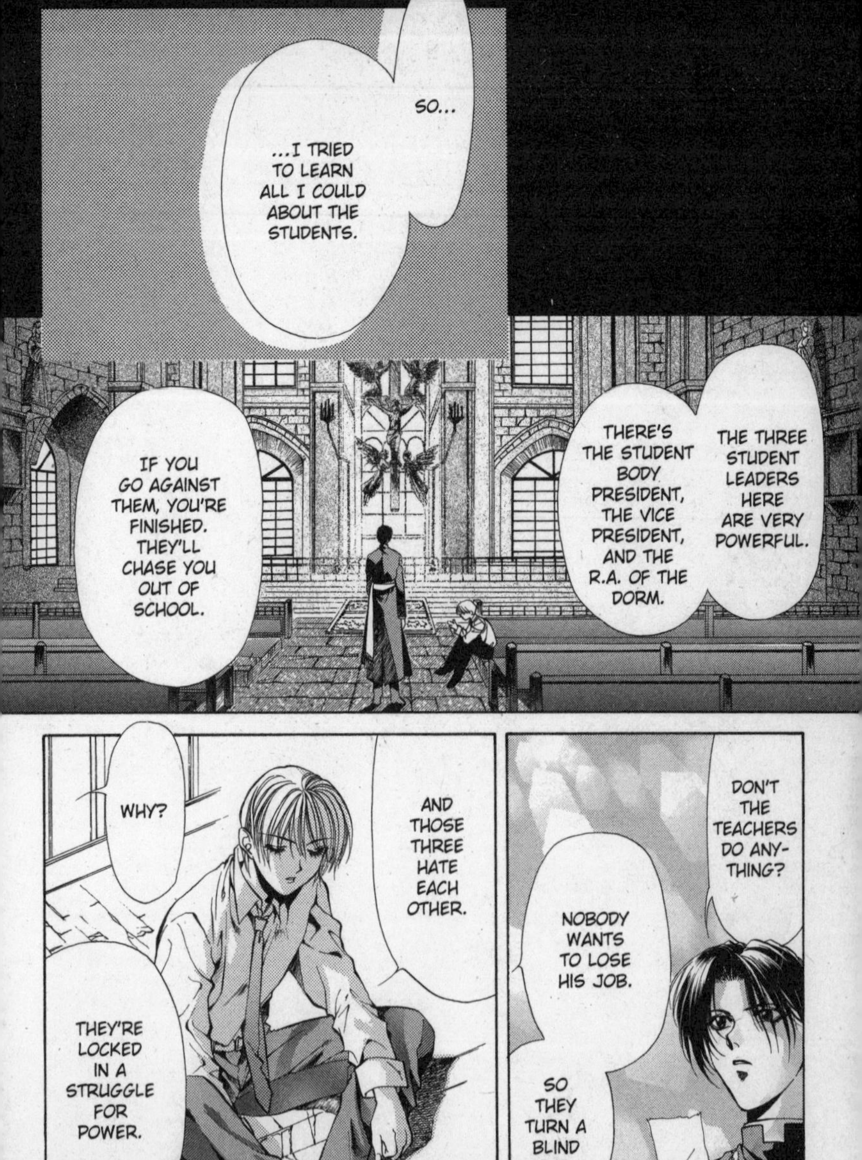
SO...
...I TRIED TO LEARN ALL I COULD ABOUT THE STUDENTS.
THE THREE STUDENT LEADERS HERE ARE VERY POWERFUL.
THERE'S THE STUDENT BODY PRESIDENT, THE VICE PRESIDENT, AND THE R.A. OF THE DORM.
IF YOU GO AGAINST THEM, YOU'RE FINISHED. THEY'LL CHASE YOU OUT OF SCHOOL.
DON'T THE TEACHERS DO ANY-THING?
NOBODY WANTS TO LOSE HIS JOB.
SO THEY TURN A BLIND EYE.
AND THOSE THREE HATE EACH OTHER.
WHY?
THEY'RE LOCKED IN A STRUGGLE FOR POWER.

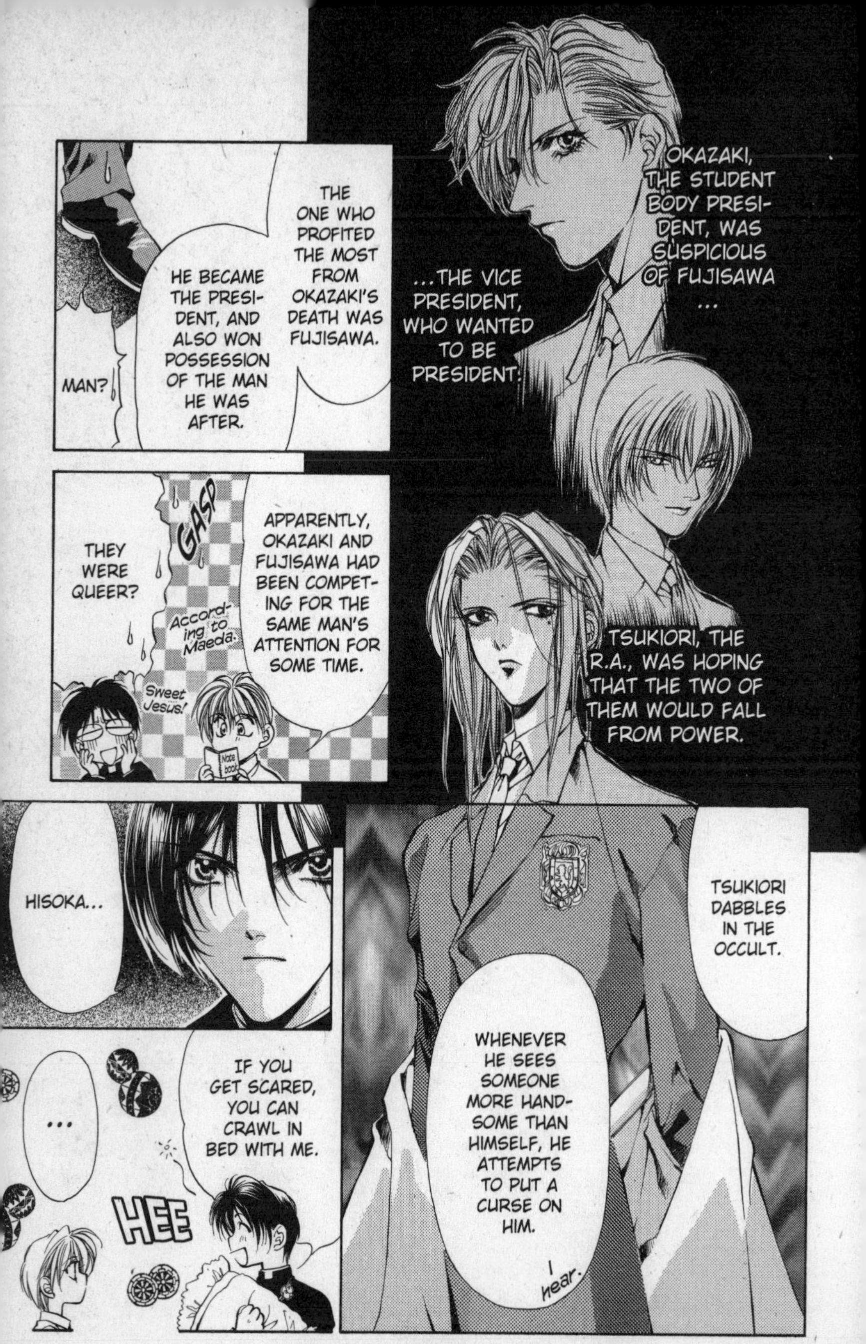
OKAZAKI, THE STUDENT BODY PRESI-DENT, WAS SUSPICIOUS OF FUJISAWA ...
...THE VICE PRESIDENT, WHO WANTED TO BE PRESIDENT.
TSUKIORI, THE R.A., WAS HOPING THAT THE TWO OF THEM WOULD FALL FROM POWER.
THE ONE WHO PROFITED THE MOST FROM OKAZAKI'S DEATH WAS FUJISAWA.
HE BECAME THE PRESI-DENT, AND ALSO WON POSSESSION OF THE MAN HE WAS AFTER.
MAN?
APPARENTLY, OKAZAKI AND FUJISAWA HAD BEEN COMPET-ING FOR THE SAME MAN'S ATTENTION FOR SOME TIME.
GASP
THEY WERE QUEER?
According to Maeda.
Sweet Jesus!
Note book
TSUKIORI DABBLES IN THE OCCULT.
WHENEVER HE SEES SOMEONE MORE HAND-SOME THAN HIMSELF, HE ATTEMPTS TO PUT A CURSE ON HIM.
I hear.
HISOKA...
IF YOU GET SCARED, YOU CAN CRAWL IN BED WITH ME.
...
HEE

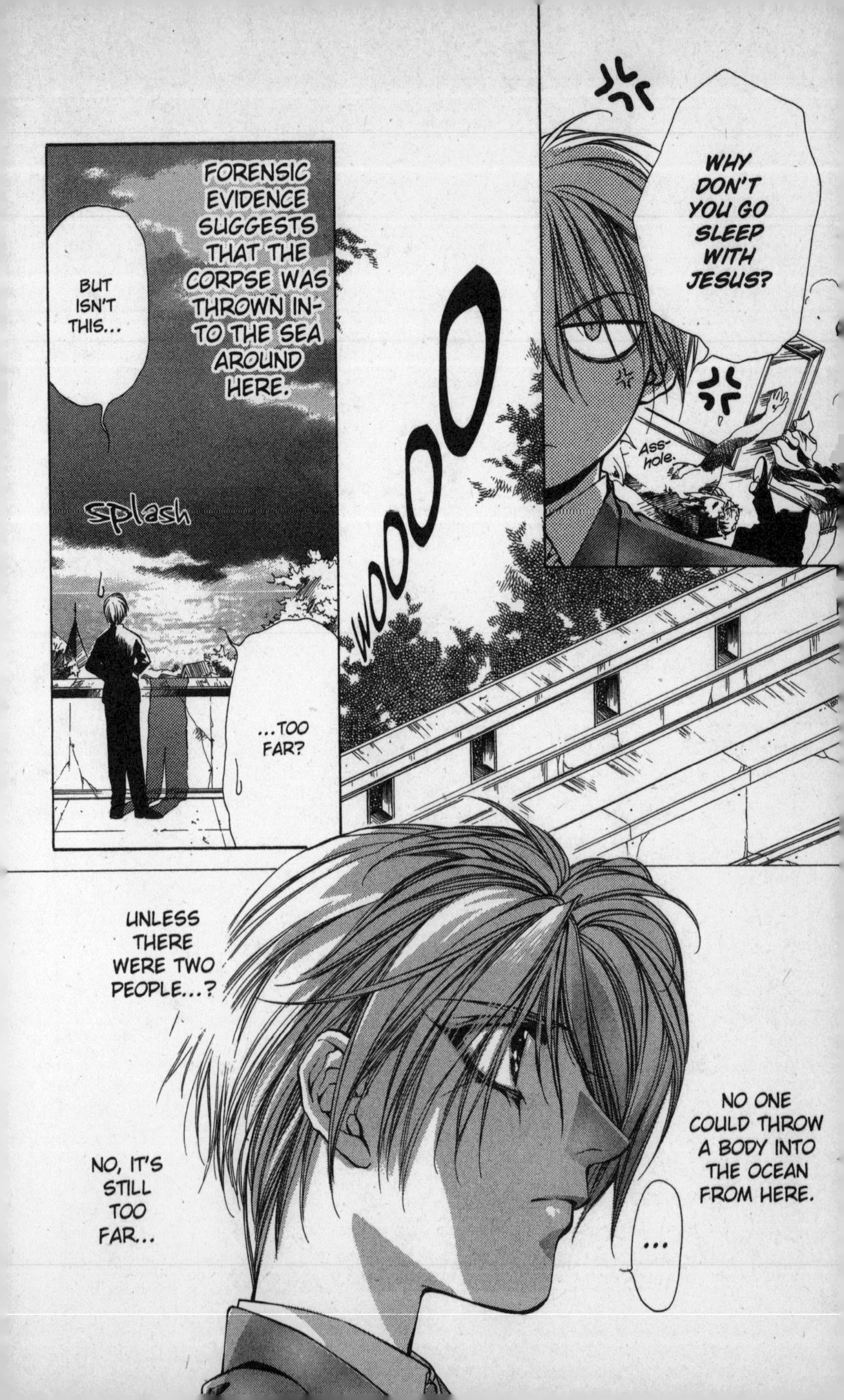
WHY DON'T YOU GO SLEEP WITH JESUS?
Ass-hole.
WOOOOO
FORENSIC EVIDENCE SUGGESTS THAT THE CORPSE WAS THROWN IN-TO THE SEA AROUND HERE.
BUT ISN'T THIS...
splash
...TOO FAR?
NO ONE COULD THROW A BODY INTO THE OCEAN FROM HERE.
...
UNLESS THERE WERE TWO PEOPLE...?
NO, IT'S STILL TOO FAR...

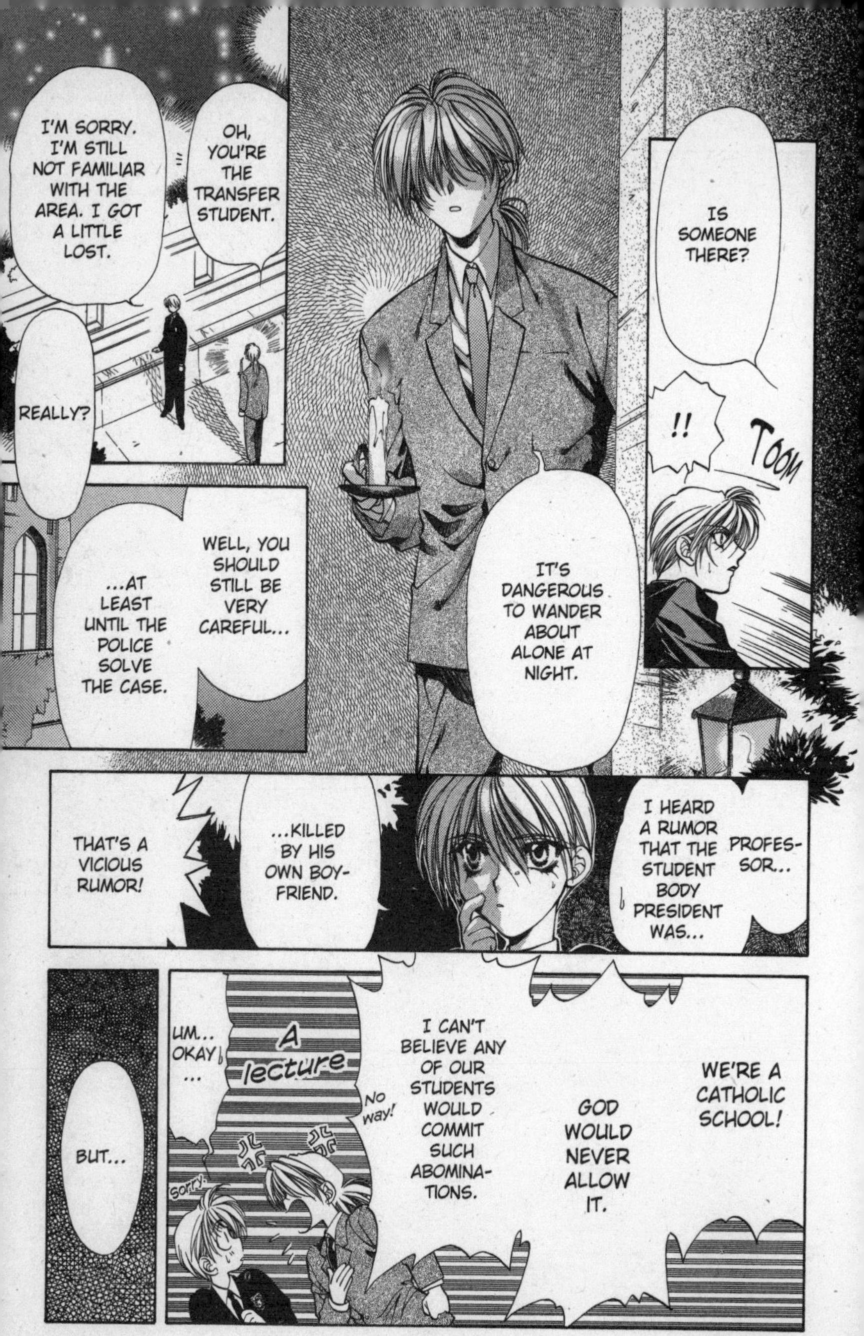
IS SOMEONE THERE?
!!
TOOM
IT'S DANGEROUS TO WANDER ABOUT ALONE AT NIGHT.
OH, YOU'RE THE TRANSFER STUDENT.
I'M SORRY. I'M STILL NOT FAMILIAR WITH THE AREA. I GOT A LITTLE LOST.
REALLY?
WELL, YOU SHOULD STILL BE VERY CAREFUL...
...AT LEAST UNTIL THE POLICE SOLVE THE CASE.
PROFES-SOR...
I HEARD A RUMOR THAT THE STUDENT BODY PRESIDENT WAS...
...KILLED BY HIS OWN BOY-FRIEND.
THAT'S A VICIOUS RUMOR!
WE'RE A CATHOLIC SCHOOL!
GOD WOULD NEVER ALLOW IT.
I CAN'T BELIEVE ANY OF OUR STUDENTS WOULD COMMIT SUCH ABOMINA-TIONS.
No way!
A lecture
UM... OKAY ...
Sorry.
BUT...

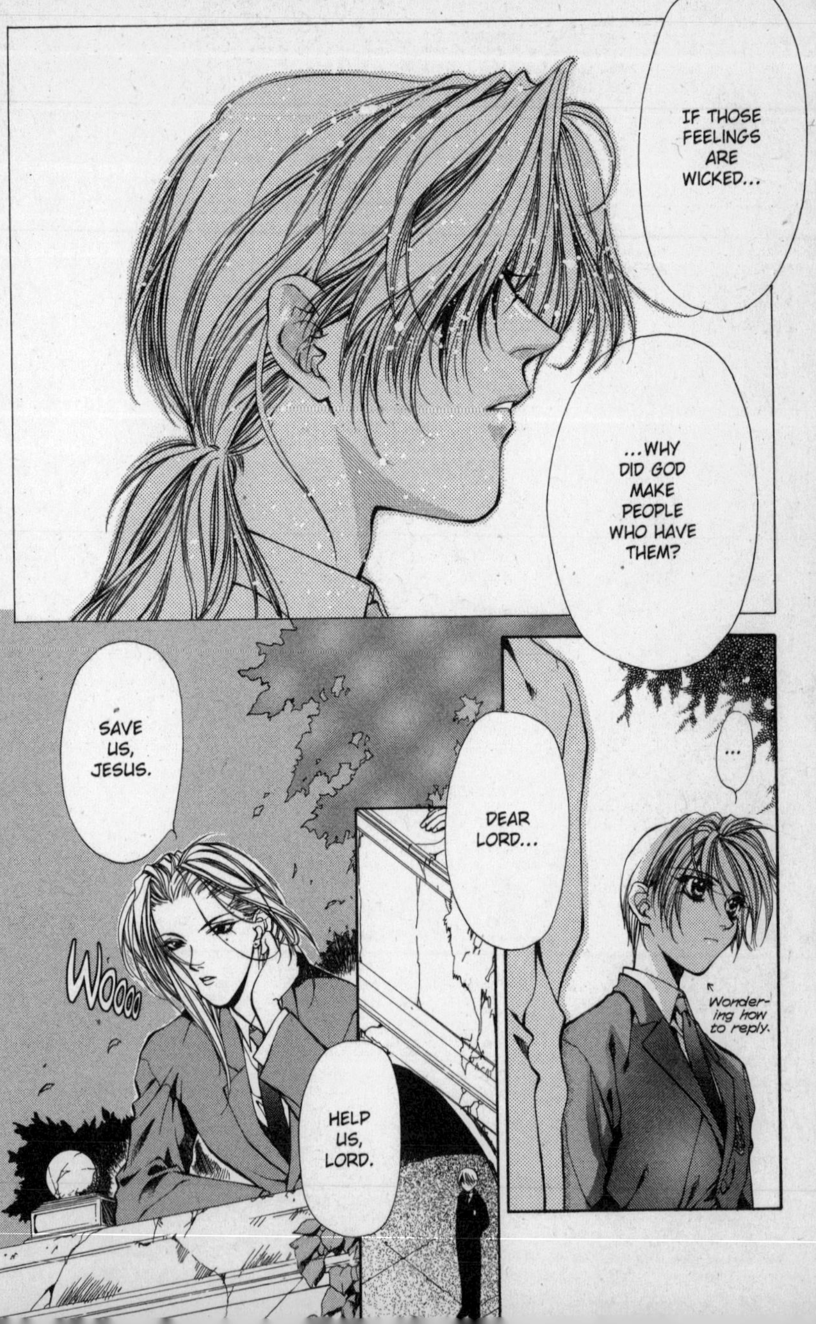
IF THOSE FEELINGS ARE WICKED...
...WHY DID GOD MAKE PEOPLE WHO HAVE THEM?
...
Wondering how to reply.
DEAR LORD...
SAVE US, JESUS.
WOOOO
HELP US, LORD.

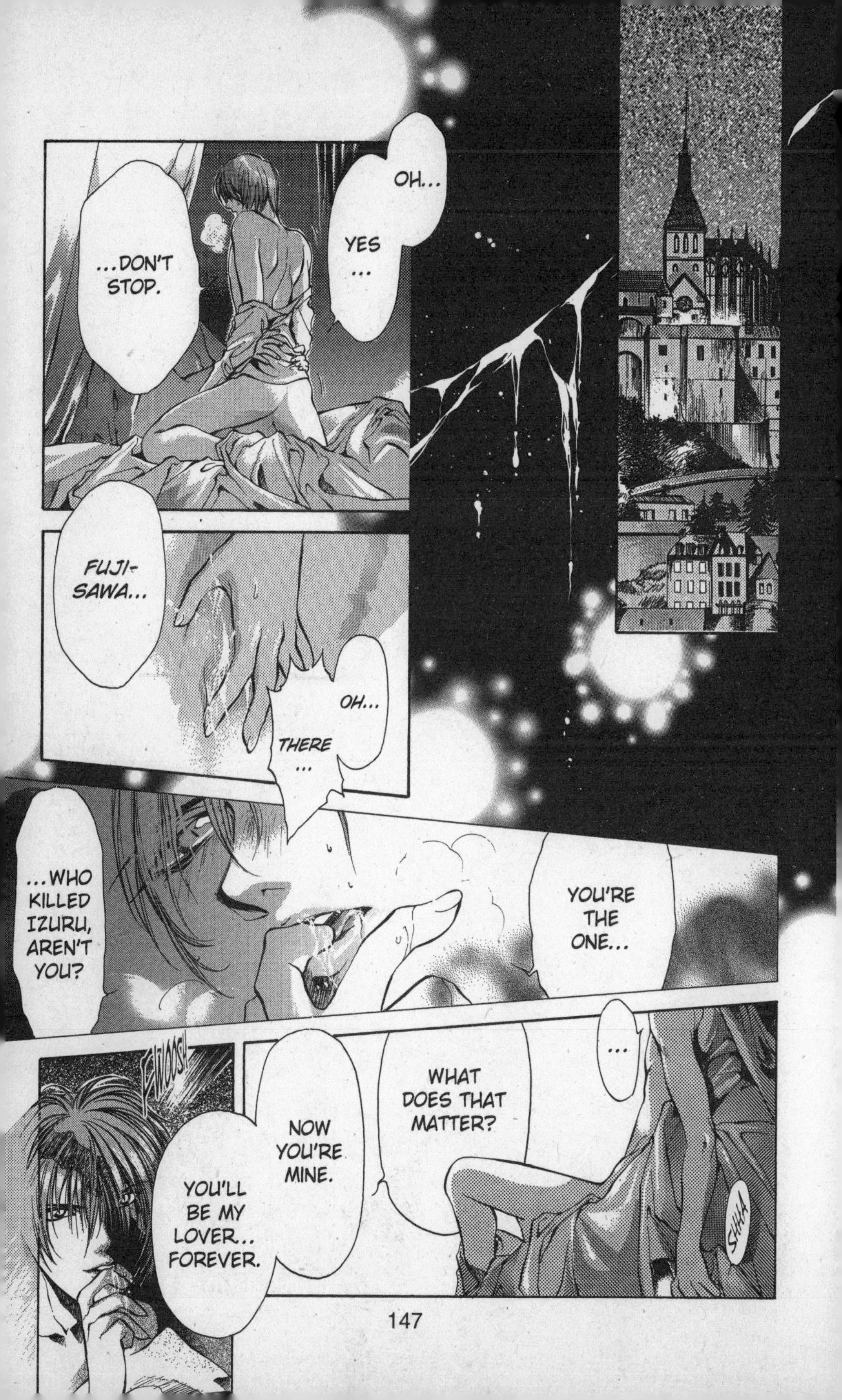
OH... YES...
...DON'T STOP.
OH... THERE...
FUJI-SAWA...
YOU'RE THE ONE...
...WHO KILLED IZURU, AREN'T YOU?
...
WHAT DOES THAT MATTER?
SHHA
NOW YOU'RE MINE.
YOU'LL BE MY LOVER... FOREVER.
FWOOSH

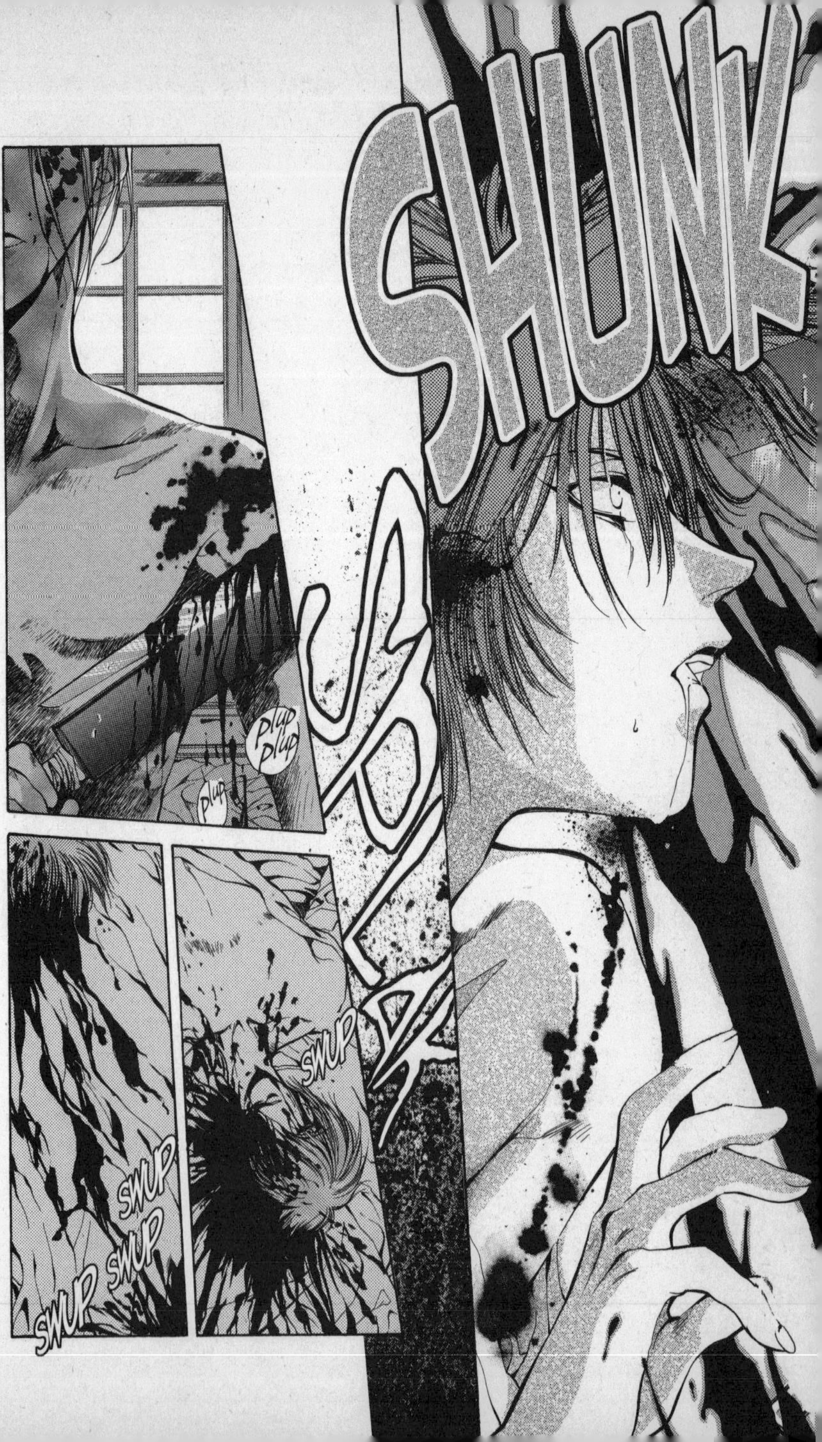
SHUNK
plup plup
plup
SWUP
SWUP
SWUP
SWUP

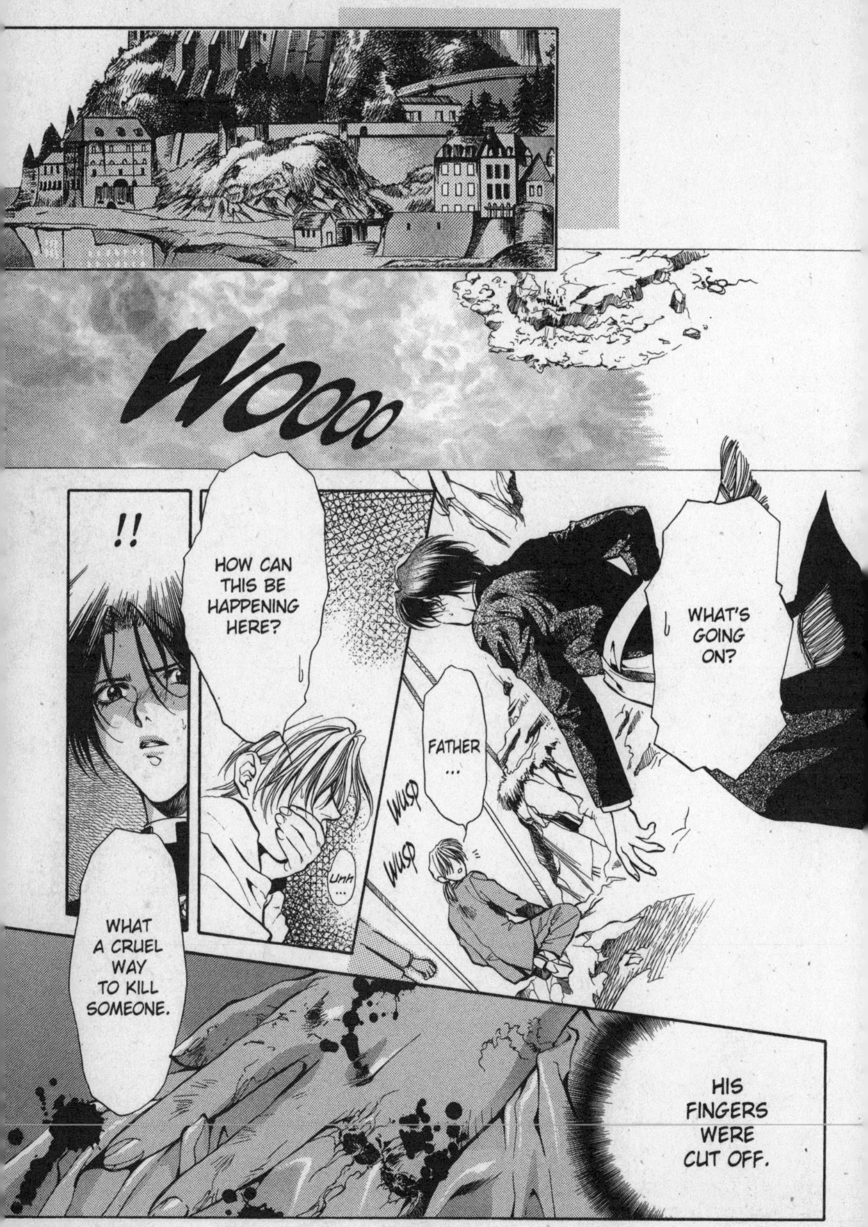
WOOOO
WHAT'S GOING ON?
FATHER...
WUSP
WUSP
HOW CAN THIS BE HAPPENING HERE?
Unh...
!!
WHAT A CRUEL WAY TO KILL SOMEONE.
HIS FINGERS WERE CUT OFF.

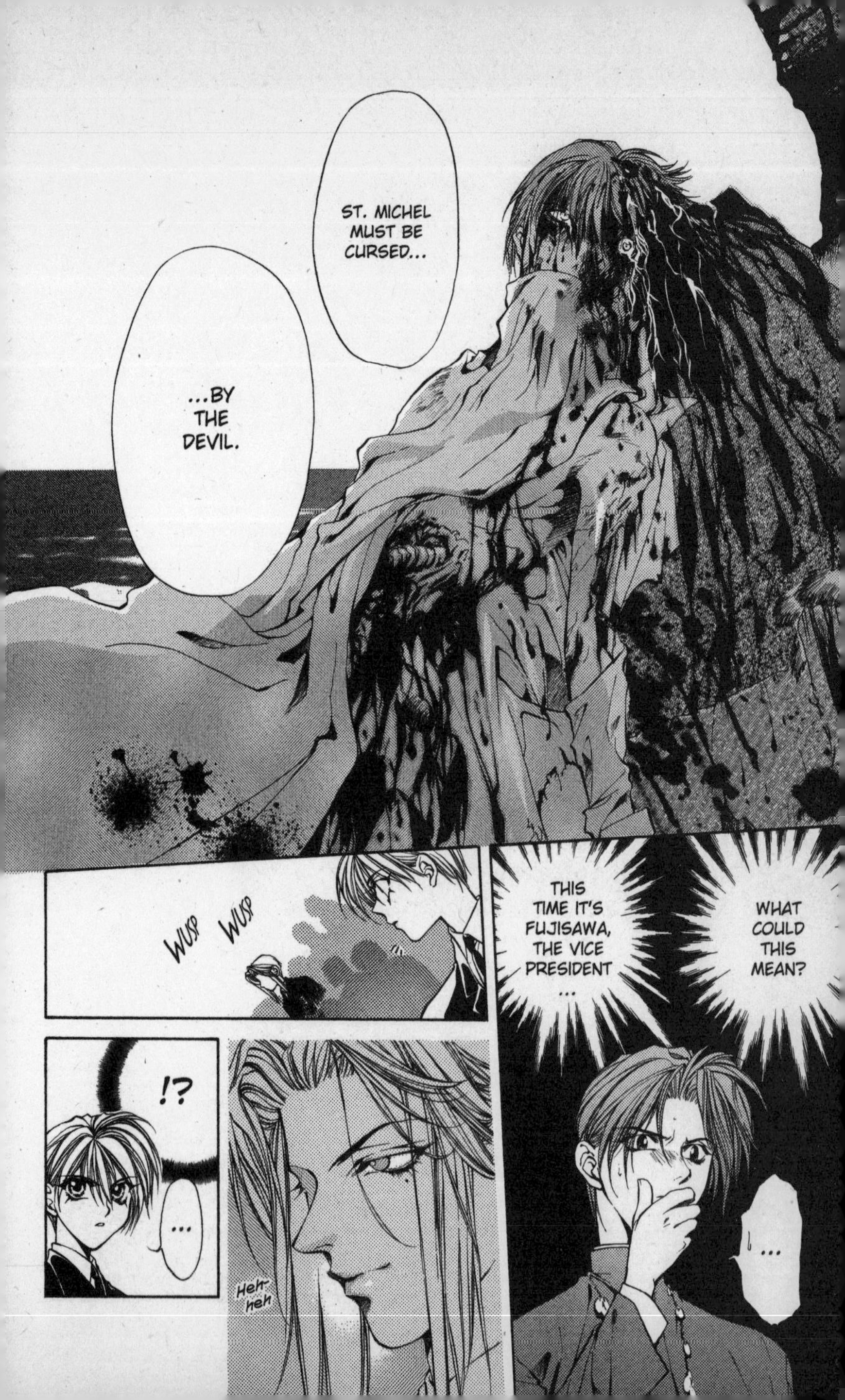
ST. MICHEL MUST BE CURSED...
...BY THE DEVIL.
THIS TIME IT'S FUJISAWA, THE VICE PRESIDENT ...
WHAT COULD THIS MEAN?
I...
WUSP WUSP
Heh-heh
!?
...

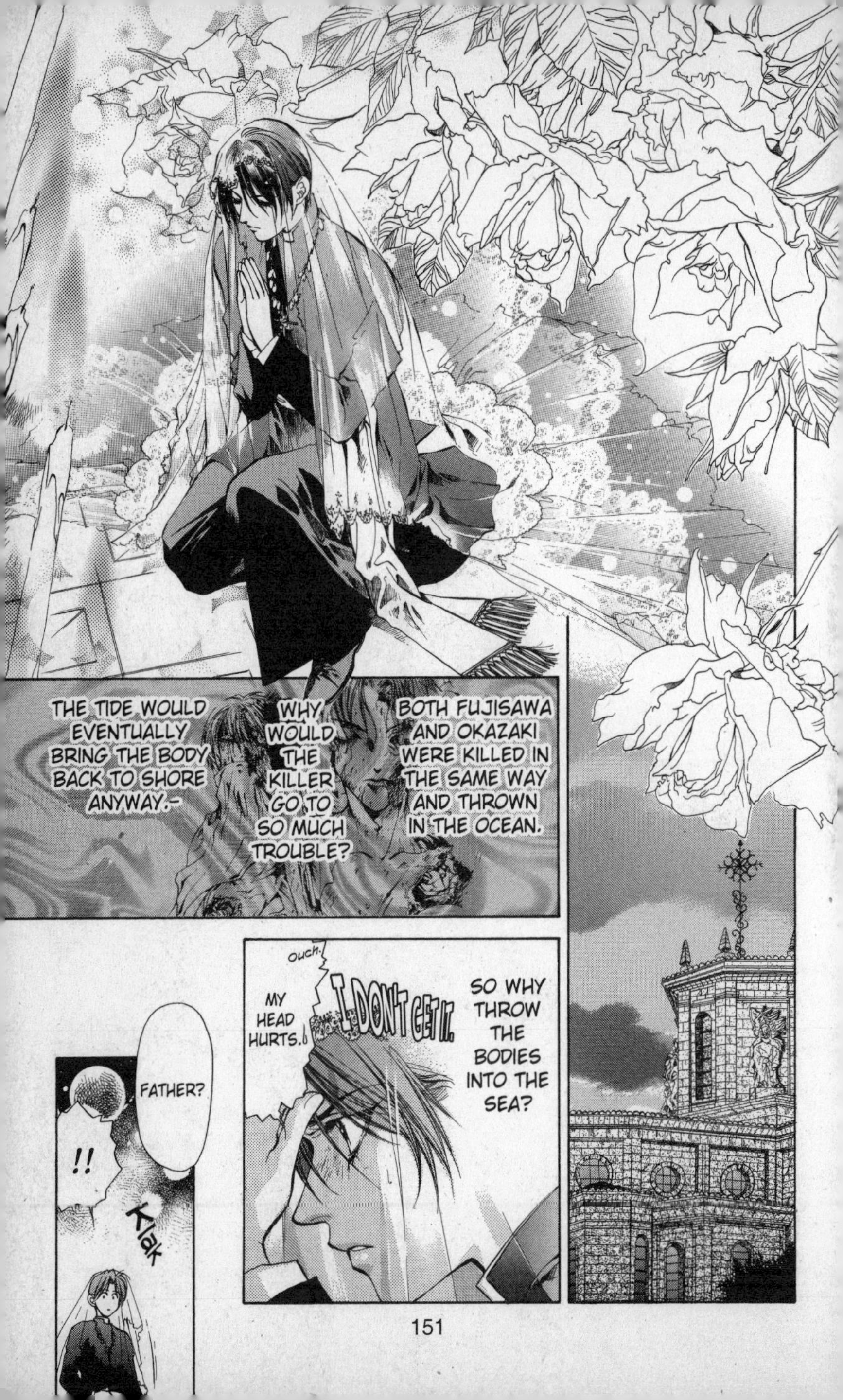
BOTH FUJISAWA AND OKAZAKI WERE KILLED IN THE SAME WAY AND THROWN IN THE OCEAN.
WHY WOULD THE KILLER GO TO SO MUCH TROUBLE?
THE TIDE WOULD EVENTUALLY BRING THE BODY BACK TO SHORE ANYWAY.
SO WHY THROW THE BODIES INTO THE SEA?
I DON'T GET IT.
Ouch.
MY HEAD HURTS.
FATHER?
!!
Klak

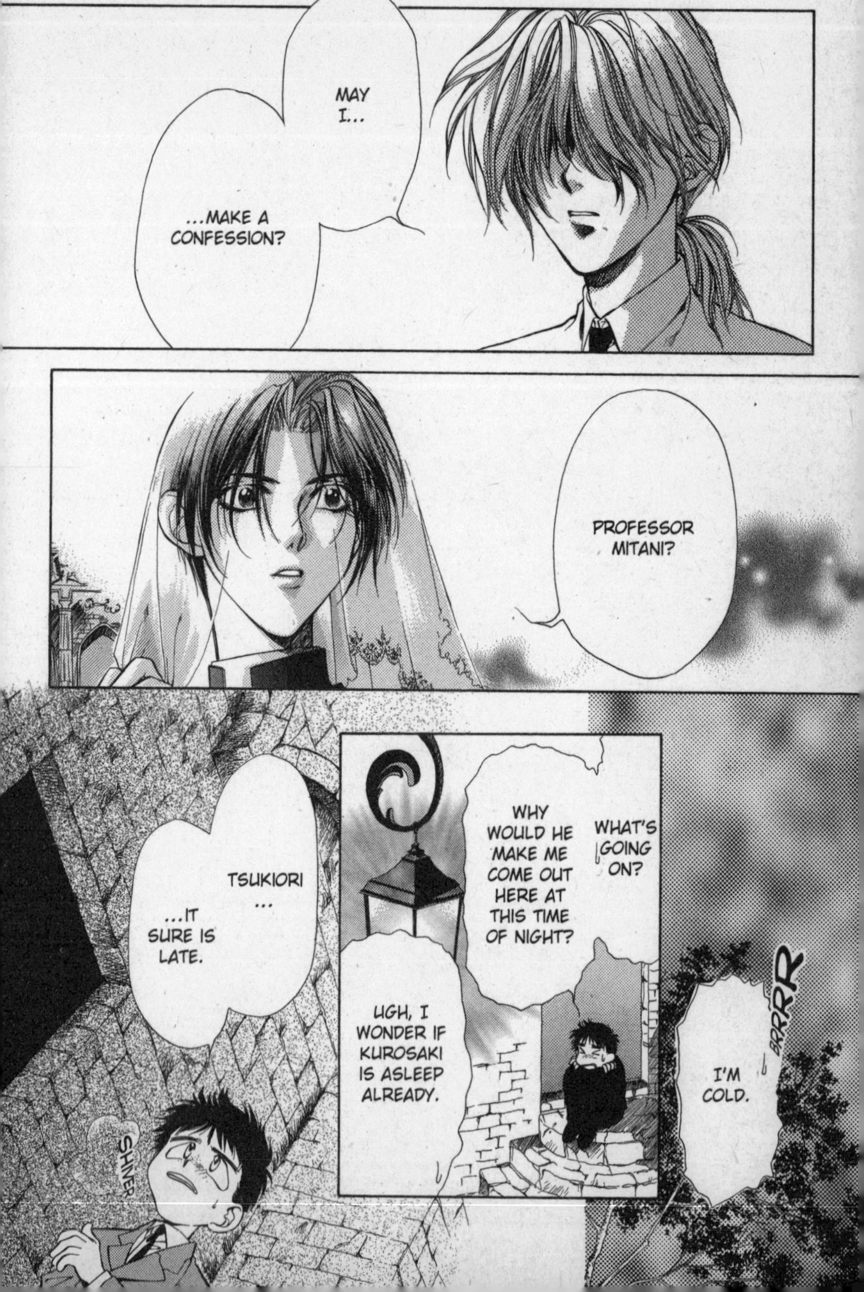
MAY I...
...MAKE A CONFESSION?
PROFESSOR MITANI?
BRRRR
I'M COLD.
WHAT'S GOING ON?
WHY WOULD HE MAKE ME COME OUT HERE AT THIS TIME OF NIGHT?
UGH, I WONDER IF KUROSAKI IS ASLEEP ALREADY.
TSUKIORI ...
...IT SURE IS LATE.
SHIVER

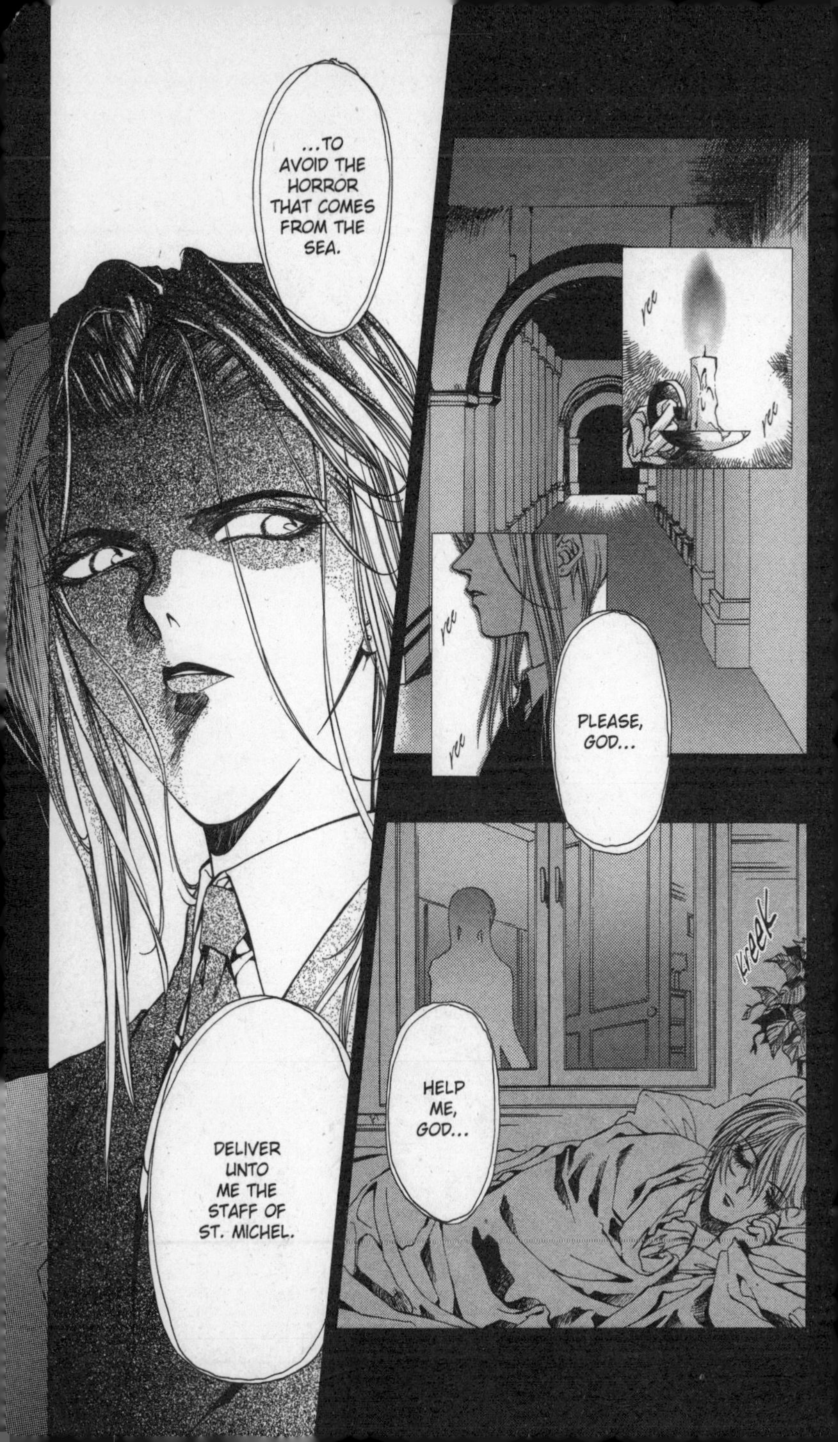
ree
ree
ree
ree
PLEASE, GOD...
kreek
HELP ME, GOD...
...TO AVOID THE HORROR THAT COMES FROM THE SEA.
DELIVER UNTO ME THE STAFF OF ST. MICHEL.

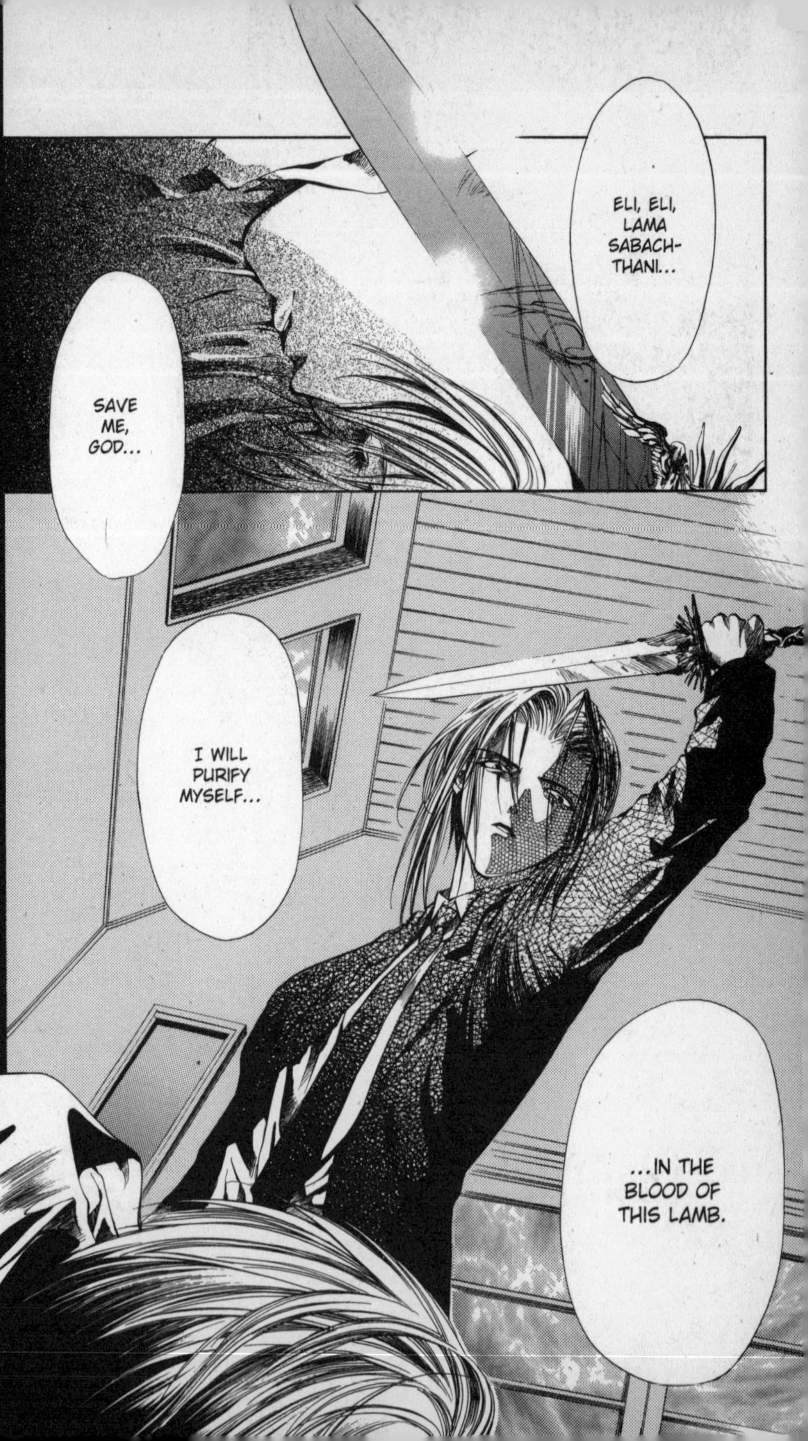
ELI, ELI, LAMA SABACH-THANI...
SAVE ME, GOD...
I WILL PURIFY MYSELF...
...IN THE BLOOD OF THIS LAMB.

CHAPTER 6

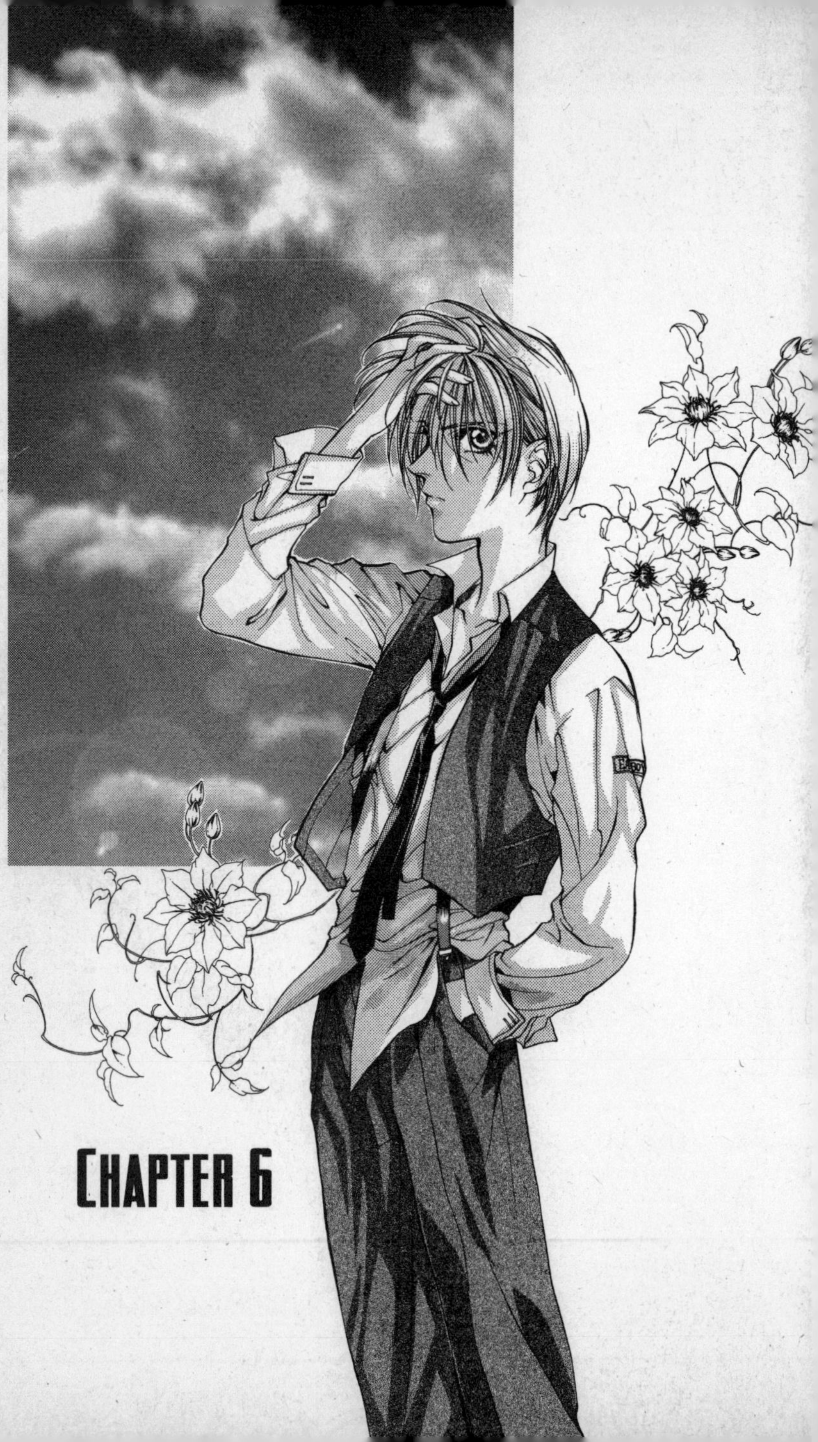

PLEASE, GOD...
HELP ME, GOD...
PLEASE, GOD...
SAVE ME.

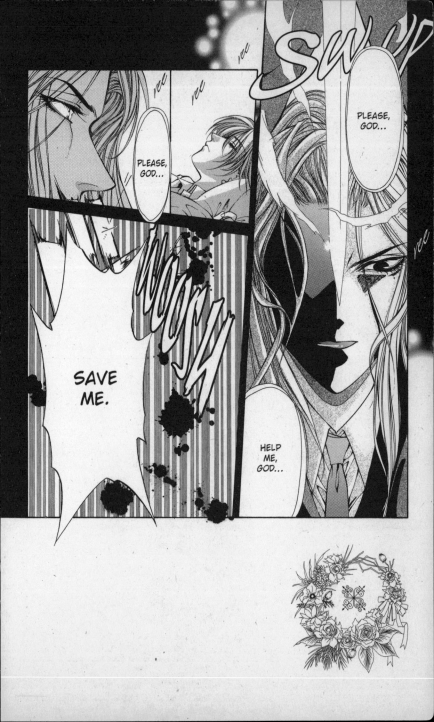

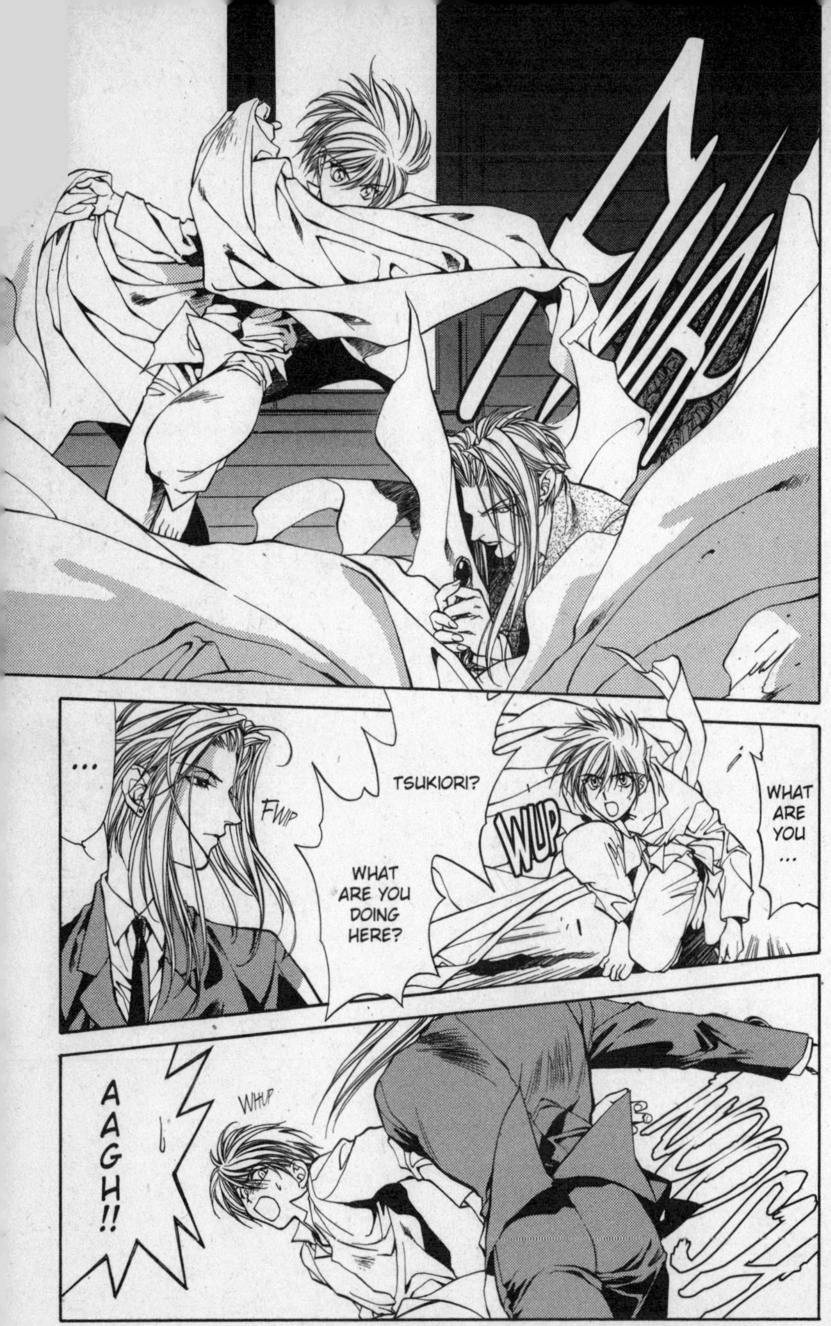
WHAT ARE YOU ...
TSUKIORI?
WUP
WHAT ARE YOU DOING HERE?
FWIP
...
WHUP
AAGH!!

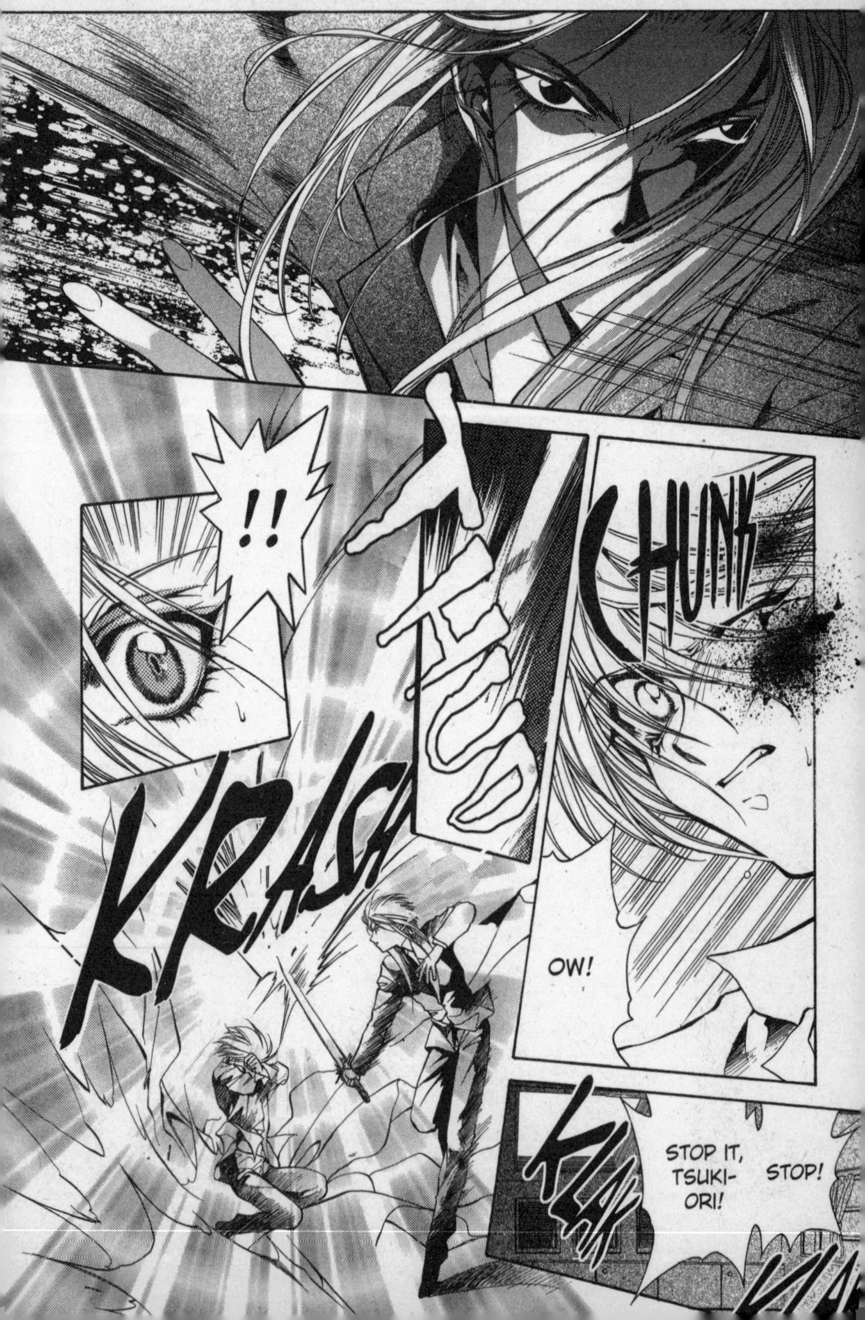
CHUNK
OW!
!!
KRAC
STOP!
STOP IT, TSUKI-ORI!
KLAK

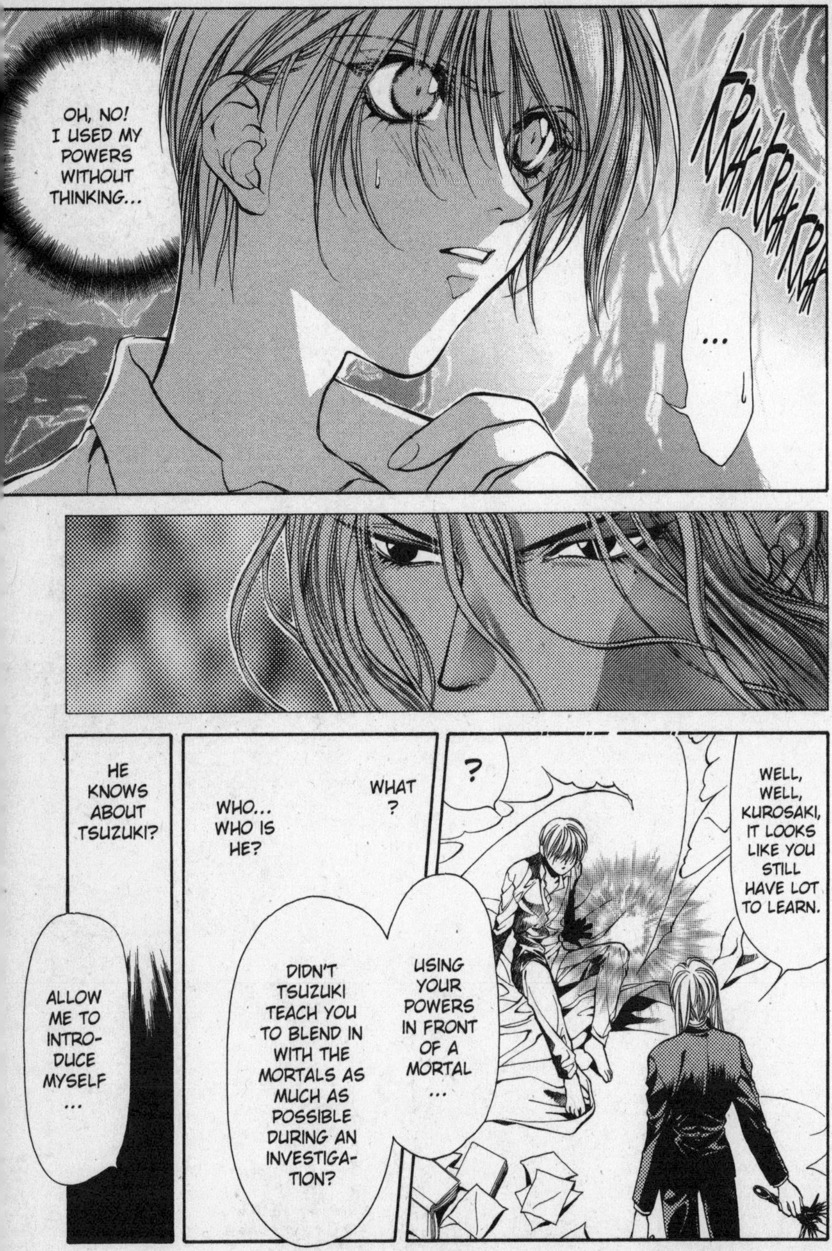
KRAH KRAH KRAH
...
OH, NO! I USED MY POWERS WITHOUT THINKING...
WELL, WELL, KUROSAKI, IT LOOKS LIKE YOU STILL HAVE LOT TO LEARN.
?
USING YOUR POWERS IN FRONT OF A MORTAL ...
DIDN'T TSUZUKI TEACH YOU TO BLEND IN WITH THE MORTALS AS MUCH AS POSSIBLE DURING AN INVESTIGA-TION?
WHAT ?
WHO... WHO IS HE?
HE KNOWS ABOUT TSUZUKI?
ALLOW ME TO INTRO-DUCE MYSELF ...

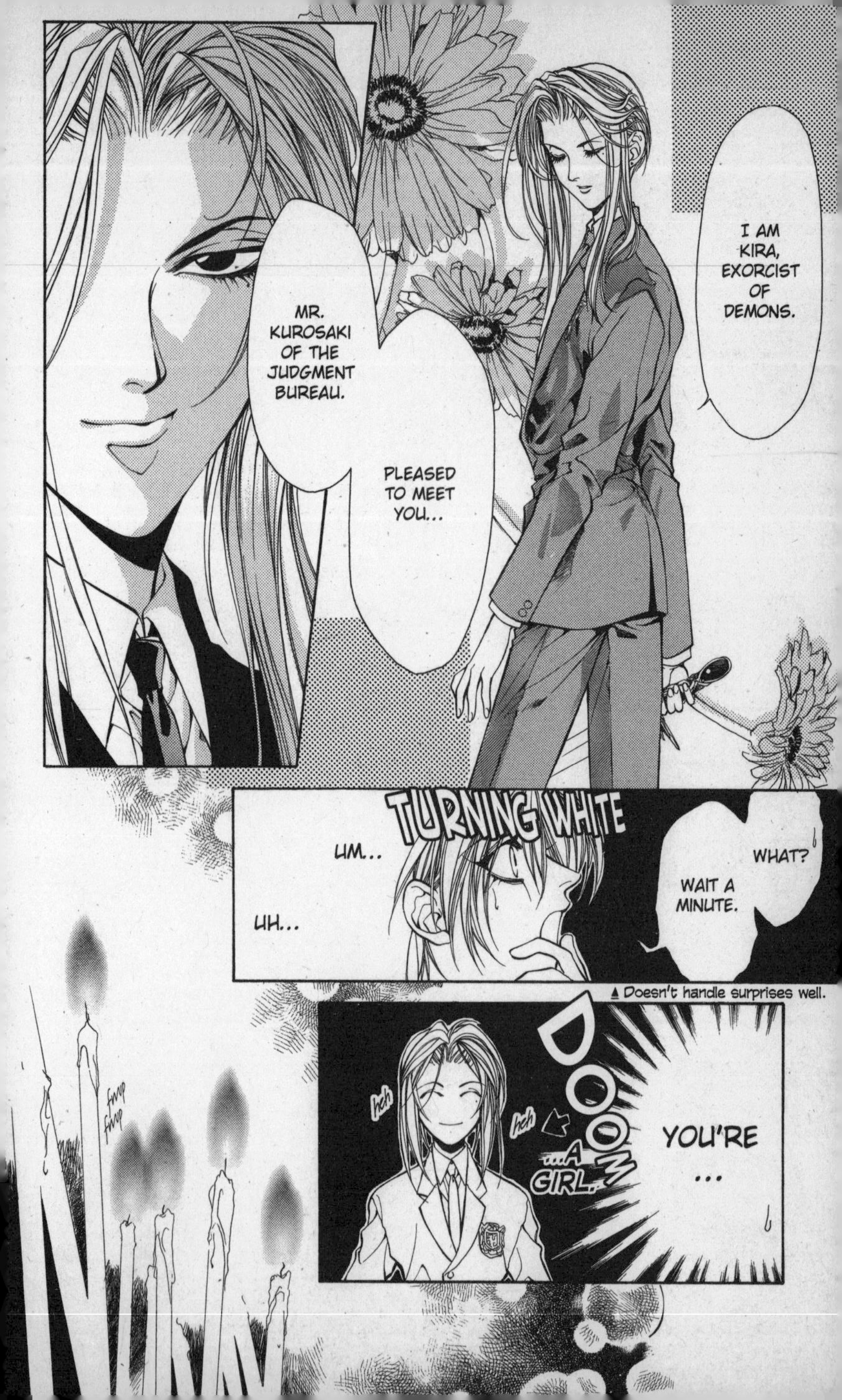
I AM KIRA, EXORCIST OF DEMONS.
MR. KUROSAKI OF THE JUDGMENT BUREAU.
PLEASED TO MEET YOU...
WHAT?
WAIT A MINUTE.
TURNING WHITE
UM...
UH...
▲ Doesn't handle surprises well.
YOU'RE ...
DOOOM
...A GIRL.
heh
heh
fwip fwip

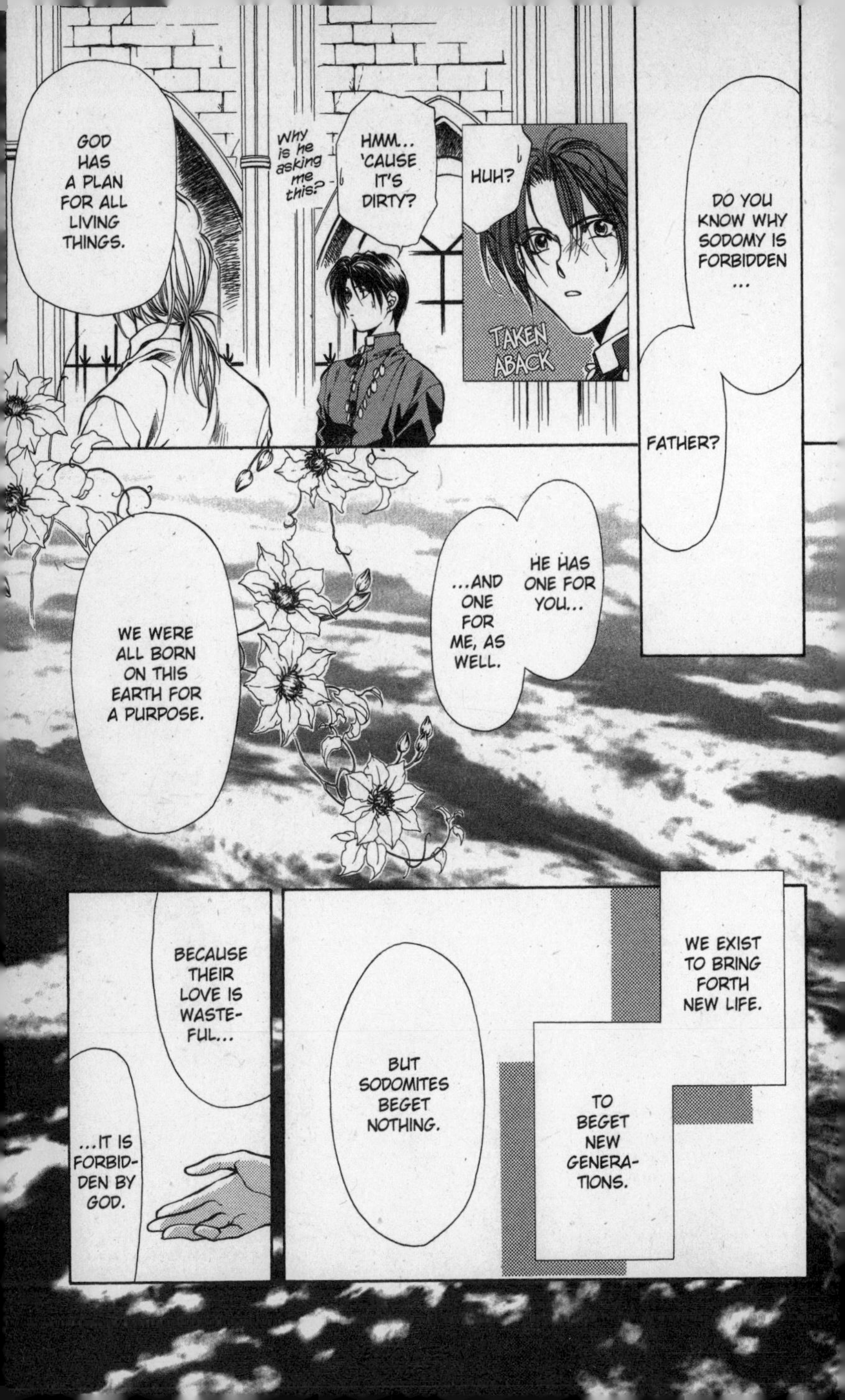
DO YOU KNOW WHY SODOMY IS FORBIDDEN ...
FATHER?
HUH?
TAKEN ABACK
HMM... 'CAUSE IT'S DIRTY?
Why is he asking me this?
GOD HAS A PLAN FOR ALL LIVING THINGS.
HE HAS ONE FOR YOU...
...AND ONE FOR ME, AS WELL.
WE WERE ALL BORN ON THIS EARTH FOR A PURPOSE.
WE EXIST TO BRING FORTH NEW LIFE.
TO BEGET NEW GENERA-TIONS.
BUT SODOMITES BEGET NOTHING.
BECAUSE THEIR LOVE IS WASTE-FUL...
...IT IS FORBID-DEN BY GOD.

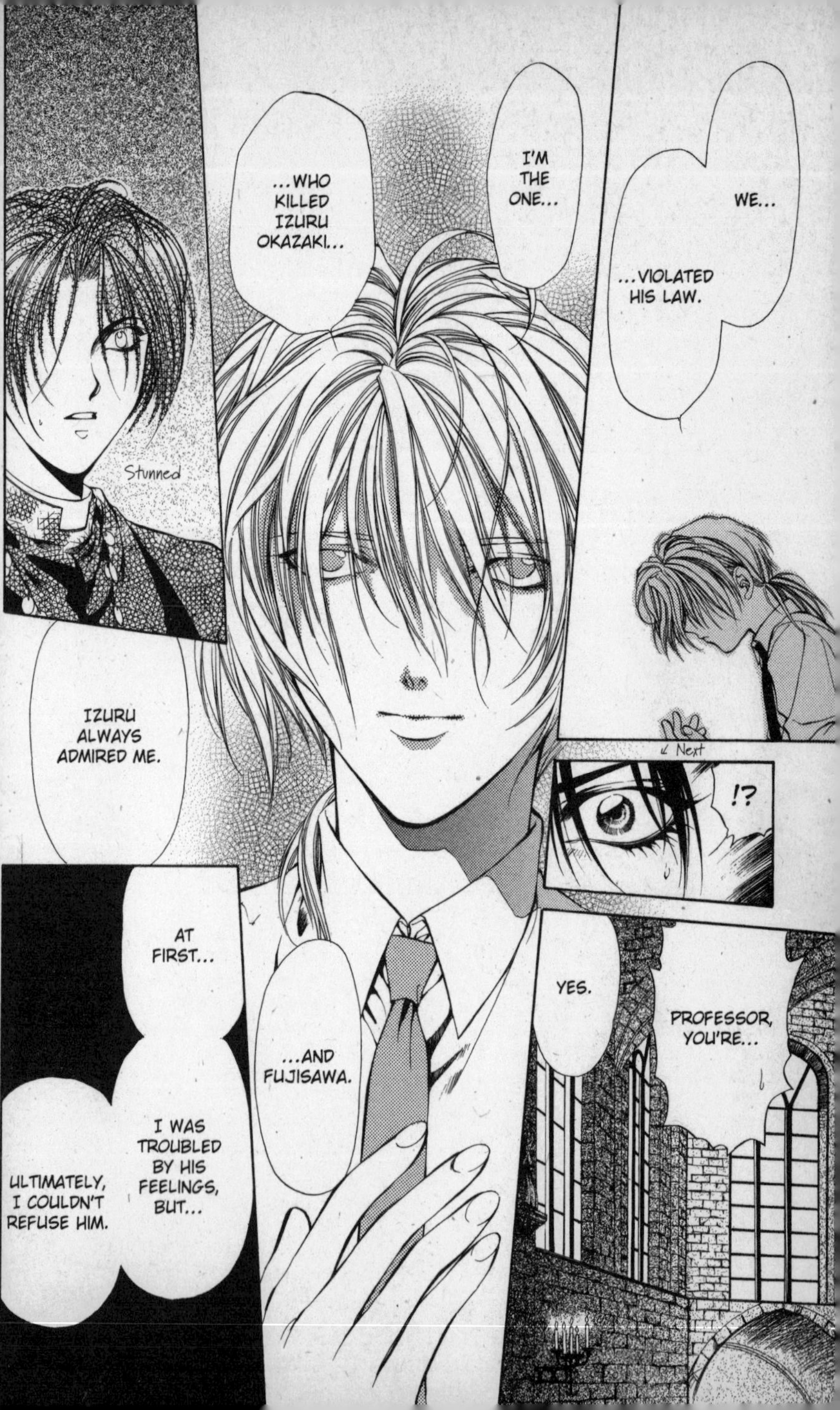
WE...
...VIOLATED HIS LAW.
I'M THE ONE...
...WHO KILLED IZURU OKAZAKI...
Stunned
Next
!?
PROFESSOR, YOU'RE...
YES.
...AND FUJISAWA.
IZURU ALWAYS ADMIRED ME.
AT FIRST...
I WAS TROUBLED BY HIS FEELINGS, BUT...
ULTIMATELY, I COULDN'T REFUSE HIM.

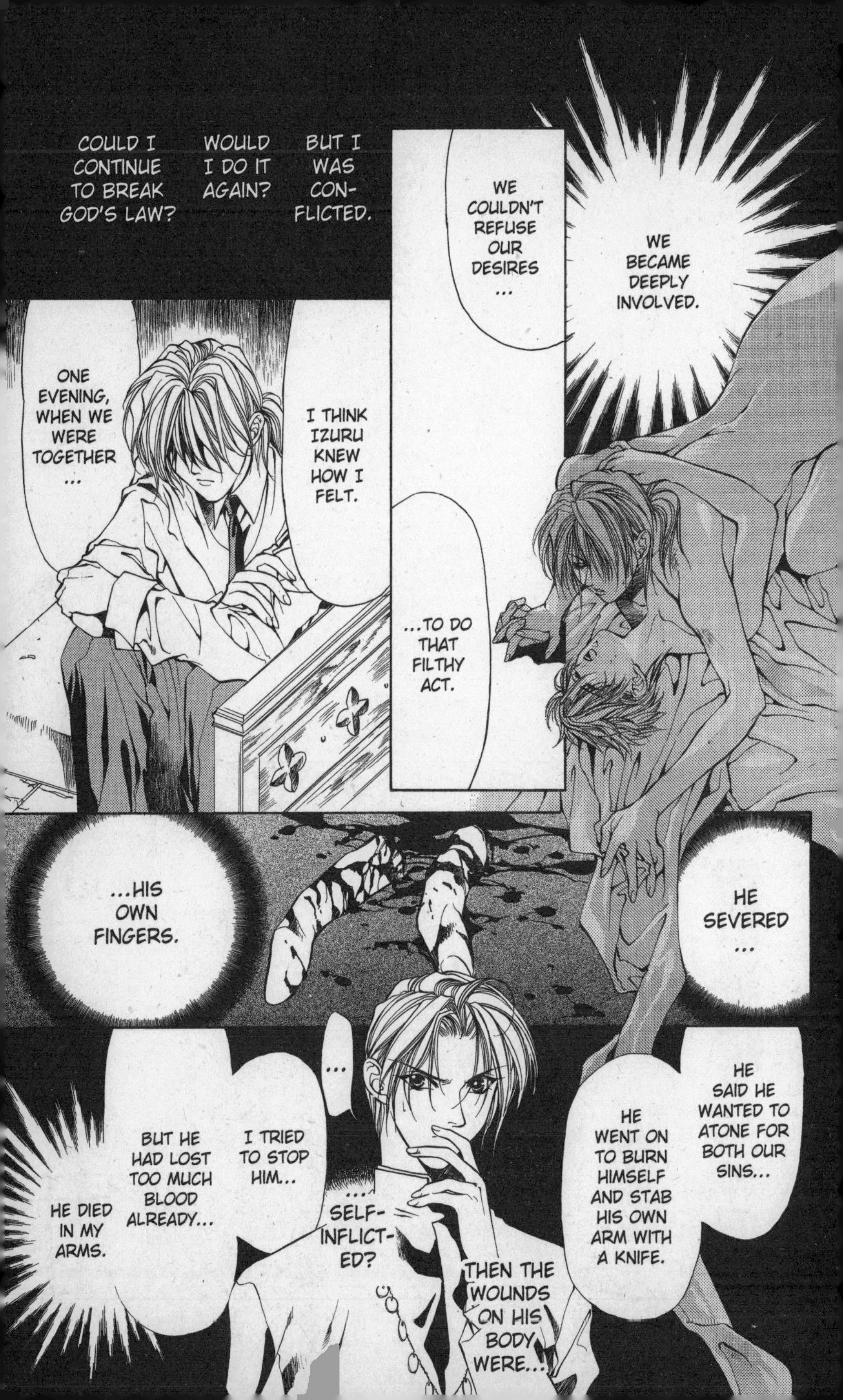
WE BECAME DEEPLY INVOLVED.
WE COULDN'T REFUSE OUR DESIRES ...
...TO DO THAT FILTHY ACT.
BUT I WAS CON-FLICTED.
WOULD I DO IT AGAIN?
COULD I CONTINUE TO BREAK GOD'S LAW?
I THINK IZURU KNEW HOW I FELT.
ONE EVENING, WHEN WE WERE TOGETHER ...
HE SEVERED ...
...HIS OWN FINGERS.
HE SAID HE WANTED TO ATONE FOR BOTH OUR SINS...
HE WENT ON TO BURN HIMSELF AND STAB HIS OWN ARM WITH A KNIFE.
THEN THE WOUNDS ON HIS BODY WERE...
...SELF-INFLICT-ED?
...
I TRIED TO STOP HIM...
BUT HE HAD LOST TOO MUCH BLOOD ALREADY...
HE DIED IN MY ARMS.

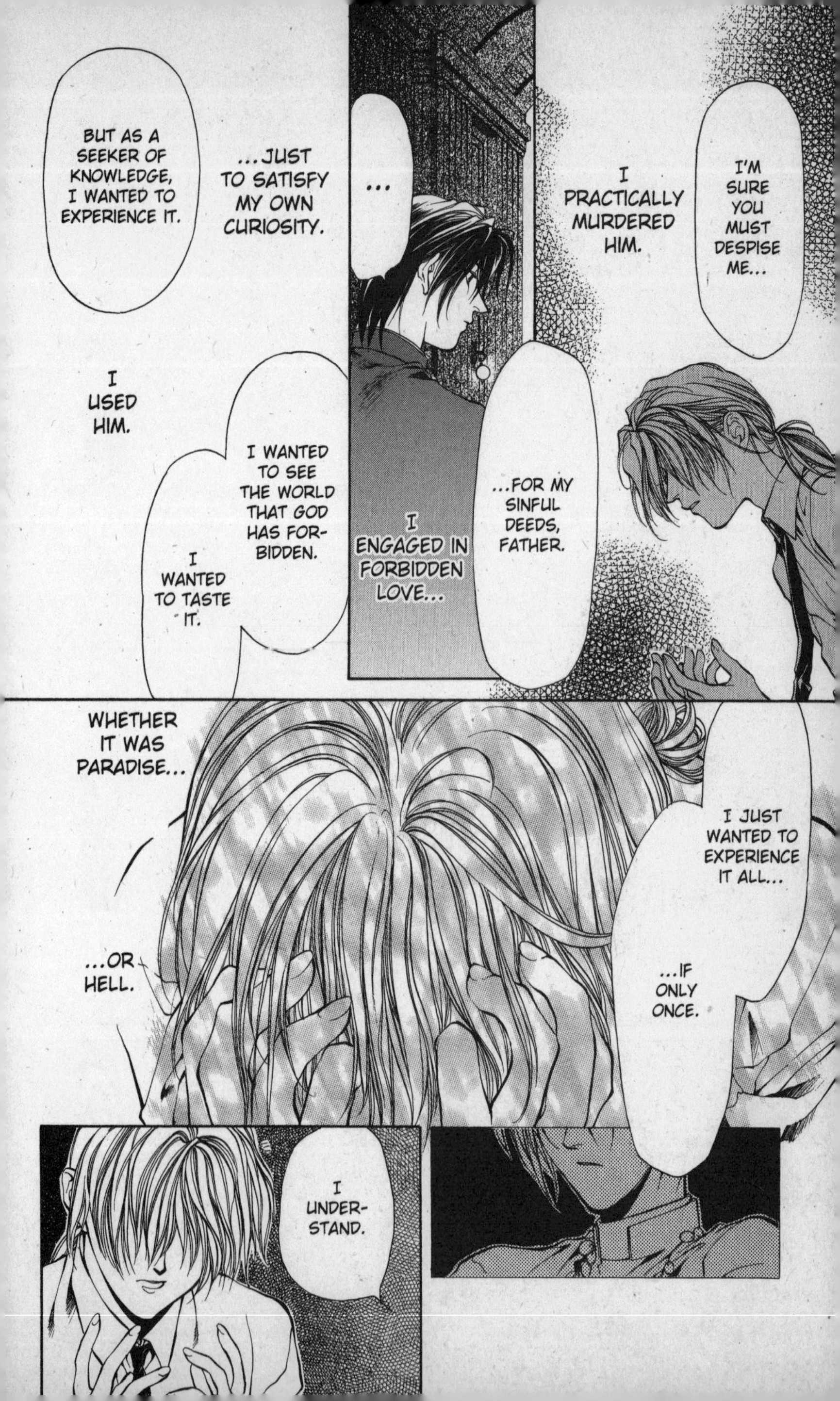
I'M SURE YOU MUST DESPISE ME...
...FOR MY SINFUL DEEDS, FATHER.
I PRACTICALLY MURDERED HIM.
...
I ENGAGED IN FORBIDDEN LOVE...
...JUST TO SATISFY MY OWN CURIOSITY.
BUT AS A SEEKER OF KNOWLEDGE, I WANTED TO EXPERIENCE IT.
I WANTED TO SEE THE WORLD THAT GOD HAS FOR-BIDDEN.
I WANTED TO TASTE IT.
I USED HIM.
I JUST WANTED TO EXPERIENCE IT ALL...
...IF ONLY ONCE.
WHETHER IT WAS PARADISE...
...OR HELL.
I UNDER-STAND.

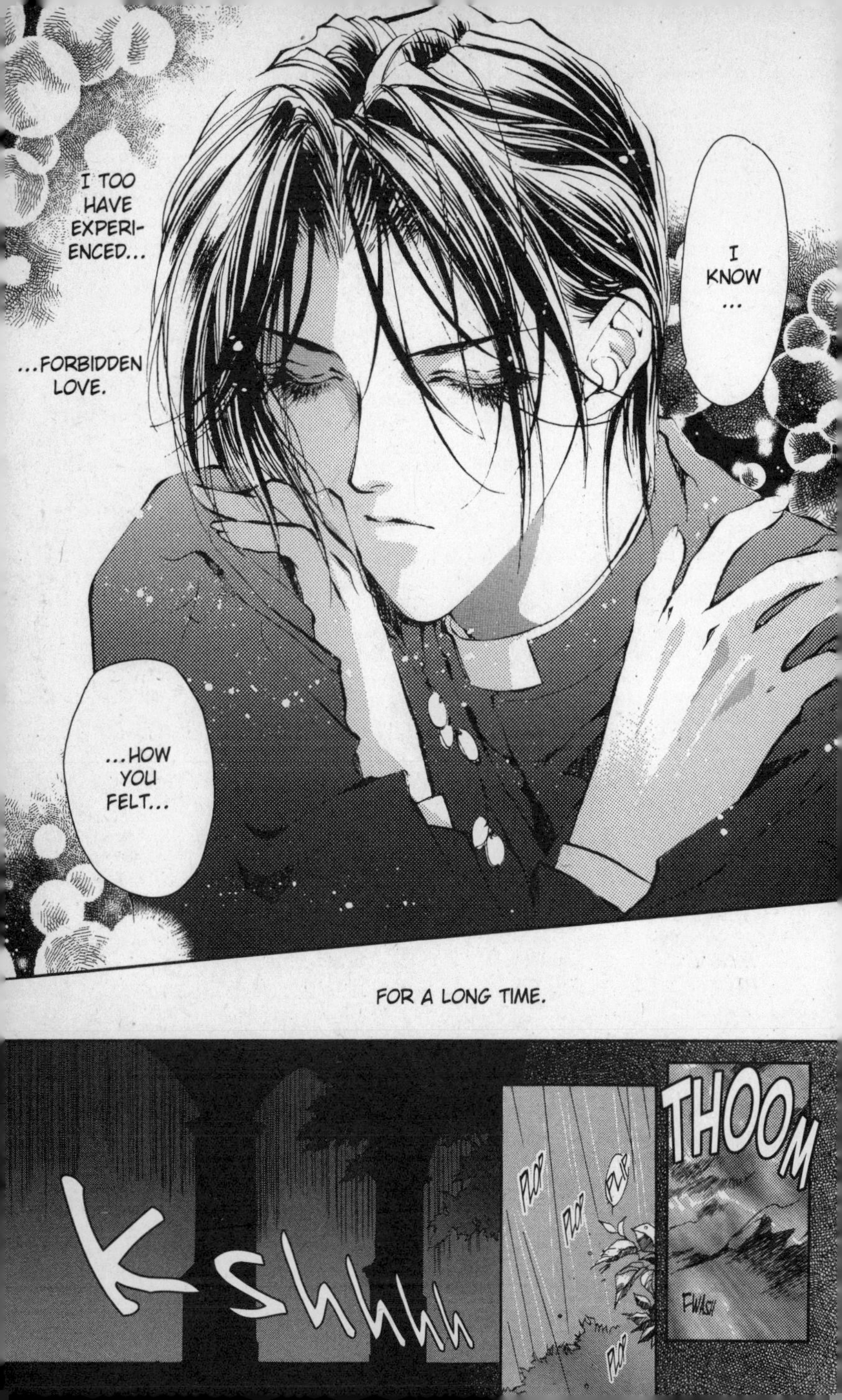
I KNOW ...
I TOO HAVE EXPERIENCED...
...FORBIDDEN LOVE.
...HOW YOU FELT...
FOR A LONG TIME.
THOOM
FWASH
PLOP
PLOP
PLOP
PLOP
Kshhhh

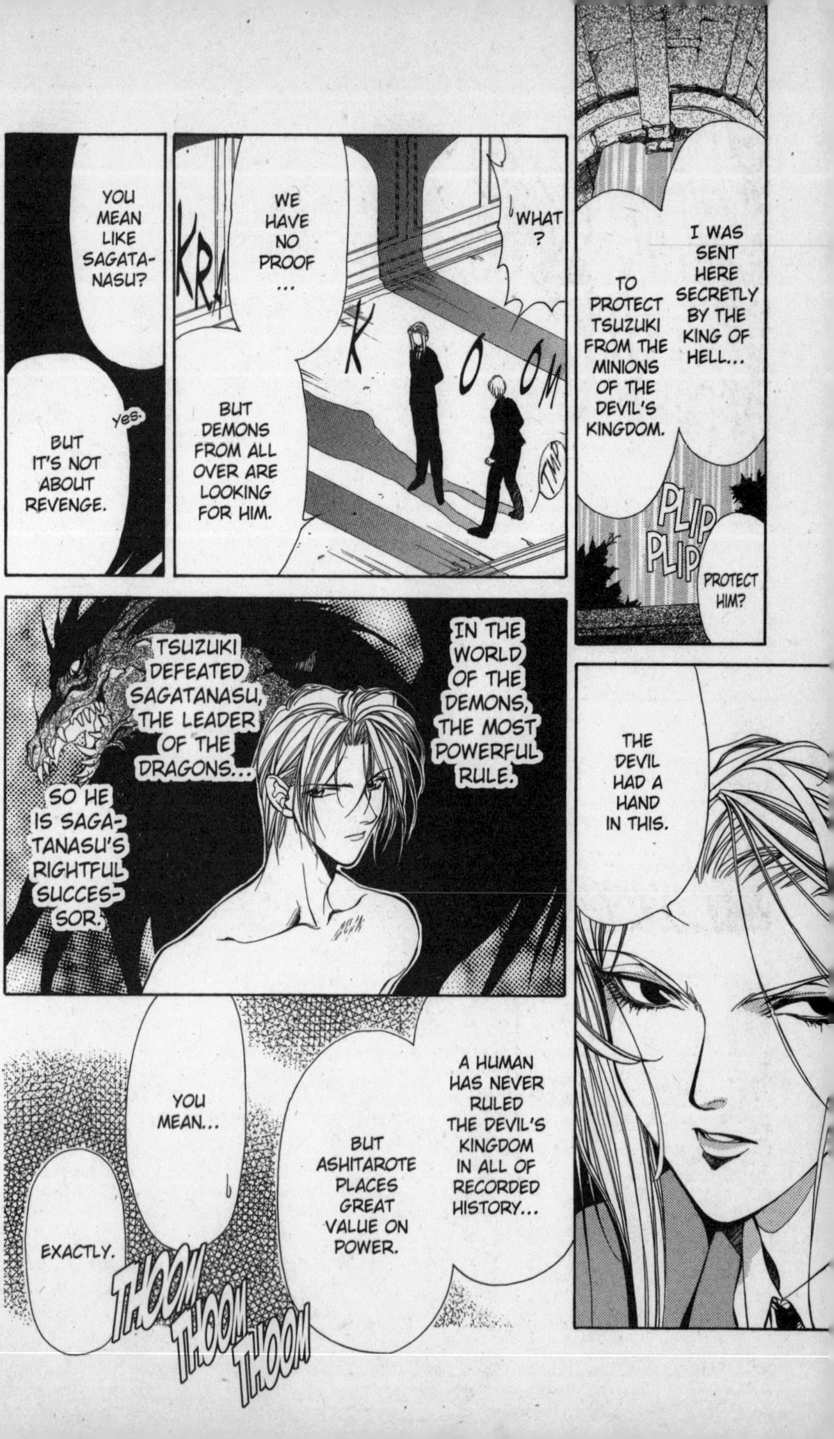
I WAS SENT HERE SECRETLY BY THE KING OF HELL...
TO PROTECT TSUZUKI FROM THE MINIONS OF THE DEVIL'S KINGDOM.
PLIP PLIP
PROTECT HIM?
WHAT?
KRAKOOM
TMP
WE HAVE NO PROOF...
BUT DEMONS FROM ALL OVER ARE LOOKING FOR HIM.
YOU MEAN LIKE SAGATANASU?
Yes.
BUT IT'S NOT ABOUT REVENGE.
THE DEVIL HAD A HAND IN THIS.
IN THE WORLD OF THE DEMONS, THE MOST POWERFUL RULE.
TSUZUKI DEFEATED SAGATANASU, THE LEADER OF THE DRAGONS...
SO HE IS SAGATANASU'S RIGHTFUL SUCCESSOR.
A HUMAN HAS NEVER RULED THE DEVIL'S KINGDOM IN ALL OF RECORDED HISTORY...
BUT ASHITAROTE PLACES GREAT VALUE ON POWER.
YOU MEAN...
EXACTLY.
THOOM THOOM THOOM

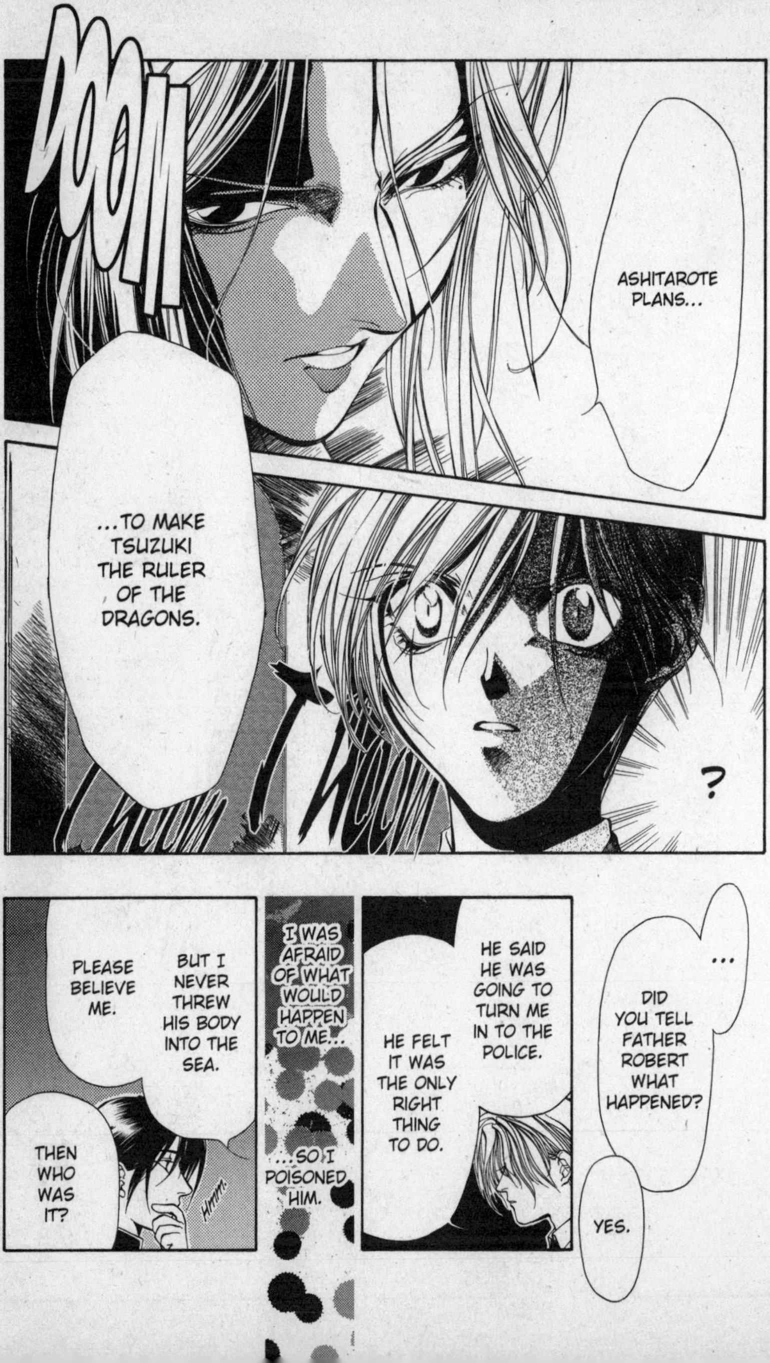
ASHITAROTE PLANS...
DOOM
...TO MAKE TSUZUKI THE RULER OF THE DRAGONS.
?
...
DID YOU TELL FATHER ROBERT WHAT HAPPENED?
YES.
HE SAID HE WAS GOING TO TURN ME IN TO THE POLICE.
HE FELT IT WAS THE ONLY RIGHT THING TO DO.
I WAS AFRAID OF WHAT WOULD HAPPEN TO ME...
...SO I POISONED HIM.
BUT I NEVER THREW HIS BODY INTO THE SEA.
PLEASE BELIEVE ME.
Hmm.
THEN WHO WAS IT?

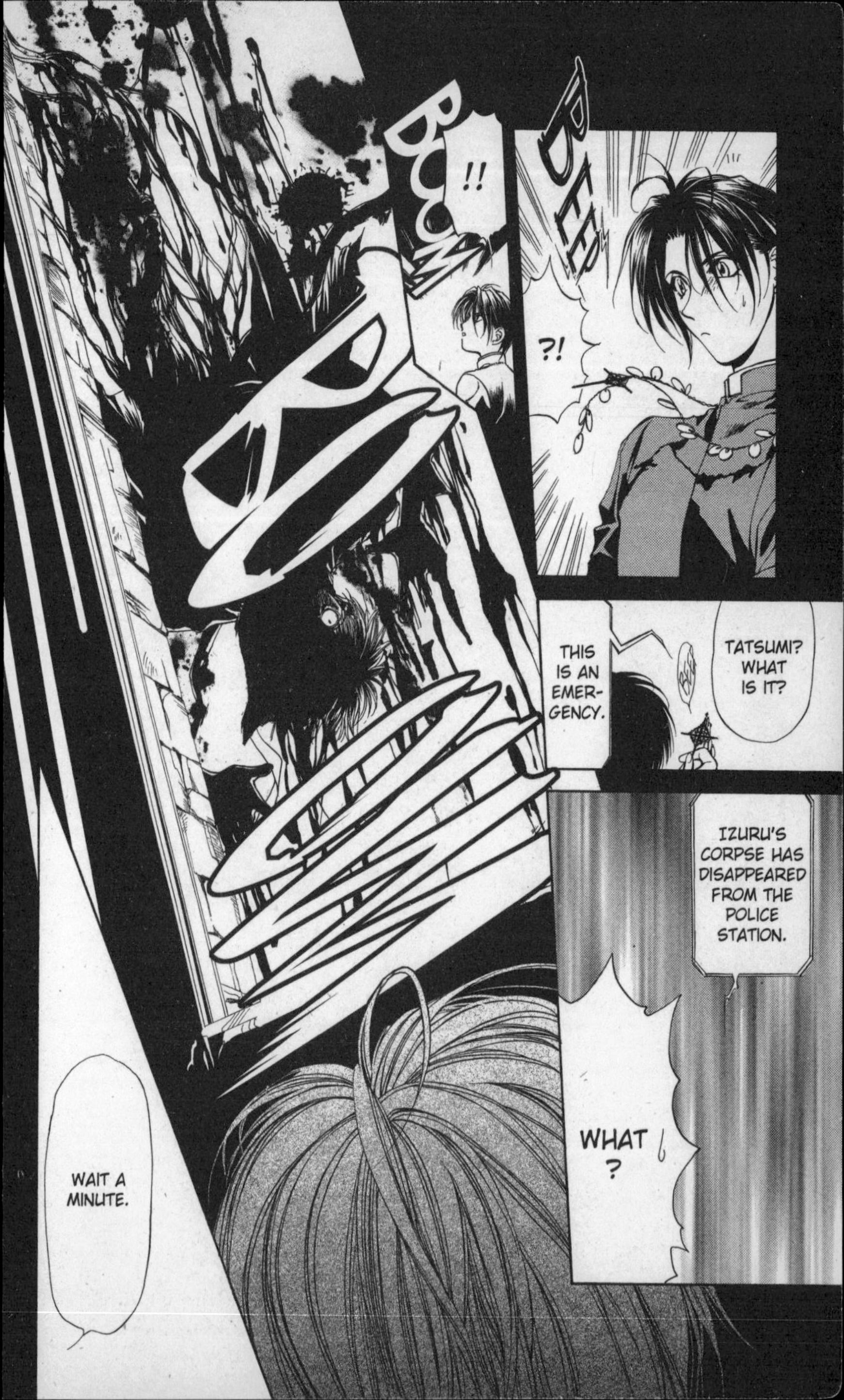
BEEP
?!
TATSUMI? WHAT IS IT?
THIS IS AN EMERGENCY.
IZURU'S CORPSE HAS DISAPPEARED FROM THE POLICE STATION.
WHAT ?
BOOM
!!
WAIT A MINUTE.

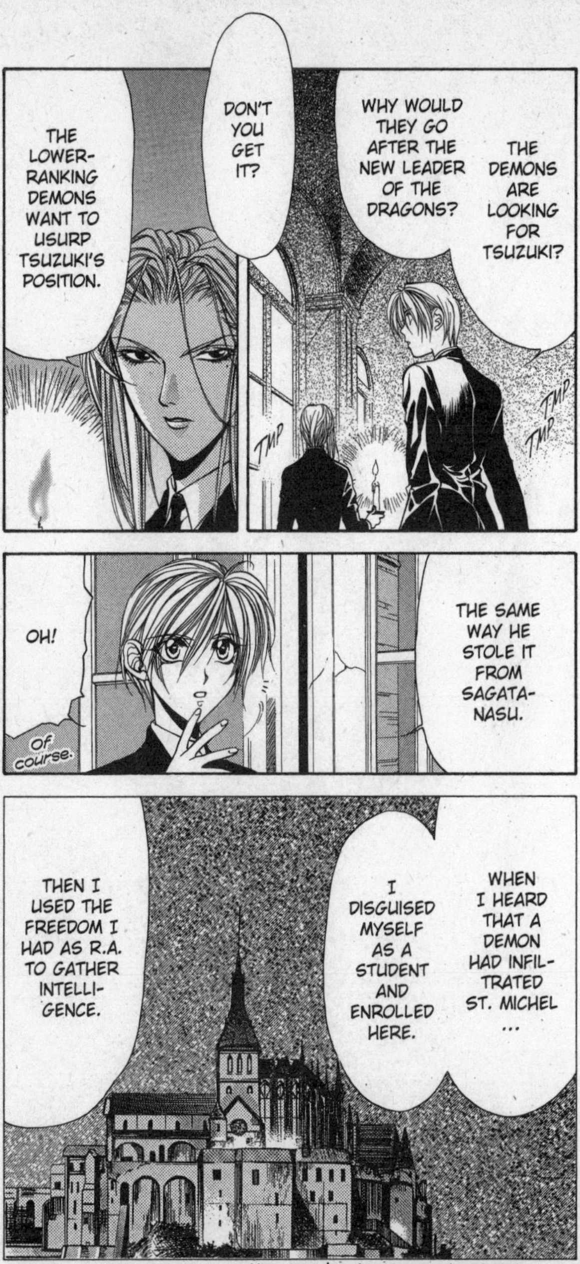
THE DEMONS ARE LOOKING FOR TSUZUKI?
WHY WOULD THEY GO AFTER THE NEW LEADER OF THE DRAGONS?
TMP TMP
TMP
DON'T YOU GET IT?
THE LOWER-RANKING DEMONS WANT TO USURP TSUZUKI'S POSITION.
THE SAME WAY HE STOLE IT FROM SAGATA-NASU.
OH!
Of course.
WHEN I HEARD THAT A DEMON HAD INFIL-TRATED ST. MICHEL ...
I DISGUISED MYSELF AS A STUDENT AND ENROLLED HERE.
THEN I USED THE FREEDOM I HAD AS R.A. TO GATHER INTELLI-GENCE.

Kira doesn't belong to any department. She's an independent agent.

Now I'd like to explore the mystery of St. Michel. (Ha) Let me explain the meaning of Kira's words "Eli, Eli, lama sabachtani." That's actually a phrase from the French author Gustave Doré's Bible (...it may exist in other versions too). It means "Please help me, God". I'm pretty sure it's Hebrew. Sorry if that's not right. Next... why is Fujisawa killed? (Ha) I didn't really have enough space to explain that, sorry. The answer is simple—because he threatened Mitani. Fujisawa wanted to black-mail Mitani into being his love slave. As for how he found out that Mitani was the murderer, well, that's a... Mystery!! This story isn't easily digested. It was a failure. I'll work harder next time.

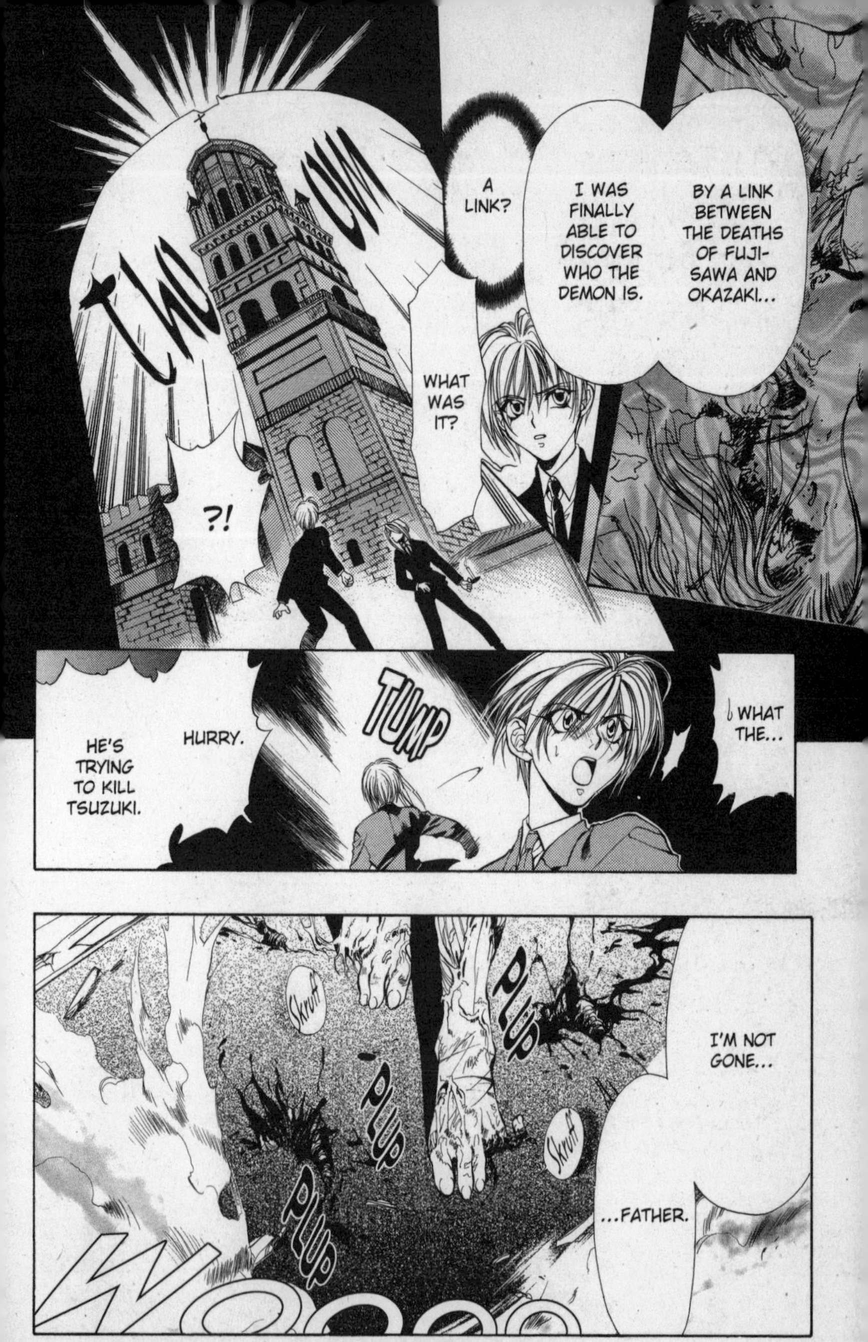
BY A LINK BETWEEN THE DEATHS OF FUJI-SAWA AND OKAZAKI...
I WAS FINALLY ABLE TO DISCOVER WHO THE DEMON IS.
A LINK?
WHAT WAS IT?
?!
WHAT THE...
TUMP
HURRY.
HE'S TRYING TO KILL TSUZUKI.
I'M NOT GONE...
...FATHER.
PLUP
Skruff
PLUP
PLUP
Skruff
PLUP

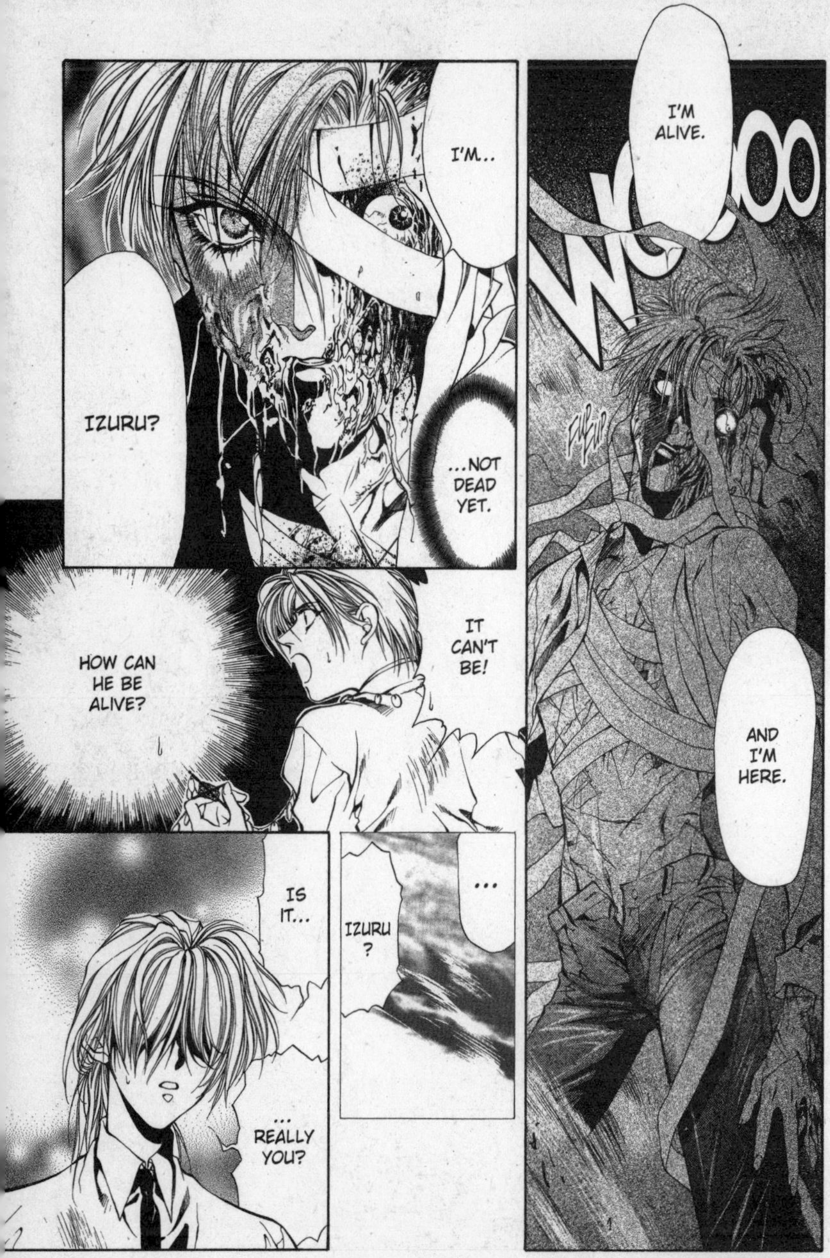
I'M ALIVE.
AND I'M HERE.
I'M...
...NOT DEAD YET.
IZURU?
IT CAN'T BE!
HOW CAN HE BE ALIVE?
...
IZURU?
IS IT...
...REALLY YOU?

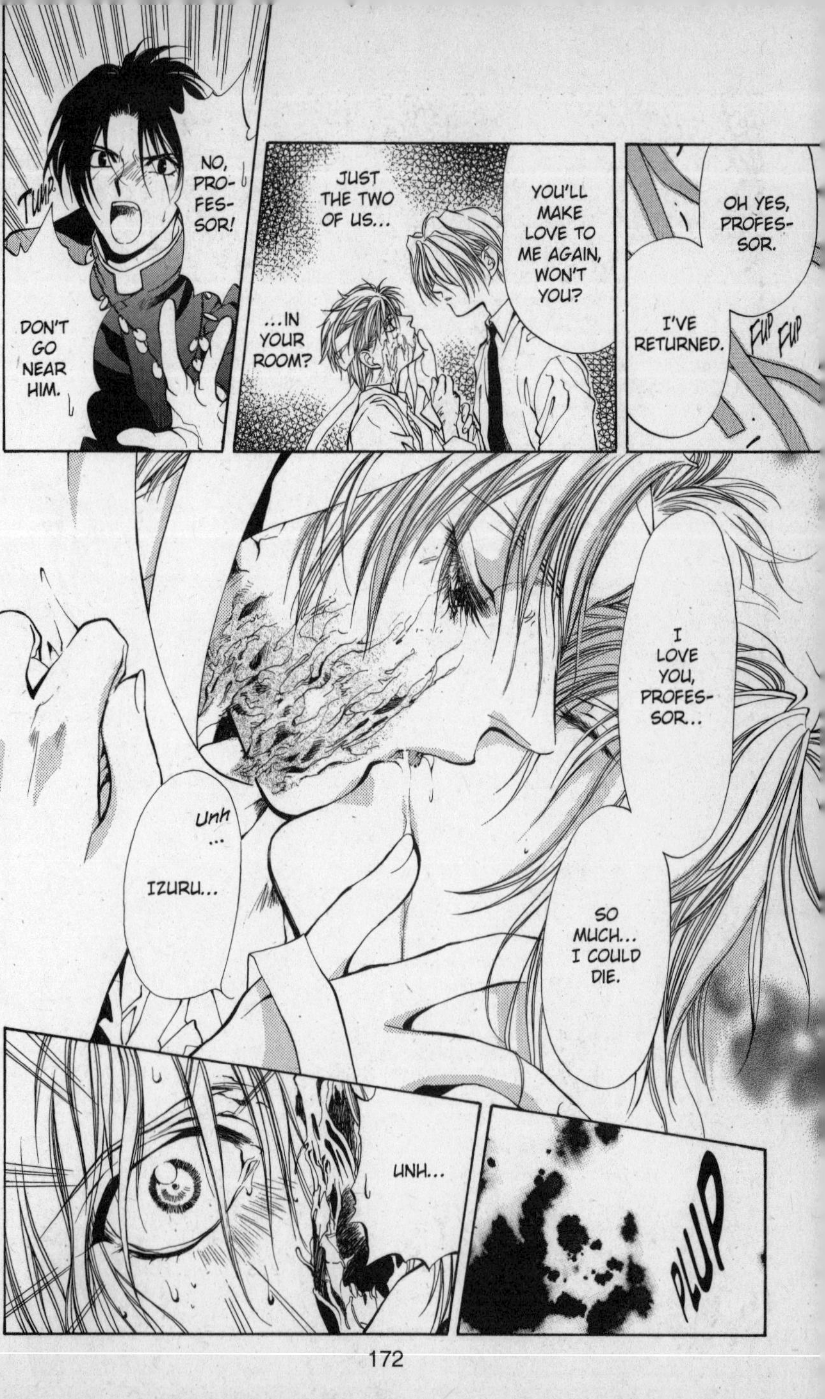
OH YES, PROFESSOR.
I'VE RETURNED.
FLIP FLIP
YOU'LL MAKE LOVE TO ME AGAIN, WON'T YOU?
JUST THE TWO OF US...
...IN YOUR ROOM?
NO, PROFESSOR!
TUMP
DON'T GO NEAR HIM.
I LOVE YOU, PROFESSOR...
SO MUCH... I COULD DIE.
Unh ...
IZURU...
PLUP
UNH...

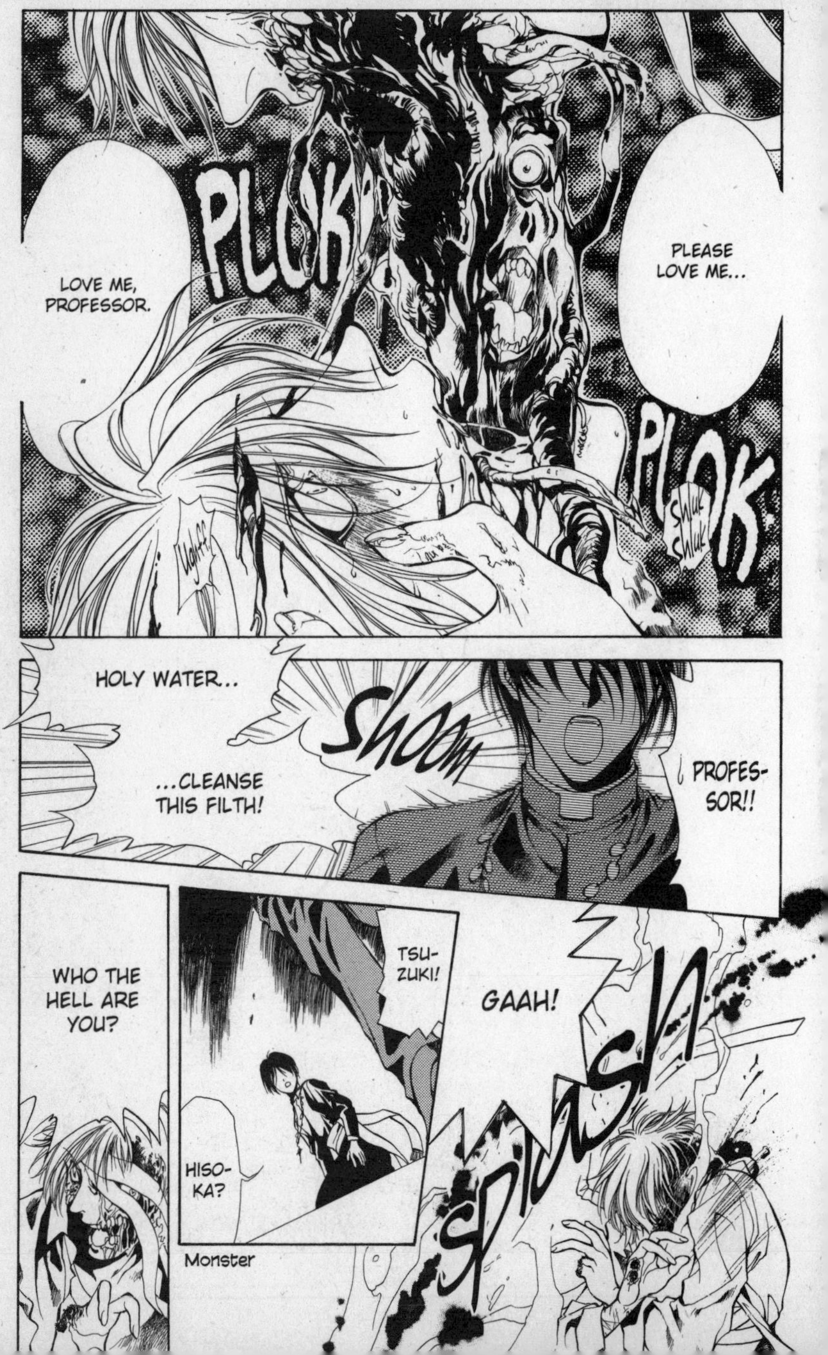
PLEASE LOVE ME...
PLOK
Shluk
Shluk
PLOK
LOVE ME, PROFESSOR.
Ughff
PROFES-SOR!!
Shoom
HOLY WATER...
...CLEANSE THIS FILTH!
Splash
GAAH!
TSU-ZUKI!
HISO-KA?
WHO THE HELL ARE YOU?
Monster

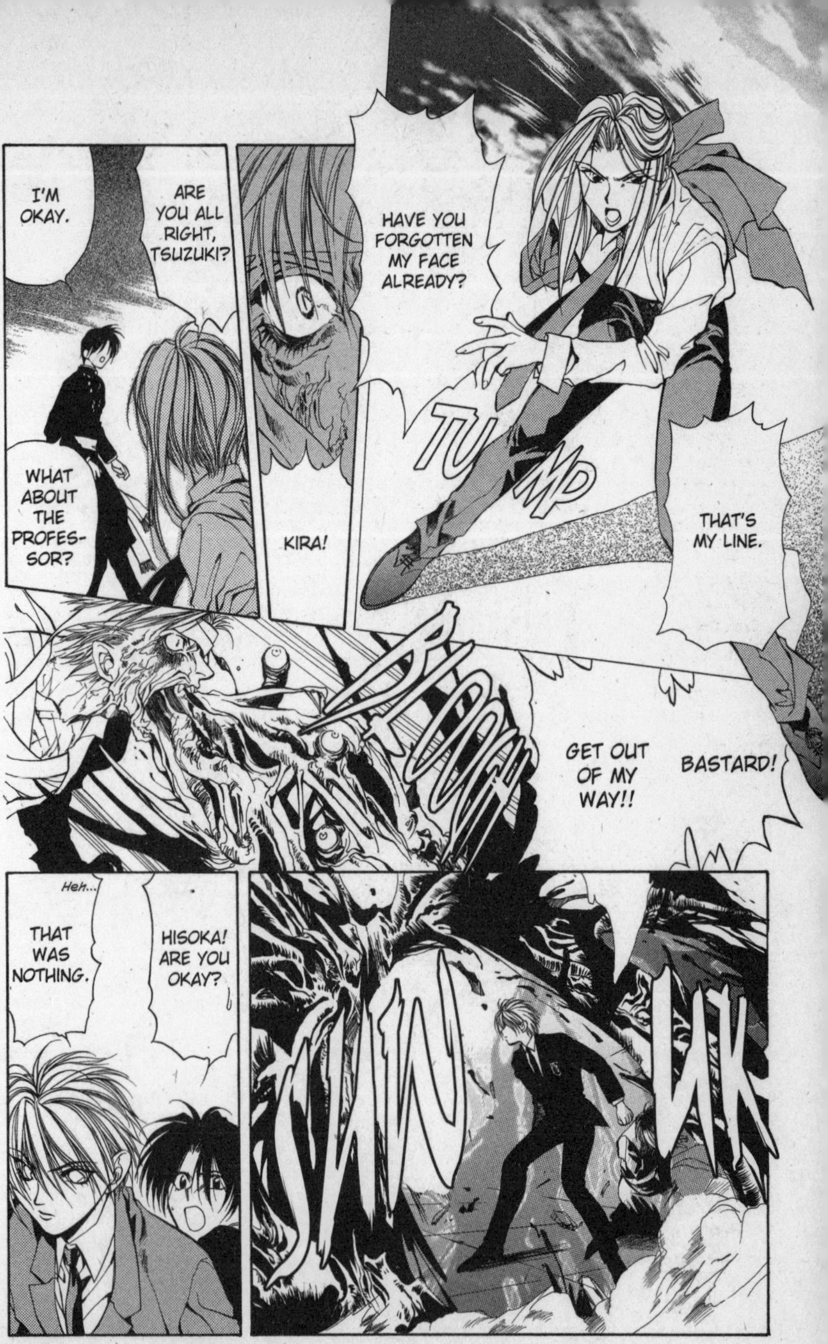
HAVE YOU FORGOTTEN MY FACE ALREADY?
TUMP
THAT'S MY LINE.
KIRA!
ARE YOU ALL RIGHT, TSUZUKI?
I'M OKAY.
WHAT ABOUT THE PROFES-SOR?
BASTARD!
GET OUT OF MY WAY!!
HISOKA! ARE YOU OKAY?
Heh...
THAT WAS NOTHING.

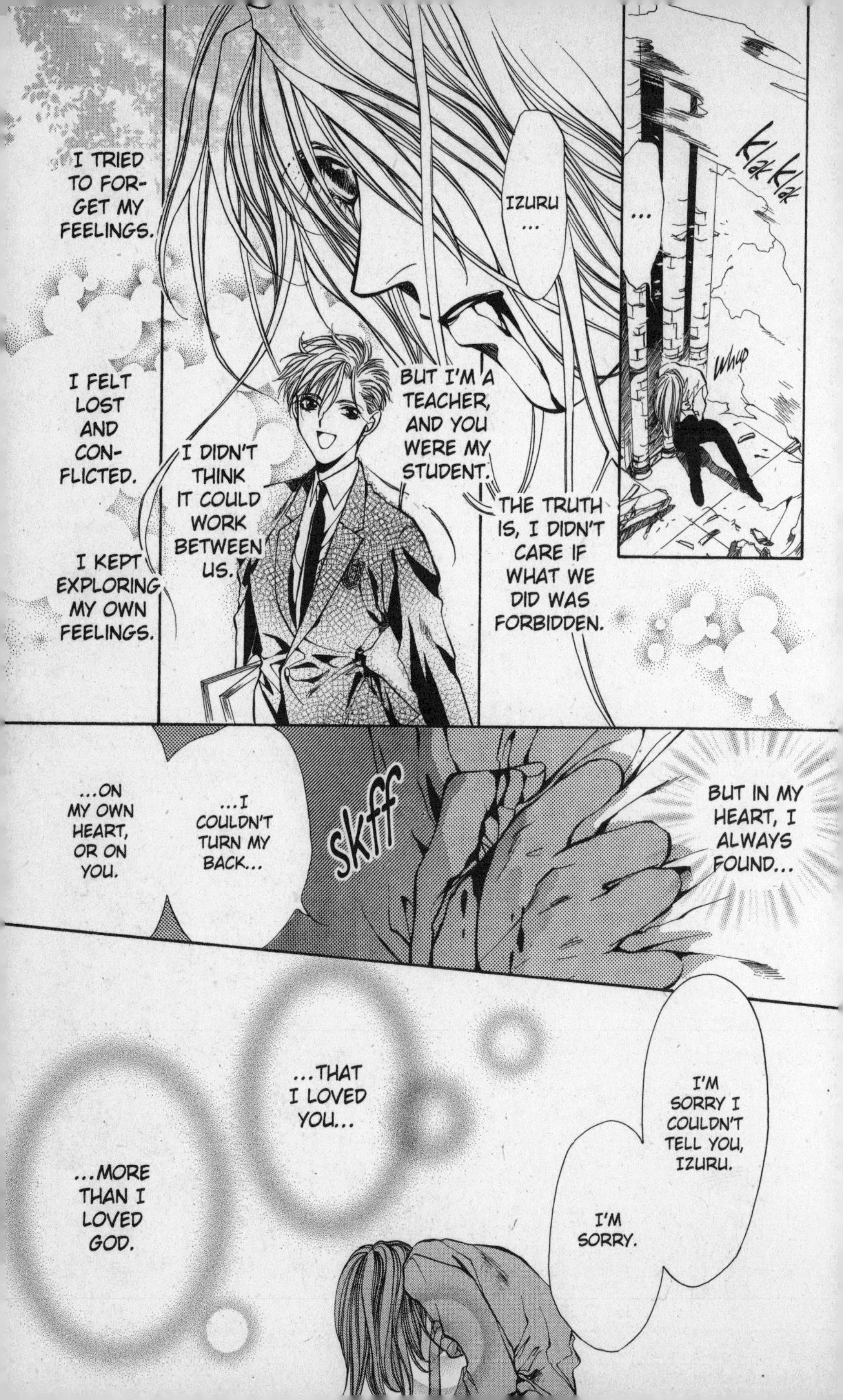

Klak Klak
...
whup
IZURU ...
BUT I'M A TEACHER, AND YOU WERE MY STUDENT.
THE TRUTH IS, I DIDN'T CARE IF WHAT WE DID WAS FORBIDDEN.
I DIDN'T THINK IT COULD WORK BETWEEN US.
I TRIED TO FORGET MY FEELINGS.
I FELT LOST AND CONFLICTED.
I KEPT EXPLORING MY OWN FEELINGS.
BUT IN MY HEART, I ALWAYS FOUND...
skff
...I COULDN'T TURN MY BACK...
...ON MY OWN HEART, OR ON YOU.
I'M SORRY I COULDN'T TELL YOU, IZURU.
I'M SORRY.
...THAT I LOVED YOU...
...MORE THAN I LOVED GOD.

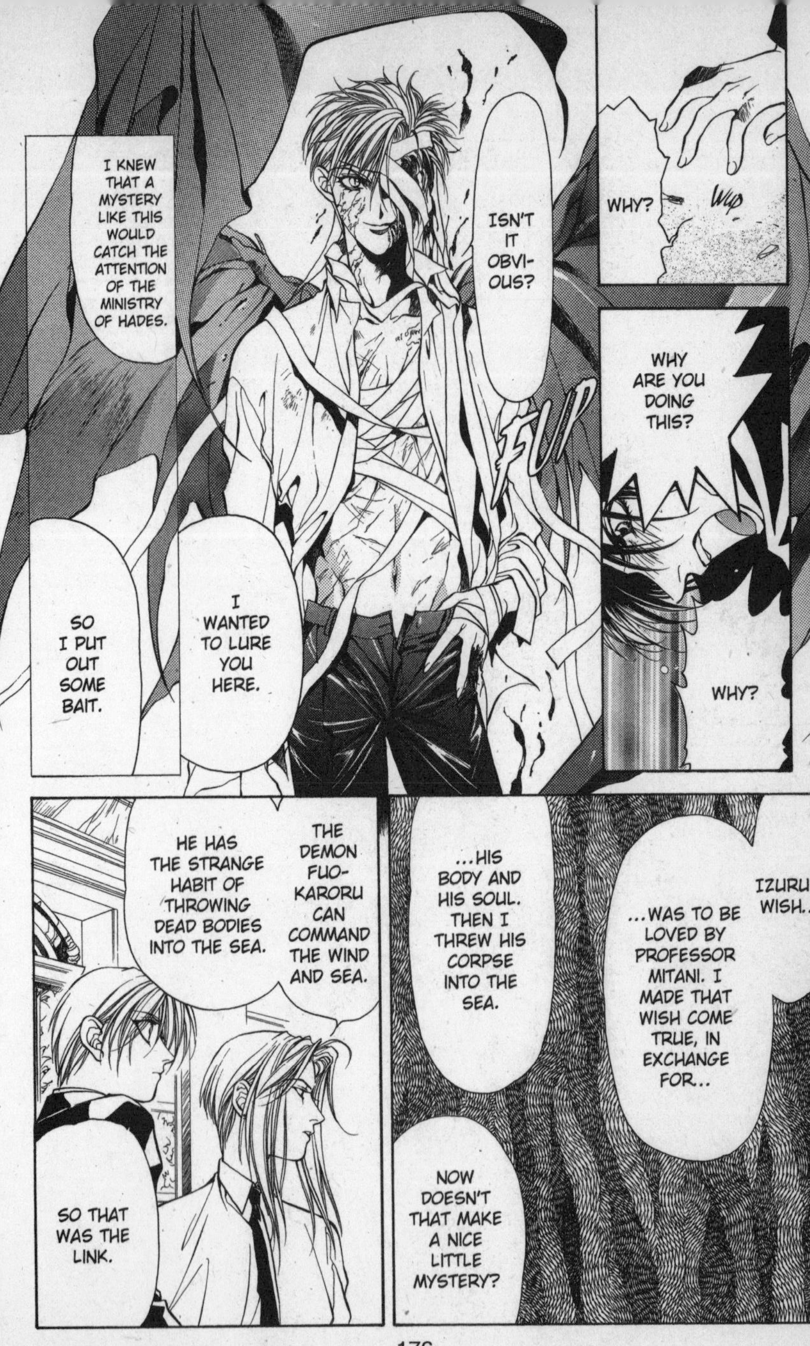
WHY?
WUP
WHY ARE YOU DOING THIS?
WHY?
ISN'T IT OBVI-OUS?
FUP
I KNEW THAT A MYSTERY LIKE THIS WOULD CATCH THE ATTENTION OF THE MINISTRY OF HADES.
I WANTED TO LURE YOU HERE.
SO I PUT OUT SOME BAIT.
IZURU'S WISH...
...WAS TO BE LOVED BY PROFESSOR MITANI. I MADE THAT WISH COME TRUE, IN EXCHANGE FOR...
...HIS BODY AND HIS SOUL. THEN I THREW HIS CORPSE INTO THE SEA.
NOW DOESN'T THAT MAKE A NICE LITTLE MYSTERY?
THE DEMON FUO-KARORU CAN COMMAND THE WIND AND SEA.
HE HAS THE STRANGE HABIT OF THROWING DEAD BODIES INTO THE SEA.
SO THAT WAS THE LINK.

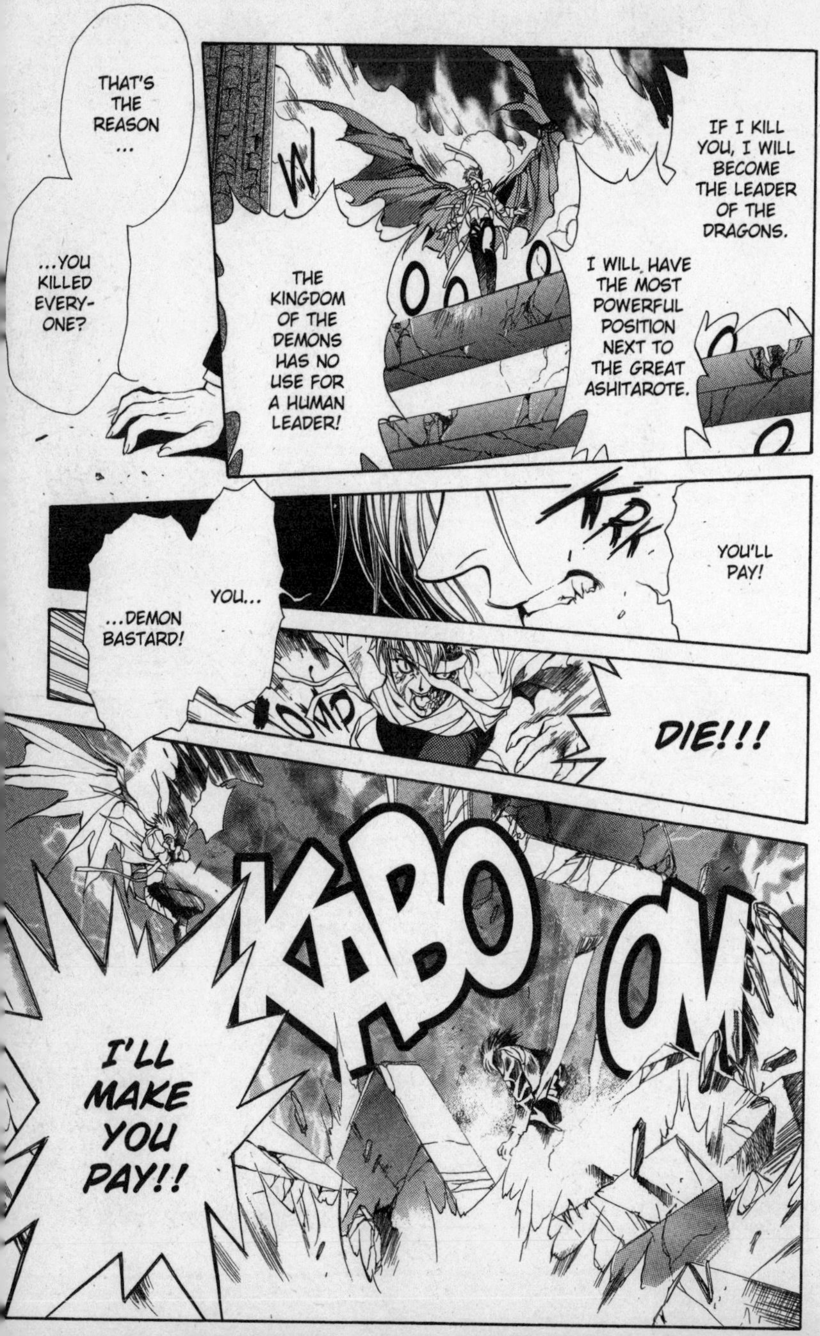
IF I KILL YOU, I WILL BECOME THE LEADER OF THE DRAGONS.
I WILL HAVE THE MOST POWERFUL POSITION NEXT TO THE GREAT ASHITAROTE.
THE KINGDOM OF THE DEMONS HAS NO USE FOR A HUMAN LEADER!
THAT'S THE REASON ...
...YOU KILLED EVERY-ONE?
KRK
YOU'LL PAY!
YOU...
...DEMON BASTARD!
DIE!!!
KABOOM
I'LL MAKE YOU PAY!!

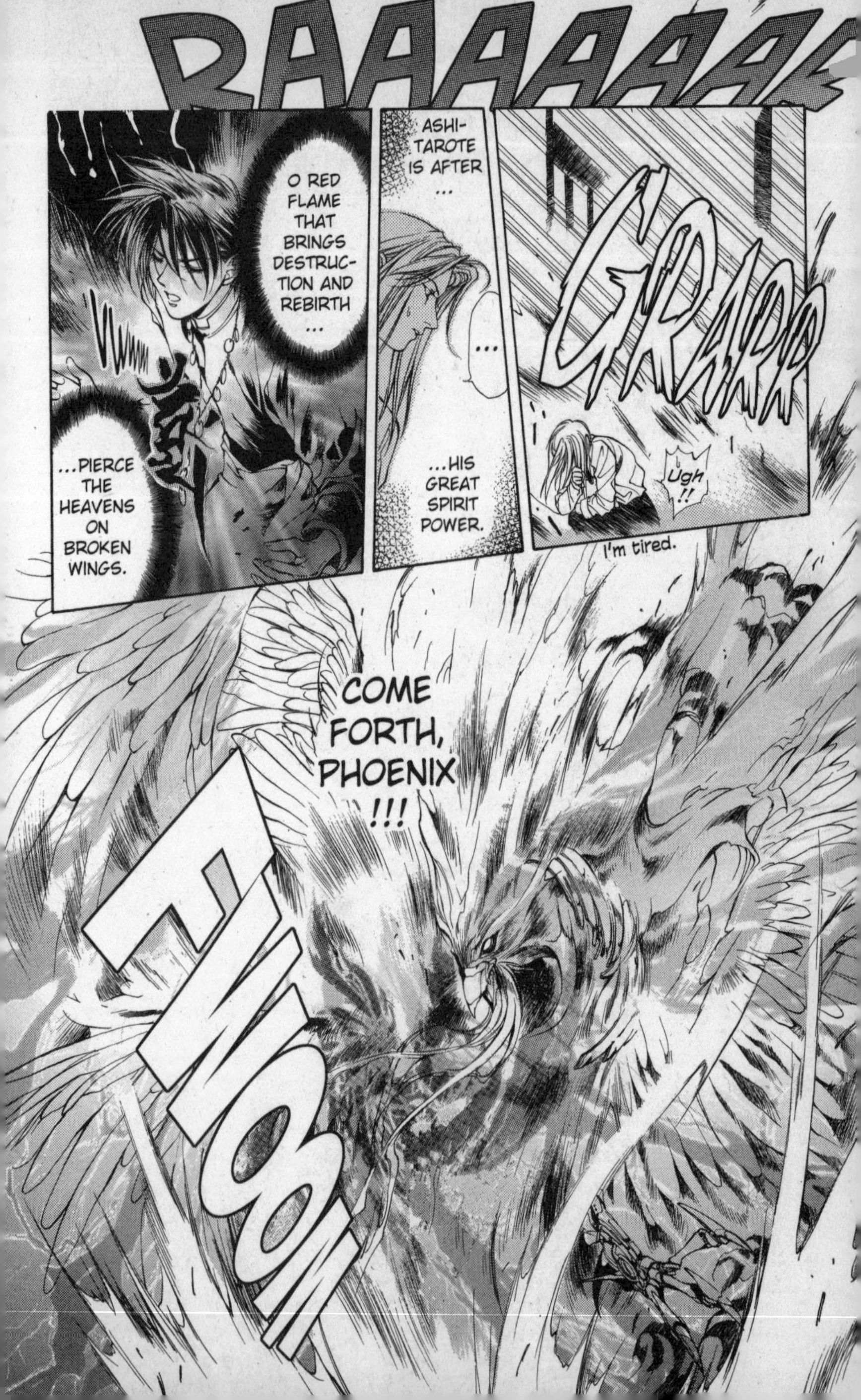

RAAAAAA
GRARR
Ugh!!
I'm tired.
ASHI-TAROTE IS AFTER...
...
...HIS GREAT SPIRIT POWER.
O RED FLAME THAT BRINGS DESTRUCTION AND REBIRTH...
...PIERCE THE HEAVENS ON BROKEN WINGS.
COME FORTH, PHOENIX!!!
FWOOM!

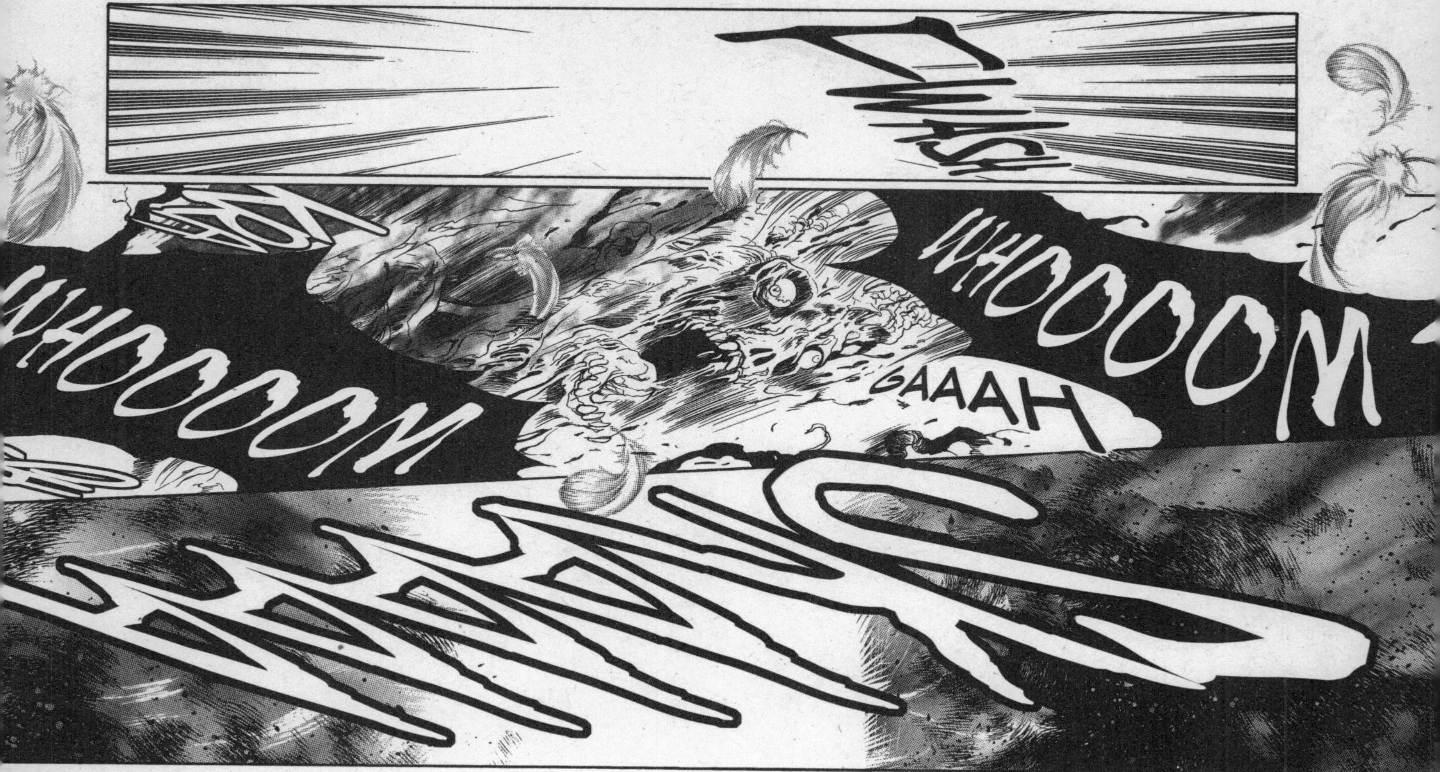
FWASH
WHOOOOM
GAAAH
WHOOOOM

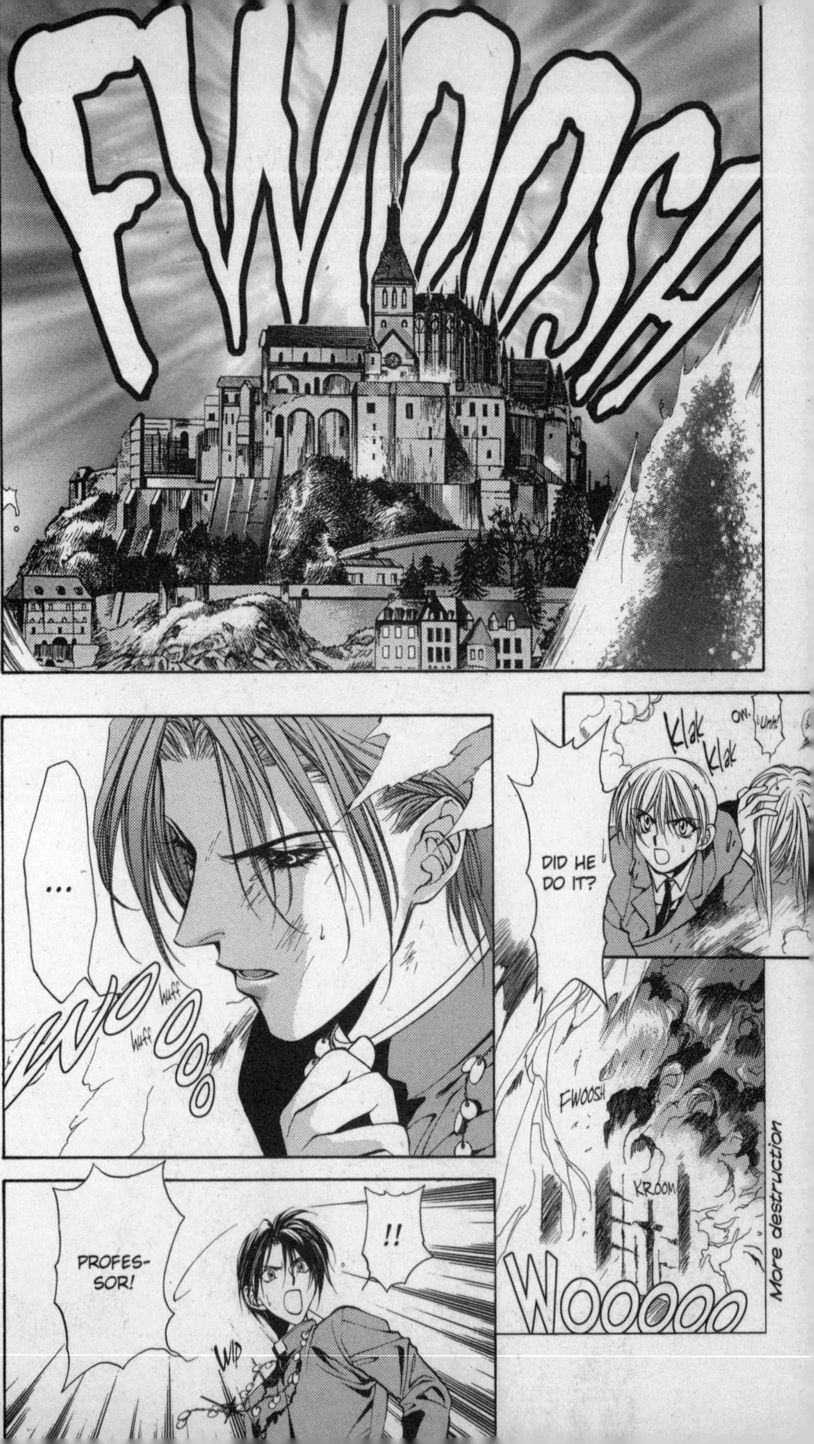
FWOOSH
Unh!
OW.
KLAK KLAK
DID HE DO IT?
FWOOSH
KROOM
WOOOOO
...
huff huff
WOOO
!!
PROFES-
SOR!
WIP
More destruction

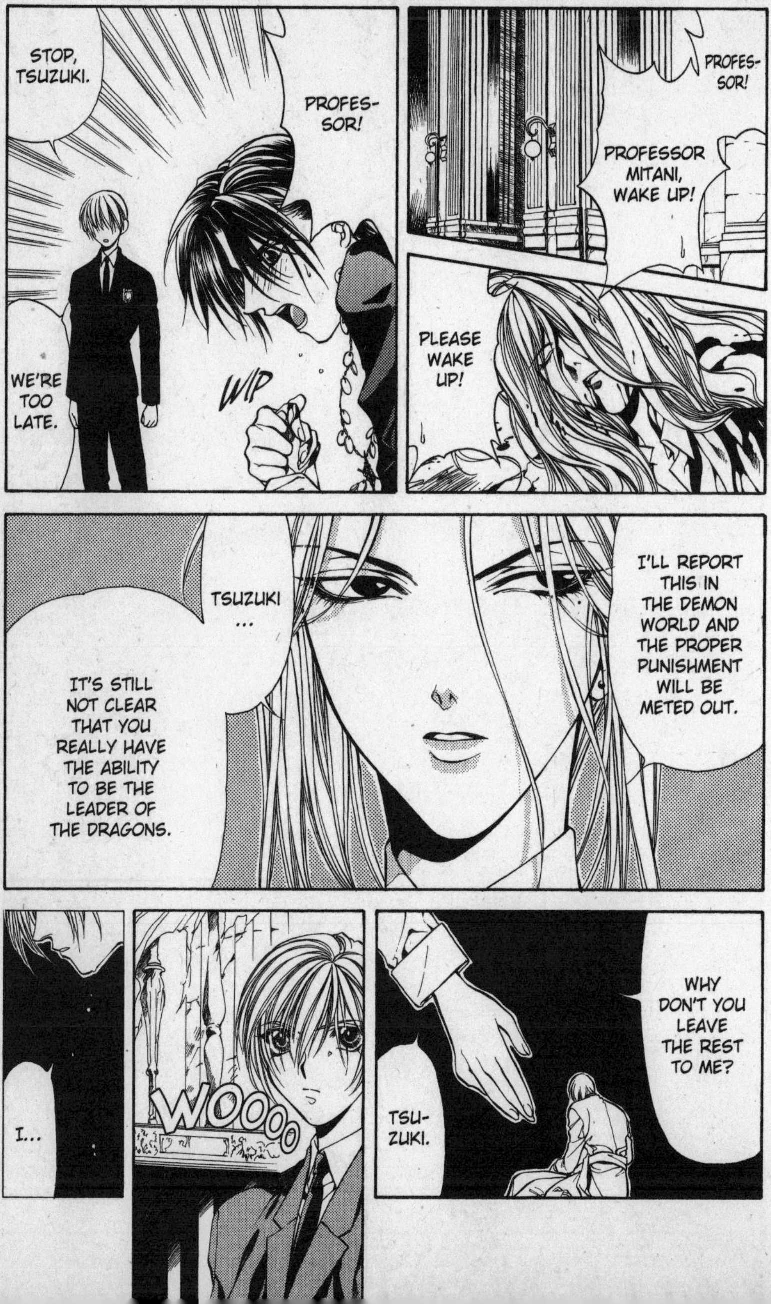

PROFES-SOR!
PROFESSOR MITANI, WAKE UP!
PLEASE WAKE UP!
PROFES-SOR!
STOP, TSUZUKI.
WIP
WE'RE TOO LATE.
I'LL REPORT THIS IN THE DEMON WORLD AND THE PROPER PUNISHMENT WILL BE METED OUT.
TSUZUKI ...
IT'S STILL NOT CLEAR THAT YOU REALLY HAVE THE ABILITY TO BE THE LEADER OF THE DRAGONS.
WHY DON'T YOU LEAVE THE REST TO ME?
TSU-ZUKI.
WOOOO
I...

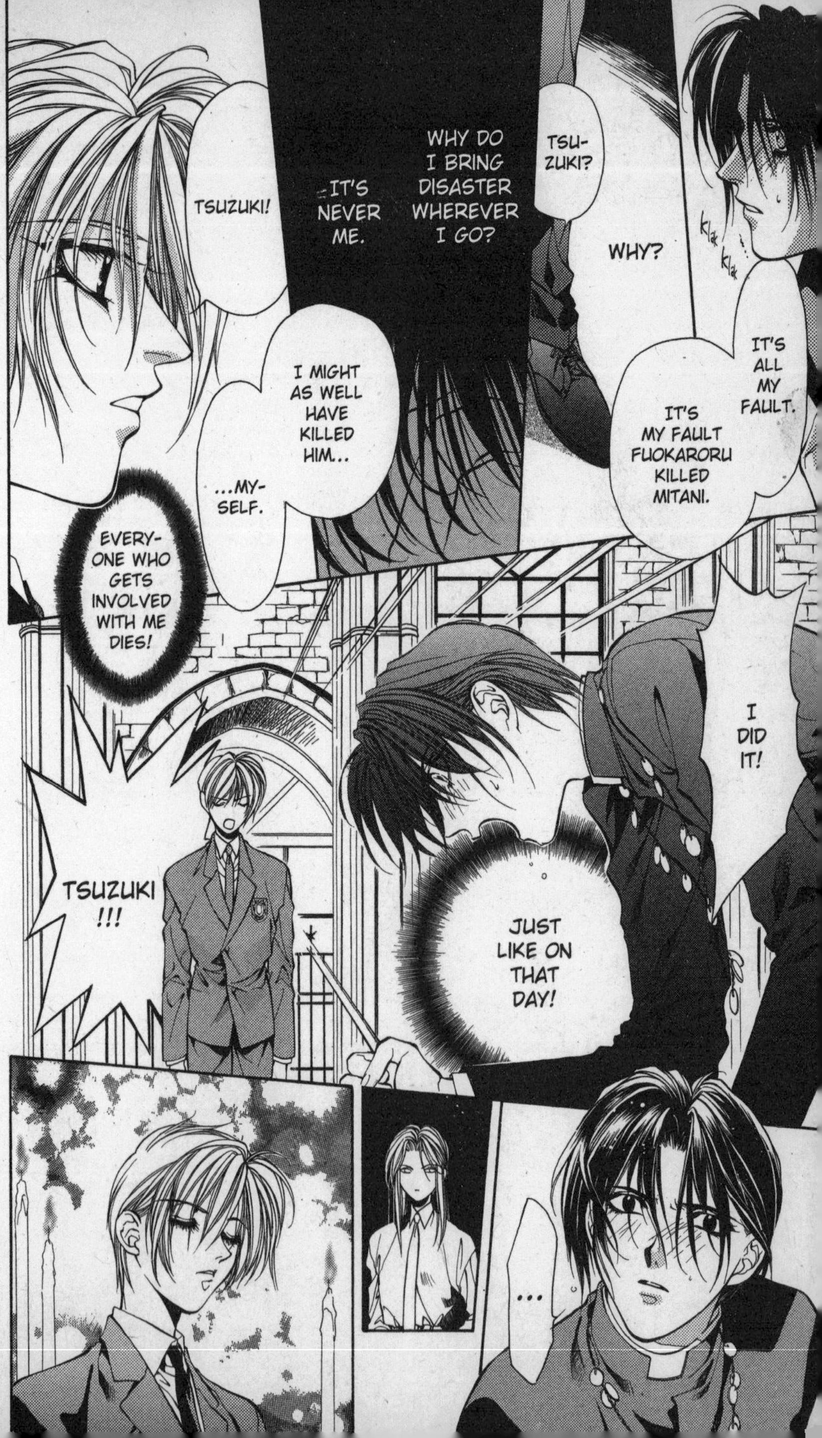
TSU-ZUKI?
WHY?
klak klak
IT'S ALL MY FAULT.
IT'S MY FAULT FUOKARORU KILLED MITANI.
WHY DO I BRING DISASTER WHEREVER I GO?
IT'S NEVER ME.
TSUZUKI!
I MIGHT AS WELL HAVE KILLED HIM...
...MY-SELF.
EVERY-ONE WHO GETS INVOLVED WITH ME DIES!
I DID IT!
JUST LIKE ON THAT DAY!
TSUZUKI !!!
...

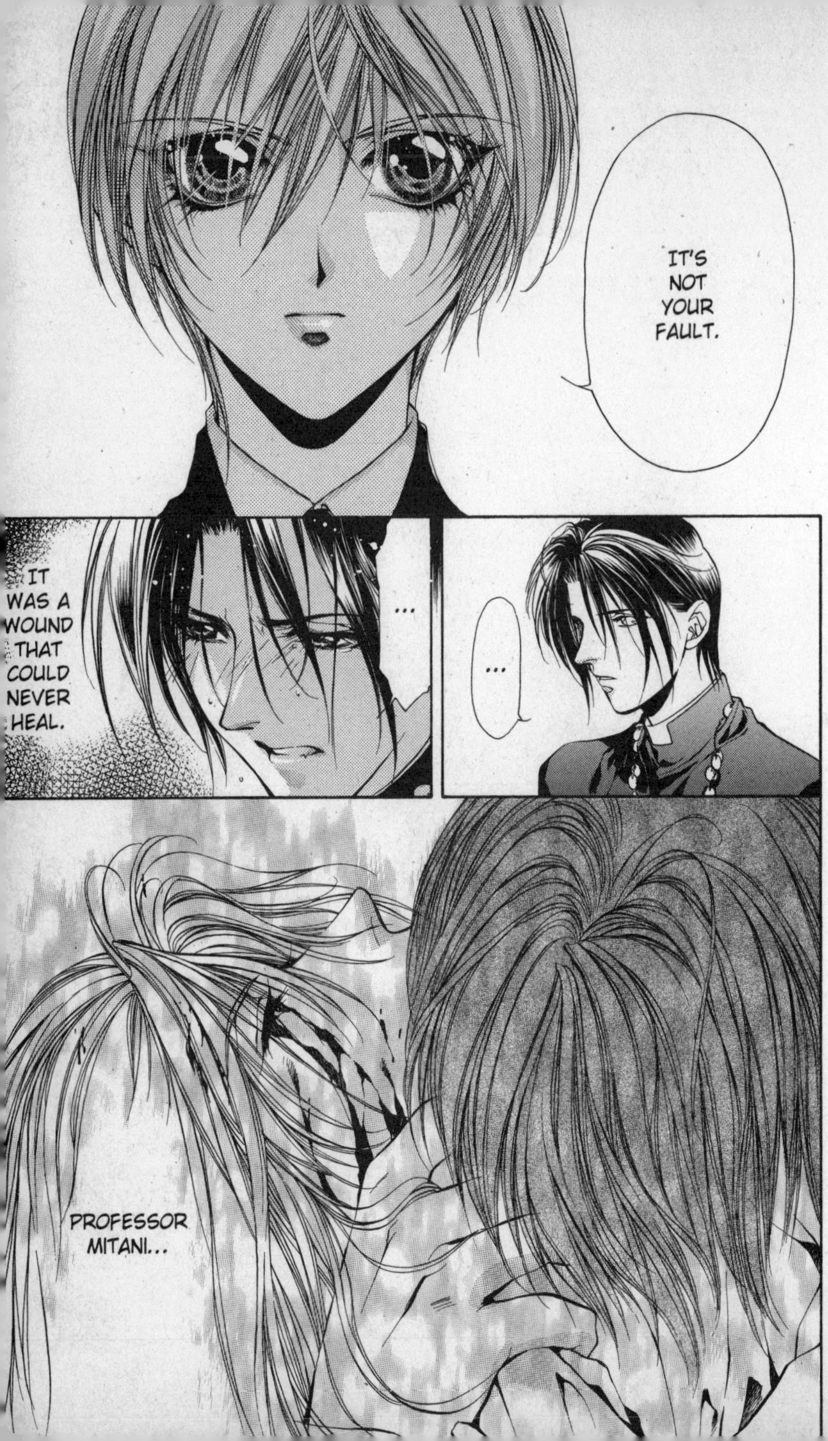
IT'S NOT YOUR FAULT.
...
...
IT WAS A WOUND THAT COULD NEVER HEAL.
PROFESSOR MITANI...

YOU TURNED YOUR BACK ON GOD FOR A TASTE OF ANOTHER WORLD.

BUT WAS THAT WORLD A PARADISE...

...OR
...

Afterward

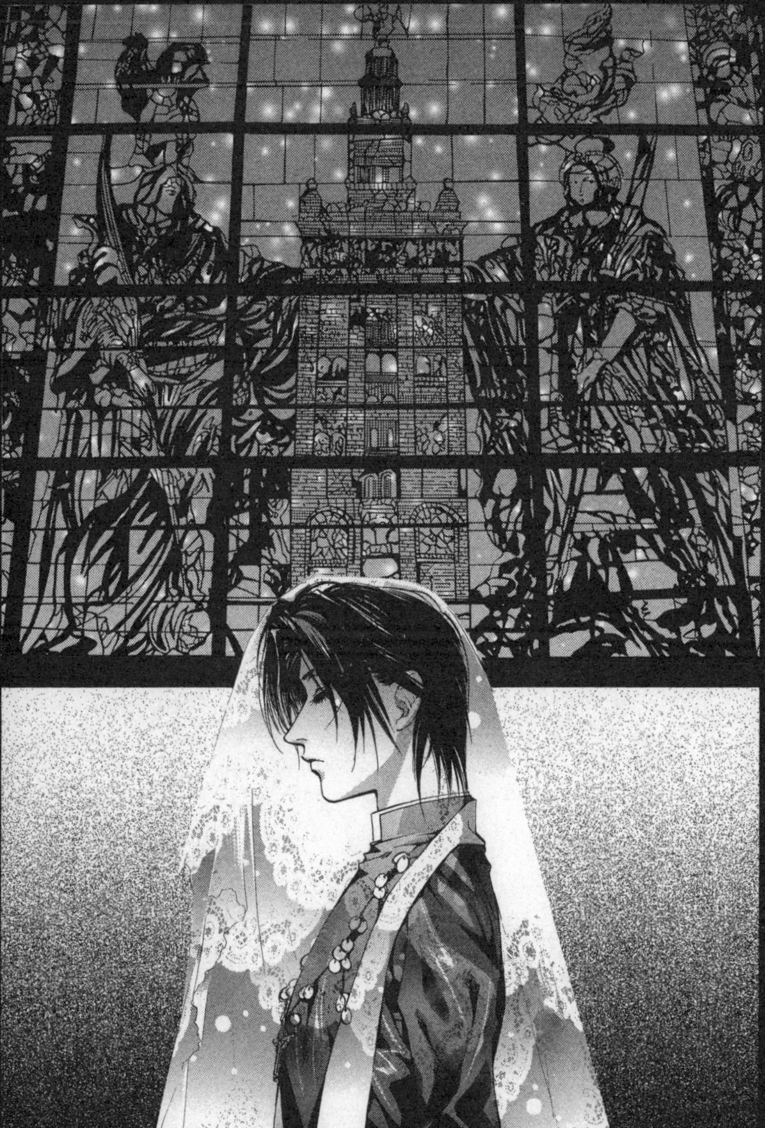

INTERMISSION

▲ This isn't my bathroom. (Ha)

AT FIRST I TRIED WRITING THIS BY HAND,
BUT AFTER ABOUT A QUARTER OF A PAGE, I
REALIZED IT WOULD BE TOO SMALL TO READ,
SO I TYPED IT. I'M SURE ALL OF THE READERS
OF THE ORIGINAL MANGA ARE AWARE OF THIS,
BUT A NEW "*DESCENDANTS OF DARKNESS*"
CD WAS JUST RELEASED! HOWEVER, IT'S NOT
ON SALE AND IT'S ONLY AVAILABLE TO THOSE
WHO REQUEST IT BY MAIL. BUT IT'S REALLY
COOL. IT'S A FULL ALBUM. THE VOICE ACTORS
ALL SOUND EXACTLY AS I HOPED THEY WOULD.
IF YOU CAN'T GET ONE YOURSELF, BORROW
ONE FROM A FRIEND.

I hate big cities, but I do love the look of buildings like this. I can't get enough of them.

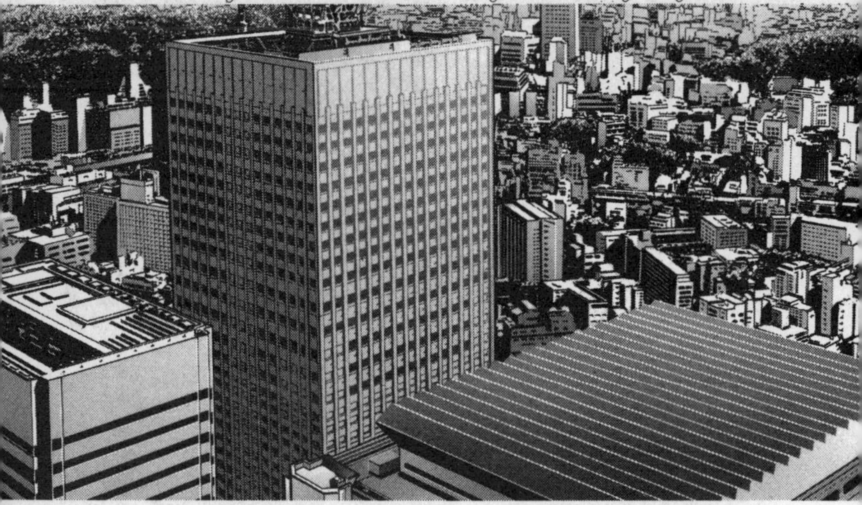

OH YEAH. I JUST BOUGHT A COMPUTER. IT'S A MAC, OF COURSE. I TOLD MYSELF THAT I WAS GETTING IT TO HONE MY ARTISTIC SKILLS. (HA!) BUT I SURF THE NET WITH IT TOO. THE PHOTO OF THE BATHROOM, ON THE RIGHT, IS ONE THAT I DIGITIZED. I ALTERED THE TONE TOO. IT WAS FUN. I'M GOING TO KEEP STUDYING SO I CAN MAKE EVEN MORE BEAUTIFUL ILLUSTRATIONS. WELL, THAT'S ALL FOR NOW. SEE YOU NEXT TIME.

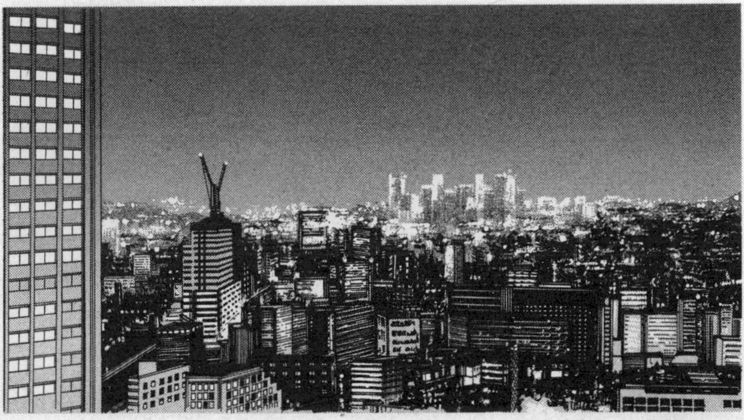

English Adaptation Notes
By Lance Caselman

[page 68] _Karuta_, the _Hyakuninisshu_ card game

Karuta is a card game played with the _Ogura Hyakuninisshu,_ an anthology of 100 poems by 100 poets, composed centuries ago in the _waka_ style (five lines of 31 syllables arranged 5, 7, 5, 7, 7). _Waka_ was a popular form of court poetry that was eclipsed by _haiku_ in the 17th century. _Karuta_ uses two decks of 100 cards. One deck has complete _waka,_ while the cards of the other deck contain only the last two lines of the poems. There are usually two players or teams of players, and one reader. Each side lays out 25 of the fragment cards, the reader reads the first lines of a _waka,_ and each side tries to find the fragment that completes it and take it off the table. If the card is taken from the opponent's area, a card from the finder's side replaces the gap. The first player or team to clear all 25 cards wins.

[page 69] _Ushinohi_ and eels

Ushinohi is a Japanese mid-summer holiday in which eel is the traditional dish. Why eel? Because the muggy heat of summer makes people feel sluggish, and eel is believed to invigorate the body. _Ushinohi_ eel is marinated in a sweet, soy-based sauce, grilled, and served over rice.

[page 69] The New Year's Bell

On New Year's Eve in Japan, Buddhist temples ring a bell 108 times to drive away the 108 worldly passions that humans must overcome to attain enlightenment. Many people gather at shrines for the event, or listen to the tolling on TV and radio. One desired effect of the ceremony is relief from the cares and worries of this world.

[page 108] Spell slips or _fuda_

Fuda, or spell slips, probably have a Chinese Taoist origin, although Buddhists use them too. They are used by magic-wielder of various kinds to cast spells or as talismans. An incantation or charm is written on a strip of yellow paper or cloth and stuck to the head of the victim or beneficiary.

[page 134] St. Michel School and Mont-Saint-Michel

Inspired by a dream, St. Aubert built a shrine to St. Michael on an island in France in 708. Over the centuries, it became the stunning Cathedral complex of Mont-Saint-Michel. The St. Michel School, though located in Japan, is unmistakably inspired by this medieval wonder.

[page 139] The Augsburg Cathedral Stained Glass Window

Five stained glass windows in the cathedral of Augsburg, Germany—including one in the image of the prophet Daniel—date from the 1140s. They are believed to be the oldest surviving examples of the art.

[pages 156 and 171] Eli, Eli, lama sabachtani

These words, translated in the King James Bible as: "My God, my God, why hast Thou forsaken me?" were spoken by Jesus at about the ninth hour on the cross, shortly before he died. The words were recorded in the book of St. Matthew 17:46 in a sort of Hebrew-Aramaic pidgin, although Jesus is believed to have spoken Aramaic. Yoko Matsushita's source seems to have been _The Bible Gallery_ by Talbot W. Chambers with illustrations by Gustave Doré published in 1880, or some translation thereof.

[page 168] Ashitarote, or Ashtaroth

Ashitarote is a variation of Ashtaroth, a dragon-riding demon from medieval demonology. Ashtaroth is usually described as a handsome aristocratic man with very bad breath. People would summon Ashtaroth (or try to) usually on Wednesday nights in order to obtain secret knowledge. He is also mentioned in the Faust tales as one of seven princes of Hell.

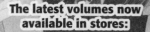

COMPLETE OUR SURVEY AND LET US KNOW WHAT YOU THINK!

☐ Please do NOT send me information about VIZ products, news and events, special offers, or other information.

☐ Please do NOT send me information from VIZ's trusted business partners.

Name: _____

Address: _____

City: _____ **State:** _____ **Zip:** _____

E-mail: _____

☐ **Male** ☐ **Female** **Date of Birth** (mm/dd/yyyy): ___/___/_____ (Under 13? Parental consent required)

What race/ethnicity do you consider yourself? (please check one)

☐ Asian/Pacific Islander ☐ Black/African American ☐ Hispanic/Latino

☐ Native American/Alaskan Native ☐ White/Caucasian ☐ Other: _____

What VIZ product did you purchase? (check all that apply and indicate title purchased)

☐ DVD/VHS _____

☐ Graphic Novel _____

☐ Magazines _____

☐ Merchandise _____

Reason for purchase: (check all that apply)

☐ Special offer ☐ Favorite title ☐ Gift

☐ Recommendation ☐ Other _____

Where did you make your purchase? (please check one)

☐ Comic store ☐ Bookstore ☐ Mass/Grocery Store

☐ Newsstand ☐ Video/Video Game Store ☐ Other: _____

☐ Online (site: _____)

What other VIZ properties have you purchased/own? _____

_____

How many anime an[...] [la]st year? How many were VIZ titles? (please chec[...])

ANIME	MANGA	VIZ
☐ None	☐ None	☐ None
☐ 1-4	☐ 1-4	☐ 1-4
☐ 5-10	☐ 5-10	☐ 5-10
☐ 11+	☐ 11+	☐ 11+

I find the pricing of VIZ products to be: (please check one)

☐ Cheap   ☐ Reasonable   ☐ Expensive

What genre of manga and anime would you like to see from VIZ? (please check two)

☐ Adventure   ☐ Comic Strip   ☐ Science Fiction   ☐ Fighting

☐ Horror   ☐ Romance   ☐ Fantasy   ☐ Sports

What do you think of VIZ's new look?

☐ Love It   ☐ It's OK   ☐ Hate It   ☐ Didn't Notice   ☐ No Opinion

Which do you prefer? (please check one)

☐ Reading right-to-left

☐ Reading left-to-right

Which do you prefer? (please check one)

☐ Sound effects in English

☐ Sound effects in Japanese with English captions

☐ Sound effects in Japanese only with a glossary at the back

THANK YOU! Please send the completed form to:

VIZ Survey
42 Catharine St.
Poughkeepsie, NY 12601

RECEIVED

MAR 1 1 2010

NORTHWEST RENO LIBRARY
Reno, Nevada

All information provided will be used for internal purposes only. We promise not to sell or otherwise divulge your information.